Modi's Bharat

Praise for *Modi's Bharat*

'A superb insight into the scale of PM Modi's grand vision for India's development and the transformative execution of that vision by an inspired government that works under him.'

Mahesh Jethmalani
Rajya Sabha MP and senior advocate, Bombay High Court

'Modi's greatest achievement is to tell the West, which thought that Indian democracy cannot scale up development like the autocratic China, that democratic India too can deliver growth and high scale success. Amit and Savio have graphically brought out with irrefutable references Modi's achievements that have made the West and the world to look at India as never before.'

S. Gurumurthy
Editor, *Thuglak*; and chairman, Vivekananda International Foundation

'Since 1947, all PMs have tried to reduce poverty and improve citizens' lives. Of them, PM Modi clearly stands out. He has ensured that almost all citizens have the necessities of life, and poverty has fallen to single digits. His ability to deliver results is extraordinary and impactful. This book exhaustively catalogues his achievements and explains why he is the best PM India has ever had.'

Dr T.V. Mohandas Pai
Padma Shri awardee and chairman, Aarin Capital Partners

'A detailed report card of the Modi decade of 2014 to 2024 that serves as a reminder of the giant strides taken in every conceivable sphere of national progress.'

Ashwin Sanghi
New York Times bestselling author and *Forbes India* celebrity 100 list

'India's transformation across all sectors under Modiji has been at a speed and scale never witnessed before. Not only is his vision grand and futuristic in nation building but he ensures it translates into real results on the ground. All this and much more, substantiated with data, have been captured in a captivating style in this book by Amit and Savio. Hope they will write its sequel as we march towards VikasitBharat@2047.'

Durga Shanker Mishra
Former secretary to Government of India
and former chief secretary of Uttar Pradesh

'While carrying out a clinical analysis of Modiji's first decade as PM, Amit and Savio have brought out the transformation and surge in development under 126 important indices with supporting facts and figures. It gives one a true extent of detail to which attention was focused to achieve spectacular results as compared to earlier decades. The authors' analyses in the two parts named "National Security Comes First" and "Top 10 Reasons Why We Wrote This Book" bring out the essence of Modiji's commitment and dedication towards propelling Bharat to restore its true place in the world order. A must-read for every Indian.'

Air Marshal Suresh Chandra Mukul, PVSM, AVSM, VM, VSM
Former chief of Integrated Defence Staff

'Excellent research by Amit and Savio, covering everything PM Modi and his government have done in 10 years, with 3,000-plus data points. I doubt even the Statistics Ministry has so much. Modi should start a "Data Compilation and Communications Department" in the PMO and hire these guys to manage it.'

Dr Anand Ranganathan
Author, professor, scientist, and TV debater

'In their second book together, Amit and Savio have insightfully captured what Modi has achieved both as Prime Minister and Politician. The duality is important given the complexity that India and its democracy is. And in doing so, the authors give you a ringside view of how India has changed and the manner in which the seeds of a future-forward India have been sown. For any one keen on understanding today's India and Indians, this is a must-read.'

Suhel Seth
Actor, author, TV panellist, and strategic brand marketing consultant

'A comprehensive data-backed compendium of Modi's 10 years, including comparisons with the Manmohan Singh regime. The book is a must-read for anyone interested in an unembellished examination of the ongoing Modi Era.'

Rahul Shivshankar
Author; consulting editor, Network 18;
and former editor-in-chief, Times Now

'In Bharat's eternal epic the Ramayana, the bear Jambavan reminds Hanuman of his great power, which he had forgotten. Today, led by its outstanding son Narendra Modi, Bharat has rediscovered its comprehensive national power based on self-confidence, self-esteem, self-reliance and self-belief. The book highlights this simple truth beautifully with facts and figures. Bharat is indisputably a global role model! Vande Mataram!'

Ambassador Deepak Vohra

Former Indian ambassador to Armenia, Georgia, Lithuania, Poland, Sudan and South Sudan

'Amit and Savio have done it again. A brilliantly researched book that tells you what happened in the last 10 years, with comparisons of what did not happen during the 10 years before Modi, which the authors aptly call the UPA-era.'

Vivek Ranjan Agnihotri

National Award–winning filmmaker and bestselling author

'This book is unique in that it doesn't just list out the achievements of the government but also gives you a sense of the Herculean effort expended in doing so—bringing nothing short of revolutionary change, while maintaining social cohesion. Moreover, the sequential and thematic nature, highlight the truly revolutionary nature of these changes—something lost upon many, because they assume this was just natural growth.'

Abhijit Iyer-Mitra

Senior fellow, Institute of Peace and Conflict Studies

'Destiny defining Ds of India—development, direct benefit transfers and diplomacy—began in 2014, and it is important to be captured and documented for future generations. Under the leadership of Narendra Modi, rapid strides have been taken up by the nation. Amit and Savio have factually captured this in the book. I wish future generations of scholars will use this book as an authentic source.'

R.V.S. Mani

Author, whistleblower and former civil servant

'This book is a statistician's delight, and a must read for all those keen to know India's journey over the last 10 years. A very interesting document that helps understand the past decade and India's story.'

Tehseen Poonawalla

Entrepreneur, venture capitalist, TV personality, and Congress supporter

'Amit and Savio have put a robust account of claims of Modi's efforts in the last 10 years in power. The book is aimed at highlighting India's purported global outreach, military, economic, social, political, technological and Hindutva growth under Modi while comparing alleged failures of UPA. For anyone interested in politics, this is a must read.'

Touseef Ahmed Khan

Advocate, Calcutta High Court; TV panellist; and TMC supporter

'As an observer and investor in the equity markets and not someone who closely follows politics, I am more interested in what successive governments have done for the Indian economy. Keeping that in mind, I believe that the Modi government has done quite a bit to improve the economy, which has been very well captured in this book. Having said that, I believe much more should be done in Modi's 3rd term, especially to improve the lives of the middle class and make things easier for investors and tax payers.'

Arun Kumar Mukherjee

Stock market guru

Modi's Bharat

A Decade of Achievements

Amit Bagaria
and
Savio Rodrigues

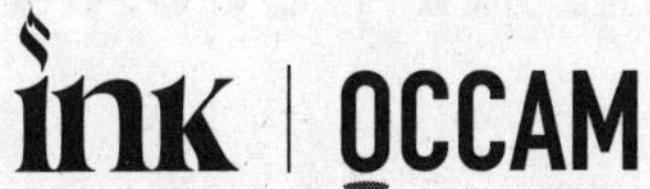

ISBN: 978-81-972231-7-4

First published in India 2025
This edition published 2025

BluOne Ink Pvt. Ltd
A-76, 2nd Floor, Sector 136, Noida
Uttar Pradesh 201301
www.bluone.ink
publisher@bluone.ink

Printed and bound in India by Thomson Press India Ltd.

Kali and Occam are imprints of BluOne Ink

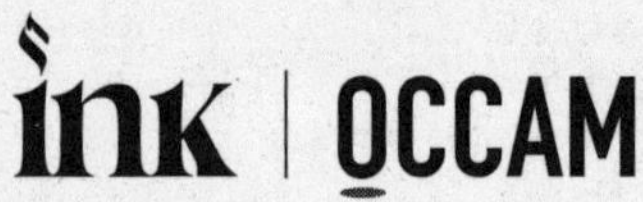

Contents

Part II: Managing the Economy

Part III: Digital India

Part IV: Unprecedented Infrastructure Development

Abbreviations

L = Lakh, Cr = Crore, LCr = Lakh Crore, M = Million, B = Billion, T = Trillion, 1L = 100,000, 1M = 10L, 1Cr = 100L or 10M, 1B = 100Cr, 1LCr = 1 Trillion, ac = acres, p.a. = per annum, or per year. ha = hectares, GW = gigawatt (1,000 MW), MW = megawatt, kmph = kilometres per hour, msft = million square feet, MT = million metric tons, MTPD = metric tons per day, mtpa = million tons per annum, SFT = square feet

A&NI	Andaman & Nicobar Islands
AAI	Airports Authority of India (100% GOI-owned)
AAP	Aam Aadmi Party
ADIA	Abu Dhabi Investment Authority
ADM	Area Denial Munition
AEW&C	Airborne Early Warning & Control Aircraft
AGMF	Advanced Guided Missile Stealth Frigate (type of Ship)
AI	Artificial Intelligence
ALH	Advanced Light Helicopter
AMCA	Advanced Multirole Combat Aircraft
APC	Armoured Personnel Carrier
ASEAN	Association of Southeast Asian Nations is a union of 10 nations: Brunei, Cambodia, Indonesia, Laos, Malaysia, Myanmar, the Philippines, Singapore, Thailand, and Vietnam
ASG	Additional Solicitor General of India, a GoI advocate
ATAGS	155mm x 52 calibre Next-Gen Advanced Towed Artillery Gun System (howitzer) indigenously developed by the DRDO

ATGM	Air-to-Ground Missile
ATM	Anti-Tank Munitions
ATMP	Assembly, Testing, Marking, and Packing (of semiconductor chips)
ATS	Anti-Terrorism Squad (of police forces)
AUH	Advanced Utility Helicopter
AUM	Assets under Management is a term that describes how much money a bank, PE firm or NBFC is managing
AYUSH	Ayurveda, Yoga, Naturopathy, Unani, Siddha, and Homeopathy
B2B	Business to Business
B2C	Business to Consumer
BIMSTEC	Bay of Bengal Initiative for Multi-Sectoral Technical and Economic Cooperation is a grouping which Bangladesh, India, Myanmar, Sri Lanka, and Thailand founded in 1997. Nepal and Bhutan became members in 2004.
BPL	Below Poverty Line
BRTS	Bus Rapid Transit System
BSF	Border Security Force
BUA	Built-up Area
BVRAAM	Beyond Visual Range Air-to-Air Missile
CAA	Citizenship Amendment Act, 2019
Cabinet	The Union Cabinet or the 'Council of Ministers' of the GoI
CAG	Comptroller and Auditor General of India is India's national bookkeeper. It audits the accounts of the GoI and all state governments.
CAGR	Compounded Annual Growth Rate
CAPF	Central Armed Police Forces; comprises Assam Rifles, BSF, CISF, CRPF, ITBP, NSG, and SSB
CBI	Central Bureau of Investigation handles cases of bribery, government or political corruption, breaches of central laws, multi-state organised crime, and multi-agency or international cases
CCPA	Cabinet Committee on Political Affairs

CCS	Cabinet Committee on Security includes the PM and ministers of Home Affairs, Finance, Defence, and External Affairs
CDS	Chief of Defence Staff
Centre	The Central Government, aka the GoI
CEO	Chief Executive Officer (in India, the more common designation for the chief executive of a company is Managing Director)
CID	Crime/Criminal Investigation Department of a police force/department
CISF	Central Industrial Security Force
CIT	Corporate Income Tax paid by companies and firms
CJI	Chief Justice of India
COO	Chief Operating Officer, the second-most senior executive in most companies
CPI	Communist Party of India
CPM	Communist Party of India (Marxist)
CRPF	Central Reserve Police Force
CSC	Common Service Centres are GOI's one-stop shops for digital services such as booking railway tickets, payment of utility bills, PAN and Aadhaar enrolment, banking, insurance services, etc.
CSIA	Chhatrapati Shivaji Maharaj International Airport, Mumbai
CVC	Central Vigilance Commission
DBT	Direct Benefit Transfer
DDA	Delhi Development Authority
DGP	Director General of Police, the top cop in an Indian state
DJB	Delhi Jal Board
DMK	Dravida Munnetra Kazhagam
DPI	Digital Public Infrastructure
DPR	Detailed Project Report, based on which most of the industrial or infrastructure projects are undertaken
DRDO	Defence Research & Development Organisation, India

DRI	Directorate of Revenue Intelligence is India's apex anti-smuggling intelligence, investigations and operations agency
DSNA	Deputy National Security Advisor
EBC	Economically Backward Classes
ED	Enforcement Directorate enforces the FEMA and the PMLA
EoDB	Ease of Doing Business
ESIC	Employees' State Insurance Corporation is a GOI entity that provides outpatient and inpatient medical services to workers and their relatives
EU	European Union
EV	Electric Vehicle
EWS	Economically Weaker Sections
F&O	Futures & Options are stock market trades where a buyer does not take pay and take 'delivery' of shares; but trades for a fixed later date and price, and pays the loss if the price is lower, or encashes profit higher. One can also do 'sell' trades in a similar fashion.
FBI	Federal Bureau of Investigation, USA's internal LEA
FCI	Food Corporation of India's responsibilities are price support for safeguarding farmer interests and distribution of PDS food grains for PDS and maintaining satisfactory stocks of food grains
FDI	Foreign Direct Investment made directly into a business, different from portfolio investments made by FPIs into stock markets
FEMA	Foreign Exchange Management Act
FIR	First Information Report (filed at a Police Station)
Forex	Foreign Exchange
FPI	Foreign Portfolio Investors are institutions that buy equity/bonds, or other corporate debt instruments through stock markets
FPO	Farmer Producer Organisation

FPS	Fair Price Shops (ration shops)
FTA	Free Trade Agreement
FY	Fiscal Year. In India, 1 April to 31 March is a 'FY'. As an example, we have used FY23 to depict financial year 2022–2023.
GDP	Gross Domestic Product is total value of goods and services produced in a country in a fixed period and is a key metric for assessing the size of a country's economy
GoI	Government of India, also referred to as the Central Government
GST	Goods and Services Tax
GTV	Gun Towing Vehicle
HAL	Hindustan Aeronautics Limited (a PSE)
HALE	High Altitude Long Endurance (type of drone)
HMV	High Mobility Vehicle with minimum 8,000kg payload
Howitzer	Artillery Gun that falls between a cannon and a mortar
I.N.D.I.A.	Indian National Developmental Inclusive Alliance
IAF	Indian Air Force
IB	Intelligence Bureau is India's internal security and counter-intelligence agency, like the FBI of USA and MI5 of UK
IEC	Information, Education and Communication
IGIA	Indira Gandhi International Airport, New Delhi
IMF	International Monetary Fund
IPS	Indian Police Service
ISI	Inter-Services Intelligence Directorate, Pakistan's spy agency
ISRO	Indian Space Research Organisation
ITD	Income Tax Department (ITD) collects direct taxes (CIT and PIT) and is authorised to investigate tax defaults, delays and frauds
ITR	Income Tax Return
J&K	Jammu & Kashmir, a Union Territory (formerly a state), for which India and Pakistan have fought 3 wars since 1947

JAM	Linking of Jandhan (bank account), Aadhaar, and Mobile
JDU	Janata Dal (United)
JICA	Japan International Cooperation Agency, which funds development projects abroad to indirectly sell Japanese systems and tech to the projects
JMM	Jharkhand Mukti Morcha
JNPT	Jawaharlal Nehru Port Trust, a port in Navi Mumbai
JNU	Jawaharlal Nehru University, New Delhi
JV	Joint Venture
L&T	Larsen & Toubro, India's largest engineering and construction company, also a defence manufacturer
LAC	Line of Actual Control is the undefined border between India and China in areas where the actual border is disputed
LACM	Land Attack Cruise Missile
LCA	Light Combat Aircraft
LCH	Light Combat Helicopter
LEA	Law Enforcement Agency
LeT	Lashkar-e-Taiba is an anti-India terrorist organisation
LNG	Liquified Natural Gas
LoC	Line of Control, the *de facto* India–Pakistan border. Also 'Line-of-Credit' given by India to other countries
LoP	Leader of the Opposition
LS	Lok Sabha, the Lower House of India's Parliament (545 members)
LUH	Light Utility Helicopter
MALE	Medium Altitude Long Endurance (type of drone)
MBRL	Multi Barrel Rocket Launcher
MBT	Main Battle Tank
MCap	Market Capitalisation of a company is the total market value of the company's shares
MEA	Ministry of External Affairs (aka Foreign Ministry)
MHA	Ministry of Home Affairs (aka Home Ministry)
MLCP	Multi Level Car Park

MMRDA	Mumbai Metropolitan Region Development Authority
MNC	Multi National Company/Corporate
MoD	Ministry of Defence
MoR	Ministry of Railways
MoS (IC)	MoS with Independent Charge of a ministry with no Cabinet Minister
MoS	Minister of State, a junior minister in India
MoU	Memorandum of Understanding
MP	Member of Parliament
MRFA	Medium Multirole Fighter Aircraft
MRO	Maintenance, Repair and Overhaul (of aircraft)
MSME	Medium, Small, and Micro Enterprises
MSP	Minimum Support Price at which government procures food grains from farmers
NBFC	Non-Banking Financial Company
NCB	Narcotics Control Bureau
NCP	Nationalist Congress Party
NCP–SCP	Nationalist Congress Party-Sharadchandra Pawar
NCR	The 55,083km^2 National Capital Region of India
NCRB	National Crime Records Bureau
NCW	National Commission for Women
NDA	National Democratic Alliance, that ran the GoI from 1998 to 2004 and has been running it under Modi since May 2014
NDRF	India's National Disaster Response Force
NER	Northeast Region (of India)
NGMV	Next Gen Missile Vehicle (high-speed Ship which uses stealth)
NGO	Non-Governmental Organisation
NGOPV	Next Gen Offshore Patrol Vessel (type of Ship)
NHAI	National Highways Authority of India
NIA	National Investigation Agency, India's main anti-terrorism LEA
NMIA	Navi Mumbai International Airport (under construction)
NPAs	Non-Performing Assets (of banks)

NPCI	National Payments Corporation of India
NREGA	Mahatma Gandhi National Rural Employment Guarantee scheme gives minimum 100 days' employment per annum to rural households whose adult members volunteer for unskilled manual work
NSA	National Security Advisor of India
NSC	National Security Council of India
NSCS	National Security Council Secretariat
NSG	National Security Guard, a paramilitary counterterrorism commando force
NTPC	National Thermal Power Corp (a PSE), India's largest power producer
OBCs	Other Backward Classes
OCI	Overseas Citizen of India
PDS	Public Distribution System that comprises ration shops
PIO	Person of Indian Origin
PIT	Personal Income Tax paid by individuals
PLA	People's Liberation Army, China's military; their air force is PLA Air Force and Navy is PLA Navy
PMJAY	Pradhan Mantri Jan Arogya Yojana
PMLA	Prevention of Money Laundering Act
PMO	Prime Minister's Office
PoJK	Pakistan-occupied Jammu & Kashmir
PPP	Public–Private Partnership
PSB	Public Sector Bank, with over 50% ownership by the RBI or GoI
PSE	Public Sector Enterprise (aka Public Sector Unit) is a company with over 50% ownership by GoI or a state government or both.
PwD	Person with Disability
RAW	Research & Analysis Wing is India's external intelligence agency or 'spy agency', like USA's CIA, UK's MI6, Israel's Mossad. It handles foreign intelligence, counterterrorism, and counter-proliferation.
RBI	The Reserve Bank of India

Recon	Reconnaissance (surveillance)
RJD	Rashtriya Janata Dal
RS	Rajya Sabha, the Upper House of Parliament
RSS	Rashtriya Swayamsevak Sangh, the 'moral' parent body of the BJP, is a volunteer-based organization that undertakes various types of social work. RSS *swayamsevaks*, or volunteers, are often the first to reach a disaster spot even before official agencies
RTI	Right to Information, an Act of Parliament through which citizens have the right to ask any ministry or government department for information
SAARC	South Asian Association for Regional Cooperation: India, Afghanistan, Bangladesh, Bhutan, Maldives, Nepal, Pakistan, and Sri Lanka
SAML	Surface-to-Air Missile Launcher
SBI	State Bank of India (the largest PSB)
SCI	Supreme Court of India, the apex court of India
SCM	Supersonic Cruise Missile
SCs	Scheduled Castes
SDG	Sustainable Development Goals of UNDP and WHO
SFIO	Serious Fraud Investigation Office investigates corporate fraud with a mandate to detect and prosecute 'white collar' crime
SGI	Solicitor General of India, the country's second highest law officer
SHG	Self-Help Group
SIT	Special Investigation Team
SP	Samajwadi Party
SP	Superintendent of Police
SPV	Special Purpose Vehicle
SS–UBT	Shiv Sena-Uddhav Balasaheb Thackeray
STEM	Science, Technology, Engineering, and Mathematics
STs	Scheduled Tribes
TDP	Telugu Desam Party
TMC	Trinamool Congress Party

UAPA	Unlawful Activities (Prevention) Act, 1967; Amended by Modi Government in 2019
UN	United Nations
UNDP	United Nations Development Programme
UPA	United Progressive Alliance, led by Sonia Gandhi was a group of political parties that ran the Central Government from May 2004 to May 2014
UPI	Unified Payments Interface
UT	Union Territory (India has 28 states and 08 UTs)
WHO	World Health Organization
WTO	World Trade Organization
YEIDA	Yamuna Expressway Industrial Development Authority

Introduction

The Gujarat*i* Model

The table of contents is as comprehensive as possible, and you can identify the topics that interest you, as not everything in this book is meant for every Indian.

Modi won his first national general election in 2014 with an absolute majority (the first in 30 years) primarily due to his 12.6 years of work as the Chief Minister (CM) of Gujarat—the 'Gujarat model' in his own words.

Gujarat's Gross State Domestic Product grew at 14.85 per cent p.a. in 20 years (FY03–23), compared to India's Gross Domestic Product (GDP) growing at 9.68 per cent. With <6 per cent of India's land area and <5 per cent of population, Gujarat contributes 8.5 per cent to the country's GDP, has 1/3rd share of total exports, and a 16.5 per cent share in total renewable energy capacity.

Gujarat is also home to the world's tallest statue and single office complex, India's first International Financial Services Centre, and greenfield Special Investment Region. It will also be the first state in India where semiconductor chips will be made.

Adani is building the world's largest Renewable Energy Park of 30GW at Khavda. At 538km^2, it is 5.12 times the size of Paris! Adani Group has committed an investment of ₹3.8LCr in the state by 2028, for copper, cement, solar panels, green ammonia/hydrogen, and PVC.

Reliance is setting up a Green Energy Giga Complex and a carbon fibre plant.

Tatas have built a military transport aircraft factory (in a joint venture or JV with Airbus), a 20GW lithium-ion battery plant, a semiconductor fab, and have started work on producing Electric Vehicles (EVs).

Nayara Energy, backed by Rosneft of Russia, plans to set up a ₹68,000Cr ethane cracker project at its refinery in Vadinagar.

ArcelorMittal is building the world's biggest single-location steel plant. Welspun has committed an investment of ₹40,000Cr to build a green hydrogen and green ammonia ecosystem.

Micron Technology of the US is setting up a ₹23,000Cr memory chip assembly and test facility that will open by early 2025.

Maruti Suzuki is building a ₹38,200Cr, 1M vehicle plant, its second in the state, which will start in FY29. It is also expanding the existing plant's capacity to 1M units/year.

None of this would be possible if Narendra Modi would not have been the chief minister (de-facto Chief Executive Officer or CEO) of the state for 12.6 years.

However, the Indian and foreign media has not been kind to Modi. Let's see some of the really surprising cover stories and story titles about India's PM, who has been elected three times in a row (2014, 2019, and 2024).

USA's *Time* magazine: 'The Modi-fication of India is Almost Complete.'[1]

UK's *Guardian*: 'India's election: fixing a win by outlawing dissent damages democracy.'[2] 'Messianic spell: how Narendra

Modi created a cult of personality.'[3] 'As India goes to the polls, can democracy deliver a better life for all of its people? – Behind a veneer of progress, injustice and inequality propped up by corruption and the caste system haunt the subcontinent.'[4] 'Narendra Modi's Hindu nationalist government is escalating its attack on civil rights.'[5] 'US should not normalize Modi's autocratic and illiberal India.'[6]

USA's *Reuters*: 'India can grow fast with or without Narendra Modi.'[7]

USA's *Bloomberg*: 'Progressive South is Rejecting Modi.'[8] 'India's Voting Machines Are Raising Too Many Questions.'[9] 'Modi's Sledgehammer Politics Are Battering Indian Democracy.'[10] 'Billionaire Press Barons Are Squeezing Media Freedom in India.'[11] The last one is truly laughable as *Bloomberg* is owned by the billionaire Bloomberg family.

UK's *Financial Times*: 'The 'mother of democracy' is not in good shape.'[12]

USA's *The New York Times*: 'Modi's Temple of Lies.'[13] 'Modi's India is Where Global Democracy Dies.'[14]

Japan's *Nippon*: 'Indian Democracy in Peril: Slide into Autocracy Likely to Continue.'[15]

France's *Le Monde*: 'India: democracy in name only.'[16] 'India's elections this year stand out for their 'undemocratic nature' – Modi is turning democracy into electoral authoritarianism.'[17] 'India's democratic regression – The autocratic bent of Indian Prime Minister Narendra Modi is clear.'[18]

UK's *The Economist*: 'Narendra Modi's illiberalism may imperil India's economic progress.'[19]

None of this is new for Modi, though, as he has been the subject of negative press for over 22 years.

Opposition leaders have also been very harsh towards Modi, especially with their words.

Rahul Gandhi called Modi a *'Panauti'* (unlucky). After the surgical strikes by the Indian Army in PoJK, Rahul accused Modi of doing *"Khoon ki Dalali"* (brokering in the blood) of Indian soldiers. He also called Modi a *jebkatra* (pickpocket): 'Have you seen how a *jebkatra* works? One person diverts your attention and the second steals your money. Diverting attention is the PM's job and (business tycoon) Adani comes from behind to take your money away. [Home Minister] Amit Shah stands nearby with a lathi to ensure nobody creates a disturbance. That's the Gujarat model. The poor and deprived sections of society will destroy it.' Rahul has been pulled up by the Election Commission, and none other than the Supreme Court of India (SCI) for some of these remarks.

His mother Sonia Gandhi called Modi '*Maut ka Saudagar*' (Dealer of Death) in 2007. Priyanka Gandhi has called Modi a *neech* (lowlife).

It is not just the Gandhis who have abused Modi. Current party president Mallikarjun Kharge said Modi is like Hitler, and a 'poisonous snake'. Anand Sharma said Modi is 'mentally sick', BK Hariprasad has called him a '*gandi naali ka keeda*' (worm of a dirty drain), Renuka Chowdhury called Modi a 'virus', Salman Khurshid called him a '*napunsak*' (impotent), Shashi Tharoor called him a '*bichchoo* (scorpion) who sits atop a Shivling'. The list is much longer.

West Bengal CM Mamata Banerjee has often called Modi 'Hitler', 'Hitler's grandfather', '*paapi*' (sinner), the 'greatest danger to the country', a 'liar' and has also said that Modi is a 'bad influence on youngsters'.

Then there are leftist journalists, activists, the so-called intellectuals and thinkers, and self-appointed historians.

Such people are referred to as the 'Lutyens Lobby' by most centrists or right-leaning people. Modi often refers to them as the 'Khan Market Gang'. This ecosystem loves the Congress party and thus hate Modi. If you watch TV debates, you have surely seen many of them.

They also don't like the fact he is not UK-educated like former prime ministers Jawaharlal Nehru, Rajiv Gandhi, Dr Manmohan Singh, and as well as many former United Progressive Alliance (UPA) ministers, but an ordinary 'villager' from a humble background, wears Indian clothes, and gives his talks/speeches in pure Hindi, which is difficult for most convent-educated people (about 75 per cent of the Lobby) to understand. But the problem is not Modi's Hindi, is it?

Members of the Lobby seem to have many chronic communicable diseases such as Hindu-hatred, Modi-phobia, BJP/RSS-hatred and so on. Sadly, our great scientists who developed an 'AatmaNirbhar' Covid vaccine in record time, have not been able to develop a vaccine for their ailments.

In May 2019, Modi became the 4th PM in history to get elected for a 2nd full term of five years, and only the 3rd to get a majority. With 354 seats, he was just eight seats short of a 2/3rd majority!

This was the 1st time since India's first election to the Lok Sabha (LS), India's lower house of Parliament in 1952 that the Congress party did not come back to power after a full 5-year term of non-Congress rule.

The 2014 Lok Sabha (LS) elections were a combination of two factors—a strong negative wave against the UPA Government (controlled by Sonia Gandhi via Dr Manmohan Singh whom she had 'appointed' as PM), combined with a pro-Modi wave, as he was already quite an enigma.

This made it easy for the Modi-led Bharatiya Janata Party/National Democratic Alliance (BJP/NDA) to sweep the 2014 polls with a clear majority, a first for India in 30 years.

'From 2004 to 2014, you had a lady who was in power but not in office, you had a man who was in office, but not in power, that's the irony,' said brand marketing guru, theatre actor, and TV panellist Suhel Seth.[20]

By the 2019 elections, the massive corruption of UPA was almost forgotten. This was a referendum on Modi's first term. In his own words in Parliament, the BJP-led NDA secured a big win in 2019 'after a trial by fire'.[21]

On Independence Day 2020, Modi became the longest-serving non-Congress PM, surpassing the 2,272 days of the first and only other BJP PM, Atal Bihari Vajpayee. On 31 May 2024, Modi became the 3rd longest serving PM after Jawaharlal Nehru and his daughter Indira Gandhi.

On 4 June 2024, Modi became the first PM in 62 years (after Nehru in 1962) to get a 3rd term. Though the BJP and the BJP-led NDA got significantly less seats than in 2019, the NDA won a comfortable majority of 55.8 per cent of the total LS seats.

By the time we finished more than 3,000 man-hours of painstaking research for this book, we had come up with a truly mindboggling 190,125 achievements of Modi in under 10 years. Yes, Narendra Modi has done almost two lakh things for WE THE PEOPLE OF INDIA by 'ending the curse of incremental thinking', in his own words.

Despite being Modi's fans and followers, both of us were shocked to find out that the PM had done so much in such a short time.

Those who still call Modi a *feku* (fraud) are either blind, or deaf, or both.

'This is the decade of high-speed connectivity, high-speed mobility, and high-speed prosperity', Modi said about India's ongoing mega development programs launched by his government. In the book, you will see how he is 100 per cent correct, and more.

We have used many abbreviations throughout the book, so we suggest you refer to the List of Abbreviations in the beginning, after the Previews (titled as 'Praise for the Book') and before this Introduction (Preface).

By the time the book is in your hand or Kindle/other reading device, a lot of the numbers mentioned here may have changed as there would be more progress and development, but that is yet another testament to Modi's work.

Please do write a review on Amazon.

Happy reading!

Part 1

National Security Comes First

Under Modi, India's defence budget went up by a staggering 145.5 per cent in 10 years.

I

Secured the Security Council

The National Security Council (NSC), headed by a National Security Advisor (NSA), operating through the National Security Council Secretariat (NSCS), is the apex body of the national security management structure in India. The NSC, NSCS, and the NSA posts were created by Prime Minister Atal Bihari Vajpayee in November 1998 when he appointed former diplomat Brajesh Mishra as India's 1st NSA.

The Strategic Policy Group (SPG, not to be confused with the PM's Special Protection Group) is headed by the NSA, and includes the Cabinet Secretary, NITI Aayog Vice Chairperson, the Chief of Defence Staff (CDS), the three service chiefs, Reserve Bank of India (RBI) Governor, eight Government of India (GoI) Secretaries, three intelligence chiefs, and the Defence Research & Development Organisation (DRDO) Chairman. The 22-member SPG is considered as the most powerful in the GoI structure after the PM and the Cabinet Committee on Security (CCS).

Though created in 1999 by Prime Minister Vajpayee, it was a much smaller body headed by the Cabinet Secretary. Modi made the NSA the SPG's head, and gave it the 'wings' necessary for it to be fully effective.

The National Security Advisory Board (NSAB), also headed by the NSA, consists of eminent experts outside of the government and provides long-term prognosis and analysis to the NSC, recommends solutions and addresses policy issues referred to it.

There used to be a 3rd organisation—Joint Intelligence Committee that analysed intelligence data from Research & Analysis Wing (RAW), Intelligence Bureau (IB), and the Directorates of Military, Naval and Air Intelligence. Modi dismantled it in October 2018 to remove duplication and transferred its responsibilities to the NSAB.

Dr Manmohan Singh had three NSAs, two were former Foreign Secretaries while the 3rd was a former Intelligence Bureau (IB) Director. He also expanded the NSCS by adding two Deputy National Security Advisor (DNSA) posts.

Modi appointed Ajit Doval who has been NSA for 10 years. An ex-IPS officer, Doval is 'the stuff legends are made of'.

Doval spent 33 years with the IB, was the youngest police officer to get the *Police Medal* after just six years' service (the norm is minimum 17 years) for his work in the Northeast—he spent long periods undercover with the insurgent Mizo National Army in Myanmar and deep inside Chinese territory; he also spent almost seven years as a spy inside Pakistan (he did not get caught as he spoke their dialects, ate their food and wore their clothes). His expertise on Pakistan is considered unrivalled.

In 1988, Doval infiltrated the Golden Temple in Amritsar posing as an Inter-Services Intelligence (ISI) agent, spied on Khalistani terrorists hiding there, gathered info on their weapons, made maps on their locations, and passed them to the National Security Guard (NSG). Almost like a Marvel comic book hero, Doval was inside the Temple when the NSG stormed in. Rajiv Gandhi awarded him the *Kirti Chakra*, India's second highest gallantry award, the first Indian Police Service (IPS) officer to get an award reserved for military personnel till then.

In 2001, Vajpayee made Doval head of two intelligence coordination bodies set up due to intelligence failures leading up to the Kargil war with Pakistan. In 2004, Dr Manmohan Singh made him Director of the IB. He retired in January 2005 and led a private life till May 2014, when Modi recalled the former spymaster as the country's 5th NSA.

If you follow newspapers or TV news, you would have seen Doval sitting right next to Modi in his meetings with important world leaders. Doval is considered the 3rd most powerful person in the Modi Government, after the PM and the Home Minister.

Modi appointed a 3rd DNSA in October 2018 and restructured the NSCS. Whereas the DNSA posts did not have clearly defined roles earlier, each DNSA now heads a wing—an ex-IPS officer (he was a former RAW chief) with strong intelligence background heads the Intelligence and Technology Wing, an ex-Indian Foreign Service (IFS) officer (he was Ambassador to several countries and a private secretary to three PMs) heads the Strategic Planning Wing, and an ex-IPS officer (former Director General of the Border Security Force or BSF) with rich internal security experience heads the Internal Affairs Wing.

In a first, Modi created two military posts in the NSCS—a Military Advisor of Lt General/Air Marshal rank (incumbent is a former Deputy Chief of the Indian Air Force or IAF), and a National Maritime Security Coordinator of Vice Admiral rank (incumbent is a former Vice Chief of the Navy).

Though the NSA has an office in the Prime Minister's Office (PMO), in 2018, Doval ensured that the Sardar Patel Bhavan in New Delhi was taken over exclusively for the NSCS. Several ministries and departments were moved out of the 5-storey building to make space.

When Modi won a 2nd term in May 2019, he extended Doval's term for five years and promoted him from Minister of State (MoS) rank to Cabinet Minister.

After winning the 3rd term in June 2024, Modi extended the 79.5-year-old NSA's term for another five years. This has made Doval one of the oldest senior government officers in India's history. Simultaneously, the PM promoted one of the three DSNAs (the ex-RAW chief) to a newly created post of Additional NSA.

2

Modernised the Armed Forces

The Modi Government is making rapid progress in modernising the nation's armed forces to overcome an unpardonable 30-year delay in the firepower procurement program. Modi has cut through long-winded arms procurement procedures of the UPA-era.

For example, not a single howitzer had been procured since the 1986 Bofors scam involving the then prime minister, Rajiv Gandhi.

From 1950 to 2013, India imported 110.59B TIV [As the actual values of arms deals are confidential, 'trend-indicator-value' (TIV) derived by the globally respected Stockholm International Peace Research Institute (SIPRI) is the most accurate 'currency' for arms trade].

This is how things changed under Modi:

ARMS & AMMUNITION IMPORTS (Source: https://armstransfers.sipri.org/ArmsTransfer/ImportExport			
Supplier Country	**Imports (1950-2013)**	**Imports (2015-23)**	**Change**
France	**3.78%**	**22.44%**	**▲ 493.7%**
Israel	**1.85%**	**12.93%**	**▲ 598.9%**
USA	**1.976%**	**10.03%**	**▲ 407.6%**
UK	**14.85%**	**2.47%**	**▼▼ 83.4%**
USSR (later Russia)	**68.804%**	**46.50%**	**▼▼ 32.4%**

This shows that India finally woke up to the reality that France, Israel and the US produce better weapons than Russia (formerly part of USSR). High imports from Russia continue, as India needs spares/ammunition for equipment bought in the past.

Since 2021, Modi Government ordered 'Made-in-India' defence equipment worth over ₹4.5LCr ($58B), and this has saved Forex of at least $261B (82.9 per cent of our Forex reserves on 16 May 2014) as this equipment would have costed at least $319B if India imported them.

Let's examine some of the crucial acquisitions of the last 10 years.

Naturally, the highest in value are aircraft, drones and ships.

AIRCRAFT and DRONES	Supplier	QTY
Tejas Mk-1A 4th-gen Multirole Light Combat Aircraft	HAL (India)	180
Sukhoi-30 MK-I Multi Role Fighter Aircraft	HAL (India)	12
Prachand multirole Light Combat Helicopter	HAL (India)	156
Dhruv Light Utility Helicopter	HAL (India)	94
Rudra Weaponised Advanced Light Helicopter	HAL (India)	32
Netra-1 Surveillance Aircraft (on *Embraer* platform)	DRDO (India)	6
Rafale Multi Role Fighter Aircraft	Dassault (France)	36
C-295 Medium Tactical Transport Aircraft (capable of landing at & taking off from unprepared fields)	Tata Advanced Systems (India) Airbus (Spain)	46 16
Medium-range Multirole Maritime Reconnaissance Aircraft	Airbus (Spain)	15
Romeo MH-60R Seahawk Helicopter *Stinger* Missiles *Hellfire* missiles	Sikorsky (USA) Raytheon (USA) Northrop Grumman (USA)	24 245 225
P8I Anti-Submarine Aircraft with Missiles & Torpedoes	Boeing (USA)	18
Apache Guardian Attack Helicopter	Boeing (USA)	28
Chinook Heavy Lift (10,886kg load) Helicopter	Boeing (USA)	15
Poseidon P-8i Naval Patrol & Anti-Submarine Aircraft	Boeing (USA)	8
MQ9B Predator High Altitude Long Endurance Drone (with 124 Air-to-Ground Missiles and 13,950kg of Bombs)	General Atomics (USA)	31
Drishti-10 Starliner Drone (can fly 36hrs at up to 30,000ft)	Adani Defence & Aerospace	4
Heron Mark-II Medium Altitude Long Endurance Drone (can have long-range missiles/other weapons; fly 44hrs nonstop at up to 35,000ft; illuminate enemy targets with lasers to help fighter jets to use long-range weapons)	IAI (Israel)	50
Mini Unmanned Aerial Vehicle (drone)		300
Heterogeneous Drone Swarm System of 100 UAVs (world's first high density swarming UAS (Unmanned Aerial System) induction for military applications	New Space Research &Tech (India)	100

SHIPS and VESSELS	Supplier	QTY
INS Vikrant Aircraft Carrier	Cochin Shipyard (India)	1
Next-Gen Missile Vehicle (heavily-armed)	Cochin Shipyard (India)	6
Scorpene-class Submarine (French technology)	Mazgaon Dock Shipbuilders (India)	9
The Navy will import 48 Heavy Weight Torpedoes for these Submarines and procure a 'significantly' higher quantity from an Indian supplier when these are developed locally		
Guided Missile Stealth Frigate (advanced)	Garden Reach Shipbuilders & Engineers (India)	3
Next-Gen Offshore Patrol Vessel	Garden Reach Shipbuilders & Engineers (India)	5
Next-Gen Offshore Patrol Vessel	Goa Shipyard (India)	7

From 1963 onwards, India bought 874 MiG-21 aircraft from Russia of which 80 crashed before 1982. It was decided that Hindustan Aeronautics Limited (HAL) would develop the Light Combat Aircraft (LCA) to replace them.

Due to prolonged delays, in 2021 (by which time 231 MiG-21s had crashed) it was decided to urgently import 126 Medium Multirole Fighter Aircrafts (MRFAs). This would take at least six years for any vendor to supply. Requests for Information (RFIs) were sent to potential suppliers in 2001. As the next step, Requests for Proposal (RFPs) were to be sent in December 2005 to technically pre-qualified suppliers.

Sonia Gandhi-led UPA came to power in May 2004 and after delays, RFPs went to six shortlisted suppliers in August 2007. Proposals came in on 28 April 2008. In January 2012, the UPA announced that the Rafale made in France was selected for exclusive negotiations. For the next two years, the UPA was unable to finalise a deal.

Due to the IAF's urgent need for two squadrons (36 aircraft), Modi personally negotiated with the French President during a visit to France in April 2015 and after their teams ironed out details in next seven months, a deal to import 36 Rafale MRFAs was signed in September 2017, with provision for 100 per cent transfer of technology to India.

Dassault of France (the manufacturer of the Rafale jets) will ensure 75 per cent fleet uptime, compared with below 50 per cent in IAF's Sukhoi fleet.

Missiles include 500km-range Scalp Air-to-Ground Missiles (ATGMs) that can hit targets well inside China or Pakistan without crossing the borders, 120km Beyond Visual Range Air-to-Air Missiles (BVRAAMs), 80km BVRAAMs, and 60km close-combat missiles.

All 36 Rafales were delivered by December 2022 and have helped leapfrog the Indian air defence and strike capability by at least 20 years.

The Modi Government has approved the purchase of 26 Rafale Marine aircraft for India's 2nd aircraft carrier; prices and terms are being finalised.

Apart from airplanes, drones and ships, massive quantities of missile systems and missiles, rocket launchers and rockets, tanks, artillery guns, etc., have also been purchased.

MISSILE & ROCKET SYSTEMS	Supplier	QTY
S-400 Triumf Mobile Surface-to-Air Missile System (the missiles that can destroy aircraft, missiles, and drones up to 400km range and engage up to 06 targets at a time)	MKB Fakel (Russia)	**5 Squadrons** **40 Launchers** 560 Missiles
BrahMos Supersonic Cruise Missile (multiple variants for Army, Navy, Air Force)	Brahmos Aerospace (Indo-Russian JV)	420
Barak-8 Surface-to-Air Missile System (multiple variants for Army and Navy)	Bharat Dynamics-IAI (Indo-Israel JV) Kalyani-RADS (Indo-Israel JV)	**58 Launchers** 1682 Missiles
Astra Mark-I BVRAAM	Bharat Dynamics (India)	248
Nirbhay Land-to-Air Supersonic Missile (1000km range)	Bharat Dynamics (India)	300
R-33 and *R77* Air-to-Air Missile	Vympel (Russia)	1000
Milan-2T Anti-Tank Guided Missile	Bharat Dynamics (India)	4960
Akash Short Range Surface-to-Air Missile	Bharat Dynamics (India)	8 Launchers
Spike Long-Range Anti-Tank Guided Missile System	Rafael Advanced Defence Systems (RADS) (Israel)	**12 Launchers** 210 Missiles
Spike New Generation Anti-Tank Guided Missile	Bharat Forge (in a JV with RADS, Israel)	NA
Spice 2000 building-blaster Bomb	RADS (Israel)	100
Pinaka Multi-Barrel Rocket Launcher	Larsen & Toubro (L&T), Tata Advanced (India)	108
Pinaka ADM Type 2 and Type 3 Rocket	Yantra India Ltd	6400
New-Generation 84mm Rocket	Carl Gustaf (Sweden)	65,000

TANKS and ARTILLERY GUNS, etc.	Supplier	QTY
T90 Arjun Mk1A Main Battle Tank	Govt Heavy Vehicles Factory (India)	602
T90S Bhishma Tanks	Govt Heavy Vehicles Factory (India)	1657
Army will order Indian-made Future Ready Combat Vehicles to replace old Russian-made T-72 tanks from 2030 onwards.		1770
Light Tanks for high-altitude warfare	Larsen & Toubro or L&T (India)	354
Close-In Weapon System with Air Defence Gun, Tracking/Search Radar	L&T (India)	61
Dhanush Howitzer Guns	Advanced Weapons & Equipment India (AWEIL)	144
Advanced Towed (Howitzer) Artillery Gun System	AWEIL, L&T, Bharat Forge, Tata ASL	307
M777 Ultra-Light Howitzer Gun (can be slung under helicopters for airlift to mountains)	BAE Systems (direct supply from USA) Mahindra Defence (made under license in India)	25 120
K-9 Vajra-T 155-mm Howitzer Guns	L&T (in a JV with Hanwha of South Korea)	100

The 26/11 Mumbai terror attacks showed that Indian security forces, including NSG's elite 'Black Cat' commandos, were inadequately equipped.

Personnel of the Mumbai Police, the Maharashtra Anti-Terrorism Squad (ATS) and even the NSG commandos did not have night-vision goggles or proper bulletproof jackets.

To meet these challenges, the Modi Government modernised personal firearms and protection equipment and the process is ongoing.

Along and near the Chinese border and Line of Actual Control (LAC), the Indian Army has erected heated shelters, bunkers, and Arctic tents with integrated arrangements for electricity, water, and toilets.

The Modi Government has purchased or ordered arms and ammunition worth over ₹23.5LCr in 10 years and the budget for the current year (FY25) plus the next four years is said to be almost ₹16LCr.

Many procurement projects were started by the UPA Government but failed to take off, critically harming India's national security interests. The standard excuse used to be 'lack of funds'.

PERSONAL and SMALL ARMS	Supplier	QTY
M2 Browning Heavy Machine Guns .50 BMG (12.7x99mm)	FN Herstal (USA)	110
Mk 48 Maximi General Purpose Machine Guns	FN Herstal (USA)	715
Negev NG7 5.56x45mm Light Machine Gun	Israel Weapon Industries	40,979
Sako TRG42 Sniper Rifle .338 Lapua Magnum	SAKO (Finland)	402
Barrett M107 A1 Heavy Sniping Rifle 50BMG calibre	Barrett Firearms Manufacturing (USA)	100
Various Made-in-India Sniper Rifles	Indian Manufacturers	4849
JVPC sub-machine Carbine Gun 5.56x30mm for close-quarters-battle	AWEIL, Kalyani Strategic Syst.(India)	425,213
12.7mm SRCG (Stabilised Remote Control Gun)	AWEIL (India)	463
SIG 716g2 Assault Rifle 7.62x51mm	Sig Sauer (USA)	145,400
FN SCAR (H) Assault Rifle 7.62x51mm	FN Herstal (USA)	1050
CMT CZ 807 Assault Rifle 7.62x39mm	Counter Measures Technologies (India)	NA
AK-203 Assault Rifle 7.52x39mm	Concern Kalashnikov (Russia)	70,000
Indo Russian Rifles has been set up in Amethi (UP) as a JV between 2 PSEs (50.5%), Concern Kalashnikov (42%), and Rosoboronexport (7.5%) to make 75,000 AK-203 rifles/year and Indian Armed Forces will buy 9yrs production		670,000
FN SCAR (L) 5.56x45mm Assault Rifle 5.56x45mm	FN Herstal (USA)	1400
AK-47 Assault Rifle 7.62x39mm (upgrades of old Russian-made rifles)	SSS Defence (India)	
Tata 360 Ballistic Vest (bulletproof jacket)		62,627
SMPP Vest (bulletproof / ballistic jacket)	SMPP Pvt Ltd (India)	186,000
EXFIL High Cut Ballistic Helmet for Special Forces	Team Wendy (USA)	<500
MKU Mukut Lightweight Bulletproof Helmet	MKU Ltd (India)	158,279
Tata Advanced Combat Helmet	Tata Advanced Systems (TASL), India	50,000
PVS-14-SOCOM helmet-mounted Night Vision Monocular	ANVS (India)	400
ECWCS (Extended Cold Weather Clothing Systems) comprising Parka Down Jackets, Gloves with Inserts, Mittens, Undershirt, Drawers, Shirt, Lined Trousers, Socks, Boots, Parka, Snow Goggles, and Sleeping Bags	Supplied by US Army (made by Harrdshell and WL Gore & Associates)	11,000 sets

If UPA did not have the funds, where did Modi get the funds from?

The answers are simple—government funds in the UPA-era probably went to the piggy banks of Sonia Gandhi and UPA ministers, whereas Modi managed to generate more money for the government by almost wiping out corruption in GoI's ministries, departments and public sector enterprises (PSEs).

Central Armed Police Forces

The Central Armed Police Forces (CAPFs) are also being provided with modern state-of-the-art weapons, equipment, and technology.

Cyber Security

Under Modi, India's forces have taken several steps for protecting and strengthening India's digital sovereignty against cybercriminals (including enemy nations such as China) that pose a threat through the misuse of the internet.

Nausena Bhawan

For 74 years, the Indian Navy's headquarters staff based in the national capital operated from 13 different buildings, most of them shared with other services. The newly built iconic '*Nausena Bhawan*' is a new state-of-the-art headquarters for the Navy. Located in Delhi Cantonment, the sprawling complex is equipped with modern facilities and cutting-edge technologies. It represents a significant step forward for the Navy, providing a centralised and technologically advanced headquarters that reflects the nation's commitment to maritime excellence and national security.

Similarly, new headquarter buildings have also been planned for the Army and the Air Force.

3

CDS and Unified Commands

On New Year's Day 2020, Modi created the Chief of Defence Staff (CDS) post as the head of the Armed Forces, chief military adviser to the PM, and head of a new Department of Military Affairs (DMA). The CDS and DMA are critical in today's era of hybrid warfare and integrated 'theatre' (or geographical) commands.

Consisting of military and civilian officers, the DMA deals with the Integrated Defence Staff Headquarters, and promotes jointness in planning, procurement, staffing, training, optimal utilisation of resources, and use of Made-in-India equipment. It coordinates between the Ministry of Defence (MoD), the three services, the nuclear/cyber/space commands, and integrates the overall combat capabilities of the nation's armed forces.

India was the only nation among the Top 10 economies with no chief military advisor to the Head of Government. The US, China, Russia, Japan, Germany, the UK, Italy, Canada, and Mexico all have one.

India has two unified commands—Andaman & Nicobar Command and Strategic Forces Command (handles the nuclear arsenal), and 17 single-service commands (Army 7, IAF 7 and Navy 3).

It is a proven fact that unified commands with representation from all three services lead to more efficient communication and planning for peacetime and wartime strategies.

The US had seven theatre commands (Central, European, Indo-Pacific, Northern, Southern, African, and Space Command) for several decades, and added a Cyber Command a few years ago. China established five theatre commands in 2016 to enhance offensive capabilities and improve their command-and-control structures.

Though it is not easy to change legacy systems of over 75 years, the first CDS, General Bipin Rawat was working to establish Integrated Tri-Service Theatre Commands till his suspicious death in a chopper crash 23 months after he became CDS.

Due to the mystery surrounding the crash, Modi took 10 months to appoint a new CDS, General Anil Chauhan, on 28 September 2022. General Chauhan is continuing the difficult tasks based on the foundations laid by General Rawat.

A consensus has been reached among all the three services on the plan. Three Integrated Theatre Commands will be established, one each for managing the China border/LAC on the north and the Pakistan front on the west, with the 3rd a Maritime Command in peninsular India.

Each will be led by a senior 3-star general (Lt General, Air Marshal or Vice Admiral). Air assets, for example, will not be owned by any single command but shift from one to another based on contingency.

A group of 102 officers (40 Army, 32 IAF, 30 Navy), in the rank of Lt. Colonels and Majors, were cross-posted to other services in May and June 2023. This initiative is aimed at areas of commonality, such as equipment like drones and the BrahMos missiles.

Common annual confidential reports have been introduced for all 2-star and 3-star generals across the three services to synergise appraisals for Tri-Service appointments.

In August 2023, the Parliament passed the 'Inter-services Organisations (Command, Control and Discipline) Bill' and the Act was notified by the GOI in mid-May 2024, paving the way for creation of the unified Theatre Commands.

4

Strengthened Border Infrastructure

The UPA hardly built roads, tunnels, bridges, or military airfields in border areas. AK Antony (Defence Minister for 7.5 years) said in Parliament, 'Independent India has had a policy … that the best defence is not to develop our borders. An undeveloped border is safer.'[1]

In contrast, Modi paid special attention to augmenting infrastructure along the Line of Control (LoC), LAC and the Pakistan and China borders.

The Border Road Organisation's (BRO) budget was increased 3.8 times. Hundreds of roads and bridges, and almost 50 tunnels have been built.

- The strategic 255km DSDBO Road connecting Leh with the Daulat Beg Oldie (DBO) military post near the LAC reduced travel time from two days to six hours. As many as 11 years after construction started in 2000, it was found that over 75 per cent of the road had been laid on the riverbed and got damaged every summer as melting snow flooded the Shyok River. About half of the ₹320Cr spent had been embezzled. Over 77 per cent of the road built over 11 years had to be realigned by Modi Government.

- The IAF landed a C-130J transport aircraft at DBO airfield.
- It also landed it on a pitch-dark night in Kargil airfield (length of only 6km against the required 9km). Kargil is surrounded by 14,000–15,000ft high mountains.
- The 1134ft Shyok River Bridge in Ladakh at an altitude of 15,300ft above sea level was completed in 7 months in October 2019, an unprecedented global achievement at this altitude.
- In September 2020, Modi inaugurated the 9km Atal Tunnel on Manali–Leh Highway. It has reduced travel time by 4–5 hours. The foundation stone was laid in June 2010 by Sonia Gandhi. Less than 45 per cent of digging work was completed in the next four years.
- The newly opened 6.5km Sonamarg Tunnel (earlier Z-Morh Tunnel) has reduced time to only 15 minutes against hours over the earlier zigzag road that ran up and down the hills. Tourist guides, roadside shop owners and hoteliers in Sonmarg say their incomes have tripled since the tunnel opened.
- An adjacent 14.2km 2-lane Zoji La Tunnel being built below Zoji La Pass between Sonmarg (Jammu & Kashmir or J&K) and Drass in Kargil (Ladakh) at a height of 11,575ft above sea level is expected to open in 2027, and together will ensure year-long movement on Srinagar–Kargil–Leh highway that is closed for over seven months/year due to heavy snowfall. This was a strategic requirement of the Army as the area is close to the LoC and vulnerable to terrorist activity. The tunnels will also connect the Amarnath Yatra base camp at Baltal (Kargil) and other places in Ladakh, boosting tourism and the economy of the region.
- Udhampur–Ramban 9.28km tunnel reduced Jammu–Srinagar travel time by over two hours. A 0.26km tunnel

on Akhnoor–Poonch Road in J&K plays a vital role in enhancing connectivity from Jammu to Poonch.

- The 2.27km Sela Tunnel in Arunachal Pradesh has reduced the travel time from Dirang to Tawang (90km from LAC, breached by China's People's Liberation Army (PLA) in the 1962 war) by 70 minutes, and ensured all-weather connectivity from Army IV Corps' headquarters in Tezpur (Assam). The Sela Pass is visible to Chinese soldiers across the LAC and the tunnel under the pass has overcome this military disadvantage. *The Chinese had reached Tezpur in 1962 as the Indian Army was not able to send tanks or armoured vehicles to Tawang. Now, with an 18ft clearance inside the tunnel, we can even send rocket and missile launchers.*
- The under-construction 4.1km 4-lane Shinku-la Tunnel will be the world's highest tunnel at 16,580ft above sea level when complete.
- At least another 20 tunnels are under construction in J&K and 11 in Ladakh.
- The National Highways Authority of India (NHAI) began 4-laning the 247km Jammu–Srinagar highway (the only all-weather road connecting Kashmir with the rest of India) in 2011. The project includes 10 tunnels of 21.5km. Only about 15 per cent was complete in three years under UPA. As of November 2024, about 88 per cent was complete and 100 per cent is expected to complete by the end of 2025. This will reduce the distance by 50km, and travel time from 9–10hrs to about five hours.
- To ease travel between Jammu and Srinagar, two more highway corridors are being built.
- The 1.32km Chenab Rail Bridge opened in August 2022. The project was approved in December 2004, during

UPA-1 and originally intended to complete in December 2009, but it was halted in September 2008 due to fears over stability and safety. Although work restarted in August 2010, there was hardly any progress until Modi became PM.

- After the Uri attack (see 'Terror-Free India'), Modi decided to set up several dams to fully utilise India's share, to send a message to Pakistan to stop terrorism activities. India is building seven dams and hydroelectric power projects of 5,134MW in Kishtwar (Kashmir). These will help reduce excess water shared with Pakistan under the 1960 Indus Water Treaty, via which the rivers of the Indus water system are split between India and Pakistan. India is under-utilising the over 7.5M acre-feet (MAF) of water from its share, allowing it to flow into Pakistan. India has sent two notices in 2023 and 2024 to Pakistan for a review of the Treaty.
- The 2,963 border villages in Arunachal Pradesh, Himachal Pradesh, Ladakh, Sikkim, and Uttarakhand are undergoing comprehensive development at a cost of ₹4,800 Cr under the 'Vibrant Village Program'.

Technological solutions are being implemented on fenced portions of the borders to make fencing smarter.

Read more in the 'Developing J&K', 'Developing Ladakh' and 'Developing the Northeast' chapters in this book.

Why was UPA not building border infrastructure? What was the Memorandum of Understanding (MoU) that the Congress party signed in August 2008 with China's ruling (and only) party, the Communist Party of China?

5

Handled the Dragon

China occupied 640–750 km^2 of Indian Territory in Eastern Ladakh during UPA Government's 2nd term. In 2013, former Foreign Secretary Shyam Saran, then chairman of the National Security Advisory Board, after his visit to the region, informed the government that a patrol of People's Liberation Army (PLA) of China had set a new LAC, occupying 640km^2 of Indian territory, but the UPA Government had hidden this fact from the nation.

Top strategic thinker Dr Brahma Chellaney wrote on 11 May 2013 in *The Japan Times*:[2]

> On the night of Apr 15, a People's Liberation Army (PLA) platoon stealthily intruded near the China–India–Pakistan tri-junction, established a camp 19km inside Indian-controlled territory, and presented India's government with the potential loss of a strategically vital 750km^2 high-altitude plateau [Depsang]… To add to India's woes, Salman Khurshid, the country's bungling foreign minister, initially made light of the deepest Chinese incursion in more than a quarter century. The garrulous minister called the intrusion just 'one little spot' of acne on the otherwise 'beautiful face' of the bilateral relationship—a mere blemish that could be treated with 'an ointment'.

Khurshid said in a May 2013 China visit that he would 'love to live in Beijing'. The *Times of India* wrote: 'Khurshid's visit took on such a rosy hue that it's difficult to believe India and China were on the verge of a border conflict just a week ago.'[3]

China's PLA made nearly 600 incursions into Indian territory between 2010 and 2013, including a 19km incursion inside Indian territory on 15 April 2013.

Starting 5 May 2020, there was a border standoff between India and China along the LAC in Eastern Ladakh. The Indian Army and Indo-Tibetan Border Police (ITBP) troops engaged in face-offs and skirmishes with China's PLA troops at several locations.

There were efforts by China to occupy Indian Territory at multiple locations. India said that 19 Indian *jawans* (soldiers) and a Colonel, plus 42 Chinese soldiers and an officer were killed in hand-to-hand combat at Galwan Valley (Ladakh) on the night of 15 June 2020.

American magazine *U.S. News & World Report* said that 35 Chinese troops including a senior officer died, quoting US intelligence sources.[4]

Rahul Gandhi regularly alleges that Modi lost territory to China—an allegation that has no proof whatsoever.

Whichever version you believe, it is abundantly clear that India had the upper hand. India did not lose an inch of territory under Modi.

Several government contracts, earlier awarded to Chinese companies, were cancelled and such moves are continuing.

The GoI started taking several measures to make it difficult to import Chinese goods into India. (In the 'Make in India' and the 'Wafer and Chips' chapters, you will see how India has finally started reducing dependency on Chinese imports).

Modi Government pressurised OnePlus, Oppo, Vivo, and Xiaomi to replace all their Chinese-owned distributors with Indian-owned ones and this has started happening. The GoI is also pressuring these companies to add more Indian executives in top decision-making leadership roles and has told them: 'otherwise alternatives may be explored'. The message is quite clear—shape up or ship out.

Many Chinese as well as Indian executives of Chinese companies in India are being investigated by government agencies including LEAs for foreign exchange violations, spying and other crimes, and some have even been arrested.

The Modi Government has also banned more than 320 Chinese apps.

6

Built Military Bases Abroad

Oman

In the Sultanate strategically located at the mouth of the Persian Gulf, India has four bases. There is an IAF base and an Indian Navy base at the port town of Duqm; the Indian Navy has berthing privileges (its vessels can enter at any time and access facilities there) at the Muscat Naval Base. In February 2018, Modi successfully negotiated the use of Omani airbases by IAF aircraft. India also has a listening station (to detect movements by sound and intercepting electronic communications) in Ras al Hadd.

Sri Lanka

In 2018, India agreed to form a JV with Sri Lanka to operate Mattala Rajapaksa International Airport (MRIA) in Hambantota, 241km southeast of Colombo. It is called the 'world's emptiest airport' due to lack of flights. The loss-making airport was funded via high-interest Chinese loans. The seaport in Hambantota is leased to China for 99 years to set off Chinese loans. Gaining control of the airport is a huge strategic gain by India. In December 2023, Sri Lanka's Ministry of Ports and Aviation confirmed that an agreement was reached to hand over the operations of MRIA to a private JV between Indian and Russian entities.

Singapore

In 2017, India and Singapore signed a bilateral agreement that allows Indian Navy ships limited logistical support, including refuelling, at Singapore's Changi Naval Base.

Vietnam

India has a naval presence in the South China Sea through the Cam Ranh Bay Naval and Air Base. In 2016, India said it would establish a satellite tracking and imaging centre near Ho Chi Minh City to keep an eye on China. It was completed by Indian Space Research Organisation (ISRO) in 2018 at an estimated cost of $23M. The centre enables ISRO to track and receive data from satellites launched from India and gives Vietnam access to images from Indian earth observation satellites that cover China and the South China Sea. It is linked with ISRO's stations in Indonesia and Brunei.

Mauritius

In 2015, India got access to North Agaléga Island, 1122km north of Mauritius, and developed an air and naval staging point for surveillance of southwestern Indian Ocean. India's Boeing P8I surveillance aircraft will also operate from there.

Seychelles

India has a listening and radar post in this island nation 1760km north of Mauritius. India supported the construction of 6 coastal surveillance radars linked with the Indian surveillance network. During a visit to New Delhi in June

2018 by Seychelles' President Danny Faure, the countries said they would work together to develop a naval base while keeping 'each other's interests' in mind.

Madagascar

India has a listening and radar post on this island nation located about 1000km west of Mauritius and about 1250km southwest of Seychelles.

The three island nations of Madagascar, Mauritius and Seychelles form a strategic triangle for India in the western Indian Ocean area.

Indonesia

A feasibility study was done to develop the strategically valuable Sabang port in Indonesia's Aceh province, located about 193km from India's southernmost tip and about 700km from Port Blair, the capital of Andaman & Nicobar Islands (A&NI). The port will allow India easier access to the Malacca Straits, a narrow stretch of the sea between Indonesia and Malaysia and one of six chokepoints along the world's maritime trading routes. A substantial chunk of the world's goods trade passes through the Straits, as does most of China's energy. Sabang can bolster India's military position vis-à-vis China in the Indian Ocean. In 2018, Indonesia's coordinating minister for maritime affairs alluded to a possible military use for Sabang. Progress slowed down due to Covid-19. A Joint Task Force to undertake projects for port related infrastructure in and around Sabang has been set up. India will help the Indonesian Air Force to maintain their Russian-made Sukhoi jets. Private Indian companies are also in talks to develop a port in Western Sumatra, which would help improve economic ties between the two countries.

Bhutan

There is an Indian Military Training Team station and base in Bhutan—a signal to show the Chinese that Bhutan is not alone. Through a strategic defence agreement, in case of any Chinese intrusion or attack, India will help defend Bhutan.

Tajikistan

Its location above PoJK and Afghanistan is strategic for India. Farkhor Air Base, 130km southeast of the capital Dushanbe, is operated by the IAF in collaboration with the Tajik Air Force. It was India's first military base outside Indian Territory. Ayni Air Base, aka Hisar Air Base, is just 10km west of Dushanbe. This is also jointly operated by the IAF and the Tajikistan Air Force. Since 2014, India has deployed Su-30 MKI aircraft in limited numbers at this base.

While some of India's foreign military bases (especially in Bhutan and Tajikistan) have been around since before his time, Modi has successfully negotiated most of the others listed above, as well as access to American and French bases mentioned in the next chapter.

Although many years late due to the complete lackadaisical attitude of the Sonia Gandhi-led UPA, India under Modi is now developing its own 'Necklace of Diamonds' to counter the part of China's 'String of Pearls' that surrounds India around its entire coastline with Chinese commercial ports or military bases in Cambodia, Malaysia, Myanmar, Bangladesh, Sri Lanka, Maldives, Pakistan, and Djibouti.

7

International Defence Treaties

India inked the 'Logistics Exchange Memorandum of Agreement' (LEMOA) with the US in 2016, a 'Communications, Compatibility and Security Arrangement' (COMCASA) in 2018, an 'Industrial Security Agreement' (ISA) in December 2019, a 'Basic Exchange and Cooperation Agreement for Geospatial Cooperation' (BECA) in 2020, and a 'Maritime Information Sharing Technical Arrangement' (MISTA) to enhance cooperation between their' navies.

The UPA stonewalled LEMOA, COMCASA, and BECA for 10 years saying they will 'compromise India's strategic autonomy'. The Modi Government has stressed there are 'enough India-specific safeguards' in these treaties to protect India's sovereign interests.

LEMOA facilitates India's use of American facilities throughout the Indian Ocean region, including at Diego Garcia (1173km south of Maldives) and various American facilities in the Persian Gulf.

Indian armed forces now have ties with the US Central Command (CENTCOM) that covers Pakistan, Afghanistan, Egypt, the entire Middle East, Kazakhstan,

Kyrgyzstan, Tajikistan, Turkmenistan, Uzbekistan), and the US Africa Command. This tie-up was very strategic. Earlier, India only had ties with the US Indo-Pacific Command that covers China, India, Japan, Australia, New Zealand, and all Asian countries except the five 'stans' that are part of CENTCOM.

BECA allows India to get highly classified geospatial intelligence including topographical and aeronautical digital data and advanced satellite imagery on a real-time basis for enhancing the accuracy of our missiles and armed drones and long-range navigation of aircraft.

COMCASA and BECA allow India to buy armed US-made drones for long-range precision strikes against targets on land and sea.

An Indo-US Industrial Security Joint Working Group aligns policies and procedures to allow one another's defence industries to collaborate on cutting-edge defence technologies.

Special Forces of India (Army's PARA SF, Navy's MARCOS, and IAF's Garud Commando Force) and the US (Army's Delta Force, Green Berets, and Rangers, US Navy SEALs, US Marines, and various groups in the US Air Force or USAF) now interact regularly.

Other Countries

In January 2018, India finalised a logistics exchange agreement with France that allows Indian access to French military facilities, including key bases at Djibouti on the Red Sea and at Réunion in the southern Indian Ocean.

The Indian Navy has trained 550 Vietnamese Navy submariners to operate Kilo-class submarines. India provided a $100M 'line of credit' in September 2014 and another

$500M line of credit in September 2016 for Vietnam to buy Indian defence equipment. The IAF trains Vietnamese pilots to fly Sukhoi aircraft.

In June 2018, Modi announced a $100M line of credit to Seychelles for acquiring Indian defence equipment. India also gifted a second Dornier aircraft for the Seychelles military.

During the Modi-era, India has signed agreements or MOUs with more than 45 countries, including Algeria, Argentina, Australia, Bahrain, Bangladesh, Botswana, Brunei, Egypt, France, Fiji, Greece, Guyana, Indonesia, Israel, Italy, Japan, Jordan, Kazakhstan, Kenya, Kuwait, Kyrgyzstan, Laos, Myanmar, Nigeria, Oman, Papua New Guinea, Philippines, Portugal, Qatar, Russia, Rwanda, Saudi Arabia, Seychelles, Singapore, South Korea, Spain, Sudan, Tanzania, Turkmenistan, UAE, Uganda, Ukraine, USA, Uzbekistan and Vietnam for collaboration on various defence and security-related issues.

8

One Rank One Pension

Within nine months of becoming PM, Modi fulfilled the 41-year-old demand of Armed Forces' veterans for 'One-Rank One-Pension' (OROP).

Demand for pay-pension equity was provoked by Prime Minister Indira Gandhi's decision in 1973 to decrease the pensions of Armed Forces personnel by 20–40 per cent and increase the pensions of civilian government employees by 20 per cent, without consulting the Forces.

In 1986, her son, Prime Minister Rajiv Gandhi implemented the 'Rank Pay' system, which reduced the basic pay of Captains, Majors, Lt Colonels, Colonels, and Brigadiers in the Army, and their equivalent in the IAF and the Navy, relative to the basic pay scales of civilian and police officers. This perplexing move created radical asymmetries between police and military ranks, affected pays and pensions of lakhs of Armed Forces' officers and veterans, and became a lingering cause of distrust, which governments over the next 28 years did little to amend.

In 2008, the Sonia Gandhi-led UPA Government discarded Rank Pay and introduced 'Grade Pay' and 'Pay bands', which instead of addressing rank, pay and pension asymmetries caused by Rank Pay, reinforced existing asymmetries.

OROP ensures payment of uniform pension to persons retiring in the same rank with the same length of service, irrespective of when they retire.

When OROP was accepted by the Modi Government, there were about 3.2M beneficiaries, of whom about 86 per cent were widows, Junior Commissioned Officers (JCOs), Non-Commissioned Officers (NCOs), and other ranks, and about 14 per cent were officers.

As per some surveys, 77 to 85 per cent of the serving personnel and veterans of the Armed Forces welcomed the move.

9

Jai Jawan

On 30 August 2022, seven former Indian Navy officers and a sailor were arrested by Qatar State Security, the intelligence agency of the Middle Eastern monarchy where 0.84M Indians comprise 28.6 per cent of the 2.94M population—the largest ethnic population in a country with about 88 per cent migrants.

The eight were employees of a consulting company engaged in advising Qatar on obtaining Italian submarines that could evade radar detection. The charges were not made public by Qatari authorities and their bail requests were denied seven times. Though India had consular access to the eight while they were in prison, Qatar told our Embassy officials that evidence suggested they passed on intelligence to Israel.

In late-March 2023, the eight men had their first court trial. On 26 October, a Qatari court handed death sentences to all eight on spying charges.

On 1 December, Modi met Sheikh Tamim bin Hamad Al-Thani, Emir of Qatar on the sidelines of a summit in Dubai. Official statements said: 'They discussed bilateral partnership and the well-being of the Indian community in Qatar.'[5] But Modi's real agenda was different. On 6 February 2024, India signed a $78B deal with QatarEnergy to buy 7.5MT/year of Liquified Natral gas (LNG) till 2028. On 12 February, Qatar released all the eight men.

'I wish to thank PM Modi because this would not have been possible (without) his personal intervention', said Capt. Navtej Singh. 'Without the intervention of PM Modi, we would not have been standing in front of you (at Delhi airport) today', added Commander Sanjeev Gupta.[6] GoI officials had been in regular touch with the eight families for 17.5 months.

On 14 February, Modi flew to Qatar to meet the Emir, the PM, and other top officials.

Also see 'Terror-free India' about how Modi and his team secured the release of an IAF pilot captured by Pakistan.

Since 2014, PM Narendra Modi has been visiting military facilities in border areas to celebrate Diwali with the *jawans*.

From Siachen Glacier in 2014, to 1965-war memorials in Punjab in 2015, China border in Himachal Pradesh in 2016, J&K's Gurez sector in 2017, Uttarakhand's Harsil in 2018, J&K's Rajouri in 2019, Rajasthan's Longewala in 2020, J&K's Nowshera in 2021, Ladakh's Kargil in 2022, Himachal Pradesh's Lepcha in 2023, and near the Indo-Pak border in Gujarat's Kutch district in 2024.

He speaks with the *jawans*, watches their song and dance performances, and makes them feel cared for. When none other than the PM comes to your border base in freezing temperatures instead of being with his own family on Diwali, which soldier would not be proud of his nation?

Where did Dr Manmohan Singh celebrate Diwali from 2004 to 2013? Or Sonia Gandhi who controlled his government, or Rahul Gandhi? How many occasions do you remember when the PM helped Indian military officers imprisoned by foreign governments?

10

Younger Fighting Force

Inside every Indian lies the heart of a soldier, willing to serve the nation. Modi's Agnipath Yojana empowers, disciplines and skills youth with military ethos but also improves the battle preparedness of the Indian Armed Forces for rapidly changing scenarios.

It is a unique opportunity for nation building based on unity in diversity through empowered, disciplined and skilled youth who can fulfil their dreams of joining the Forces to build a self-reliant and strong India. No one is better than the Forces to train and discipline the youth. Channelising their positive energy will create permanent skilled manpower for society, as the scheme will continue without an end.

Every year, 46,000 young women and men of age 17½ to 21 years who meet certain educational, physical and medical criteria are recruited as Agniveers to serve a 4-year Tour of Duty (ToD) in all three services—Army (40,000), Air Force (3,000), and Navy (3,000). This will go up to 90,000 in the 5th year and 125,000 from the 6th year onwards.

Agniveers get a monthly pay of ₹30,000 in the first year, going up to ₹40,000 in the 4th year, including hardship/risk/dress/travel allowances, rations, free medical care at military hospitals, and Canteen Stores Department (CSD) benefits—defence employees can purchase items including groceries, liquor, and cars at subsidised rates from the CSD. They contribute 30 per cent of monthly pay to a Corpus Fund and GoI matches it, so the effective CTC is ₹4.68L in the 1st year, going up to ₹6.24L in the 4th year. On completion of the 4-year ToD, an Agniveer gets a tax-free 'SevaNidhi' amount of ₹11.71L. They get premium-free life insurance of ₹48L, Ex Gratia of ₹44L for death attributable to service, and full pay for unserved tenure, including the SevaNidhi component. Disability compensation is a one-time Ex Gratia of ₹44L for 100 per cent disability, ₹25L for 75 per cent disability, and ₹15L for 50 per cent.

On completion of the 4-year ToD, all the Agniveers are given an opportunity to apply for continuing to serve with the Forces, and 25 per cent are selected for a 17-year 'permanent commission' with the Army/IAF/Navy.

The other 75 per cent leave with certification and/or higher education credits, as well as a financial package and bank loan options. They also get 10 per cent reservations and five years' age relaxation in recruitment by the CAPFs, including BSF, CISF, CRPF, RPF, and SSB.

In the prime of their youth, the 75 per cent will be mature, disciplined, dynamic, motivated, and skilled via the best possible training and hands-on experience, including team skills and camaraderie. They will have ample opportunities in civil society. For example, India hires more than 480,000 private security officers/guards each year, which can absorb all 34,500 Agniveers discharged by the Forces each year during the first 4 years, 67,500 in the 5th year and 93,750 annually from the 6th year onwards.

In the first 14-day recruitment cycle, the Army received over 3.5M applications, Navy 0.955M (82,000 women) and IAF almost 0.75M.

The Army trained the first 19,000 Agniveers in 2023 from January to June (24-week basic course) and August (31-week advanced course). The curated courses had a heavy focus on using hi-tech simulators and involved gruelling, high-intensity training comprising physical fitness, combat engineering training and basic trade training. They further underwent seven weeks on-the-job training in the unit where they will serve for four years. Training of the 2nd batch started in July 2023.

In March and August 2023, the first batch of about 3,000 Naval Agniveers, including 312 women, graduated after undergoing 16-week training programs. In the Air Force, 2,280 Agniveervayu, including 153 women, successfully completed a 22-week training program.

Apart from benefits for the nation and the Agniveers, the Forces get more diverse, energetic, fitter, and resilient youth suited to the changing dynamics of today's conflict that uses technologies such as artificial intelligence (AI), cyber warfare, space-based surveillance and reconnaissance. Youth today eat better, run faster and longer, are better versed with technology, and easily adapt to rapid changes. The average age of serving personnel will keep getting younger over the years and the high defence pension expenditure will gradually come down.

There were about 1.75M applicants in 2023 and over 1.95M in 2024 (42.5 times the number of posts), which shows the popularity of the scheme.

Congress has promised to cancel the Agniveer scheme if it is elected. The key word is 'if'.

11

Reinforced the Agencies

The 'NIA (Amendment) Act 2019' gave more teeth to the National Investigation Agency (NIA). It empowered the NIA to probe terror attacks targeting Indians and Indian interests abroad, and investigate human trafficking, fake currency, manufacture/sale of prohibited arms, and cyberterrorism.

The 'Unlawful Activities (Prevention) Act 1967' or 'UAPA' enabled the GoI to designate an organisation as a terrorist organisation but not individuals as terrorists. When India designated Lashkar-e-Taiba (LeT) as a terrorist organisation, Hafiz Saeed started Jama'at-ud-Da'wah. Each time, the new outfit would have to be re-designated.

After Modi's 2019 UAPA Amendment, if Maulana Masood Azhar is designated as a terrorist, any organisation associated with him is automatically a terrorist organisation. Most major countries and the UN designate individuals as terrorists. It was high time India did it. As of December 2024, there were 45 'Terrorist Organisations' designated by the NIA.

Earlier an investigating officer had to get the approval of a state's Director General of Police (DGP) to seize properties relating to terrorism in that state. The Federal Bureau of Investigation (FBI) in the US, Ministry of State Security

(MSS) in China, *Federal'naya Sluzhba Bezopasnosti* (FSB) in Russia, and similar agencies in other countries never needed approval from any state or city police department for any kind of ops in that state/city. With UAPA 2019, if an NIA officer is investigating, the DG of NIA can approve attachment of property in any state. Let's look at some data:

NIA & ED see Huge Improvement in Results	Earlier	Modi-era	Change
NIA—Cases Registered	28.4/year from Jan2009 to May2020	379.2/year from Jun2020 to Feb2024	▲ 1235%
NIA—Convictions	4.9/year from Jan2009 to May2020	53.6/year from Jun2020 to Feb2024	▲ 994%
ED—Cases Registered	~1400 during UPA	~4810	▲ 244%
ED—Properties Attached	₹5000cr during UPA	₹101,500cr	▲ 1930%
Sources: Several MHA, NIA & ED Press Releases; Modi Speeches **Note:** Some of this data may be subject to ±7.5% variation			

In 2023 alone, the NIA conducted 1,040 searches/raids and arrested 625 persons (114 *jihadis*, 76 Left-Wing Extremists (LWEs), 65 ISIS operatives, 47 absconders, 45 human traffickers, 28 accused of terrorism and organised crime), filed 513 chargesheets, and 74 were convicted. It also attached 240 properties worth ₹55.9Cr.

The NIA has arrested more than 90 Kashmiri separatists, and most are in jail. Many were funded by Pakistan. A total of 403 properties worth more than ₹730Cr were attached, and some destroyed with court permission, and over ₹100Cr lying in bank accounts was frozen.

Such actions had not been taken for 30 years. The NIA registered 32 cases of terror financing, whereas before 2014, there was no case registered. J&K's State Investigation Agency (SIA) registered 51 cases whereas earlier the need for a SIA was not felt.

More than 125 separatist leaders were provided 'official' security by the Central/State Government for decades. *Yes, we taxpayers were paying for the security of anti-India people. Call that irony or by its real name—'vote-bank politics'.* Modi withdrew all security in February 2019.

More than 7,500 properties of Pakistani nationals and 131 of Chinese nationals have been vested in the Ministry of Home Affairs (MHA)'s Custodian of Enemy Property for India and put up for e-Auctions from time to time.

Revenue service officers from Central Bureau of Investigation (CBI), Directorate of Revenue Intelligence (DRI), Enforcement Directorate (ED), Income Tax Department (ITD), and Serious Fraud Investigation Office (SFIO) are now being trained by the IB and RAW in intelligence tradecraft; the National Institute of Securities Markets on investigating economic crimes; State Bank of India Institute of Consumer Banking on money laundering; National Law University on legal aspects/matters; and by the National Academy of Direct Taxes on forensic accounting and digital forensics.

This is also a first for India.

12

Terror-free India

RVS Mani was a senior Internal Security officer in the Home Ministry during 2006– 2010. His book *The Myth of Hindu Terror:* says that Mani was summoned in May 2006 by Home Minister Shivraj Patil. In the minister's cabin, Congress leader Digvijaya Singh and Maharashtra IPS officer Hemant Karkare sought information on terrorist attacks, while Patil sat, unconcerned. (*Singh had publicly hugged Zakir Naik, an Islamic preacher banned by many countries, who had said that a man has the right to beat his wife, and those who convert from Islam and then speak against Islam should be killed.*) Mani wrote:

> They were not happy that Muslims were aiding terrorists. The first seed of the canard was sown that 'Hindu terror' existed and this decree led to many knots among various security and intelligence agencies. The attitude of the government and intent to cover every terror incident as 'saffron' and the ambivalence in acting against the real perpetrators was making India cannon fodder.

26/11 @ Mumbai

On 26 November 2008, 10 LeT terrorists infiltrated South Mumbai via sea and attacked the iconic Taj Mahal Hotel,

Oberoi Trident Hotel, Chhatrapati Shivaji (rail) Terminus, and many other locations—they killed 166 and injured over 350. RAW had given inputs about the possibility of an attack, but no action was taken by the UPA at the Centre or the Congress Government in Maharashtra. The surprised police were no match for heavily armed terrorists. Despite attacks on many public places with TV coverage, Maharashtra's police agencies and government took very long to see what was happening—it was 4 hours after the attacks began that the CM requested GoI to send the NSG. The Navy's MARCOS commandos were called to the Taj Mahal Hotel, but reached after 3 hours, though their base is very close. Security Ops were hampered due to live TV coverage. Handlers from Pakistan told the terrorists details about the Ops. Only 2 days later the media was directed to show 'deferred' footage.

Two journalists who had helped the terrorists with live TV coverage were bestowed Padma Shri awards in 2008 by the Sonia Gandhi-led UPA Government.

Though Mumbai had a huge population and had several terrorist acts, there was no NSG centre; its commandos had to fly in from Manesar (Haryana). The NSG chief asked for an aircraft, but it was in Chandigarh. RAW provided an Ilyushin-76 but it could only accommodate 120. Three trips were needed to ferry the 300 NSG commandos. The 1st flight was delayed by over 75 minutes because Shivraj Patil insisted on flying with them and reached the airport late. When the NSG commandos did reach Mumbai the next morning, they did not have detailed layouts of the buildings under attack. But the terrorists had this info due to prior reconnaissance. Though Mumbai ATS had recorded conversations between terrorists and their handlers, these were not passed quickly enough to the NSG. *Clearly, something was very wrong!*

Mani wrote:

On 26/11, almost all top MHA officials were in Pakistan. Indo-Pak Home Secretary (HS) Level Talks were scheduled in Islamabad on 25 November. Inclusion of Addl. Secy. (Border Management) Anwar Ahmad in the Indian team was unprecedented. It was at the behest of some political command. He had the 2nd highest rank, after the HS. When two or more officers give differing views to the leader, the senior has a higher chance of prevailing. Their stay was extended till 27 Nov. Delegates were reluctant, but Ahmad advised the HS to extend. After meeting Pakistan's Interior Minister on 26/11 afternoon, the Indians were taken to a resort in the Pir Panjal mountains, where phone network is weak. Pakistan's agenda was evident. Was there a mole in India's team? Two RAW and IB Jt. Secretaries (JS) had detailed inputs of a potential attack but could not prevail upon the HS about not staying an extra day. One JS returned early on 26 Nov, citing urgent work. There would be a better response to the attack with lesser casualties/ damages if the HS and his team were in Delhi. Why did the delegation extend? Why did the HS not listen to the RAW/IB assets instead of Ahmad? Mumbai has several experienced forces. The CISF [Central Industrial Security Force] is specialised in securing facilities like hotels and could have salvaged the situation before the NSG arrived. The CRPF [Central Reserve Police Force] battalion at Navi Mumbai could go as immediate reinforcement and first aid. But with no clearance from the HM, timely action could not be taken, and these forces remained immobile and unused even as terrorists wreaked havoc.

On the terrorists entering via a fishermen's colony, Mani wrote, 'They do not tolerate a stranger passing their colony. It is stupid to believe that 10 strange men, armed to the teeth walked through around 7:30pm. Did people from the community help them? If so, who were they? I suspect a politician wearing the mantle of being the community's leader.'

Abdul Rahman Antulay (Union Minority Affairs Minister and former Maharashtra CM) is mentioned by Mani, so the implication is clear. Mani wrote:

> Maharashtra's Additional Chief Secretary (Home), Chitkala Zutshi was in Taj. She was escorted out with the attack in progress, without a scratch. No one else escaped. Zutshi was responsible for securing the same places that were penetrated. Still, she was at the Taj. Inputs about a possible attack were shared with Maharashtra's Chief Secretary, DGP, and the Home Department. The terrorists came from the same route about which she had inputs. Her presence and escape cannot be a mere coincidence. In call transcripts between the handlers and attackers, a handler says, 'There are three ministers and a government secretary in your hotel. Find those 3–4 persons and get whatever you want from India.' Under such circumstances, how was Zutshi left unscathed in the attack and how did she escape? The terrorists could not reach so many locations without local support. Inputs like who were in the Taj Hotel could not be without backing of an institutional-level mechanism or some strong political group's backing. We had intelligence inputs on a possible attack from the sea route. Several of our coastal security establishments had prepared for it. But there was apparently some intervention from the topmost political office, instructing 'restraint'.
>
> Ajmal Kasab was caught alive. Investigations were leading to Pakistan's involvement. At this juncture, Antulay did a media interview about a conspiracy to kill his favourite police officer [Karkare], undermining the investigative process.

> What was his agenda? Anyone joining the dots cannot rule out the possibility that many members of the governments [Centre and State] or persons having the blessings of the governments had partnered, harboured, and covered up for the perpetrators. These are strong words, but I have seen records, been privy to many discussions, and therefore such an inference is being drawn.

All of India's Internal Security Forces, including the 'Black Cat' commandos of the National Security Guard (NSG), were found to be inadequately equipped even with simple things like automatic guns, life vests, headgear, boots, etc.

There was ample proof of Pakistan's involvement. Interior Minister Rehman Malik said that Javed Iqbal, who acquired VoIP phones in Spain, plus 3 others had been arrested, and acknowledged that Ajmal Kasab was a Pakistani. In October 2009, Pak-American David Headley and Tahawwur Rana were arrested and charged by the FBI in the US. Two Pakistanis were arrested in Italy. In December 2009, FBI charged an ex-Pak Army major. In March 2010, Headley disclosed that ISI was involved in the attacks. The Delhi Police arrested Pakistani Abu Hamza, the terrorists' main handler, deported from Saudi Arabia. Hamza was present in the control room in Pakistan and revealed that an LeT man and a Pakistan Army Major visited India to survey targets in Delhi and Mumbai. Headley had spent several days in Mumbai to survey potential targets and to plan the attacks.

The defence chiefs proposed IAF airstrikes on terror camps in PoJK, but this was rejected by the UPA government (*who else but Sonia Gandhi could take this decision?*).

Mani refers to what took place in the MHA when P Chidambaram became home minister 4 days after 26/11—

how the NIA acted as the home minister's favourite and as a 'big brother' to other agencies, and how it propagated 'Hindu Terror' and 'Saffron Terror':

> In every case assigned to NIA, they overlooked the initial evidence and replaced it with evidence supporting the Hindu Terror narrative. The interrogation report of Headley was submitted to Chidambaram by the NIA team that had gone to Chicago. The NIA was accused of excising vital portions before submitting at court. The security establishment knew that the NIA submitted a full report containing the full testimony to Chidambaram.

Other Terror Attacks in UPA-era

At least 51 attacks took place in 29 cities outside of J&K, the Northeast region (NER) and Maoist areas—Delhi and Mumbai (8 each), Hyderabad (4), Bangalore (3), Pune and Ahmedabad (2 each), Chennai, Jaipur, Lucknow, Coimbatore, Ludhiana, Varanasi, Madurai, Ayodhya, Patna, and 14 other cities and more than 2,170 persons died in these attacks. How many places outside J&K/NER/Maoist-infested areas have been attacked in the Modi-era?

Over 30 of the 51 attacks were by Pakistan-based or Pakistan-sponsored groups, yet no action was taken. Rather, UPA ministers and officials regularly met with the Pakistanis, pretending to be besties.

The way the police handled the 8 Sept 2006 bombings in Malegaon (Maharashtra) was full of unpardonable flip-flops. Most of the 45 deaths were Muslims as the blasts took place after Friday prayers at a cemetery adjacent to a mosque. The Maharashtra Police suspected five groups—LeT, Jaish-e-Mohammed (JeM), Students' Islamic Movement of India

(SIMI), Harkat-ul-Jihad-al-Islami (HuJI), and Bajrang Dal; but did not release any evidence. Later, the police said the methods were similar to mosque attacks for which 16 Bajrang Dal members were arrested but not charged. Maharashtra ATS said there was no evidence of involvement of any Hindu Group as only Islamist outfits could get RDX. A SIMI man was arrested. Mumbai's DGP said the main conspirator is from LeT and co-conspirator from SIMI. On 28 November, he said two Pakistan nationals were involved, and the ATS has arrested six SIMI activists.

In November 2011, all the 8 men were released on bail after 5 years in jail. In 2012, Chidambaram asked the NIA to take over and 'look at the Hindu terror angle'. The NIA arrested 4 Abhinav Bharti members and filed chargesheets in May 2013.

In February 2007, there were blasts in the Delhi–Lahore Samjhauta Express and about 70 people died. Mani wrote:

> A Karachi-based terror outfit claimed responsibility. Bharti Arora, then SP (Police and Railways) of Panipat, confirmed this. The investigating officer reaffirmed it. In dossiers shared by India with Pakistan, there is a reference to it. Isn't this acknowledgement of Pakistan's involvement? The official position (in 2007) was that the attackers were a group of Hindus. If that was the case, why did it get included in the Pakistan dossiers?

Two other bombings killed nine persons at Malegaon (Maharashtra). Mani wrote:

> Original information from police said it was the handiwork of Ahl-e-Hadith. Two arrested persons confirmed they were

> from SIMI and went to Pakistan for weapons training. By mid-2008, the Maharashtra ATS began taking over Malegaon and other cases. There was a speed and alacrity with which this was taken out from local police and assigned to ATS, headed by Hemant Karkare. The narrative changed immediately. The involvement of Ahl-e-Hadith was trashed. Reports were received (at the MHA in Delhi) from Mumbai about involvement of Hindu organisations. In the July 2006 Mumbai blasts, it took 5–6 months when it was easier for ATS to arrest the suspects. In Malegaon, it took just 35 days for the same ATS to arrest a serving Army officer, Lt Col Purohit. In these 35 days, some time would have been lost in getting clearances from Army HQ for charging a serving officer. It is hard to digest that in less than a month, wisdom dawned on the ATS that Malegaon was the handiwork of Hindu terror groups, although field-level police personnel continued to report that Ahl-e-Hadith was involved.

It is mind-nerving how the Sonia Gandhi-led UPA tried to blame all terrorism incidents in India on Hindu nationalist and Saffron groups.

Let us move on to the Modi-era.

Uri Surgical Strike

Four terrorists of ISI-controlled JeM attacked an Indian Army camp in Uri (J&K) on 18 September 2016—18 soldiers died.

Modi did not sit silent. The message was bold and unlike any other PM before Modi—India will strike back. Ten days after the attack, four teams of 70–80 Indian Army personnel, including Special Forces commandos crossed the LoC just after midnight to attack targets up to 1.2km inside PoJK and returned by 4:30am. The GoI said that 30–40 terrorists and 2–9 Pakistani soldiers were killed.

Modi gave the Army a 'free hand' to plan and execute the 'surgical strike'. He told the troops to not think about success or failure and be back 'before sunrise'. A day earlier, Modi told water ministry officials 'blood and water can't flow together', referring to the Indus Waters Treaty. In the chapter 'Strengthened Border Infrastructure', we wrote what Modi is doing about it. In 2021, Modi revealed that the date was changed twice, keeping in mind the safety and security of the troops.

Balakot Airstrikes

On 14 February 2019, an explosives-laden car rammed into a bus near Pulwama, part of a 78-vehicle convoy moving CRPF personnel from Jammu to Srinagar; and 40 CRPF men died in the resultant blast. This was the biggest terror attack on India's Armed Forces in J&K and again, the JeM was responsible. Modi's CCS told the military to take revenge. Addressing an election rally in Jhansi (Uttar Pradesh) on 15 February, Modi said, '*Agla kadam humaari sena uthaayegi, samay bhi woh chunenge, jagah bhi who teh karenge, aur tareeka bhi unka hoga*' (next step will be by our forces, they will decide the time, place and method).[7]

In the wee hours of 26 February, 16 IAF jets (with support from Airborne Early Warning & Control Aircraft or AEW&C aircraft and an air refuelling tanker) executed airstrikes in Balakot (Pakistan) and destroyed JeM's biggest terror training camp with precision-guided bunker-buster missiles and bombs.

Since 1971, this was the first time India struck on a target deep inside Pakistan—50km from the LoC and 81km from Uri. India's assessment was that 250–300 JeM terrorists and their trainers died, though Pakistan claimed that India only bombed shrubs and trees.

Most shockingly, Rahul Gandhi, Arvind Kejriwal, Mamata Banerjee, and some Indian publications and journalists echoed Pakistan's version.

On the next day (27 February), the Pakistan Air Force conducted airstrikes in J&K but was not able to hit any important targets as its 12 jets were met with IAF's jets and had to turn back.

There was a dogfight, with the IAF and the PAF each losing a jet. Wing Commander Abhinandan Varthaman, flying a 45-year-old IAF MiG-21 that was hit by a missile, ejected, and parachuted onto a field near a village in PoJK. The local villagers beat him with sticks. He was rescued from the villagers by Pakistan Army *jawans* and taken into captivity.

As soon as he got the news, PM Modi told the chief of RAW to speak with his counterpart in the ISI to immediately release the IAF pilot. When the RAW chief did not get a positive response, Modi dialled US President Donald Trump and Chinese President Xi Jinping, hinting that India would attack Pakistan if the IAF pilot was not released immediately. China was also told that India would destroy infrastructure of the China Pakistan Economic Corridor (CPEC), an important road corridor built by China that connects Kashgar in China with Pakistan's Gwadar Port (operated by China) on the Arabian Sea, crossing PoJK, Islamabad, and Lahore.

India even moved hundreds of tanks and missile batteries, and lakhs of soldiers to the LoC and the Pakistan border, to show the Chinese and the Pakistanis that the threat was serious.

Due to American and Chinese pressure, Pakistan had to release Abhinandan, who returned to India within 58 hours from the time his aircraft was shot down. To save face, PM Imran Khan announced that Pakistan had released him as a 'gesture of peace'.

India did not just stop there.

Financial Action Task Force (FATF) is an intergovernmental body based in Paris (France) that is responsible for setting global standards on anti-money laundering (AML) and combating the financing of terrorism (CFT).

The FATF identifies jurisdictions with weak measures to combat AML/CFT in two FATF public documents that are issued three times a year—the 'Black List' (High Risk Jurisdictions that are subject to a Call for Action) and the 'Grey List' (Jurisdictions that are under Increased Monitoring).

Countries under the Grey List are considered as a safe haven for supporting terror funding and money laundering. As of February 2024, the FATF had reviewed 131 countries and jurisdictions and publicly identified 106 of them (naming them either on the Black List or Grey List). Of these, 82 made the necessary reforms to address their AML/CFT weaknesses and were removed from the process.

Despite several counterclaims and lies by Pakistan, India provided enough evidence to the FATF to get Pakistan on the Grey List in March 2019, and it remained on the List till October 2022. Pakistan had been on the Grey List in 2008-09 as well as 2012–15.

In addition, the UN listed JeM's founder Maulana Masood Azhar as a global terrorist. As a permanent UNSC member, China had been regularly vetoing this for years.

Results

Let's see if Modi has succeeded in his 'War on Terror'. The data is from the Institute of Conflict Management's South Asia Terrorism Portal (SATP)[8], and not the GoI.

Terrorism can never be wiped out anywhere, but it is evident that Modi Government's strict actions have managed to significantly reduce it.

Terrorism Incidents and Deaths	UPA (2006-2013)	MODI (2015-2024)	Reduction
Total Terror Incidents in J&K	10,690 Avg. 1,336	3,674 Avg. 367	▼ 72.5%
Civilian Deaths in J&K	1,117 Avg. 140	357 Avg. 36	▼ 74.3%
Security Forces Deaths in J&K	840 Avg. 105	575 Avg. 58	▼ 44.8%
Total Terror Incidents in NER	13,832 Avg. 1,729	6,899 Avg. 690	▼ 60.1%
Civilian Deaths in NER	1,917 Avg. 240	589 Avg. 59	▼ 75.4%
Security Forces Deaths in NER	427 Avg. 53	141 Avg. 14	▼ 73.6%
Total LWE Terror Incidents	8,516 Avg. 1,065	7,371 Avg. 737	▼ 30.8%
Civilian Deaths due to LWE	2,487 Avg. 311	839 Avg. 84	▼ 73.0%
Security Forces Deaths due to LWE	1,646 Avg. 206	481 Avg. 48	▼ 76.7%
ALL-INDIA Terror Incidents	30,348 Avg. 3,794	19,002 Avg. 1,900	▼ 49.9%
ALL-INDIA Civilian Deaths	6,335 Avg. 792	1,889 Avg. 189	▼ 76.1%
ALL-INDIA Security Services Deaths	2,946 Avg. 368	1,212 Avg. 121	▼ 67.1%

In early April 2024, UK's *Guardian* newspaper alleged that India's RAW had hired paid assassins to kill about 20 suspected terrorists inside Pakistan.

Defence Minister Rajnath Singh responded by saying that India would go inside Pakistan to kill terrorists who have killed Indians.

Modi said, 'Today, there is a strong Modi Government, hence terrorists are killed in their turf.'[9]

The *Guardian* underestimated the number, as around 34 Pakistani terrorists have been '*killed by unknown men*' or otherwise died of unnatural causes in 2023 and 2024 alone.

Hats off to the Modi government.

NATGRID

A few weeks after 26/11, Home Minister Chidambaram announced NATGRID, a framework to connect approved (security and law enforcement) User Agencies with designated data providers by leveraging information technology, to enhance the country's counter terrorism capabilities. A budget of ₹1003Cr was approved in June 2012—it took the UPA Government 3.5 years to even sanction the budget but work to build the infrastructure that was required did not start.

As soon as the Modi Government came to power, it sanctioned a Data Centre and Business Continuity Planning at New Delhi, and a Data Recovery Centre at Bengaluru. Civil work for all these was completed in 2020 and the facilities were 100 per cent ready by 2021.

NATGRID has developed NATSTAR Connectors with in-house resources, and these have been operationalised by connecting 11 User Agencies and 10 Providing Organisations. NATGRID connectivity has already been extended to all states/union territories.

13

War on Kashmir Separatism

The beauty of the soul of Kashmir was suppressed due to extremism and Islamic radicalism for decades since 1989. Terrorism robbed the future of Kashmiris, especially youth. Instead of playing cricket, they played with stones.

J&K was amongst India's top five tourist destinations until 1988, with 722,000 tourists visiting that year. This fell to just 6,287 in 1991.

More than 42,000 people were killed because Article 370 (see the chapter titled 'RIP, Article 370') gave impetus to separatism, a movement by many organizations to detach from India—some who want to merge with Pakistan and others who want an independent nation. This seeded Pakistan-sponsored terrorism.

Kashmir had 730 incidents of 'organised' stone pelting in 2015, which went up to 2,653 in 2016 in the aftermath of security forces killing 'India's Most Wanted' terrorist Burhan Wani, 'commander' of the militant group Hizbul Mujahideen.

Pelting came down to 1,412 incidents in 2017 and 1,458 in 2018 but went up again to 1,999 in 2019 (including 618 in August, the month when Article 370 was repealed).

There were 255 incidents in 2020 (90.4 per cent reduction from 2016) 76 in 2021 (97.14 per cent reduction from 2016), just 10 in 2022, and zero in 2023 as well as 2024.

112 civilians lost their lives and 6,235 were injured due to stone pelting during 2016–2021. Many separatist leaders used to say that stone pelting is a form of resistance used to challenge India. They believe that India is a foreign nation and that Kashmiris are not Indians.

Before 2019, crowds of 25,000–200,000 used to gather at funerals of terrorists in Kashmir, but after Article 370 was abolished, there have been no such occurrences because the Modi Government decided to bury a terrorist quietly at the spot he is killed, with full religious rituals.

Incidents of stone pelting have also stopped as the Modi Government has barred them (and their family members) from holding Indian passports, as well as GoI/state government jobs and contracts.

Persons with Pakistan-based 'connections' encouraging terrorism, and/or whose phone records show promotion of terrorism, have similar curbs.

These 'terrorists' were given a free hand by past Central and state governments because of 'vote-bank politics', to appease their community, which is certainly not a minority in J&K.

You have already seen detailed data on terror incidents and deaths in the previous chapter. Data aside, any 'normal' person who lives in the Kashmir Valley or visits often can vouch for the fact that terrorism has reduced drastically, especially after October 2019, and stone pelting has completely stopped.

With the revocation of Article 370, the future of the youth of Kashmir is not black; rather the black board of the school has become their future, expressed Home Minister Amit Shah.[10]

Young boys as well as girls were paid wages by the separatists to indulge in stone pelting; today instead of a career in throwing stones they can lay a foundation stone for proper job opportunities.

Kashmir is fast becoming a part of India again.

14

War on Northeast Insurgency

In May 2023, Manipur saw ugly ethnic clashes between the Meitei (more than 53 per cent of population), who are predominantly Hindu and mainly live in Imphal and the prosperous valley around it, and the Kuki-Zo tribal group (about 16 per cent of population), who are mainly Christian and live in the hills. These clashes were spurred on by stakeholders in the ₹70,000Cr narcotics trade and a proxy war by China.

People from both communities have left their villages as violence has been raging for a year and shows no sign of stopping—393 temples and 317 churches were burned down. Hundreds have lost their lives and thousands have become homeless.

An effort to mitigate the angst and reconcile differences is on by the Modi Government, but the scars will take quite a long time to heal, and violence continues off and on, although with a lower intensity.

The Myanmar civil war (which has been on since the country's independence from Britain in 1948) further escalated tensions in Manipur with an influx of Kuki-Chin illegal immigrants. Over 40,000 illegal immigrants from Myanmar live in Mizoram and over 4,500 are in Manipur.

There have been several incidents of violence and insurgency in Manipur ever since Independence, something that plagues Nagaland as well, as past Congress governments at the Centre neglected development of the region.

Violence in Manipur started when the British classified the populace into 'Hills' and 'Valley,' each governed by different laws. In 1951, Nehru gave Scheduled Tribes or ST status to the Kukis but not the Meiteis. The Meiteis' demand for ST status could shift political power and influence due to the sheer size of their community and potentially disenfranchise the Kukis and Nagas, stoking further ethnic tensions.

Manipur has 34 ethnic-based militant groups (10 from the Meitei, 22 from the Kuki, and 2 from the Naga communities); many are funded by China and Pakistan. Violent clashes between Nagas and Kukis went on from 1992 until 1999.

Hindu Meiteis and Muslim Meiti-Pangals have clashed many times even though they are part of the same ethnic group. Over 120 civilians and security personnel and over 60 militants have died since 2001.

An attack by two Naga militant groups in Manipur in June 2015 killed 18 Indian Army soldiers. The next day, on Modi's orders, 70 of the Army's 21st Para SF Commandos carried out a cross-border operation inside Myanmar and eliminated 38 militants in less than 50 minutes.

The GoI will fence the 171km unfenced stretch of the 1,643km border with Myanmar and end the 'Free Movement Regime', which allows people living on both sides to travel within 16km into each other's territory without a visa.

In November 2023, the GoI and Government of Manipur signed a Peace Agreement with United National Liberation Front (UNLF), the oldest Meitei armed group of Manipur. It was the first time that a valley-based Manipuri armed group agreed to return to the mainstream by shunning violence and agreeing to honour the Constitution and laws of India. Following this, leaders and cadres of National Revolutionary Front Manipur joined UNLF in December. This development is likely to give a momentum to efforts of GoI to restore peace and normalcy in Manipur. It will encourage other Meitei militant outfits to join the peace process and pursue their demands in a democratic manner, besides giving a boost to Modi's vision of 'Insurgency-free and prosperous Northeast'.

An accord was signed between GoI, Assam Government and United Liberation Front of Assam (ULFA) in December 2023. Another tripartite agreement was signed between GoI, Tripura Government and Tipra Motha in March 2024.

Since 2014, peace accords were signed with 13 separatist/ militant organisations in the Northeast region and nearly 10,000 youth gave up arms.

15

War on Maoists/Naxals

Between 2001 and 2024, as many as 3,987 civilians and 2,652 security personnel were killed by Maoists/Naxals aka LWEs in different parts of India.

To make India 100 per cent Maoist/Naxal-free and tackle LWE in a systematic manner, Operation 'SAMADHAN' (**S**mart leadership, **A**ggressive strategy, **M**otivation & training, **A**ctionable intelligence, **D**ashboard-based KPIs/KRAs, **H**arnessing technology, **A**ction plan for each theatre, **N**o access to financing) was MHA's strategy.

This included setting up 195 new CAPF camps, 400 fortified Police Stations, solar lights, and 3G/4G mobile towers; Joint Task Forces along inter-State boundaries to improve intelligence sharing and coordination; using trackers for weapons; biometrics in smart guns; a unique ID number for gelatine sticks and explosives; at least one drone or mini-drone for each CAPF battalions in LWE hotbeds; increased helicopter support for operations with more flying hours; and fast-tracking of road and rail connectivity.

Indian Army and Special Forces (such as the specialised anti-LWE Greyhounds of Andhra Pradesh and Telangana Police) were summoned to train other police forces.

The Prevention of Money Laundering Act (PMLA) was reviewed to ensure that funds flowing to LWE groups are choked.

Around 5,000 post offices and 4,885 mobile towers were set up in 90 Naxalism-hit districts, and in the 30 most-affected districts, 1,298 bank branches and 1,348 ATMs were opened.

For the first time in four decades, the number of deaths of civilians and security forces has been reduced to under 110 for five successive years from 2020 to 2024.

The area under LWEs' influence has been brought down from over 18,000 square km. when Modi became PM, to less than 8,500 square km. in November 2024, a reduction of more than 53.3 per cent.

The year 2024 broke all records—apart from 296 naxals being neutralised, 992 were arrested and 837 surrendered during the year.

16

War on Drugs

Almost 3.8 per cent of total household spending in rural India in FY23 was expenditure on *paan* (betel leaf), tobacco and intoxicants.

The global drug trafficking trade in 2023 was worth a staggering $725B (₹60.18LCr). In 2021, over 296M persons (3.775 per cent of the then global population) used drugs regularly, 23 per cent higher than the previous decade. The number of people who suffer from drug use disorders skyrocketed to 39.5M, (more than 45 per cent in 10 years).

It is a shocking truth that the drug epidemic is worse in India—home to over 90M drug users (6.3 per cent of India's estimated population in 2023), with a large number in the 10–17-year age group.

Unfortunately, India is located right between the 'Death Crescent' (Iran, Afghanistan and Pakistan) and the 'Death Triangle' (Myanmar, Laos and Thailand). Nepal is also a big source of drugs coming into India.

Smuggling of narcotics not only impacts the economy but also compromises the borders through narco-terrorism.

Modi wants to make India drug-free by 2047.

His government's 3-point strategy is simple but effective. With a 'Bottom to Top' and 'Top to Bottom' approach, it aims to (1) Strengthen institutional structure, (2) Increase coordination among various narco-agencies and Law Enforcement Agencies (LEAs), and (3) Initiate extensive nationwide public awareness campaigns.

The government initiated a campaign in June 2022 to destroy seized drugs, and on a single day more than 140,000kg were destroyed. In just 7 months, 1.2M kg of drugs worth over ₹12,000Cr were destroyed.

UPA Government destroyed less than this quantity in its entire 10-year tenure. Due to corruption, a large portion of seized drugs came back into the markets.

Let's look at figures of seizures and other data:

Modi's War on Drugs	UPA (2006-2013)	MODI (2015-2022)	CHANGE
OPIUM seized	18,952 kg	48,301.4 kg	▲ 154.9%
HEROIN seized	8251 kg	29,420.8 kg	▲ 256.6%
GANJA (Cannabis) seized	1,042,275 kg	4,146,208 kg	▲ 297.8%
HASHISH (Charas) seized	32,630 kg	35,551.8 kg	▲ 9%
COCAINE seized	366.5 kg	931.4 kg	▲ 154.1%
OPIUM cultivation destroyed (in acres)	34,586 (2008-2013)	49,549 (2015-2020)	▲ 43.3%
CANNABIS cultivation destroyed (acres)	19,999 (2008-2013)	70,104 (2015-2020)	▲ 251%
Cases Registered in Police Stations	1257	3891 (up to 2023)	▲ 209.5%
Drug-related Arrests	1363	5924 (up to 2023)	▲ 334.6%
Value of Seized Drugs	₹768Cr	₹22,000Cr	▲ 2765%
SOURCES: Annual Reports at https://narcoticsindia.nic.in/ and bit.ly/3X4Crdw			

In a major crackdown, the Narcotics Control Bureau (NCB) busted the 'Zambada Cartel' (aka Sinaloa Cartel) of Mexico that was doing business via the darknet and arrested 65 persons between 2021 and 2023, seized more than 43,500 blots of LSD ('acid') worth over ₹24Cr, 472gm of MDMA ('ecstasy') worth almost ₹1.9Cr, 2.23kg of imported curated marijuana worth around ₹1.12Cr, and ₹56.03L in cash.

The NCB is working with foreign LEAs to get information on global cartels operating in this part of the world. Intelligence sharing and Controlled Delivery Operations (CDOs) are being carried out with neighbouring countries.

The National Integrated Database on Arrested Narco-Offenders (NIDAAN) portal was launched in July 2022 and the National Database of Offenders of Foreign Origin (NDOFO) portal in March 2023. As of November 2023, more than 95,000 offenders of foreign origin were in the NDOFO system.

A National Toll-Free Helpline for Drug Abusers 14446 was also set up.

Grants for National Action Plan for Drug Demand Reduction were released to 310 NGOs (non-governmental organisations) up to FY22, through which 740,616 persons benefited.

Nasha Mukt Bharat Abhiyaan (NMBA), launched on 15 August 2020, brings together the NCB, state and district governments, police, NGOs, hospitals, etc., so that they can work in a coordinated manner to make India drug-free. It is operational in 372 districts. NMBA programs were also held in 17,000 border villages in 18 states/UTs. The participation of 411,887 educational institutions and over 8,000 trained 'Master Volunteers' has ensured that NMBA has reached a whopping 49M youth across India up to December 2024.

NMBA has covered 326,132 villages in 52 months and 140.54M persons have been sensitised on substance abuse, including 29.37M women. More than 2.776M persons have been treated and rehabilitated.

Events like Nashe se Azaadi, Naya Bharat, Nasha Mukt Bharat, and NMBA Interaction with National Cadet Corps (NCC) are regularly organised to engage and connect with youth and other stakeholders.

More than 16.7M students from 99,595 educational institutions participated in the National Drug Free Pledge.

Facilities opened by the Modi Government up to 2023 for handling drug abuse include 22 State Level Cordination Agencies, 660 Integrated De-addiction and Rehabilitation Centres for Addicts, 76 Outreach and Drop-In Centres, and 49 Community Peer-led Intervention Centres, All have been geo-tagged for easy access to those in need.

There has been a 42 per cent increase in the number of persons seeking counselling and de-addiction services.

17

Tightened Noose on NGOs

The Foreign Contributions Regulation Act (FCRA) 2010 regulates acceptance/utilisation of foreign contributions/ hospitality by Indian individuals/organisations and prohibits their acceptance/utilisation for any activities detrimental to India's national interest.

Modi Government amended it 3 times, with minor changes in 2016 and 2018, and then followed by major changes in September 2020 that were approved by the Parliament. FCRA 2020 had several new provisions, amid concerns by NGOs that it will further tighten channels of funding from abroad. But that was the very purpose of this legislation.

Why were the changes important? Annual foreign contribution inflows had nearly doubled from 2010 to 2019. Many recipients of foreign funds had not utilised the funds for the purpose/s registered. It was also suspected for very long that many NGOs had been indulging in converting gullible Hindus, especially Scheduled Castes (SCs), Scheduled Tribes (STs) and Other Backward Classes (OBCs), to Christianity or Islam.

People studying this trend say India's Muslim population is more realistically 17–22 per cent, against 14.2 per cent counted in the 2011 Census. Likewise, the Christian population could be 4–7 per cent, against 2.3 per cent in the Census. This is because many Hindu converts do not change their name or religion in government records, to continue receiving government benefits as SCs/STs/OBCs. Six out of 10 of my (Amit's) employees converted to Christianity between 1998 and 2008 but did not change their names or religion in official records. This is first-person evidence.

NGO activists funded by foreign countries (which are mostly economic or political adversaries of India) and organisations linked with them have been opposing nationally important projects in mining, power generation, ports, and other infrastructure for decades, by confusing gullible non-Leftist citizens and media persons via misguided environmental concerns. Why should foreign-funded NGOs be allowed to derail India's growth story? The new FCRA 2020 helps in close monitoring of these NGOs.

The acclaimed series *Rocket Boys* hinted at CIA's involvement in the air crash that killed Dr Homi Bhabha ('father of India's nuclear program'), and the suspected poisoning of Dr Vikram Sarabhai, founder of ISRO. Years before *Rocket Boys* came out, I (Amit) wrote the same in my book *USAma: Is USA the World's Largest Terrorist?*

FCRA 2010 prohibited members of a legislature or political party, candidates standing for election, editors/publishers of newspapers, and judges from receiving foreign donations. FCRA 2020 added public servants (as defined under the old Indian Penal Code (IPC).

Aadhaar details of all office-bearers is now mandatory. Transfer of foreign grants to a partner organisation or an associated person has been banned.

Earlier, a registered person could accept foreign funds in a single branch of any bank but could open any number of accounts in other banks to spend the funds. FCRA 2020 mandates that receipts can only be in a designated 'FCRA account' in a Delhi branch of SBI. No other funds can be received or deposited in this account.

Recipients could use up to 50 per cent of funds for administrative expenses. FCRA 2020 has reduced this to 20 per cent.

Automatic renewal of permissions granted for receiving foreign funds has been done away with.

By September 2024, Modi Government had cancelled licenses of 20,712 NGOs found to be violating provisions of the FCRA. Many of these were engaged in the illegal conversion of Hindus to Christianity or Islam. Another 14,867 licenses were deemed as expired.

Against the 35,579 cancelled or expired licenses, there were 16,111 active NGOs under FCRA in November 2024.

18

Better and Speedier Justice

In December 2023, the Indian Penal Code 1860 (IPC) was replaced by the Bharatiya Nyaya Sanhita Bill, the Criminal Procedure Code 1898 (CrPC) by the Bharatiya Nagarik Suraksha Sanhita Bill, and the Indian Evidence Act 1872 by the Bharatiya Sakshya Bill.

The soul of these three new codes is to protect the rights given by the Constitution to Indian citizens. Many provisions have been made to deal with crimes against women and social problems affecting them.

Let's examine some of the most important features of the new codes:

- State-of-the-art tech has been incorporated. The definition of documents has expanded to include digital records, SMS, e-mails, desktop/laptop, server/phone logs, websites, browsing history, location evidence, etc. Days of huge piles of papers in court proceedings are over.
- Entire process from First Information Report (FIR) to case diary to chargesheet to judgement will now be digital. Earlier, only appearance of the accused in court was possible via video conferencing and that too is quite recent. Now, the entire trial, including cross questioning and witness statements will be done via video conferencing.

- Investigation and recording of evidence in Trial and High Courts and Appellate proceedings can now be done digitally.
- Videography by the police is compulsory during search and seizure. No chargesheet will be valid without such recording. This will protect innocent citizens from being implicated on false charges.
- With 'Zero FIR', citizens can lodge complaints at any police station regardless of where the crime took place.
- Within 15 days of a complaint being registered, it will have to be forwarded to the concerned police station.
- Every district and police station will designate an officer who will inform the family of an arrested person online and in person.
- It is compulsory for the police to give the status of the complaint to the complainant within 90 days and every 15 days thereafter.
- There is now a provision of e-FIR.
- The time limit for filing chargesheet has been fixed for 90 days, and depending on the situation, a court may give permission for further 90 days—within 180 days the investigation has be completed and forwarded for trial.
- Courts will be bound to give notice of framing of charges to the accused person within 60 days.
- Judges will have to give decisions within 30 days of completion of arguments—decisions will not be pending for years as is the case now.
- Decisions of the courts must be made available online within seven days.
- Neither Central nor any state/municipal government can withdraw a case of imprisonment of seven years or longer without hearing the victim.

- Community service has been introduced as a form of punishment. This is common in many Western countries, but India did not have it.
- Scope of Summary Trial in small cases has been increased, offences punishable up to three years are included in Summary Trial—with this provision alone, over 40 per cent cases will be completed in Sessions Courts without the need to go to higher courts.
- The Superintendent of Police (SP) in-charge of the jurisdiction will have to testify in court after seeing the file, earlier the concerned officer was not required to appear in Court—this will enable quick testimony and quick justice.
- The government must decide on permission for trial against a civil servant or police officer within 120 days, otherwise it will be treated as deemed permission and the trial will start.
- Victim's statement with video recording is compulsory in sexual violence cases. Provision to criminalise sexual intercourse based on false promises of marriage, employment, or promotion, or on the basis of false identity has been introduced.
- In all cases of gang rape, there is now a provision of 20 years' jail sentence or life imprisonment.
- Death penalty for rape of girls below 18 years of age.
- Snatching/theft of mobile phones and/or chains from women will now be punishable.
- Punishment for exploiting women by cheating.
- Punishment for crime against children increased from seven to ten years.
- Properties of declared criminals can be attached.
- Many different types of new harsh punishment against inter-state gangs and organised crimes.

- Seven years/life imprisonment/death penalty for mob lynching. *And the Opposition accuses the BJP of encouraging mob lynching by Hindu groups.*
- 10 years or life imprisonment if a victim gets permanent disability or is brain dead.
- There were many cases of getting pardon from sentences for political gains, now death penalty can be changed to life imprisonment, life to minimum seven years and seven years to minimum three years—no culprit will be spared.
- 10 years for criminals who run from custody.
- Fines have been increased for many crimes.
- Handcuffing of suspects in grave offences to produce them in courts was not allowed; you must have seen films/series where prisoners had coir ropes tied to a policeman's hand. This has been amended.
- There was no clear definition of 'terrorism' earlier—crimes like secession, separatism, armed insurgency, subversive activities, challenging the integrity, unity or sovereignty of India have been defined for the first time and the rights have been given to confiscate properties of the accused. The court will order this on the cognisance of the investigating police officer.
- A Sessions Court Judge, after following the due process, will carry out a trial and sentence a person who is declared as a fugitive in absentia, no matter where in the world he may be hiding. He will have recourse to Indian laws and courts to appeal against the sentence.

With 313 changes to completely reform our Criminal Justice System, everyone will get justice within a maximum of three years.

It has been ensured that criminals are punished, and provisions have been made to prevent the police from misusing their powers.

Isn't it surprising that for 66.8 years, no Government of India ever thought about changing the 163-year, 151-year and 125-year-old British-era laws?

Due to continuous prodding by none other than the PM himself, all courts in India are now clearing cases faster.

According to data from the National Judicial Data Grid as reported by India Justice Report, the number of cases disposed of in 2024 exceeded the number of cases that were filed during that year.

District courts disposed of 13.4M cases in 2024, while 10.5M cases were filed. In 2023, these courts had cleared only 3.14M cases, with around 7.6M cases filed. High courts disposed of over 1.2M cases in 2024, while over 1.1M cases were filed. The SCI cleared 36,969 cases in 2024, with 21,753 new cases being filed. In comparison, in 2023, the SCI disposed of 6,114 cases, while 9,447 new cases were filed.

19

Oil and Gas Security

India spends around ₹16.8LCr on oil and gas imports per year. Our 48 assets in 22 countries equal 30.71 per cent of domestic production. Under Modi, India acquired assets in Oman, Russia, and the UAE, and invested $1.6B more in an oil project in Brazil.

A new Hydrocarbon Exploration and Licensing Policy freed up gas prices and gave explorers freedom to carve their blocks and a common license to extract all forms of hydrocarbons. Several regulatory changes were made to ease upstream operations.

In July 2020, India signed an agreement to store crude oil in strategic petroleum reserves (SPRs) in the US, not for just emergencies but also for trading to capture any price advantage.

Modi approved underground crude storage facilities of 6.5MT to increase emergency stockpiles from about 9.5 days to about 21.2 days. Indian refiners maintain 65 days of crude storage, and when added to the SPR storage achieved/ planned, takes total storage to about 86 days.

Here are some import deals signed in the Modi-era for Liquified Natural Gas (LNG):

LNG IMPORT DEALS SIGNED by PSEs in MODI-era				
Quantity/yr.	**Deal Signed In**	**From**	**Till**	**Supplier**
7.5MT	2024	2028	2048	QatarEnergy (Qatar)
3.5MT	2017	2018	2038	Cheniere Energy (USA)
2.633MT	2012 (renegotiated in 2017 from 2.5MT, extended by 3yrs)	2018	2035	Gazprom (Russia)
2.5MT				Securing Energy for Europe (Germany)
2.3MT	2017	2018	2038	Dominion Energy (USA)
1.2MT	2023	2026	2041	ADNOC Gas (Abu Dhabi)
1.0MT	2023	2026	2036	Vitol Asia (Singapore)
1.0MT	2024	2028	2042	ADNOC Gas (Abu Dhabi)
0.8MT	2023	2026	2036	TotalEnergies Gas & Power (France)
0.5MT	2023	2026	2036	ADNOC Gas (Abu Dhabi)
Between Aug2015 and Jan2018, the Modi Govt got India's Oil & Gas PSEs to renegotiate LNG import deals signed during the UPA Govt with Qatar, Australia, and Russia; and all three countries reduced the prices.				

In 2017, a Russian consortium led by Rosneft invested $13B to purchase a 20MT refinery and a network of petrol pumps in India. In 2023, Gas Authority of India Limited did the world's first ship-to-ship LNG transfer to reduce shipping costs by $1M and emissions by 7MT of CO_2. India also started paying the UAE in rupees for oil. An MoU was signed with Guyana for importing crude, participation of Indian companies in exploration and production there and cooperation in crude refining.

Oil refining capacity of PSEs went up from 120.066mtpa in FY14 to 259.9mtpa in FY24 (up 116.5 per cent) and with projects currently underway, will further go up to 450mtpa by 2029 (up 274.8 per cent).

While India pays $80 per barrel for imports, the cost of domestic manufacturing is only $12–13 per barrel.

India's Global Biofuels Alliance initiative to bring governments and global organisations together for developing/ deploying biofuels got 22 countries and 12 organisations to join in just a month.

Part II

Managing the Economy

20

Growing, Growing, Grown

From the world's 10th largest economy in 2014, the efforts and work done by the Modi Government resulted in India becoming the 5th largest in 2022, a 6-place jump in eight years.

India is expected to surpass Japan in 2026 and Germany the very next year to become the 3rd largest economy in 2027—based on post-Covid growth rates of the three nations.

Dr Manmohan Singh was PM for 10 years. He had four economics degrees, was a former chief economic advisor and then economic affairs secretary in the finance ministry, RBI governor, deputy chairman of the Planning Commission, and finance minister. Under him, the Congress projected India will become the 3rd largest economy by 2044. Modi has ensured that India achieves that milestone 17 years earlier. *What were Dr Singh and Congress thinking?*

India is now the world's 3rd largest energy consumer, 4th largest refiner, and 3rd largest automobile market (from 6th in 2014). Indians are also buying more expensive cars with each passing year.

Sales of luxury homes (apartments costing ₹4Cr and higher) grew a whopping 75 per cent in 2023 across India.

UPA Government ministers called India a 'poor country'. In 2013, Morgan Stanley placed India in the 'Fragile Five', a group that comprised five emerging economies (countries) with weak macroeconomic fundamentals including low growth, high inflation, high external deficit, and impaired state of public finances.

Ten years later, India is the world's fastest growing major economy for the 9th consecutive year! During UPA's last 3 years, China and Indonesia grew faster.

For the last 20-odd months, dozens of global business leaders and economists have been saying, 'India's time has come'. Read more in the Appendix at the end of this book.

Let's look at some data:

MANAGEMENT OF THE ECONOMY (Economist vs. *Chaiwallah*)				
WHAT	**Source**	**FY 2014** (except where stated)	**FY 2024** (except where stated)	**CHANGE**
GDP (nominal)	GOI	₹113.55 LCr	₹295.36 LCr	▲ 160.1%
Share of World's GDP	IMF	2.40% (2013)	3.57% (2023)	▲ 48.8%
Per Capita Net Income	RBI	₹79,118	₹184,205	▲ 132.8%
Forex Reserves	RBI	$304.2 B	$645.58 B	▲ 112.2%
External Debt to GDP	RBI	23.3% ▲30.9% from FY04	18.65%	▼▼ 20.0%
External Commercial Borrowings (CAGR)	RBI	21% (FY04-14)	4.5% (FY14-23)	▼▼ 78.6%
Remittances from OCIs	RBI	$65.482 B	$102.769 B	▲ 56.9%
Patents Granted/yr	https://ipindia.gov.in/trade-marks.htm	7,156	26,899	▲ 275.9%
Designs Registered/yr		5810	13,072	▲ 125.0%
Trademarks Granted/yr		88,875	232,838	▲ 162.0%
Geographical Indicators/yr		21.5	42.0	▲ 95.35%
Active Companies & LLPs	MCA	977,272	20,32,843	▲ 108.0%

In the UPA era, the ₹:$ exchange rate rose from ₹44.06 to ₹68.80 (up 56.15 per cent) in just 28 days of August 2013.

Forex reserves declined from $321.98B in August 2011 to $275.49B in August 2013. India had reserves for about six months' imports, down from 17 months in FY04.

In the pretext of responding to the 2008–09 global financial crisis, while saying India was not affected by it, UPA expanded borrowing and did not relent.

It's net market borrowings increased nearly 9.7 times in eight years to $4.9LCr in FY13. In addition, the UPA Government resorted to additional funding of $1.16LCr through 364-day treasury bills.

Not only did the UPA borrow heavily, but the funds were applied unproductively. Capital expenditure (which funds infrastructure) almost halved from about 31 per cent of total government expenditure (excluding interest payments) in FY04 to about 16 per cent in FY14. Expenditure was directed towards short-term populist measures under the direction of Sonia Gandhi. Under Modi, the share of Capex was about 28 per cent in FY24.

Many eminent personalities have made different projections for the GDP that India will have in 2047, when the nation becomes 100 years old.

PROJECTIONS of INDIAN GDP by 2047 (100th anniversary of Independence)			
Who made the projection?	Who is this person?	Projection	Growth Rate required for 24 continuous years
Nirmala Sitharaman	Finance Minister of India	$30 Trillion	9.696%
Bibek Debroy	Chairman, Economic Advisory Council to the Prime Minister	$20 Trillion	7.779%
Mukesh Ambani	Industrialist; Chairman, Reliance Industries	$35 Trillion	10.434%
Dr Arvind Panagariya	Chairman, 16th Finance Commission; 1st Vice Chairperson, NITI Aayog	$27 Trillion	9.195%
AVERAGE OF THE FOUR PROJECTIONS		**$28 Trillion**	**9.368%**

The top industrialist (Asia's richest and world's 9th richest man as of 31 December 2024, as per *Forbes* magazine's World's Billionaires List) should know ground realities better than a politician or two economists, but whoever is finally proved right, Modi's Bharat is on the right track to achieve hitherto undreamt-of targets.

Based on the average 9.368 per cent growth rate that is definitely very ambitious, India's GDP is expected to cross $5T in 2028, $10T in 2036, and $15T in 2041.

21

Expenditure and Poverty

Growing personal expenditure of citizens is the best example of rising incomes. Let us see data from the latest Household Consumption Expenditure Survey[1] (HCES) 2023–24 that mapped the personal expenditure of 154,357 rural households and 107,596 urban households for the period August 2023 to July 2024.

Personal Expenditure and Poverty	Source	FY 2012	Aug 2023 to July 2024	CHANGE
Urban Monthly Per Capita Expenditure	HCES	₹2630	₹6996	▲ 166.0%
Urban Poverty Line	SBI	₹1000	₹1929	▲ 92.9%
Rural Monthly Per Capita Expenditure	HCES	₹1430	₹4122	▲ 188.3%
Rural Poverty Line	SBI	₹816	₹1622	▲ 98.8%
Rural Expenditure / Urban Expenditure		54.37%	58.92%	▲ 8.37%
Indians with Multidimensional Poverty	Niti Aayog	29.17% (FY14)	11.28% (FY23)	▼▼ 61.33% in 9 years
Poor persons in urban India as % of total urban population	SBI	13.7%	4.6%	▼▼ 66.4%
Poor persons in rural India as % of total rural population	SBI	25.7%	7.2%	▼▼ 72.0%

What could be a better example of the success of Modinomics than the whopping increases in household expenditure?

Furthermore, the share of the expenses on food has reduced by 8 per cent for the urban population and by 12.3 per cent for the rural population in 12 years, which means that people now have more spare money to spend on other things.

In FY24, the rural poverty ratio dropped to below 5% for the first time in history. It was 26% in FY12, the 8th year of the UPA Government.

22

Prices under Control

Controlled price rise, despite the COVID-19 pandemic which forced the Modi Government to substantially increase its healthcare and social sector spending, increased the spending power of middle classes.

As per the World Bank, India's compounded average consumer price inflation was 6.068% per cent during the 9 years from 2014 to 2023 compared to 12.084 per cent in UPA's 10 years (down 49.8 per cent).

As per the International Monetary Fund (IMF), consumer inflation was 6.189 per cent in Modi's entire 10 years, compared to 11.309 per cent in UPA's 10 years (down 45.3 per cent).

It is quite evident that both the numbers (World Bank and IMF) are about the same.

It must be noted that UPA had inherited an inflation of only 4.488 per cent from Vajpayee's 6.18 years as PM.

Modi was able to keep inflation at half of UPA's levels despite much higher welfare spending due to COVID-19 and a massive 183.65 per cent increase in overall government expenditure compared with the UPA-era.

Yes, a chaiwallah managed prices better than an economist.

As per an RBI report, the weighted average tax rate under the Goods and Services Tax (GST) regime rate fell from the 14.4 per cent that the consumers paid on taxes such as Central Sales Tax, VAT, Purchase Tax, Service Tax, Octroi, Entry Tax, Surcharge, Cess, etc., in July 2017, when GST started, to 11.6 per cent in 2019, giving consumers savings of 19.44 per cent in just two years. The GST regime has helped Indian households save over ₹47,000Cr/month from December 2017 to November 2024.

While the interest rate on bank loans during most of the UPA-era ranged from 10.25 per cent to 15.75 per cent p.a., it came down to a low of 6.45 per cent and a maximum of 9.7 per cent (reduction of 37.1 per cent—38.4 per cent) from Modi's 2nd year.

23

End of Tax Terrorism, Reduced Black Money

Modi did not print currency to manage a 183.65 per cent increase in government spending compared with the UPA; neither did he import crores of Indian rupees from Pakistan.

By reducing taxes and introducing other tax reforms, Modi and his team have been able to substantially increase tax compliance.

The number of persons declaring a taxable income of more than ₹1Cr has gone up more than 5-fold in these 10 years.

Due to the increase in the tax exemption slabs for individuals, the middle class is saving a whopping ₹2.5LCr per year in taxes.

Measures such as GST, Jandhan Aadhaar Mobile (JAM) linking, and Unified Payments Interface (UPI) have greatly helped in reducing any new generation of black money.

About 11M outstanding direct tax demands up to ₹25,000 (till FY10) and up to ₹10,000 (for FY11–FY15) were withdrawn to resolve petty tax disputes dating back to 1962. In some cases, resolutions would cost as much as 10–50 times the ITD's claim amounts.

Data on Taxation & Tax Collections

Particulars	FY14	FY24	Change
No PIT for Income up to	₹2.2 lakhs	₹7.0 lakhs	▲ 218.2%
Tax Rate for existing Domestic Companies and LLPs not availing any tax concessions	30%	22%	▼▼ 26.7%
Corporate Tax Rate for certain types of New Domestic Manufacturing Cos.	30%	15%	▼▼ 50.4%
44AD—Presumptive Tax for Retail Businesses with Revenue below ₹3Cr	There was no such provision	Tax payable on Presumed Profit of 8% of Revenue (non-digital) OR 6% of Revenue (digital)	
44AD—Presumptive Tax for Professionals with Gross Receipts below ₹75 lakhs	There was no such provision	Flat Rate of 8% Tax on 50% of Gross Receipts	
No. of people who filed an ITR[1]	38M	83.4M	▲ 119.5%
Net Direct Tax Receipts[2]	₹6.386 LCr	₹19.58 LCr	▲ 206.6%
Corporate Income Tax (CIT)[3]	₹3.947 LCr	₹9.11 LCr	▲ 130.88%
Personal Income Tax (PIT)[4]	₹2.429 LCr	₹10.44 LCr	▲ 329.8%
PIT as a % age of CIT	61.54%	114.6%	▲ 86.2%
Average Time for IT Refunds[5]	93 days	10 days	▼▼ 89.3%
Gross GST collections[6] (GST was introduced in Jul2017)	₹9.875 LCr in FY19	₹20.18 LCr	▲ 104.4% in 5yrs
Persons with over ₹1Cr Income[7]	68,263 in FY17	216,000+ 31 Dec2023	▲ 216.4% in 6yrs

1 Several Media Reports; 2,3,4 bit.ly/3yCyCIl 5 bit.ly/3wT3QVe 6 bit.ly/3ViNuP3 7 bit.ly/3X4VRPt

GST has been a game changer, as the GST returns of a business are mapped with that of its suppliers, due to everything being online. It is virtually impossible for a business to avoid GST registration as its customers need 'input credit'.

Let's say an unregistered entity wants to provide security guards to a GST-registered supermarket. The supermarket will not agree as it can deduct GST paid to a registered security agency from the GST that it must remit to the government. It works similarly for all types of manufacturers, traders and providers of various services.

Except exempt goods such as water, raw foods, milk, tea, coffee, grains, vegetables, fruits, eggs, fish, meat, sugar, life-saving drugs, vaccines, sanitary pads, human blood, newspapers, books, *kumkum*, *bindis*, etc., and exempt services like air/bus fare below ₹1,500 per trip for private operators and unlimited for railways and state government transport corporations, certain medical and legal services, etc., almost everything else has GST; and now that the administration of GST is completely online, there is no escaping from it.

Once you get on the GST network, your revenues and expenditure are automatically mapped with the ITD, so your Income Tax Returns (ITR) cannot have different data than your GST returns.

The gross GST collections in the first nine months of FY25 were ₹16.33LCR, which is 9.1% per cent higher than the same period of the previous financial year. The net Direct Tax collections increased by 16.45% till 17 December 2024.

Overall, in the 10 years of Modi Government, Direct Tax collections went up by over 182%.

Since a taxpayer's Income Tax Permanent Account Number (PAN) is also linked with Aadhaar, it makes it easier for the tax department to track transactions that have an Aadhaar connection.

Even the ITD administration is completely online now. Dividends paid by companies, banking and credit card transactions above certain amounts, TDS deducted, everything is now being mapped.

Gone are the days when you could meet an Income Tax Officer or Assistant Commissioner and bribe her/him to reduce your tax. Tax Assessment has become 'faceless' so you don't even know whom to meet. Tax compliance has become hassle-free, ending the era of 'Tax Terrorism' prevalent during the UPA-era. However, we are not trying to say that the generation of black money in India is finished completely.

Of the 80.9M persons who filed ITRs for FY24, only around 31.9M paid tax (the rest reported zero income). This is only 4.09 per cent of India's working population excluding farmers (who are completely exempt from income tax) and 3.415 per cent including farmers. Compare this to 78.3 per cent paying taxes in France, 61.3 per cent in Germany, 59.7 per cent in the UK, and 50.1 per cent in the US.

If taxpayers can go up to just 7 per cent of non-Agri income earners in 5 years, the taxpayer base will go up to 57.44M by FY29 and assuming a conservative 8.5 per cent CAGR in incomes, Modi 3.0 can aim to more than treble Personal Income Tax (PIT) to ₹32.274LCr in FY29 compared with ₹10.575LCr in FY24. Imagine what this will do to the economy.

Moreover, if just 1 per cent of the richest farmers pay income tax, this will add ₹2.5LCr to the tax kitty and can pay for the treatment of 2.5M families under Pradhan Mantri Jan Arogya Yojana (PMJAY).

Of course, the prime minister must have already thought about it and there will probably be a smile on his face when he reads this.

24

EoDB, Reforms, Bankruptcy

The UPA mostly slept on reforms, assuming that what had been done by prime ministers PV Narasimha Rao and Vajpayee was enough. The Modi Government quietly did much more and witnessed significant results.

Ease of Doing Business (EoDB)

There were huge improvements in India's rank in the World Bank's Ease of Doing Business (EoDB) Index and many of its components.[2]

WORLD BANK'S EASE OF DOING BUSINESS RANKINGS			
Index / Parameter	2014 Rank	2019 Rank	Improvement
Ease of Doing Business (Overall)	**142**	**63**	**▲ 55.63%**
Construction Permits	182	52	**▲ 71.43%**
Getting Electricity	111	24	**▲ 78.38%**
Protecting Minority Investors	34	7	**▲ 79.41%**
Trading Across Borders	132	80	**▲ 39.39%**

India was listed in the 'Top 10 Improvers' for the 3rd consecutive year in 2019. As it takes time for the effect of reforms, we would have seen even greater improvements by

2023 if the World Bank had not discontinued the 'Doing Business' report after 2019.

The data on active companies and LLPs in Chapter 20 of this book shows how all this has significantly stimulated economic activity.

National Single Window System (NSWS) was launched in September 2021 to further improve the EoDB. On the NSWS portal, a business can apply for 657 Central approvals from 32 ministries and 6,787 approvals from 31 states/UTs. As of January 2023, NSWS received 420,000 unique visitors from 157 countries. More than 150,000 investors used the KYA (Know Your Approvals) module of NSWS to know the list of approvals they required for their specific business cases. A total of 75,599 approvals were granted out of over 123,000 applications.

Centre for Processing Accelerated Corporate Exit was set up by to facilitate voluntary winding up of companies in less than 100 days, against two years earlier; as many as 11,855 companies wound up in the first 15 months.

Central Registration Centre was established to accelerate services for incorporating new companies and LLPs.

By January 2023, the government had:

- Implemented 7,496 business reforms.
- Repealed 1,506 Central laws.
- Reduced over 40,000 compliances.
- Decriminalised over 3,500 laws/rules related to minor technical or procedural defaults.
- Started a paperless, online e-Bill System for all central procurement, enabling suppliers/contractors to submit digitally signed bills/claims online and track their status from anywhere.

- Started the PARIVESH portal for online submission/monitoring of proposals for Central/State/district environment/forest/wildlife/Coastal Regulation Zone (CRZ) clearances with automatic updating of application status at each stage.
- Enabled transparent 'quality-based' criteria for the evaluation of complex tenders, as against only 'lowest cost' criteria earlier.
- Mandated payment of 75 per cent of running bills by government entities to contractors and vendors of good as well as services within 10 days.
- Notified rules for settling disputes via conciliation.

Work is going on rapidly on:

- Digitisation of manual processes and interventions
- Standardisation/removal of overlapping compliances.
- Integration of thousands of Central/state-level systems through IT bridges.
- Single-point access for all citizen-centric services.
- Central Processing Centre to process all corporate compliances forms.
- Unified document filing and authenticity checking processes at all central/state departments to avoid duplication and process requests quicker.

Jan Vishwas Bill was enacted in August 2023 to amend 42 Central Acts to reduce pressure on the justice system, address technical and/or procedural defaults without imposing severe penalties, and establish a balance between severity of offense and prescribed punishment.

The GoI has offered milestone/outcome-based interest-free loans of ₹75,000Cr to states to pursue reforms.

Insolvency and Bankruptcy Code (IBC)

Laws for recovering dues/insolvency/bankruptcy were fragmented across 6–7 legislations due to which corporate default/insolvency/bankruptcy cases would not get resolved for years or even decades.

Around 5–6 very senior and minimum 40 other practising lawyers were/are Congress leaders. They were happy making money, while lenders (mostly banks and financial institutions) were not able to recover their overdue loans.

This is what Modi did:

- Created a 'Bankruptcy Legislative Reforms Committee' in August 2014.
- Got the IBC formulated and passed by the Parliament in May 2016.
- Set up National Company Law Tribunal (NCLT) in June 2016 as the adjudicating authority to manage the insolvency resolution process.
- Set up Insolvency and Bankruptcy Board of India (IBBI) in October 2016 as the regulator for overseeing insolvency proceedings.
- Set up National Company Law Appellate Tribunal (NCLAT) as the sole organisation to adjudicate appeals against NCLT decisions.

The NCLAT's decisions can only be appealed before the SCI. No other court is allowed to entertain cases on matters in the IBC or adjudicated by NCLAT.

Bankruptcy/insolvency resolution is now very smooth, compared with the previous 69 years. The IBC has rescued 3,171 distressed companies in eight years, compared with resolution in less than 3,500 companies in 29.5 years under the earlier mechanism, the Board of Industrial and Financial Reconstruction (BIFR).

Till June 2024, about 32.1 per cent of creditors' claims (₹3.40LCr) had been already recovered from 1,005 resolved cases.

NCLT had ordered 2,376 companies to be liquidated.

Till December 2023, creditors withdrew 27,514 insolvency cases involving defaults of a whopping ₹9.75LCr before their applications were admitted at the NCLT, suggesting they had either recovered money or forced debtors to settle dues by threatening IBC proceedings.

Single Demat Account

The Modi Government is working with the depositories as well as regulators and exchanges to have a Single Demat Account for all types of investments, including shares, mutual funds, fixed deposits, insurance, Public Provident Fund, and Post Office deposits.

The Single Demat Account will also allow transactions of all types of financial assets.

Single Demat will do away with the need to do multiple KYCs for every type of account or investment.

The preparation of infrastructure and software will obviously take time as multiple regulators and stakeholders are involved in the process.

25

Record Foreign Investment

Modi Sarkar's Foreign Direct Investment (FDI) policy has catalysed gross inflows[3] of a record $667.404B, compared to $305.277B in 10 years of UPA (up 118.6 per cent) despite the COVID-19 pandemic and global conflicts including the Russia–Ukraine war, Israel–Hamas/Hezbollah wars, etc.

This is because most foreign investors now believe that not only is there long-term political stability in the country but also enormous economic development that have led to unprecedented investment opportunities (see 'Appendix' at the end of the book).

India's Forex reserves went up by $333.8B in Modi's first decade as PM. They had gone up by $196.3B during the decade of UPA-rule.

Invest India

National Investment Promotion and Facilitation Agency (Invest India), which was set up in 2009 by the UPA, was given new wings by Modi.

It offers a one-stop solution to global as well as domestic investors and handholds them from the day they start exploring India till their fund deployment and beyond. Apart from tailor-made incentive offers, it mediates between government and companies.

FOREIGN DIRECT INVESTMENT COMMITMENTS of $2B and above NOTE: this is not an exhaustive list; SOURCES: Various media announcements from time to time		
Crown Prince of Saudi Arabia	Sovereign Wealth Fund PIF has AUM of $620B	**$100B**
EFTA	Iceland, Liechtenstein, Norway, and Switzerland	**$100B**
Investment Corporation of Dubai	AUM of $275B	**$75B**
ArcelorMittal-Nippon Steel	Revenue $127.71B; MCap $46B (combined)	**$39B**
Amazon (USA)	Revenue $574.8B, MCap $1.89T	**$26B**
Blackstone (USA)	World's No.1 PE firm, AUM $1000B	**$17B**
KKR-Global Atlantic (USA)	World's No.2 PE firm, AUM $711B	**$10B**
Google / Alphabet (USA)	Revenue $307.4B; MCap $1.915T	**$10B**
Warburg Pincus (USA)	AUM of $83B	**$10B**
Brookfield Asset Management (Canada)	AUM of $900B	**$10B**
Temasek Holdings (Singapore)	AUM of $288B	**$10B**
Advent (USA)	AUM of $91B	**$5-10B**
EQT Group AB (Sweden)	AUM of $252B	**$7B**
Bain Capital (USA)	AUM of $180B	**$7B**
Vedanta Group (UK)	Revenue $17.444B; MCap $3B	**$6B**
Coca Cola (USA)	Revenue $45.754B; MCap $258.2B	**$5B**
Abu Dhabi Investment Authority	Sovereign Wealth Fund; AUM of $993B	**$4-5B**
Mitsubishi UFJ (Japan)	AUM of $2.622T	**$4-5B**
Mizuho Bank (Japan)	Japan's 3rd largest Bank; AUM of $1.8T	**$3.8B**
Canadian Pension Plan Investment Board	AUM of $437.4B	**$3.6B**
Accenture (USA)	Revenue $64.11B; MCap $225B	**$3B**
The Carlyle Group (USA)	World's No.5 PE firm; AUM of $426B	**$2.7B**
CVC Capital Partners (Luxembourg)	AUM of $201.4B	**$2.4B**
Vinfast (Vietnam)	Revenue $1.198B; MCap $10.15B	**$2B**
Qualcomm	Revenue $35.82B; MCap $189.5B	**$2B**

Its more than 400 professionals are handpicked from the best universities/companies, and they serve as investors' pro bono guides, from assisting with land acquisition to highlighting projects for investment, to showcasing cutting-edge innovation and startups.

Invest India has built a tool called 'I-chat Policy' to incorporate the policies and regulations of all states/UTs on a common platform.

'Investors can come and say I'm going to invest in automotive tyres; show me the incentives from different states. It will make them a list table of, say, five states and say that these are the policies,' explained Nivruti Rai, chief of Invest India. It will not be only used for India, Rai added. 'We intend to work with Brazil and a few other countries to incorporate their policies and "train" the model to compare policies across countries. So, Brazil can use it for Brazil, but Brazil can also use it to compare with India, Malaysia, whichever country's policies we put in. India will catapult on the shoulder of technology. And we will use every single technology.'[4]

The platform will also be used internally. Invest India will publish monthly results of important sectors that are driving investments.

26

AatmaNirbhar in Arms

Until the end of 2021, you could read several articles in Indian media (especially the leftist media) that Modi's Make-in-India has failed in defence manufacturing. Today, most critics have been silenced as Indian companies have made huge progress, from BrahMos missiles and drones to the Tejas LCA, military transport aircraft, advanced military helicopters, submarines, and even an aircraft carrier. Since FY20, defence imports have come down by 21 per cent.

The value of *AatmaNirbhar* production in FY24 was about ₹126,887Cr (up 189 per cent from about ₹43,900Cr in FY14). The Ministry of Defence (MoD) has set a target of ₹1.60LCr for FY25 and ₹3LCr by FY29.

Russia has agreed to set up JVs in India to make components and spares of Russian-origin arms and weapon systems with Transfer of Technology. This will greatly enhance defence production in India as about 62-65 per cent of arms and weapon systems being used by Indian armed forces is of Russian-origin.

HAL's capacity to make Tejas LCA was trebled to 24 jets/year and will go up by another 16 jets/year by 2027. A new helicopter factory started in February 2023 to make 30 choppers/year, which will go up to 90/year in two phases.

Soon, HAL will also start making Flight Refueller Aircraft, advanced engines for MiG-29s, Jet Engines for Tejas and future aircraft via a technology transfer from GE (USA), helicopter engines in a JV with Safran (France), as well as Drones and Multi Mission Tanker Transport Aircraft in a JV with Israel Aerospace Industries (IAI) HAL has also started designing a Medium Lift Multirole Helicopter to be ready by 2031 and a 5th generation Advanced Medium Combat Aircraft to be ready by 2038.

DRDO tested the 5000+km range Agni-5 missile with MIRV (Multiple Independently Targetable Re-entry Vehicle) technology. An MIRV payload means a single missile carrying 2–3 nuclear warheads, each programmed to be released at different speeds with different trajectories to hit different targets hundreds of kilometres apart. So far, only China, France, Russia, the UK, and the US had this technology.

You can see the 'Modernised the Armed Forces' chapter to see the major equipment made by Indian companies.

Here are the details of what else some major public sector defence companies make:

- Cochin Shipyard has set up India's first International Ship Repair Facility that will also serve ships of the US Navy.
- Hindustan Shipyard is now producing 44,000-ton Fleet Support Ships.
- Garden Reach Shipbuilders and Engineers now makes Marine Diesel Engines for Navy ships with German Rolls Royce technology.
- Mazagon Dock Shipbuilders manufactures Destroyers, Missile Boats, Corvettes, Advanced Guided Missile Stealth Frigates (AGMFs), and other ships/vessels.
- BEML makes Gun Towing Vehicles (GTVs) and High Mobility Vehicles (HMVs).

- Mishra Dhatu Nigam makes titanium/other super alloys, ultra-high strength and other specialty steels for aircraft/rockets/satellites; Advanced bulletproof jackets/helmets/other armour products.

The 31 MQ-9B Predator armed drones that India is buying from General Atomics of the US (see chapter 'Modernised the Armed Forces') for $3.9B will be assembled in India, with the American company investing in India and sourcing over 30 per cent of the components from India. General Atomics will also provide expertise and consultancy to DRDO and Indian companies to develop such high-altitude (25,000 feet), long-endurance (27 hours) drones in India.

Coming to the private sector, some companies already included in the chapter 'Modernised the Armed Forces' also make additional equipment. Some others that were not included in those Tables are:

- L&T—Nuclear-powered Submarines, Interceptor Boats, Corvettes, Missile Vessels, Floating Dry Docks, Rocket Anti-Tank Munitions (ATMs), High-powered Radars, and more.
- Tata Advanced Systems—Missiles, ATMs, GTVs, and Electronic Warfare Systems.
- Kalyani Strategic Systems (Bharat Forge)—Rocket Launchers, ATMs, GTVs, and HMVs.
- Force Motors—Light Strike Vehicles.
- Adani Defence and Aerospace—Missiles and Ammunition.
- Ashok Leyland and JSW Gecko—GTVs and HMVs.
- Another 45+ private companies make various electronics, parts, components, assemblies, and other systems for the defence sector. There were just 5–7 such companies in 2014.

Lockheed Martin and Tata Advanced Systems have tied-up to bid for India's Medium Transport Aircraft (MTA) acquisition. The companies will establish a Maintenance, Repair & Overhaul (MRO) facility for the C-130J transport aircraft that will support the C-130Js in service with the IAF and C-130Js from other country's air forces. In addition, subject to approvals from the US and Indian governments, the two could start manufacturing the C-130J in India, subject to this aircraft winning the MTA contract.

Many top corporate houses such as Tata, Adani, L&T, Mahindra, Ashok Leyland (Hinduja Group), and Bharat Forge entered the complex business of defence manufacturing for the first time. Congress governments could not make this happen in 66.8 years.

Indian companies have received MoD's orders of over ₹4.5LCr under the Make-in-India program since 2021 alone. Obviously, these companies will produce and sell (in the domestic and export markets) equipment of far greater value in times to come.

iDEX or Innovations for Defence Excellence is a flagship initiative of the MoD that has the following programs:

- Defence India Startup Challenge (with Atal Innovation Mission) to support startups, Micro, Small, and Medium Enterprises (MSMEs), and innovators to create prototypes and/or commercialise products/solutions for defence and security.
- SPRINT Challenges for encouraging indigenous technology for the Indian Navy was launched in July 2022—over 110 contracts have been awarded to private sector companies.

- Mission DefSpace was launched at DefExpo Gandhinagar in October 2022 with 75 'Defence Space Challenges' for the private sector.
- ADITI was launched in March 2024 to promote innovations in 30 critical and strategic defence technologies. Technology challenges faced by the Armed Forces are presented to Indian startups and innovators who have to come up with solutions; 17 challenges were announced at the launch. Proposals that meet technical needs will get government grants up to ₹25Cr for development in a pre-defined timeframe. The first order of ₹200Cr for Anti-Drone Systems was given in 15 days to a startup.

iDEX got 7,500+ applications within seven months.

In a historic decision taken in September 2020, the Modi Government allowed 74 per cent automatic FDI and 100 per cent with government approval with restrictions on companies with links to China and Pakistan (it had been increased from 26 per cent in the UPA-era to 49 per cent by Modi Government in November 2014).

The first foreign company to get 100 per cent FDI permission was Saab of Sweden to make Carl-Gustaf M4 Shoulder-Fired Rockets.

Until December 2023, FDI of ₹5,077Cr had come in the defence sector.

A historic decision taken in 2022 made it mandatory for the Armed Forces to buy 75 per cent Made-in-India equipment. In an ever-changing geopolitical world, today's friend can become tomorrow's enemy, or a not-so-good friend. Therefore, Modi's *AatmaNirbhar* policy secures India from potential future threats.

'It's extremely essential to have a robust and effective defence industry ecosystem, including indigenous research, design, development, and production capacities', said the then Army chief, General Manoj Pande.[5]

There are 219 startups in the defence equipment sector.

Restructuring of DRDO

Since 1958, the DRDO has been the MoD's main agency responsible for the R&D of defence technologies and products. Currently, the DRDO Chairman reports to the defence ministry, and there are huge project delays and cost overruns—as many as 23 of the 55 high-priority 'mission mode' projects are behind schedule.

A Defence Technology Council will be created directly under the PMO and will be assisted by a proposed Department of Defence Science, Technology, and Innovation. The DRDO Chairman and Secretary, R&D, MoD will report to this Council. The DRDO's role will be limited to R&D, assisted by academic institutions and startups. Further product development and manufacturing will be handled by PSEs and private companies.

Exports and Export Opportunities

India exported arms and ammunition worth ₹21,083Cr ($1.9B) in FY24, compared with ₹1,153Cr in FY14 (up 1,728.5 per cent). Indian manufacturers had exports of ₹16,069Cr in the first 9 months of FY25.

Over 100 companies export arms/ammunition/assemblies/ components to about 135 countries including France, Israel, Russia, and Spain.

India has already exported BrahMos missiles worth $375M to the Philippines and deals of $700M with Vietnam and $450M with Indonesia are being negotiated.

HAL has submitted cost proposals for 68 Tejas LCAs and 30 Advanced Light Helicopters (ALHs) to five countries. There are also export requests for Cochin Shipyard's Aircraft Carrier. The value of these alone will be over ₹93,000Cr.

As per an Oxfam International report released in May 2023, all countries together spent an estimated $112B/year on arms imports between 2018 and 2022.

The top 5 exporters (USA, Russia, France, China, and Germany) together accounted for 75.9 per cent of the total arms exports.

India did not figure in the Top 25 exporters.

Considering exports of $1.9B in FY23, India may have been placed around No.30-32 that year and is poised to be around No.12-15 in 2026.

If world arms exports grow in line with world GDP at a Compounded Annual Growth Rate (CAGR) of 3.4 per cent, the value will be $276B in 2047, when India as per Modi's vision becomes *Viksit Bharat* (a developed nation).

If Indian arms exports grow at a conservative CAGR of 14 per cent, exports of $44.1B in FY47 will give India a 16 per cent market share and make us the 3rd largest arms exporter in the world.

To promote arms exports, the Modi Government posted defence attachés in 11 new countries. An attaché's job is to promote her/his country's interest in the host country, in the field of the attaché.

Why did the Congress and their supporters mock the Make-in-India program for the defence industry for so many years? Is it because they wanted India to continue depending on arms imports forever, as it is much easier to get kickbacks from foreign companies than Indian ones, especially PSEs?

27

Make in India

Nehru believed India could not do labour-intensive manufacturing. In 1950, India's share of world population was about 14.5 per cent and share of world GDP was about 4.2 per cent, giving us a GDP:Population Ratio (GPR) of 0.29. Today India's share of world population has gone up to 17.76 per cent and share of world GDP has fallen to about 3.5723 per cent, thus lowering the GPR further to 0.2 per cent—a fall of over 31 per cent.

The US has a GPR of 6.12, China 0.962, and Russia 1.0. If India had proper economic policies, we could be on par with China or Russia. At half of China (GPR 0.481), our current GDP would be $8.925T and Per Capita Income around $5900 (₹490,300), and we would not have to wait till the year 2035 to reach close to a $9T economy.

The major blame for this must go to Nehru and his daughter Indira who ruled India for 88.2 per cent of the first 37.2 years since India became an independent nation. They were abject failures as prime ministers, and this topic is not debatable as the numbers prove the point.

Share of manufacturing in India's GDP was around 17.85 per cent in FY22 and 17.05 per cent in FY23. It has been continuously falling since FY96, when it peaked at 19.6 per cent. Something urgently needed to be done to get the private sector to expand existing factories and set up new ones, and also to get new companies to enter manufacturing.

Due to 'Jayanthi tax', a nickname for the bribe one had to pay to UPA environment minister Jayanthi Natarajan (July 2011–December 2013) for environmental clearance of any industry/project, average time to get approvals went up from 86 days (pre-Jayanthi) to 316 days (post-Jayanthi). Modi Government has brought it down to 70 days, while the forest cover has gone up by over 17,600 km^2 in 9.5 years.

From 6th in 2014, India is world's 3rd largest vehicle maker today.

The Technology Development Fund for defence manufacturing has 5,408 companies engaged in R&D for indigenising 164 defence technologies under the guidance of the DRDO.

Here are some announced or expected mega investments:

NEW MEGA INVESTMENTS ANNOUNCED FOR MAKE-IN-INDIA

SOURCES: Estimates based on various media announcements from time to time

Who is Investing	For Manufacturing What	Amount
Adani Group	Conventional and Green Energy; Consumer Products; Solar Panels; Green Ammonia/Hydrogen; Cement; Pharma; PVC; Copper; etc.	₹9.5 Lcr
Reliance Industries	Oil & Gas Exploration and Production; Petrochemicals; Semiconductors; New Energy (Fuel Cell Systems, Solar Photovoltaic Panels, Green Hydrogen); Power Electronics; etc.	₹9.0 Lcr
Tata Group	Aircraft & Aircraft Components; MROs; Defence Equipment; Electronics; Automobiles (incl. EV); Conventional and Green Energy; Semiconductors; Metals; Chemicals; Consumer Products (Watches/ Eyewear/Beverages/Edibles, Jewellery, etc.)	₹8.0 Lcr
ArcelorMittal Nippon Steel	Steel; Mining; Pellet production	₹3.2 Lcr
Aditya Birla Group	Renewable Energy; Textiles & Fabrics; Mining; Aluminium & Alloys; Cement; Chemicals; Paints; etc.	₹3.0 Lcr
JSW Group	Steel; Cement; Power; Passenger & Commercial Vehicles (incl. EV)	₹90,000cr
Vedanta Group	Oil & Gas; Aluminium; Power	₹50,000cr
Others in Semiconductors		₹4.0 Lcr
Others in Automobiles and Auto Components		₹1.2 Lcr
Others in Green Ammonia and Green Hydrogen		₹90,000cr
Pharma Industry		₹75,000cr
Private Cos—Other Sectors		₹3.0 Lcr
Public Sector Enterprises	Oil & Gas; Power; Mining; Defence Equipment; Steel & Metals, etc.	₹18 Lcr

The PLI Success

Modi Government started Production Linked Incentive (PLI) schemes in March 2020 to create manufacturing champions. It covers 15 sectors with a subsidy outlay of ₹2.23LCr.

Till March 2024, 755 applications (including 176 MSMEs) had been approved; investments had crossed ₹1.23LCr, employment of over 790,000 persons had been generated (against potential of 6M jobs), and goods worth over ₹8.61LCr had been sold (against an assessment of ₹30LCr by FY28) including exports of over ₹3.2LCr.

SECTOR for PLIs (Production Linked Incentives) Source: https://www.investindia.gov.in/production-linked-incentives-schemes-india	AMOUNT
Electronics	₹38,645cr
Automobiles and Components	₹25,938cr
Electronics Components	₹25,700cr
High-efficiency Solar PV modules	₹24,000cr
Advanced Chemistry Cell Battery Storage	₹18,100cr
IT Hardware	₹17,000cr
Pharmaceuticals	₹15,000cr
Telecom and Networking Products	₹15,000cr
Food Processing	₹10,900cr
MMF Apparel, MMF Fabrics and Products of Technical Textiles	₹10,683cr
Faster Adoption and Manufacturing of Electric Vehicles (FAME)	₹10,000cr
Bulk Drugs	₹6940cr
Specialty Steel	₹6322cr
White Goods	₹6238cr

There are smaller PLI outlays for Medical Devices, Drones, and Drone Components.

Automobiles and Auto Components

The Indian Auto industry undertook over 500 localisation projects across 11 key component categories in FY20 and FY21 to reduce net imports by 5.8 per cent (reduction of ₹7018Cr). They are now investing about ₹57,000Cr in FY24–FY27 to reduce auto parts imports by another ₹25,000Cr.

Their target is to reduce China's share in imports from 32 per cent in FY20 to 24–25 per cent by FY28 and the industry is confident they will honour this commitment made to Modi.

Promoting New Technologies

The Modi Government is working rapidly to promote several new and emerging technologies.

It has set up an Innovation Fund of ₹1LCr to provide finance for research in deep-tech ventures in advanced technologies. Loans of up to 50 years' duration at zero or very low interest rates will be given to youth to invent/develop new technologies and products.

Quantum Technologies and Robotics

The ₹8,000Cr National Mission on Quantum Technologies and Applications will help support the development of 4 Quantum research parks and 21 Quantum hubs across the country.

In February 2023, Innogress signed an agreement with the Government of UP to build Indraprastha Quantum Data Center in Greater Noida in a JV with GAN Tech (UK). Innogress will also set up Greater Karnavati Quantum Computing Tech Park in Gujarat.

In June 2023, it set up the 'Greater Noida Robotics Tech Park'.

Global robotics company Addverb (backed by Reliance) has 2 factories in UP that produce 150,000 robots/year.

India has as many as 594 startups in Robotics.

Artificial Intelligence (AI)

In March 2024, the Modi Government approved a ₹10,372Cr AI Mission till FY29. This will cover creation of computing infrastructure in PPP mode, developing compute power, AI models, Apps, talent, and data platforms—and 100,000 GPUs (compute capacity) will be made available to startups, R&D facilities, universities, and other educational institutions as a service by the government.

Nvidia is the world's largest producer of chips that make AI work. Its market capitalisation is $3.492T (trillion) as of 24 January 2025, making it the largest public company in the world by market value.

'There is an opportunity for India to become "the AI factory of the world" as more and more infrastructure becomes available', Nvidia's MD for South Asia Vishal Dhupar said.[6]

Aircraft and Drones

Embraer (Brazil) is the world's 3rd largest passenger aircraft maker. It is speaking with several potential Indian partners to make three types of E2 aircrafts (80–90 seats, 97–114 seats, and 120–146 seats).

Airbus in a JV with Tata Group is setting up a Final Assembly Line for its H125 helicopter for the Indian domestic market and exports to neighbours. It will be the first private helicopter plant in India. The H125 holds six passengers and a pilot and is the only chopper to land on Mt Everest. Providing last mile connectivity to remote areas, the H125 will contribute to tourism and will also be used for emergency medical services, disaster management and law enforcement missions.

You will recall that Tata Group has already set up a plant to produce Airbus C295 military transport aircraft. The Group is also investing ₹2,300Cr in Karnataka on setting up an MRO facility for aircraft.

Airbus has signed contracts with five to six Indian companies (including Tata Group) to make components for its commercial (passenger) aircraft, including its widely popular A320neo as well as the A330neo and the wide-body A350.

The 43ac Boeing India Engineering and Tech Center opened in January 2024 to develop next-gen products and services for aerospace and defence industries, with 3,000+ engineers engaging in R&D for new-age technologies such as AI/Machine Learning, Industrial Internet of Things (IoT), Model-Based Engineering, and advanced manufacturing for global markets.

Israel Aerospace Industries is setting up a defence MRO hub in Gurugram.

There are 237 startups in Aviation and 539 in the Drone sector.

ONGC Sea Survival Centre

Oil and Natural Gas Corporation (ONGC, a PSE) is India's largest crude oil and natural gas company. The Mumbai High offshore field located 176km west of Mumbai produces 11.45mtpa of crude oil—53.3 per cent of ONGC's total and 39.2 per cent of India's total.

To save time, ONGC staff/consultants use helicopters to get there. Due to rough weather over the Arabian Sea, there have been many helicopter crashes.

ONGC has come up with an innovative solution. The ONGC Sea Survival Centre (SSC) opened in February 2024. It is an advanced marine aviation and rigorous sea survival training facility with helicopter crash simulations under rough sea conditions.

Apart from ONGC, the SSC will be used by the Navy, Coast Guard, the IAF, and by commercial airlines (those flying helicopters).

Conclusion

In March 2024, based on new orders, upturn in inventories, and higher job creation, the HSBC India Manufacturing Purchasing Managers' Index or PMI Index reached a 16-year high of 59.1.

Modi has set a target for 25 per cent of GDP from manufacturing by 2047. That requires a 10.6 per cent CAGR over the next 22 years.

28

Electronics and Telecom

This sector is a huge Modi-era success story:

MODI GOVT's SUCCESS in ELECTRONICS and TELECOM				
PARTICULARS	**FROM**	**TO**	**CHANGE**	**TIME**
Electronics Manufacturing Value[1]	$29B (FY14)	$105B (FY24)	▲ **262.1%**	10 yrs
Exports of Electronics, IT, and Telecom Products[2]	$4.15B (FY14)	$28.534B (FY24)	▲ **587.6%**	10 yrs
Mobile Manufacturing Factories[3]	2 (FY14)	205 (FY24)	▲ **10,150%**	10 yrs
Mobile Phones Made-in-India[4] (in number of units)	58M (FY15)	389M (FY23)	▲ **570.7%**	8 yrs
Production Value of Mobile Phones Made-in-India[5]	$2.3B (FY14)	$50B (FY24)	▲ **2073.9%**	10 yrs
Mobile Phone Exports[6]	$0.237B (FY15)	$15.584B (FY24)	▲ **6476%**	9 yrs
Made-in-India Mobile Phone Share in Domestic Market[7]	19% (2014)	99.2% (2023)	▲ **422%**	9 yrs
Apple's Production in India	₹16,750Cr[8] (FY21)	₹116,900Cr[9] (FY24)	▲ **597.9%**	3 yrs

SOURCES: 1 & 5 — https://bit.ly/Elec-Tele; 2 & 3 — bit.ly/3wZyrjV; 4 — bit.ly/3X3ekMm; 6) bit.ly/3VjIrxP; 7) bit.ly/45acLyk; 8 — bit.ly/3X1s0Hy; 9 — bit.ly/4bBVn85 **NOTES:** Some data may be ±5%; Some FY24 estimates are based on data reported till Feb2024

Revenue increase of 2,073.9 per cent in mobile manufacturing versus a lower quantity increase of 570.7 per cent shows that more expensive handsets are now being Made in India, and this is substantiated by Apple's figures. Apple achieved over ₹85,500Cr in iPhone production in India during April–October 2024, of which around ₹60,000Cr were exports.

This was a 37 per cent increase compared to the same period of 2023. The month of October 2024 alone had over ₹17,200Cr in iPhone production.

More mobile factories are coming up, including two of Google and Tata's third iPhone plant.

Foxconn, Pegatron, and Wistron made iPhones of over ₹1.11LCr in FY24 (market value ₹1.65–1.95Cr, depending on country) of which 37 per cent were exported. This exceeded the PLI targets given by Apple to the GoI.

Around 80 per cent of all the telecommunications equipment used in the world's fastest 5G rollout in 2023 was Made in India.

Corning (USA), in a JV with Optiemus (India), is setting up a factory in Tamil Nadu to make cover glass for mobiles.

Foxconn of Taiwan, the world's largest contract manufacturer in electronics, is investing over ₹22,000Cr in a 300ac campus near Bengaluru Airport.

Rayprus Technologies of Taiwan, that makes precision camera and lens modules for iPhones, is setting up its own factory in this campus, and so are 5 other component makers.

Wistron of Taiwan is setting up a ₹4,000Cr unit in Karnataka for making laptop computers.

Indian Electronics and Semiconductor Association has projected that India's electronics market will be ₹24.9LCr in FY27—that will take the total growth to a massive 1,280 per cent in 13 years. Projected revenues of ₹9.5LCr for mobile manufacturing in FY26 will take total growth to a whopping 4926.5 per cent in 11 years.

Between 2022 and 2024, MNCs opened more than 225 new Global Capability Centres across India.

There are 3,918 startups in technology hardware and 1,123 in telecom and networking products and services.

29

Wafers and Chips

Nehru announced plans for India to make chips back in 1962 but only the government's Semiconductor Lab (SCL) came up in 1984 at Mohali. For 37 years, no PM was able to attract any Indian/foreign private sector companies in the sector. In 2007, Intel (then the world's largest chipmaker) said that in 2006 it invested $3.5B in chip plants in China and Vietnam after the Indian Government (UPA) dragged its feet.

Modi started the India Semiconductor Mission (ISM) with a budget of ₹83,000Cr for 50 per cent project cost subsidy to manufacturers.

There is also a Design Linked Incentive (DLI) scheme to offset the various difficulties (especially the shortage of capital) faced by domestic manufacturers involved in semiconductor design.

ChipIN is a one-stop centre for chip designers that aims to provide access to state-of-the-art Electronic Design Automation (EDA) tools to 85,000 students at BTech, MTech, and PhD level to design semiconductor chips. Companies such as Siemens, Synopsys, Cadence Design Systems, Ansys, and Keysight Technologies provide EDA tools to researchers and startups in partnership with ChipIN.

The GoI received nine bids for a ₹10,000Cr modernisation of SCL. The bidders included Tata Group, Tower Semiconductor (Israel) and Texas Instruments (USA). Modi wants an Indian company to execute the project as SCL designs and makes chips for the defence and space sectors, where confidentiality is a must.

Qualcomm of the US (revenue $33B) that makes semiconductor tech for mobiles, IoT products and automobiles, opened a design centre in Chennai. The company invested $1B in India in 2024 and is open to buying Made-in-India chips from Tatas and others.

Announced investments in semiconductors are ₹571,613Cr (see Table). Over 120,000 advanced tech jobs and 150,000 indirect jobs are expected to be created.

SEMICONDUCTOR ECOSYSTEM COMING UP IN INDIA

WHO	Foreign Partner	WHAT	WHERE	WHEN	Investment	Source
SRAM & MRAM Group (UK)		Semiconductor Fab	800 acres in Chhatrapur (Odisha)		₹200,000Cr	1
Tata Electronics	Powerchip (Taiwan)	India's first Fab (3bn chips/yr)	Dholera (Gujarat)	Dec 2026	₹91,000Cr	2
Adani	Tower Semicon (Israel)	Semiconductor Fab	Taloja (Maharashtra)		₹83,950Cr	3
Sharp (Japan)		Semiconductor Display Fab	1000 acres in Guj/Maha/TN		₹34,000Cr	4
Tata Electronics		Outsourced Semiconductor Assembly and Testing (OSAT)	Jagiroad (Assam)	Nov 2026	₹27,000Cr	5
Micron Technologies (USA)		Chip Assembly, Testing, and Packaging (ATMP) plant	Sanand (Gujarat)	Ph-1 by Feb 2025	₹22,516Cr	6
CG Power	Renesas (Japan), Stars Micro (Thailand)	ATMP	Sanand (Gujarat)		₹7,600Cr	8
Zoho		Making Compound Chips	Awaiting Government Approval		₹5,900Cr	9
Simmtech (South Korea) and 05 other global companies		Chip Components	Sanand (Gujarat)	2025	₹4,800Cr	10
HCL Tech	Foxconn (Taiwan)	OSAT	Noida (UP)		₹3,900Cr	7
AMD (USA) — Technostar		Global Design Centre	Bengaluru	Nov 2023	₹3,340Cr	11
Keynes Technology India		ATMP (6.3M chips per day)	Sanand (Gujarat)		₹3,307Cr	12
Foxconn (Taiwan) in a JV with Applied Materials (USA)		Chip Making Tools	Bengaluru		₹2,100Cr	13
L&T Semiconductor Technologies		Fabless Chip Design Centre	Chennai	May 2024	₹830Cr	14
03 Others		OSAT plants	Various		₹9,370Cr	
12 others		ATMP plant proposals received by Govt of India			₹72,000Cr	15

SOURCES: 1) bit.ly/SRAM; 2) bit.ly/TataSC; 3) bit.ly/TowerIN; 4) bit.ly/SharpIN; 5) bit.ly/TataOSAT; 6) bit.ly/MicronIN; 7) bit.ly/HCL-Fox; 8) bit.ly/CGP-Sanand; 9) bit.ly/ZohoChip; 10) bit.ly/Micron-Vendors; 11) bit.ly/AMD-BLR; 12) https://ga7a.short.gy/odlkyd; 13) bit.ly/Fox-AM; 14) bit.ly/LTST-Chip; 15) bit.ly/ATMP-12

'India designs the world's most complex chips with three lakh design engineers. After the design, the second thing in the value chain are fabs. Then comes ATMP [Assembly, Testing, Marking, and Packing]. Investments in the domestic semiconductor sector will be at least ₹7.5LCr by 2028, making India one of the top five semiconductor manufacturing nations by 2028,' said Ashwini Vaishnaw, Union Minister of Electronics, IT, Communications, and Railways.

The Indian Electronics and Semiconductor Association projects the local semiconductor market at ₹8,300Cr by FY30.

More than 115 Indian startups are engaged in the semiconductor ecosystem.

30

Green Hydrogen and Ammonia

The National Green Hydrogen Mission has given legs to the sector.

Green Hydrogen & Green Ammonia Projects in India

WHO	WHAT	WHERE	WHEN	Investment	Source
IndianOil + L&T + ReNew (India) Joint Venture		Gujarat and Odisha	2026-27	₹3.00 LCr	1
NTPC Green Energy	0.438mtpa Green Hydrogen	Pudimaka (Andhra)	2026-2032	₹1.85 LCr	2
	1mtpa Green Hydrogen, Green Ammonia, and Green Methanol	Maharashtra	2026-2032	₹80,000Cr	3
Reliance Industries	3.6mtpa Green Hydrogen	Jamnagar (Gujarat)	2025	₹1.45 LCr	4
	3mtpa Green Ammonia, 0.6mtpa Green Hydrogen	Kandla (Gujarat)	2026-27	₹24,000Cr	5
Adani Group	3mtpa Green Hydrogen	Mundra (Gujarat)	2025	₹1.30 LCr	6
Acme Cleantech	1.3mtpa Green Ammonia with Green Hydrogen; 4.5GW Solar Power	Gopalpur (Odisha) Kalahandi (Odisha)	2027	₹58,219Cr	7
	5GW Solar PV, 1.5GW Electrolyser; 1.1mtpa Ammonia Synthesis Loop	Thoothukudi (TN)	2025-26	₹52,474Cr	
	1.2mtpa Green Hydrogen and Green Ammonia; 4.95GW Solar Power	Mangaluru (Karnataka)	2027	₹51,865Cr	
Welspun New Energy	Green Ammonia and Green Hydrogen	Bulandshahr (UP)		₹40,000Cr	8
	Green Ammonia and Hydrogen in JV with Gujarat Pipavav Port	Gujarat	2026-27	₹40,000Cr	9
	0.7mtpa Green Ammonia	Kendrapada (Odisha)	2026-27	₹13,860Cr	10
Essar Future Energy	1mtpa Green Hydrogen	Jamnagar (Gujarat)	2028	₹30,000Cr	11
Avadaa Green H2	0.5mtpa Green Hydrogen and Green Ammonia	Gopalpur (Odisha)	2026	₹23,500Cr	12
L&T	2.5mtpa Green Ammonia, 0.5mtpa Green Hydrogen	Kandla (Gujarat)	2025	₹20,000Cr	13
ReNew E-Fuels	0.1mtpa Green Ammonia 0.5mtpa Green Methanol	Malkangiri (Odisha)	2026-27	₹19,400Cr	14
	0.06mtpa Green Ammonia 0.3mtpa Green Methanol	Rayagada (Odisha)	2026-27		
Hygenco Green Energies	0.2mtpa Green Hydrogen	Prayagraj (UP)		₹16,000Cr	15
AM Green Hydrogen	5mtpa Green Ammonia	Kakinada (Andhra)	2026	₹15,000Cr	16
Sembcorp (Singapore)	0.72mtpa Green Ammonia	Ganjam (Odisha)	2026	₹13,000Cr	17
Waree Clean Energy	1.2mtpa Green Ammonia	Jagatsinghpur (Odisha)	2026	₹12,480Cr	18
Torrent Power	10mtpa Green Ammonia	Gujarat		₹7,200Cr	19
EG Solwin Hybrid	0.3mtpa Green Ammonia	Gopalpur (Odisha)	2026	₹6,330Cr	20
GAIL (India)	1.57mtpa Green Hydrogen	Vijaipur (MP)	May 2024	NA	21

SOURCES: 1) bit.ly/IOC-LT-Renew; 2) bit.ly/NTPC-AP; 3) bit.ly/NTPC-Maha; 4) bit.ly/RIL-Jam; 5&13) bit.ly/RIL-Kan; 6) bit.ly/AdaniGH; 7) bit.ly/AcmeGH; 8 &15) https://ga7a.short.gy/u8pE3E; 9) https://ga7a.short.gy/Wyty7g; 10 &17) bit.ly/WE-Semb; 11) bit.ly/EssarH2; 12) bit.ly/AvaadaH2; 14) bit.ly/REF_Od; 16) https://bit.ly/AMG-AP; 8) bit.ly/WaareeCE; 19) https://ga7a.short.gy/rutd4T; 20) bit.ly/EGSHPL; 21) bit.ly/GAIL-GH

Yes, a whopping ₹12.83LCr of investments have been committed to this sector, and there must be more that we may have missed.

The Government has awarded 0.412MTPA capacity to 10 companies for production of green hydrogen with a total subsidy of ₹3,055Cr.

Further, 16 companies were given incentives of ₹4,440Cr to set up electrolyser plants of 3GW/year in the first two tranches; 17 more companies have submitted bids.

L&T got the highest allocation of 300MW/year and in February 2024 commissioned India's first indigenous electrolyser—a pilot plant of 1MW, expandable to 2MW.

Adani's Gigafactory will be expanded in two more phases to 9mtpa by 2035–36, with a cumulative investment of around ₹3.6LCr.

Acme Cleantech set up the world's 1st solar-based green hydrogen and green ammonia plant in Rajasthan in 2021. The company is targeting 10mtpa green hydrogen/ammonia by 2030. It operates 1,501MWp solar power assets and more than 3,600MWp are under construction.

VO Chidambaram, Kolkata, Deendayal, and Paradip ports are being developed as Green Hydrogen/Ammonia Hub Ports.

31

EVs and Batteries

Electric car sales in India reached 90,996 units in FY24 (up 1,666 per cent in three years). EVs accounted for 2.53 per cent of all passenger cars and SUVs sold in India.

Including all other vehicle types, over 1.683M EVs were sold in India (up 1771 per cent in three years). 6.07 per cent of all buses, 5.4 per cent of all 2-wheelers and a whopping 54.3 per cent of all 3-wheelers were EVs.

The EV market is heading towards sales of ₹73,000Cr by 2025 and ₹2.7LCr by 2030.

India was imposing 100 per cent import duty on cars priced over $35,000 (cost, insurance + freight) and 35 per cent below that threshold. On 15 March 2024, after massive lobbying by Tesla and other global EV makers, the GoI announced a reduction in import duty to 15 per cent on cars above $35,000 up to 5 years and up to maximum of 8,000 cars/year for all foreign EV makers provided they do: (1) Minimum investment of $500M (₹4100Cr) for local manufacturing; (2) Minimum 25 per cent value addition by 3rd year and 50 per cent by 5th year in India.

As of 31 December 2024, India had a total of only 10,137 E-buses on the road. In 2023 alone, about 160,000 e-buses were sold in China and 6,354 in Europe.

National Electric Bus Program aims to deploy 50,000 E-buses on national highways by 2027. Further, the Pradhan Mantri E-Bus Sewa will acquire 10,000 E-buses for ₹57,613Cr (with ₹20,000Cr subsidy) to operate in 169 cities on a Public–Private Partnership (PPP) model.

Modi wants to replace about 800,000 diesel buses with E-buses by 2030. This will reduce pollution and create jobs in manufacturing and maintenance.

About ₹11–13LCr will be required for 800,000 E-buses.

4-wheeler EV Factories coming up in India

WHO	Annual Capacity	WHERE	WHEN	Investment	Source
Maruti Suzuki	600,000 EVs & 1M Hybrids	Haryana & Gujarat	2025	₹75,000Cr	1
JSW Group (with Volkswagen)	300,000 Passenger EVs 100,000 Commercial EVs	Cuttack (Odisha)		₹40,000Cr	2
Tesla (USA)		Gujarat/Maha/TN		₹16,500++Cr	3
Hyundai (S. Korea)	75,000	Chennai	2025	₹20,000Cr	4
Tata Motors	200,000 (initially)	Ranipet (TN)	2025	₹18,000Cr	5, 6
Vinfast (Vietnam)	150,000	Thootukudi (TN)	July 2025	₹16,200Cr	7
Mahindra	60,000 EVs	Chakan (Maharashtra)	2029	₹10,000Cr	8
Mahindra	Electric 2-wheelers & 3-wheelers	Zaheerabad (Telangana)	2024	₹1,000Cr	9
Foxconn (Taiwan)	Has Expressed an Interest in making about 150,000 EVs per year in India				10
Kia (South Korea)	10,000 EVs	Tamil Nadu	2025	NA	11
Switch Mobility (Ashok Leyland)	2500 e-Buses expandable to 5000	Lucknow (UP)	2024	₹2,000Cr	12
Olectra Greentech	5000 e-Buses expandable to 10,000	Hyderabad	July 2024	₹790Cr	13
PMI Electro Mobility	1500 e-Buses expandable to 3000	Pune (Maharashtra)	2025	₹300Cr	14
EaseMyTrip				₹200Cr	15
Volvo	Company has announced it is considering an EV plant in India; it may be in a JV with Eicher Motors				16

SOURCES: 1) bit.ly/MS-EV; 2) bit.ly/JSW-VW; 3) bit.ly/TeslaIN; 4) bit.ly/HY-IN; 5) bit.ly/TM-EV; 6) bit.ly/TaMo-EV; 7) bit.ly/VF-TN; 8) bit.ly/MM-EV1; 9) bit.ly/MM-EV2; 10) bit.ly/Fox-EV; 11) bit.ly/Kia-EV; 12) bit.ly/SM-AL; 13) bit.ly/OG-Hyd; 14) bit.ly/PMIEM; 15) https://bit.ly/EMT-eB; 16) bit.ly/VOL-EM

The GoI is keen that public transport in India goes all electric and is providing incentives to state governments to set up the supporting infrastructure. Under this scheme, The GoI is considering providing incentives of ₹25–27/km to run E-buses.

India's demand for Lithium-ion (Li-ion) cells and batteries is expected to be 150–160GWh by 2030.

The GoI has a scheme for viability gap funding for the battery energy storage systems (BESS) industry, under which it provides financial support of up to 40 per cent of the capital cost.

New Advanced Chemistry Cell Battery Pack and Lithium-Ion Cell Factories

WHO	Technology From	CAPACITY per Year	WHERE	INVESTMENT	Source
Ola Electric	Developed in-house in India	5GWh (expandable to 100GWh)	Krishnagiri (TN)	₹7,614 Cr	1
JSW Group	Exploring potential partners	10GWh (expandable to 50GWh)	Cuttack (Odisha)	Total ₹40,000 Cr in EVs and Batteries	2
Agratas Energy (Tata Group)	Not announced	20GWh (expandable to 40GWh)	Sanand (Gujarat)	₹13,000 Cr	3
Reliance Industries	Faradion (UK), 100% owned by Reliance Industries	20GWh EV Cells and Packs, Battery Chemicals, Containerised Energy Storage Solutions	Jamnagar (Gujarat)	₹12,000 Cr	4
Amara Raja Advanced Cell	Developed in-house in India	16GWh Li-ion cells, 2GWh NMC Cells, and 5GWh of battery packs	Divitapalli (Telangana)	₹9,500 Cr	5
International Battery Company (USA)		10GWh by 2028	Bengaluru Rural	₹8,000 Cr	6
GODI India		12.5GWh	Telangana	₹8,000 Cr	7
TDS-G, a JV between Suzuki (50%), Toshiba (40%), and Denso (10%)		Not Known	Hansalpur (Gujarat)	₹7,300 Cr	8
TDK (Japan)		Not Known	Sohna (Haryana)	₹7,080 Cr	9
Exide Energy	SVOLT Energy Tech (China)	12GWh	Bengaluru	₹6,000 Cr	10
Lucas TVS	24M Technologies (USA)	5GWh (expandable to 10GWh)	Tiruvallur (TN)	₹2,500 Cr	11
Simple Energy	C4V (USA)	1GWh (expandable to 5GWh)	Shoolagiri (TN)	₹1,230 Cr	12
NSure Reliable Power Solutions	ARCI, IIT Madras, Chennai	1GWh (expandable to 5GWh)	Malur (Karnataka)	₹1,050 Cr	13
Munoth Industries	Tianjin Lishen Battery (China)	0.54GWh (expandable to 1.25GWh)	Tirupati (Andhra Pradesh)	₹799 Cr	14
Li Energy	SafeREnergy (Australia)	2GWh (expandable to 7GWh)	Thondi (TN)	₹285 Cr	15
Nexcharge (JV between Exide Energy and Leclanché SA (Switzerland)		1.5GWh	Prantij (Gujarat)	₹250 Cr	16
Log9 Materials	Developed in-house in India	50MWh (expandable to 1GWh)	Bengaluru	₹230 Cr	17

Sources: 1) bit.ly/Ola-Li; 2) bit.ly/JSW-cell; 3) bit.ly/AE-Li; 4) bit.ly/RIL-bat; 5) bit.ly/A-Raja; 6) bit.ly/IBC-bat; 7) bit.ly/Godi-bat; 8) bit.ly/TDS-G; 9) bit.ly/TDK-J; 10) bit.ly/EE-Li; 11) bit.ly/L-TVS; 12) bit.ly/SE-bat; 13) bit.ly/Nsure; 14) bit.ly/Munoth; 15) bit.ly/Li-E; 16) bit.ly/Nexcharge; 17) bit.ly/Log9

32

Record Exports

India's share of global exports shrunk from 2.2 per cent in 1951 to 1.2 per cent in 1964. Nehru had 17 years to lay the foundation for increasing the share of manufacturing and exports but failed.

Let's look at some export data:

Record Exports	From	To (FY24)	Increase	Period
All Products & Services	$314.416B (FY14)	$778.22B	▲ 147.5%	10 years
Electronic & Telecom Products	$4.15B (FY14)	$28.534B	▲ 587.6%	10 years
Medical & Scientific Instruments	$363M (FY 20)	$2.428B	▲ 568.9%	4 years
AYUSH & Herbal Products	$106M (FY20)	$649M	▲ 512.3%	4 years
Marine Products	$1.249B (FY 20)	$7.372B	▲ 490.2%	4 years
Cars, Ships, Aircraft & Parts	$5.147B (FY20)	$29.236B	▲ 468.0%	4 years
SOURCE: https://dashboard.commerce.gov.in/commercedashboard.aspx				

Sourcing by Boeing increased from $250M in 2013 to $1.25B in 2023 (up 400 per cent).

India's mobile phone exports surpassed $20.4B during calendar year 2024, which was a 44 per cent increase from the exports during calendar year 2023.

Walmart, the world's largest retailer has announced that it is increasing exports from India to $10B/year by 2027. Its imports to the US from India were around 25 per cent in January–August 2023 as against just 2 per cent in 2018 (up 900 per cent in 5 years).

Amazon exported Made-in-India products valued at more than $8B in 2023. It is projecting $20B in e-commerce exports from India by 2025 (up 566.7 per cent in 2 years).

USA's leading EV-maker Tesla sourced automobile components (parts) worth around $1.7–1.9B from India in FY24, compared to around $1B in FY23. As per some reports, Tesla may increase this to almost $15B by FY29.

33

MSMEs, PM Mudra Yojana

MSMEs are the backbone of the Indian economy, contributing to about 25 per cent of GDP and over 40 per cent of manufacturing output.

The Udyam Assist Platform (UAP) was launched to bring Informal Micro Enterprises (IMEs) under the formal ambit for them to avail the benefits under Priority Sector Lending.

Udyam registration is a mandatory certification for MSMEs. As of December 2024, there were over 57.98M registered enterprises (69,087 Medium, 733,532 Small and almost 57.18M Micro enterprises), with almost 245.264M employees, which translates to over 25.5 per cent of India's total working-age population.

Pradhan Mantri Mudra Yojana (PMMY)

PMMY was launched by Modi in April 2015 for providing loans up to ₹10L to the non-corporate, non-farm, Medium and Small Enterprises and individuals.

Mudra has three products—'Shishu' for loans up to ₹50,000, 'Kishore' for loans from ₹50,001 to ₹5L and 'Tarun' for loans of ₹5–10L. Borrowers who have been prompt in paying earlier loans can get higher amounts as a 2nd or 3rd loan for further growth.

Modi 3.0 will increase the upper limit of PMMY loans to ₹20L.

Almost 477.04M loans were disbursed in 108 months up to March 2024 at an average of 4.417M loans/month.

An amount of ₹28.095LCr was disbursed, at an average loan amount of ₹58,895. This shows that borrowers are mostly in the 'Shishu' category, although the average loan amount has gone up from ₹38,117 in FY16 to ₹80,840 in FY24 (up 107.5 per cent).

About 336.5M women got 71 per cent of the loans and 44.6 per cent of total loan amount; SC/ST/OBCs got 50.8 per cent of the loans and 34.94 per cent of the total loan amount; and minorities got 11.32 per cent of the loans and 8.82 per cent of the loan amount. The East and Northeast regions got 29.7 per cent of the loans, South 28.5 per cent, North 24.2 per cent, and West 17.6 per cent.

Clearly Mudra follows '*Sabka Saath, Sabka Vikas*'.

Credit Guarantee Schemes

During COVID-19, the Emergency Credit Line Guarantee Scheme (ECLGS) provided much-needed additional credit to over 13M MSMEs. Hospitality and related services, especially those in the Micro and Small Enterprises (MSE) sector, suffered the most. The ECLGS was extended up to March 2024. Till FY24, 9.176M guarantees of a whopping ₹6.78LCr had been approved.

Credit Guarantee Trust for Micro and Small Enterprises (CGTMSE) scheme motivates first generation entrepreneurs towards self-employment by providing credit guarantee funding for third-party guarantee/collateral-free loans of up to ₹2Cr. Guarantees on coverages range from 85 per cent for Micro enterprise up to ₹5L, and 75 per cent for others, and 50 per cent of the coverage is for retail activity.

PM Employment Generation Programme (PMEGP)

PMEGP gives monetary subsidy for setting up new projects/units costing maximum ₹50L in manufacturing and ₹20L in business/services sector. Any individual of age 18+ (minimum Class-8 pass for projects above ₹10L in manufacturing and above ₹5L in business/services) can apply. Self-Help Groups (SHGs) (including those Below Poverty Line or BPL), registered Societies, Production Cooperative Societies, and Charitable Trusts are also eligible.

In general category, the subsidy rate is 15 per cent in urban areas and 25 per cent in rural areas; the beneficiary must put in 10 per cent of project cost from their own funds. For special categories (women, minorities, PwDs, SC/ST/OBC, ex-servicemen, transgenders, and people from hill and border areas, aspirational districts, and the Northeast region) the subsidy is 25 per cent in urban areas and 35 per cent in rural areas, with beneficiary's own contribution reduced to 5 per cent. The balance project cost is provided by banks in the form of term loan and working capital.

Existing PMEGP/Mudra units can get a 2nd loan for upgradation, with project cost of maximum ₹1Cr in manufacturing and ₹25L in the business/services sector. Subsidy is 20 per cent in hill/Northeast states and 15 per cent in other places and the beneficiary must put in 10 per cent on their own.

In eight years till FY24, 737,433 persons got subsidies (women 40.9 per cent, minorities 11.02 per cent, SCs 9.3 per cent, STs 5.18 per cent, and OBCs 39.48 per cent).

Cluster Development Schemes

MSE Cluster Development Program aims at the growth of MSEs by addressing advancements in sustainable and green manufacturing technology, market access, skills and quality, etc.; creating infrastructural facilities including flatted factory complexes in existing clusters of MSEs and industrial areas; and setting up Common Facility Centres for testing, training, raw material depot, effluent treatment, complementing production processes, etc.

Other Programs and Schemes

Scheme of Fund for Regeneration of Traditional Industries or SFURTI aims to get traditional artisans and industries into clusters to support them to become competitive for long-term sustainability.

The GoI gives support of ₹2.50Cr to 500 artisans and up to ₹5Cr to 500 artisans (maximum 90 per cent financial assistance for hard costs such as factory and machinery and 95 per cent in hill/Northeast states) engaged in sectors such as handicrafts, textiles, coir, khadi, bamboo, Agri-processing, honey, etc., enabling them to set up production facilities with modern machinery.

There is support with raw materials, marketing, business development, and digitization, and 100 per cent financial assistance up to ₹25L for soft costs in skill development, exposure visits, buyer-seller meets, etc.

The Modi Government made a huge ₹50,000Cr equity infusion into the MSME Self-Reliant India Fund.

There is a Raising and Accelerating MSME performance (RAMP) program with an outlay of ₹6000Cr.

ASEEM, e-Shram, National Career Service, and Udyam portals provide live, organic databases, delivering Government-to-Consumer (G2C), Business-to-Consumer (B2C), and Business-to-Business (B2B) services relating to credit facilitation, skilling, and recruitment, and are being interlinked.

Production of Khadi and Village Industries (KVIs) went up from ₹26,109Cr in FY14 to over ₹1.08LCr in FY24 (up 313.7 per cent). Sales of KVI products went up from ₹31,154Cr to almost ₹1.55LCr (up 397.5 per cent). Employment went up from 13.038M persons to around 18.622M persons (up 42.8 per cent).

There are as many as 32 Modi Government schemes for the MSME sector.

34

Startup India

India had more than 157,300 GoI-recognised startups as of December 2024, compared with only about 350 startups in FY14. Around 5,500 new Startups are registered monthly.

Despite the challenges due to a prolonged funding winter since COVID-19, Indian startups got over $88.2B between 2021 and 2024.

As of July 2024, there were 118 Unicorns (valuation of $1B and above) in India with a combined valuation of over $350B of which 20 were women-led.

India now has the 3rd highest number of Unicorns in the world, after the US (1,000+) and China (330+).

Indian startups have created over 1.72M direct jobs.

The GoI has many funding schemes, including a Startup India Seed Fund Scheme (SISFS), a Startup India Investor Connect platform that uses AI for matchmaking, a Credit Guarantee Scheme for Startups (CGSS) and a Fund of Funds for Startups (FFS) Scheme through which it provides funding to Alternate Investment Funds (AIFs), which then invest in startups. Nearly ₹13LCr funding had been secured by Indian startups by December 2024.

35

Robust Stock Markets

India has two primary domestic stock exchanges. As of September 2024, 5,505 companies were listed on the Bombay Stock Exchange (BSE), which started the trading of equities in 1957, and about 2,620 companies were listed on the National Stock Exchange (NSE), which started in 1994.

NSE was the world's No.1 stock exchange for five years in a row in derivatives contracts in 2023. In February 2024, NSE overtook Shenzhen's Stock Exchange to become the world's No.1 equity cash market exchange in number of trades. On 5 June 2024, NSE handled a record number of 19.71B orders and 285.5M trades in just 6 hours 15 minutes.

Let's look at what Modinomics has done for investors, despite the world being at a virtual standstill for 19 months due to COVID-19.

MARKETS BOOM & ZOOM	FY14	FY24	CHANGE
BSE Market Cap	₹74,153cr	₹377,362cr	▲ 408.9%
NIFTY500 Multicap 50:25:25 Index	3032.80	13,850.10	▲ 356.7%
NIFTY MidSmallCap 400	2762.41	16,549.90	▲ 499.1%
NSE Active Investors (Equity-Cash)	5.25M	47.9M (Sep 2024)	▲ 812.4%
NSE Cash Market Turnover	₹28.085-Lcr	₹201.034-Lcr	▲ 615.8%
Total FPI Investments in Equity & Debt	₹51,649cr	₹339,066cr	▲ 556.5%

Sources: https://www.moneycontrol.com/; https://www.bseindia.com/index.html; https://www.nseindia.com/

NSE's individual investors are from 99.84 per cent of all Pin Codes in India. The exchange added 86.88M new investors between June 2016 and November 2024. In fact, more than 81.5% of NSE's total investors (as of November 2024) have been added in the last 10.5 years.

During the first two terms of Modi, Foreign Portfolio Investors (FPIs) or Foreign Institutional Investors (FIIs) invested almost ₹8.82LCr in India.

JP Morgan of US is the world's largest bank with a market cap of $581B (₹48.5LCr) on 30 June 2024. On 22 September 2023, JP Morgan included GoI's Fully Accessible Route (FAR) Bonds in its 'Emerging Markets Index'. This illustrated India's attractiveness for investors always hunting for credible investments. FPIs bought GoI Bonds of $10.7B in 193 working days since JP Morgan's announcement.

Bank of America (the world's 2nd largest bank by market cap), HSBC of Hong Kong (6th largest) and Citigroup of US (15th largest) also included the GoI's FAR Bonds in their indices and projected $107–120B investment flow to India.

Bloomberg of US is a $13B company that provides information that helps investors make critical financial decisions and move financial markets worldwide on a real-time basis. Bloomberg has evolved billions of data points into relevant and actionable insights trusted by tens of thousands of business and finance professionals. On 5 March 2024, Bloomberg included GoI's FAR Bonds in their 'Emerging Market Local Currency Government Index' (total Assets Under Management or AUM of index funds that track BEMLCGI is $6.18T, 1.656 x India's GDP) and said, 'We will continue to keep reviewing India for Bloomberg's Global Aggregate Index' (total AUM tracking BGAI is $13.65T).

MSCI of USA (formerly Morgan Stanley Capital Int'l) is a $2.53B company that provides equity/debt/real estate indices, multi-asset portfolio analysis tools, etc. The MSCI Emerging Markets Index (AUM $1.3T) is a selection of equity stocks that tracks financial performance of key companies in fast-growing nations. India's weightage went up from 9 per cent in 2020 to 18.84% as of October 2024 (up 109.3 per cent), whereas China's came down from 34.2 per cent to 24.72 per cent (down 27.7%).

When Modi became PM, sellers of equities got their money 3 days after the sale (T+3); now they get it the next day (T+1). From April 2024, a T+0 settlement went live on a trial basis for 25 traded stocks. In addition, the top 500 stocks (by market capitalization) will have a T+0 settlement option from 31 January 2025. The US is still struggling to get to T+1.

While it is true that the Indian stock markets went down from their highest-ever value recorded on 27 September 2024 by almost 11.9 per cent on 22 January 2025 (before this book went for printing), this was primarily because most of the world feared that the new Trump presidency will adversely affect the economies of most countries other than the US; and most experts feel that a resilient Indian economy (except minor bumps for 2–3 quarters) will make the markets strong again.

36

Healthier Banks

Gross Non-Performing Assets (GNPA) of banks is the sum of all loans where the recovery is impossible or very challenging. These are also called 'bad loans'.

A bank only discovers whether a loan has become bad (Non-Performing Asset or NPA) or not after the deadline for repayment has expired. Since corporate loans have an average tenure of 3–7 years, estimates for the combined GNPAs of all banks can best be done by looking at the 3rd, 4th, and 5th year after a government has left office.

Prime Minister Vajpayee left office in May 2004 and the average GNPA (as a percentage of Gross Loans) of all banks combined was only 2.3 per cent in FY08.

The UPA left office in May 2014 and the average GNPA of all banks had shot up to 11.2 per cent (up 387 per cent) by FY18. This was largely because of political interference by the UPA Government's leaders in the commercial lending decisions of PSBs. What was even worse, gross advances by PSBs rose from ₹6.6LCr in March 2004 to ₹39LCr in March 2012 (up 491 per cent).

Under Modi, the GNPAs of all banks came down to 2.8 per cent by FY24 (down 75 per cent).

According to a Credit Suisse Bank report published in March 2014, the top 200 companies with an 'interest coverage ratio' of <1, owed about ₹8.6LCr to banks. Nearly 44 per cent of those loans were yet to be recognised as NPAs. That would have added another 6.7 per cent to the GNPA ratio, taking it to a shameful 19.33 per cent.

In a September 2018 response to a Parliamentary panel, UPA-era RBI Governor Raghuram Rajan, a critic of Modi said: 'A larger number of bad loans originated in 2006-2008'. He said that too many loans were given to 'well-connected' promoters with a history of default and blamed PSBs for inadequate due diligence, and that 'PSBs continued financing promoters even while private banks were getting out'.[7] Rajan continues to be a favourite of Rahul Gandhi.

Let us look at some data that shows how the performance of banks (especially PSBs) has improved in the Modi-era.

HEALTH OF INDIAN BANKS

(GNPA = Gross Non Performing Assets or 'bad loans'; PSB = Public Sector Bank)

PARAMETER	FY14 (except where stated)	FY24 (except where stated)	CHANGE
All Banks—Average GNPA	9.867%	2.8%	▼▼ 71.6%
PSBs—Average GNPA	12.63%	3.7%	▼▼ 70.7%
PSBs—Net Profit	₹37,096 Cr (FY21)	₹146,162 Cr	▲ 169% in 3yrs
PSBs—Net Interest Margins	2.45%	3.1%	▲ 26.5%
PSBs—Return on Assets	0.5%	1.3%	▲ 160%
PSBs—Return on Equity	8.48%	13.8%	▲ 62.7%

Sources: bit.ly/RBI-2014 and bit.ly/RBI-2024

Until June 2024, banks had already recovered bad loans of a huge sum of ₹11.8LCr. This money became available to do healthier lending.

New credit (new loans sanctioned) since 2016 has been under intense scrutiny by the RBI, and the percentage of new loans becoming NPAs has also been continuously coming down.

All this did not happen by magic, but rather by continuous efforts by the finance ministry and the RBI, prodded by none other than Modi himself, and of course with the cooperation of the banks, as they were also interested in cleaning up their books to get better valuations in the stock markets (see the next chapter).

There were 27 PSBs in India in May 2014 and Modi merged them into 12 in his first six years. An RBI paper released in February 2023 said that bank mergers in India had been beneficial to the banking sector as the financial performance and efficiency of acquirers had improved post-merger.

37

Rise of the Public Sector

Let's look at some statistics that will show us how the PSEs have performed during Modi's regime. We shall compare 15 PSEs with 15 iconic private companies by revenue, profit, and MCap (market capitalisation).

PUBLIC Sector Company (PSE)	Revenue	Net Profit	MCAP
	From FY12-14 to FY21-23		15Apr19 to 10Apr24
Fertilizers & Chem Travancore (FACT)	▲ 87.6%	▲ 1907%	▲ 1628.3%
Rail Vikas Nigam (RVNL)	▲ 307.6%	▲ 191.4%	▲ 1006.8%
Hindustan Aeronautics (HAL)	▲ 70.4%	▲ 71.8%	▲ 862.1%
Shipping Corp. of India (SCI)	▲ 17.8%	▲ 3024%	▲ 518.5%
Cochin Shipyard	▲ 70.7%	▲ 117.8%	▲ 391.8%
Bank of Maharashtra	▲ 41.7%	▲ 169.7%	▲ 410.4%
Housing & Urban Dev Corp. (HUDCO)	▲ 147.4%	▲ 143.2%	▲ 347.4%
Power Finance Corporation (PFC)	▲ 335.2%	▲ 329.5%	▲ 312.8%
REC Ltd.	▲ 176.4%	▲ 159.2%	▲ 301.6%
Chennai Petroleum Corp. (CPC)	▲ 6.7%	▲ 7122%	▲ 260.0%
National Aluminium (NALCO)	▲ 84.3%	▲ 178%	▲ 186.9%
Mishra Dhatu Nigam	▲ 54.5%	▲ 113.7%	▲ 207.5%
RITES	▲ 116.3%	▲ 70.2%	▲ 170.3%
Steel Authority of India (SAIL)	▲ 200.3%	▲ 216.5%	▲ 139.0%
State Bank of India	▲ 82.2%	▲ 140.8%	▲ 140.3%

NOTE: The sources for all data in the three tables in this chapter are https://www.moneycontrol.com/; https://www.bseindia.com/index.html; and https://www.nseindia.com/

We chose these companies not because they have the highest MCap increases (they don't), but as a mix of large/mid/small-cap companies in 13 diverse businesses. The start date is 15 April 2019 as (a) many PSEs got listed between August 2017 and April 2019; and (b) 5 years is a long enough period for comparison.

As FACT, Shipping Corp. and Chennai Petroleum made aggregate losses during FY12–14, to make a proper comparison and not give ∞ (Infinity) as the net profit growth percentage, we added losses of FY12–14 to the profits of FY21–23 and divided the obtained total by ₹1Cr to arrive at the growth.

It is another story altogether how these companies made aggregate profits of ₹8,661Cr in FY21–23 (Modi-era), versus aggregate losses of ₹3,425Cr in FY12–14 (UPA-era).

Now let's see the 15 iconic private sector companies.

PRIVATE Sector Company	Revenue From FY12-14 to FY21-23	Net Profit From FY12-14 to FY21-23	MCAP 15Apr19 to 10Apr24
Adani Enterprises	▲ 74.8%	▼ 27.7%	▲ 2177.2%
Bharti Airtel	▲ 52.1%	▼ 14%	▲ 250.9%
Larsen & Toubro (L&T)	▲ 112.7%	▲ 329.5%	▲ 183.0%
ICICI Bank	▲ 130.9%	▲ 177.8%	▲ 179.7%
Bajaj Finance	▲ 340%	▲ 472%	▲ 139.7%
Reliance Industries	▲ 72%	▲ 209.8%	▲ 122.0%
Infosys Ltd.	▲ 197%	▲ 131.1%	▲ 105.8%
Asian Paints	▲ 166.9%	▲ 204.5%	▲ 100.5%
Tata Consultancy Services (TCS)	▲ 200.2%	▲ 157.9%	▲ 85.7%
Maruti Suzuki	▲ 121.1%	▲ 135.3%	▲ 71.3%
Wipro Ltd	▲ 96.3%	▲ 74.1%	▲ 68.6%
ITC Ltd.	▲ 93.5%	▲ 109.9%	▲ 40.0%
Hindustan Unilever	▲ 100.9%	▲ 155.2%	▲ 32.9%
Kotak Mahindra Bank	▲ 247.4%	▲ 456.5%	▲ 30.3%
HDFC Bank	▲308.3%	▲ 454.5%	▼ 35.8%

See how the growth of PSEs has benefitted the GoI:

GROWTH OF PSEs	FROM	TO	CHANGE
Net Worth of all 254 PSEs	**₹9.5 Lcr** (FY14)	**₹17.33 Lcr** (FY23)	▲ **82.4%** (9yrs)
Nifty PSE Index	**2846.20** (02May14)	**10,222.00** (02May24)	▲ **259.1%**
Dividends to Govt of India (excl. financial sector CPSEs)	**₹25,921cr** (FY14)	**₹69,222cr** (FY24)	▲ **167%**
Total Market Cap of PSBs (GOI-owned Banks)	**₹333,199cr** (31Mar20)	**₹1,647,291cr** (01Apr24)	▲ **394.4%** (4yrs)
Nifty PSU Bank Index	**2942.25** (02May14)	**7586.15** (02May24)	▲ **157.8%**

Compared with the 394.4 per cent increase in the aggregate MCap of all 12 Public Sector Banks (PSBs), the MCap of all 18 private banks grew just 137.6 per cent to ₹30.039LCr.

Modi energised PSEs in a way that 13 PMs before him could not, especially the six PMs who had five years or more on the job to do so.

Let's see an example of apathy in Dr Singh's tenure. The ₹27,000Cr electric locomotive factory in Madhepura (Bihar) was to be set up to make 800 locomotives of 12,000HP in 11 years. Though approved by UPA in February 2007, work did not start for 7.25 years, as the Cabinet could not decide if GoI should run the project by itself or via a JV with a private player. Modi went the JV route with Alstom SA of France under the Make-in-India program and the factory was completed in March 2018. It has delivered 378 coaches as of April 2024. Alstom also makes the NamoBharat trains (see chapter 'Delhi Capitals' in this book) as well as coaches for Metros in many cities.

In the Modi-era, a JV between the GoI and Wabtech will soon start exporting Made-in-India locomotives from its plant at Marhowra in Bihar.

38

Labour Reforms

Even 77 years after Independence, almost 57.7 per cent of India's 784.7M non-farm workforce is in the unorganised sector and do not have access to the benefits enjoyed by the organised sector. The working class was also entangled in a web of multiple labour legislations.

Between 2015 and 2019, the Modi Government had nine tripartite discussions with all the Central Trade Unions, Employers' Associations, and representatives of state governments on labour reforms.

The Code on Wages, Code on Social Security, Occupational Safety, Health and Working Conditions Code (or OSH Code), and the Industrial Relations Code replaced 29 old Central labour laws. Salient features of the new codes include:

- Guarantee minimum wages, Employees' State Insurance Corporation (ESIC), and pension benefits to all workers in organised and unorganised sectors, including plantation and mine workers, contract and gig workers (those working for tech platforms such as Ola, Swiggy, Dunzo, etc.). The minimum wage is determined based on skill level, nature of work and state/region.
- Guarantee of timely payment of wages to workers.
- Equal remuneration for male and female workers.

- Aadhaar-based Universal Account Number (UAN) for easy portability of EPFO and ESIC accounts.
- Employers with over 20 workers to post all vacancies online.
- Requirement of minimum service for eligibility of gratuity removed for fixed-term workers.
- 'Inspector Raj' to end by changing the role of an inspector to an advisor and facilitator for workers.
- Issue of Appointment Letters and free annual Health Check-up by employers has been made mandatory.
- Under the 'One Nation-One Ration Card' scheme, an Inter-State Migrant Worker (ISMW) can get ration in the state s/he is working while her/his family can avail of rations in the state they reside in.
- Only workers appointed by a contractor were recognised as ISMW. Now, workers can register as ISMW on the national portal, and s/he gets a legal identity to avail the benefits of various social security schemes.
- Helpline in each and every state for resolution of the ISMWs' grievances.
- Instead of the earlier 240 days, now if a worker has worked for 180 days, s/he is entitled to one day leave for every 20 days of work done.
- Women given right to work at night at their consent and employer must ensure adequate arrangements for safety and other facilities.
- If an organised sector worker loses her/his job, s/he will get financial aid and other benefits under Atal Bimit Vyakti Kalyan Yojana, like 'unemployment allowance' prevalent in many Western nations.
- On retrenchment, an employer shall give 15 days' wages to the worker losing her/his job for re-skilling (to be credited directly to the worker's bank account).

- Only Trade Unions with 51 per cent voting rights shall be recognised for negotiating and making agreements with employers. In establishments in which no single Union gets 51 per cent of the votes, a 'negotiating council' of Trade Unions must be established for making agreements with employers.
- For industries, registrations have come down from eight to one, licenses from four to one, and number of returns to be filed also from four to one.
- It is now easier for employers to hire and fire workers, thereby making India a more attractive country to do manufacturing business.
- Maximum jail term for employer-offenders reduced from seven to three years.

Since labour is a 'concurrent subject' in the Constitution (which means that both the Centre and the states have jurisdiction), the states must frame rules and regulations for the labour codes to be rolled out. As of December 2024, all states and UTs had prepared draft rules on the four codes, that are now expected to be rolled out in the first half of 2025.

The old labour laws helped everyone (especially corrupt *babus* or officials) except the workers themselves. The new codes benefit the workers as well as the employers. They will go a long way in strengthening the weakest component of India's economy—manufacturing.

Part III

Digital India

'Digital India is my dream for India. When I say, "Digital India" it is not meant for the rich but for those who are poor. I dream of a Digital India where technology ensures the citizen–government interface is incorruptible.'

—Prime Minister Narendra Modi

39

India Is JAMmin'

One of the key needs of a growing economy is using technology to contribute to citizens' ease of living. After the launch of the Digital India Mission on 1 July 2015, almost 97 per cent of all Indians are using affordable technology in their day-to-day lives.

'JAM' (JanDhan–Aadhaar–Mobile) refers to linking of a person's Jan Dhan account with her/his Aadhaar and Mobile. It has played a pivotal role in increasing financial inclusion, revolutionised transparency of governance, and gone a long way in plugging leakages. In April 2018, the World Bank said that leakages of pension payments dropped by 47 per cent. Let's look at some numbers:

Success of JAM	FY2014	FY2024	CHANGE	Sources
Mobile Phone Subscribers	905M	1199M	▲ 32.5%	1
Mobile Broadband Subscribers	69.9M	884M	▲ 1119.5%	1
Data Consumption/user/month	0.08GB	20.06GB	▲ 24,975%	1
Cost of Mobile Data	₹269/GB	₹14/GB	▼▼ 94.8%	2
Aadhar Numbers Issued	610.1M	1379.8M	▲ 126.2%	3
Annual DBT Transfers	₹7367.7cr	₹691,360cr	▲ 9,284%	4
Schemes Linked to DBT	28	315	▲ 1025%	4
PMJDY Accounts	116.9M	525.0M	▲ 349.1%	5
Digital Payment Transaction Volume (FY18 to FY24)	20.7B (FY18)	168.3B (FY24)	▲ 713% in 6yrs	6

Sources: 1) bit.ly/COAIAR; 2) bit.ly/DataIND; 3) bit.ly/AadhaarDB; 4) bit.ly/DBT-DB; 5) bit.ly/PMJDY-ac; 6) bit.ly/DigiPTV

All of these are awe-inspiring increases, especially the 9,284 per cent increase in Direct Benefit Transfers (DBTs). Under DBT, funds of government schemes and subsidies are directly transferred to citizens' bank accounts, thereby plugging leakages. India saved around ₹3.65LCr up to March 2024 due to DBT, over 1.12 per cent of India's GDP, in this period.

5G service reached over 165M users and over 8,000 locations within 5 months of its launch.

Aadhaar is now also available as PVC cards, e-Aadhaar and mAadhar, as well a 'masked' Aadhaar.

A World Bank survey found that only about 36 per cent Indians had a bank account in 2012 and 43 per cent of these were not used. In August 2014, Modi launched Pradhan Mantri Jan Dhan Yojana (PMJDY) to ensure access to banking, loans, insurance, and pensions to everyone, especially underserved weaker sections and low-income groups.

PMJDY account owners can maintain zero balance, get a RuPay debit card with inbuilt accident insurance of ₹1L, and various government benefits are transmitted directly via DBT. In the first 6 months, nearly 0.897M PMJDY accounts were opened daily. In December 2024, 55.7 per cent of account holders were women, average balance per account was ₹4,428 and 68.4 per cent had RuPay debit cards.

Mode of Digital Payment SOURCE: https://rbidocs.rbi.org.in/rdocs/PSUPDFs/PAYMENTSYSTEM052024422E68282C6C44A5AAB4C0B45E15D725.PDF	**Share (May 2024)**
RTGS	69.48%
NEFT	15.82%
BHIM UPI	9.36%
IMPS	2.77%
NACH	1.37%
Credit Card	0.75%
Debit Card	0.20%
Others (including FASTag, Mobile/Net Banking)	0.25%

40

47 years' work in 10 years

The National Payments Corporation of India (NPCI), an initiative of the RBI and Indian Banks' Association was started in January 2010. With over 60 banks as shareholders, it is an umbrella organisation that operates a robust payments and settlements infrastructure.

Pre-Modi-era products include National Financial Switch (ATMs); IMPS; AEPS ('Anytime, Anywhere' authentications with Aadhaar without OTP to withdraw cash, send money and do online transactions); RuPay (secure card payment network with protection from 'phishing'); and NACH (for corporates and banks to register mandates for bulk push and pull paperless transactions).

Modi started UPI or Unified Payments Interface (multiple bank accounts in any bank's single app, 'Peer to Peer' collect request scheduled and paid as per requirement, and more); *99# (dial *99# on non-internet phones to send/receive interbank funds, check balances, set/change UPI PIN, etc. through an interactive menu in 13 languages); BHIM App (instant payments or collections using mobile number and UPI ID); BharatQR (scan QR code to make payment); RuPay Credit Card (link digital card to UPI for safe payments by scanning QR code); Bharat BillPay (regular payments like electricity, phone, DTH/OTT, gas, water, insurance, Systematic Investment Plans (SIPs), school fees, FASTag recharge, municipal taxes, etc. 'Anytime Anywhere' with cards, UPI, net/mobile banking, wallets, kiosk, ATM, bank branch, etc., with instant SMS confirmation); RuPay NCMC Card (contactless debit card with offline wallet for low-value payments); UPI LITE (single-factor authentication for instant transactions below ₹500); UPI AutoPay (e-mandates for recurring payments); UPI-ATM (withdraw cash from any bank's enabled ATMs without using a card); Hello! UPI (navigate UPI App in regional languages by touch or voice and make payments by speaking in your language); credit line on UPI (access pre-sanctioned credit lines from banks for low-ticket loans. Leveraging AI, banks can identify opportunities for customers and merchants with high UPI payments. Since customer data is available through the UPI system, banks can start from low-ticket credit lines and go higher based on consumer behaviour and repayment patterns. This will foster economic growth and enhance financial inclusion); UPI Lite X (no need of Internet connection on your or recipient's phone. From lifts to basements and flights, transactions are done offline).

UPI for Secondary Market started its Beta phase in January 2024 the equity cash segment on stock markets, initially for limited HDFC and ICICI bank customers. Investors can block funds in their accounts, which will only be debited by Clearing Corporations on trade confirmation during settlement. Clearing Corporations will process pay-outs on a T+1 basis. The Beta facilitator was Groww as the brokerage; and BHIM, Groww and YES PAY NEXT as the UPI Apps. Many other 'Qualified Stock Brokers' will be able to offer this facility from February 2025.

NRIs with mobile numbers from countries like Australia, Canada, Hong Kong, Oman, Qatar, Saudi Arabia, Singapore, the UAE, the UK, and the US can use UPI without an Indian mobile number.

Indians can use UPI for paying via QR scans at certain retail outlets in Bhutan, France, Mauritius, Nepal, Qatar, Singapore, Sri Lanka, and the UAE.

Soon to on-board will be Bahrain, Belgium, Cambodia, Hong Kong, Japan, Malaysia, Maldives, Netherlands, Oman, Philippines, Saudi Arabia, South Korea, Switzerland, Taiwan, Thailand, the UK, and Vietnam.

Inbound international travelers from almost all countries can now also use an 'UPI One World' wallet.

Cost per payment transaction has come down from around ₹700–800 to just ₹20–25, a massive reduction. Due to this and the ease of use, the number of UPI transactions increased from 6.12M/day in February 2018 to 539.68M/day in December 2024 (up 8,718% in under 7 years).

A sizable 76 per cent of all bank account holders in India now make or receive digital payments.

Value of UPI transactions grew from ₹683.08Cr/day in February 2018 to ₹74,990.32Cr/day in December 2024 (up 10,878% in under 7 years).

As of July 2024, India had 216,352 ATMs, 10.443M points of sale (PoS; like Micro ATM devices), 334.83M QR codes, 980.46M debit cards, and 104.57M credit cards.

NPCI Bharat BillPay Ltd (NBBL) is now a separate entity with the name of Bharat Connect. In October 2023, it got into the B2B segment, whereby Bharat Connect-enabled sellers can issue multiple invoices to buyers who can pay multiple invoices in a single transaction via UPI, net banking, cards, wallet, IMPS, and cash. Bharat Connect can become huge by on-boarding big-ticket sellers, such as manufacturers and distributors, as billers who can leverage enabled channels and modes to facilitate payments from buyers such as retailers in lieu of goods and services.

As of December 2024, Bharat Connect had 36 Biller Operating Units with 22,113 Billers, 67 Customer Operating Units and 1,649 Agent Institutions.

During Oct-Dec 2024, it had 5.12M average daily transactions with a transaction value of ₹2,236Cr per day.

No other country in the world has such a massive digital public infrastructure (DPI). Banks' costs of onboarding customers in India have decreased from almost ₹2,000 to less than ₹10 due to this DPI.

In September 2023, the World Bank praised India's DPI and especially the 'JAM trinity', and its transformative impact under the Modi Government, specifically naming his government. It said India has achieved remarkable landmarks in just 6 years, accomplishments that would typically have taken 47 years to realise.

Senior Congress leaders P Chidambaram (a former union finance minister) and Shashi Tharoor said even as recently as in 2020 that digital payments will not work in India.

41

eFGORST

The eTaal Portal was conceived to measure/analyse eServices of Central/state/UT governments and take actions wherever required. It measures the impact of 4,317 eGov initiatives (eServices) with a real-time view of all e-transactions via an Integrated Visual Interface. Many tax payments are also analysed.

Using web service, AI and power business intelligence or BI, eTaal is based on automatically shared transaction counts. Robust Web Application Programming Interface (API) Security Frameworks ensure safe, secure and authentic data, and protection from unauthorized access, use, modification, or disclosure.

eTaal uses historical data and statistical modelling to forecast future trends and events for the stakeholders to make informed decisions. The model compares data with other data of similar size, nature, and impact to help users understand projects requiring attention, and to identify potential problems beforehand to take suitable actions to overcome those well in advance.

An Interactive Chatbot built on Neural Machine Translation tech that used AI responds to exact queries in real-time. It can understand free-flowing conversation and automate tasks. Average query response time is 27 seconds and resolution rate is 98.72 per cent.

The dashboard facilitates quick analysis of transaction data in tabular/graphical forms enabling users to drill down to lowest level without compromising on privacy, security or integrity of the Apps.

We had to look at the mind-numbing numbers three times as we couldn't believe what we saw! eTaal measured as many as 305.267B eTransactions in 2024, or a whopping 834.062M daily transactions.

FASTag

National Electronic Toll Collection via FASTag has helped reduce congestion and reduced corruption. Average waiting time at toll plazas has reduced from 12.2 minutes to just 47 seconds. As of November 2024, there were over 101.752M FASTags, and more than 1,650 FASTag-enabled toll plazas. Toll collection went up to ₹69,425Cr in 2024 compared with ₹8,068.7Cr in 2019 (up 760.4 per cent in 5 years). FASTag tolls as a percentage of total road tolls went up from 16.1 per cent in FY18 to 97.9 per cent in FY24 (up 508 per cent in 6 years).

Govt eMarketplace (GeM)

To enhance transparency, efficiency, and speed in government procurement, GeM was created in August 2016. It provides e-bidding, reverse e-auction and demand aggregation to facilitate government buyers to achieve best value for their money.

The numbers in this table show the remarkable growth:

Success of GeM (Government eMarketplace) https://gem.gov.in/statistics		
2.1M vendors of 11,888 product and 323 service categories connected online with 374,358 Govt buyers		
Financial Year	**GMV Transacted**	**Growth**
FY 2019-20	₹8505Cr	
FY 2020-21	₹65,957Cr	▲ 675.5%
FY 2021-22	₹106,000Cr	▲ 60.7%
FY 2022-23	₹201,463Cr	▲ 90.1%
FY 2023-24	₹403,718Cr	▲ 100.4%
TOTAL BUSINESS SINCE INCEPTION (GMV)		**₹959,477Cr**
Money Saved by Ministries, Govt Depts, and PSEs		**₹108,300Cr++**

ONDC

The Open Network for Digital Commerce (ONDC) was launched on 29 April 2022 to enable small businesses to capitalize on the benefits of digital commerce by creating a level playing field. By November 2024, it had over 649,000 sellers (85 per cent small enterprises) and was facilitating almost 14.4M orders per month.

Rapid Assessment System (RAS)

RAS was developed to improve the quality of online and offline service delivery, websites and Apps of GoI and all state/UT governments. It is a configurable, performant, scalable, and secure platform. The form builder can power surveys, polls, feedback, etc., quickly, with minimum efforts.

Built-in Analytics provide insights at a granular level. The platform supports Role Based Access Control for all functionalities, making it an end-to-end solution for feedback requirements by all departments of all governments.

As of June 2024, there were 771.1M feedback requests for 2,613 services of 456 integrated government departments.

ServicePlus

ServicePlus meta-data-based e-Service delivery network delivers electronic services to citizens. Its mobile App is quick-to-learn and easy-to-use with minimal effort and very low skillsets. The vision is to make all government services accessible to each citizen in his/her locality through common service delivery outlets, and ensure efficiency, transparency and reliability of such services at affordable costs to realise his/her basic needs. As of June 2024, there were 3,353 services on the system. Almost 303.6M applications were received, of which 91.46 per cent were satisfactorily disposed. More than 350,000 applications come daily.

TeleStack

About 77,000 towers are functional under the indigenously developed Telecom Technology Stack. The Modi Government will start scaling it up in a very big way with the installation of 20,000 more towers and compete with Huawei, ZTE, Samsung, Nokia, and Ericsson in the coming years. It is looking to export a full range of indigenously designed 4G and 5G stacks to use the technological developments as a key foreign policy tool. India has received inquiries from more than 15 telecom operators and nine nations including Egypt, Kenya, Mauritius, and Papua New Guinea.

42

App *hi* App

Modi Government launched over 30 Apps for ease of living. Here are a few:

- **Aarogya Setu** was launched within eight days of the first lockdown to help limit the spread of COVID-19 with Bluetooth-based contact tracing, mapping of likely hotspots, and dissemination of relevant information.
- **CoWIN** was launched on the day vaccination started. Even developed countries like the UK and the US were issuing 'paper' vaccination certificates when India was issuing digital ones on our mobiles.
- **DigiLocker** provides each citizen a dedicated cloud account of 1GB to store, access, share, and verify authentic documents and certificates such as Aadhaar, passport, driving licence, vehicle registrations, mark sheets, income/caste certificate, etc., uploaded in a digital format by the original issuers. By the end of 2024, DigiLocker had 439.37M registered users and 8.49B verified issued documents from 1,865 issuers.
- **DigiYatra** facilitates easy movement through airport security with a facial scan, eliminating the need for document verification by CISF, thus reducing queues at 24 airports by September 2024, and ramping up quickly.

Till December 2024, over 9M active users had used the convenient DigiYatra facility over 44M times.

- **IRCTC Rail Connect** had 122.1M active users as of FY24, with about 38,000 daily additions. About 1.238M tickets were booked daily @ 860/minute. Indian Railways will soon launch a 'SUPER APP' with real-time updates on train status, ticket booking, complaint registration, and other features. It will consolidate 12 existing Apps including Bhasha Sangam, Indian Railways PNR, National Train Enquiry System, IRCTC Air, IRCTC Rail Connect, Rail Madad, Rail Saarthi, Food on Track, PortRead, Satark, TMS-Nirikshan, and UTS.
- **UMANG** was launched in November 2017 in 23 languages and gives access to 2,101 services provided by government departments. In December 2024, UMANG had 73.4M users who had done 5.1606B transactions and regularly do an average of about 94.7M transactions every month.
- **eSakshya** helps the police in recording and managing evidence in criminal cases.
- **Mera Ration 2.0** streamlines the distribution of subsidised foodgrains to ration card holders across India.
- **NSP OTR** facilitates a One Time Registration (OTR) for students seeking scholarship, with Aadhaar-linked facial recognition.

43

Digital Rural India

The world's biggest rural telecom project BharatNet provides access to Gram Panchayats to all telecom service providers, Cable TV operators, OTT platforms, and other content providers for broadband connectivity, so that they can offer citizens Apps for e-Health, e-Education, e-Governance, etc., in rural/remote India.

As of December 2024, 692,498km of OFC has been laid compared with just 6,577km in FY14 (up 10,429 per cent)—with 214,313 Gram Panchayats (almost 80 per cent of all Gram Panchayats) connected; over 1.197M Fibre-To-The-Home (FTTH) and 656,345 broadband connections; and 104,574 WiFi hotspots set up in rural and remote areas, that have a monthly data consumption of 139.5 GB.

As of FY24, there were 974 Digital Villages with 220,081 persons registered for education; 881,160 households for human healthcare (over 4.207M consultations done); 221,269 households for veterinary healthcare (210,225 consultations done); 11,259 for training in 5 skills.

PMGDISHA

Prime Minister Gramin Digital Saksharta Abhiyaan or PMGDISHA is a free 20-hour course that is training 60M persons in rural areas on operating computers, tablets, smartphones, emails, browsing Internet, searching for information, enabling them to become digitally literate so that they can access government services and start using digital banking via BHIM UPI.

As of March 2024, 439,631 Common Service Centres (CSCs) were registered as training centres, 73.5M people registered for the scheme, of which 63.9M were trained and 47.8M candidates (45 per cent female) were certified.

Digital Ration Cards

The Modi Government has achieved 100 per cent digitisation of all 195.176M ration cards, a huge feat for a country as diverse and expansive as ours—99.5 per cent of ration cards are Aadhaar-seeded, 52.5 per cent are mobile number-seeded and 20.9 per cent are bank account-seeded.

Bhu-Aadhaar

Unique Land Parcel Identification Number (ULPIN) or Bhu-Aadhaar is a 14-digit ID assigned to a land parcel based on its latitude and longitude coordinates. The purpose is to help develop land banks through an Integrated Land Information Management System. As of December 2024, computerization of Record of Rights was completed in 626,210 villages (95.56% of total). Almost 32.58M Cadastral Maps (70.2% of total) were digitized. Computerization of Registration was completed in 95.73% Sub-Registrar Offices (SROs) and Integration of SROs with Land Records was completed in 88.56% of all SROs.

In order to implement ULPIN and generate geo-referenced data of the Land Parcels, geo-referencing of Cadastral Maps have been completed in 355,899 villages (54.31%). ULPINs have been issued in 214,842 villages (32.78%).

Common Service Centres

Unfolding in the heartlands of India is an inspiring tale of innovation and entrepreneurship, led by VLEs or Village Level Entrepreneurs who manage CSCs.

CSCs are one-stop shops for digital services such as booking railway tickets, payment of utility bills, PAN and Aadhaar enrolment, banking, insurance services, etc. There were 577,806 active CSCs in November 2024 (up 588.2 per cent from May 2014) that had done 36.99M transactions.

The over 480,000 VLEs plus staff at about 150,000 IndiaPost offices have being trained to assist buyers, sellers and service providers with registrations; product catalogue upload and management; order acceptance, fulfilment and invoice generation functions on the GeM portal.

As part of Modi Government's policy, women from marginalised communities and lower-income groups are encouraged to establish CSCs in rural areas, becoming agents of social change, thereby fostering empowerment of the entire society.

In the first 326 days of FY24, CSCs facilitated 140M banking transactions worth over ₹65,000Cr including 120M Digipay transactions; issued over 120M Ayushman Bharat Health Account (ABHA) cards and over 100,000 Jeevan Pramaan life certificates for pensioners; registered over 10M workers on the e-Shram portal; and processed 800,000 passport and 200,000 PAN Card applications.

In 2023, they facilitated 1.6M Aadhaar enrolments; 45M Pradhan Mantri Fasal Bima Yojana (PMFBY) applications; 30M electricity bill payments of ₹4,263Cr; 3.9M IRCTC ticketing transactions; 150,000 ITRs; 45,471 Tele-Health Consultations; 1.506M Agri Tele-Consultations; registered 5.9M Tele-law cases; and issued 4.4M Pradhan Mantri Shram Yogi Mandhan (PMSYM) cards.

Grameen eStore

Today's buyers do not just need a lot of options while shopping, they also want things at their doorstep. Our way of shopping has changed. Even a villager no longer needs to go to a city to buy a Maruti car, an Oppo mobile or fashionable clothes. S/he can buy these from home with just one click. No, not from Amazon or Flipkart or Meesho.

It is possible through CSC Grameen eStores (CGeS), a concept that has not only changed the way villagers' shop, but also established new dimensions of employment and development. Today, there are more than 400,000 CGeS spread across more than 15,000 Pin Codes across the length and breadth of the country.

Setha Singh Rawat of Ajmer (Rajasthan) runs 'Darzi Online' as its VLE. He used to run a tailoring business with 3 women. When his shop had to be closed due to COVID-19, he joined a CSC. Rawat now runs a business that sells hoodies, laptop bags, shirts, and a lot more, has 75 employees and did business of ₹1.75Cr in 2022.

It is through these eStores that all goods have become just a click away for remote villages. Select the item, make payment, and the shopping is done! No going to a shop to see the goods or meet the shopkeeper, no counting cash. Most big brands are associated with the CGeS. Items are way more affordable than on any other website as the App eliminates middlemen. Startups in every state transact with the CGeS as they get better sales and margins. The eStores have a wide range of local handicrafts, groceries, consumer durables, and believe it or not—automobiles.

Since its launch in 2020, CGeS is making rapid progress. In FY21, eStores did a business of ₹50L. This increased to ₹22.39Cr in FY22, ₹50.88Cr in FY23, and an estimated ₹92Cr in FY24. Today, 480,156 VLEs run eStores that cater to 644,715 customers. It has emerged as a major medium for women's empowerment. Kharidu Sunita sells Tata Croma, TTK Prestige, Whirlpool, Vivo, and Crompton products in Perecherla (Andhra Pradesh). She employs 12 villagers of which 10 are women.

Grameen eStores are creating employment opportunities on a large scale and presenting a new saga of village development by directly connecting local manufacturers and farmers with consumers.

PM VISHWAKARMA

Launched on 17 September 2023, this scheme provides support to artisans/craftspeople engaged in 23 traditional trades, including recognition via certificate and ID card, toolkit up to ₹15,000, training for skill upgradation, stipend of ₹500/day, collateral-free loan up to ₹300,000, incentives for digital transactions, and marketing assistance such as branding, product advertisements, and quality certification. The scheme aims to cover all Gram Panchayats, Nagar Panchayats and Urban Local Bodies. VLEs have played a pivotal role in raising awareness about government schemes and enrolling maximum beneficiaries.

In one year, almost 24.883M applications were received and almost 2.168M artisans/craftspeople were registered (over 54.4 per cent women) of which over 900,000 completed basic training on 24 trades at training centres. Of the registered persons, 33.8 per cent are tailors, 19.4 per cent are brick masons, and 17.6 per cent are carpenters.

Cybersecurity Ambassadors

Cybercrime is on the rise, with phishing and malware becoming common. Due to the COVID-19 lockdowns, people started relying more on computers and smartphones and students started studying online. There were over 1.158M cyberattacks in 2020 (up 194 per cent compared with 2019). Rural citizens, especially women and old people were most affected, as they were easy targets.

CSC e-Governance Services partnered with Capgemini, CISCO, IBM, Kyndryl, Oppo, Samhita-CGF, etc., to promote cybersecurity awareness and make rural women Cybersecurity Ambassadors.

560,000 women (age 18–45) are being trained on cyberstalking, social media/financial frauds, the modus operandi of fraudsters, and various reporting methods. This enables them to harness economic opportunity through career prospects as cybersecurity personnel.

SVAMITVA

The SVAMITVA (Survey of Villages Abadi and Mapping with Improvised Technology in Village Areas) scheme was launched in April 2020 to map the whole of rural India, prepare digital maps, identify properties, and issue 'Property Cards' to the rightful owners. By December 2024, drone surveys were done in 310,540 villages, 266,140 maps were handed over to states, over 100.05M land parcels were digitised, and over 15.02M Property Cards had been distributed to the owners.

eGramSwaraj

This is a software application for Gram Panchayats that has an integration with the Public Financial Management System (PFMS). By December 2024, 249,729 Panchayati Raj Institutions onboarded the eGramSwaraj PFMS.

44

India Stack Global

India's leadership in digital technologies and our experience of implementing digital transformation projects at a scale of billions and trillions can be easily shared globally.

There have been continuous requests from various countries for India to contribute to the Global Digital Public Goods repository. The lessons from India Stack are there for the world to adopt—of course, India is not going to give it for free.

India Stack Global was launched to showcase the India Stack and its building blocks to prospective customers around the world. Currently, 15 key projects/platforms are on the India Stack, and the information is available on the India Stack portal in all the six languages of the UN.

- **Aadhaar** (almost 1.412B ID cards generated, over 128B authentications done, more than 22B eKYCs done, DBT disbursal of $477.69B in government welfare schemes as of December 2024, with savings of $44.59B)
- **UPI** (over 329B digital payment transactions with a value of more than $6.42T)
- **CoWIN** (handled peak of 2.5B API hits)
- **DigiLocker** (439.37M users with 8.49B verified issued documents)

- **Aarogya Setu** (218.2M downloads, 935.88M tests)
- **Diksha** (world's largest, most diverse school education platform that offers engaging learning material, relevant to the prescribed school curriculum, to teachers/students/parents; 17.6M users; 180.5M enrolments; 5.59B learning sessions; 365,000 e-Contents; 144.3M completed courses)
- **UMANG** (73.4M users; 5.1606B transactions)
- **E-Sanjeevani** (230,314 Doctors; 16,895 Hubs; 131,231 Spokes; 332.52M Patients served)
- **GeM** (375,000+ government buyers; 11,204 product and 332 service categories $134.8B order volume)
- **API Setu** (3,246 APIS; 1,871 organisations)
- **e-Office** (1,177 organisations; over 1.26M users; 3.89M eSigns; 956.4M eFiles; 3.91B receipts)
- **e-Hospital** (more than 1,140 hospitals; 466.94M registrations; 36.46M inpatient admissions; 15.08M discharge summaries)
- **POSHAN Tracker** (98.993M beneficiaries, tracks last mile service delivery through 1.333M Anganwadi workers)
- **e-Courts** (3,580 district/taluka court complexes and 39 High Courts onboarded; 2.99M district court cases disposed/month; 1.25B orders/judgments available online; ₹350Cr estimated savings due to free and open-source software)
- **NCD Platform** (543M persons enrolled in National Non-Communicable Diseases; 41M facilitated for treating hypertension/diabetes; 86M ABHA Health IDs created)

Part IV

Unprecedented Infrastructure Development

Indian cities are choking to death due to downright neglect by past governments. The Modi Government has invested 11.3 times more than the UPA Government in urban India.

The number of fuel retail outlets countrywide went up from 52,248 in April 2014 to 93,115 in November 2024 (up 78.2 per cent).

45

SBM and JJM

Though drinking water and sanitation are state subjects, seeing the pathetic 'state' of affairs, on 15 August 2014, Modi announced Swachh Bharat Mission (SBM), a drive to build toilets, make India 'Open Defecation Free (ODF)', and improve waste management.

Swachh Bharat Mission-Grameen (Target Villages = 585,439, Target Districts = 763)	**Quantity**	**Average**	**Increase over UPA**
Individual Household Latrines in Villages	115.037M	33,161/day	▲ 477%
Community Sanitary Complexes	234,438	68/day	
	Household	**Community**	
Waste Collection and Segregation Sheds		262,801	None of this infrastructure was ever built in any Village by the UPA or by any Govt prior to Modi's in 66.8yrs
Vehicles to transport Non-Degradable Solid Waste		401,085	
Compost Pits	2.399M	733,819	
Biogas plants for Biodegradable Waste Management	45,192	10,893	
Plastic Waste Management Units	2822		
Drainage Facilities	1,093,873		
Soak/Leach/Magic Pits for Grey-water Management	6.801M	1,563,901	
Phytorid / DEWATS Waste Water Treatment Systems		112,878	
Faecal Sludge Treatment Plants		2876	
Kitchen Gardens	12.78M		
Waste Stabilisation Ponds 3/5	32,181		**% of Total**
Waste Bins	81,500	311,000	
Villages with Liquid Waste Management (March 2024)	467,664		79.9%
Villages with Soid Waste Management (March 2024)	302,265		51.63%
ODF+ Villages (March 2024)	532,559		91.0%
ODF+ Gram Panchayats (March 2024)	227,194		89.35%
SOURCE: https://sbm.gov.in/sbmgdashboard/statesdashboard.aspx			

Wasn't Sonia Gandhi's UPA supposedly a 'welfare government'?

What were Congress governments doing all these years? Only 39 per cent of Indian villages had sanitation facilities in 2014. What could be more pathetic and tragic than this?

Rural women had to defecate in open fields behind bushes or trees mostly after sunset to protect themselves from the lecherous desires of disgusting men. Lakhs of women have been raped on their way to or back from the fields. Modi has given dignity to 420M females.

SBM-Grameen led to many economic and socio-economic benefits, and India achieved WHO's Sustainable Development Goal (SDG) 6.2 (Sanitation and Hygiene) as much as 11 years ahead of the stipulated timeline.

Swachh Survekshan Grameen Survey in 2022 **Source:** bit.ly/SSGS-2022	**% age**
266,296 citizens in 17,559 villages (709 Districts) via face-to-face interactions, plus 51.3+M citizens via mobile APP and Web portal, 24,610 village-level waste management assets, 17,548 IEC locations, 16,797 Govt schools, 16,654 Anganwadi centres, 14,408 panchayat bhawans, 14,977 religious places, 8042 health facilities, 5778 haats/bazaars, and 9216 other public places	
Households with Access to Toilet	**95.4%**
Public Places with Access to Toilet	**74.6%**
Minimal Stagnant Water within Public Place Premises	**93.1%**
Minimal Littering within Public Place Premises	**84.2%**
Households aware of Safe Menstrual Hygiene Practices	**94.6%**
Villages with Community-level Composting Arrangement	**24.0%**
Arrangement for door-to-door/fixed point Waste Collection	**32.9%**
Citizens who said Solid Waste Management works had started in their village	**62.7%**
Villages with Community Soak/Magic Pit/Waste Stabilization Pond	**35.7%**
Citizens who said Liquid Waste Management works had started in their village	**63.8%**
Citizens who said Sanitation Situation Improved since October 2014	**84.0%**
Citizens Satisfied With Solid/Liquid Waste Management Work in their village	**68.4%**
Districts with Integrated Plan for End-to-End Management of Plastic	**88.2%**

What would be the findings before Modi launched SBM? Your guess is as good as ours.

Due to SBM, millions of households (especially the poor) are saving around ₹50,000/year each on healthcare costs.

Urban India was not any better—most of the 4,715 cities and towns had pathetic sanitation infrastructure. In 66.8 years, states did not use taxes and central grants for development. Projects were approved, contracts were awarded, bills were submitted and paid, reports were generated showing work was complete; but sadly, no work happened except in the state capitals and major cities where politicians were scared that citizens would raise their voice. In all other cities and towns, the money was pocketed by politicians and bureaucrats.

<table>
<tr><th colspan="2">Swachh Bharat Mission-Urban</th><th>Source: https://sbmurban.org/</th><th>% of Target</th></tr>
<tr><td colspan="2">Individual Household Latrines in Towns</td><td>63,74,355</td><td>108.6%</td></tr>
<tr><td colspan="2">Community and Public Toilets</td><td>636,826</td><td>125.5%</td></tr>
<tr><td colspan="2">Door-to-Door Solid Waste Collection</td><td>93,756 Wards</td><td>97.5%</td></tr>
<tr><td colspan="2">Wards with 100% Waste Segregation</td><td>87,540 Wards</td><td>91.0%</td></tr>
<tr><td colspan="2" rowspan="2">Daily Waste Being Treated</td><td>130,000+ Tons/day</td><td>80.3%</td></tr>
<tr><td colspan="2">Only around 18% was being treated in 2018</td></tr>
<tr><td colspan="2">Legacy Waste Quantity Remediated</td><td>114.6MT</td><td>48.6%</td></tr>
<tr><td colspan="2">ODF Towns</td><td>4,576</td><td>97.1%</td></tr>
<tr><td colspan="2">ODF+ Towns</td><td>3,913</td><td>83.0%</td></tr>
<tr><td colspan="2">ODF++ Towns</td><td>1,429</td><td>30.3%</td></tr>
<tr><th>Liquid Waste Management Infrastructure</th><th>Capacity (MLD)</th><th>Liquid Waste Management Infrastructure</th><th>Capacity (MLD)</th></tr>
<tr><td>Sewage Treatment Plants</td><td>47,335</td><td>Fecal Sludge Treatment Plants</td><td>0.1187</td></tr>
<tr><th>Solid Waste Management Infrastructure</th><th>Capacity (TPD)</th><th>Solid Waste Management Infrastructure</th><th>Capacity (TPD)</th></tr>
<tr><td>Biomethanation Plants</td><td>4,412</td><td>Material Recovery Facilities</td><td>83,093</td></tr>
<tr><td>Waste-to-Compost Plants</td><td>120,166</td><td>Waste-to-Energy Plants</td><td>20,135</td></tr>
<tr><td>Solid & Liquid Resource Management Facilities</td><td>13,804</td><td>Construction & Demolition Waste Recycling Plants</td><td>48,187</td></tr>
</table>

Lakhs of rural women are earning money as *rani mistris* after getting trained as masons who can build toilets. Incidents of sexual violence against women have come down drastically. Rural women are refusing to marry grooms if they don't have a toilet in their house.

Exactly five years after launching SBM, on 15 August 2019, Modi announced the *Jal Jeevan Mission* (water is life mission) to provide 55 litres of piped water per person per day to rural households, with the catchphrase Har Ghar Jal (water in every house).

Jal Jeevan Mission (Rural)	**Quantity**	**% of Total**	**Increase**
TOTAL 193,190,347 Households *FTC = Functional Tap Connection* **Source:** bit.ly/JJM-R			
Households with FTCs (15 Aug 2019)	32,362,838	**16.75%**	
Households with FTCs (30 June 2024)	**149,690,207**	**77.48%**	**▲362.54%**
Supply in Schools	Hand Wash (856,191); Toilets/Urinals (741,388); Grey Water Reuse (129,714)		
Anganwadi Centres	Hand Wash (799,517); Toilets/Urinals (585,699); Grey Water Reuse (119,702)		
100% coverage States	A&N Islands, Arunachal Pradesh, D&NH and D&D, Goa, Gujarat, Haryana, Himachal Pradesh, Mizoram, Puducherry, Punjab, Telangana		
90% coverage States	Bihar, Ladakh, Lakshadweep, Nagaland, Uttarakhand		
80% coverage States	Assam, J&K, Maharashtra, Sikkim, Tamil Nadu, Uttar Pradesh, Tripura		
75% coverage States	Chhattisgarh, Karnataka, Manipur, Meghalaya		
70% coverage States	Andhra Pradesh and Odisha		
60% coverage States	Madhya Pradesh		
50% coverage States	Jharkhand, Kerala, Rajasthan, West Bengal		

New connections averaged 81,765/day in FY24.

In the case of water also, the situation was not better in urban India. In 2018, 45.5 per cent of urban households didn't have safe drinking water and 75.25 per cent didn't have sewerage/septage coverage.

In October 2021, the GoI launched AMRUT 2.0 to provide safe water to 26.8M households in 4,378 towns and 26.4M sewer connections with septage management in 500 AMRUT cities, with infrastructure for source sustainability, rainwater harvesting, groundwater recharge, and management of household wastewater for reuse.

The data in the Table below is as of FY24.

AMRUT 2.0 Mission (URBAN) Source: Ministry of Housing and Urban Affairs	**Quantity**	**% of Target or Total**	**Increase**
Households with New FTCs	**20.03M**	**74.8%** of target	
Total Households with FTCs	52.11M	**88.5%** of total	▲ 62.4%
Households with New Sewer Connections	**15.4M**	**58.2%** of target	
Total Households with Sewer Connections	29.97M	**50.9%** of total	▲ 105.7%
Parks Developed	**2697**		
Saplings Planted	**6.277M**		
Rainwater Harvesting Structures Installed	**583,229**		
Water Bodies Rejuvenated	**5032**		
New Water Bodies Developed	**72,051**	(Under AMRUT SAROVAR Mission)	
Water-logging Points Eliminated	**3471**		
Establishments Using Treated Water	**51,194**		

46

emPOWERed India

An incredible sum of ₹17.1LCr has been invested in the power sector by the Modi Government and further ₹17.5LCr is in the pipeline.

In April 2014, about 28.6M homes in 18,374 villages had no electricity connections. Under SAUBHAGYA, this was reduced to 'zero' in less than 20 months. The International Energy Association called it the 'largest and fastest expansion of access to electricity in the world'.

After decades of 'load-shedding', India has become a power-surplus nation. See the data on the next page.

As much as 47.1 per cent of India's installed power capacity and 40.2 per cent of transmission capacity was added in just 10 years by the Modi Government.

More than 260GW of generation capacity and over 90,000CKm of transmission lines are under construction.

As much as ₹1.23LCr was invested to strengthen rural distribution systems.

Power distribution companies (DISCOMs) are recovering from UPA-era legacy of high debts. RDSS is a result-linked scheme with a budget of ₹3.04LCr for FY23–26 to improve quality, reliability, and affordability of power supply through a financially sustainable and efficient distribution sector.

POWER Sector Source: https://npp.gov.in/dashBoard/trans-map-dashboard	FY2014	FY2024	CHANGE
Total Power Generation Capacity	235.089 GW	**444.757 GW**	**▲ 89.2%**
Share of RE in total capacity	30.55%	**45.36%**	**▲ 48.5%**
Power Supply in Rural Areas	~12hrs/day	**~20.8hrs/day**	**▲ 73.3%**
Power Supply in Urban Areas	12.4hrs/day	**23.75hrs/day**	**▲ 91.5%**
Transmission Lines (Circuit-Km)	291,020 CKm	**486,517 CKm**	**▲ 67.2%**
Inter-Regional Transfer Capacity	36 GW	**117 GW**	**▲ 225%**
Sub-Stations Added/Upgraded		**6974 nos.**	
HT/LT lines Added/Changed (Circuit-Km)		**835,000 CKm**	
Addition in Transformer Capacity		**699,206 MVA**	
AT&C Losses (see next page)	~27%	**20.8%**	**▼ 23%**
Unpaid Dues of GENCOs	₹1.40 Lcr	**₹44,000cr**	**▼ 68.6%**

NEW RULES FOR POWER SECTOR COMPANIES

- Dues of Govt Departments have to be Paid
- Subsidy declared has to be Paid
- Energy Accounting & Audit has to be up to date
- Tariff has to be up to date

It aims to reduce AT&C (aggregate technical and commercial) losses to 12–15 per cent pan-India by FY25. AT&C loss is Energy Loss (technical loss + theft + billing inefficiency) plus Commercial Loss (payment default + collection inefficiency). RDSS also reduced the gap between the Average Cost of Supply and Average Realisable Revenue.

To reduce losses and modernise, public sector DISCOMs and state power departments get funds for distribution infrastructure and prepaid smart meters. Almost 18.27M smart meters had been installed by December 2024.

Under new electricity rules, penalties are imposed on distributors for not giving new electrical connections within 3 days in cities, 7 days in suburban towns, and 15 days in villages. To get new connections of up to 10KW, only two documents are required now, and no demand charge estimation is needed up to 150KW.

Why did the UPA keep India under darkness for over 12 hours a day? Why did they allow the power sector bleed to near bankruptcy?

The largest power outage in history happened in July 2012, leaving 620M people in darkness and putting national security at risk, even as 24GW of capacity was idle due to coal and gas shortage.

Were the people in government all busy in filling their pockets and the pockets of Sonia Gandhi's family?

47

Green Light

Modi has walked the talk on reducing the nation's carbon footprint. India has surpassed all targets committed at different forums or summits, especially the UN Conference of the Parties (COP) summits.

GREEN ENERGY	FY2014	Aug 2024	CHANGE
Renewable Energy (RE) Capacity	71.81 GW	**205.389 GW**	**▲ 186.0%**
Share of RE in total capacity	30.55%	**45.81%**	**▲ 50.0%**
Solar Power Capacity	2.5 GW	**87.212 GW**	**▲ 3,388.5%**
Wind Power Capacity	21 GW	**47.075 GW**	**▲ 124.2%**
Natural Gas Pipelines	15,340 km	**23,391 km** (Dec 2023)	**▲ 52.5%**
LNG Terminals Storage Capacity	22 mtpa	**47.7 mtpa**	**▲ 116.8%**
Piped Natural Gas (PNG) Connections (Domestic)	2.22 M	**11.82 M**	**▲ 432.4%**
PNG (Commercial & Industrial)	NA	**63,450** (Apr 2024)	**NA**
About 98% of India's population now has PNG connections.			
Cities with LNG Pipelines	27	**61**	**▲ 126%**
Energy Savings Per Year (toe*)	3.02M toe	**50.8M toe**	**▲ 1,582%**
Nationally Determined Target (NDC) of 40% Installed Capacity from Non-Fossil Fuel Sources achieved in CY2021—**9 years ahead of schedule**			
Reducing Emissions Intensity by 33% achieved in CY2019—**11 years ahead of schedule**			
***toe** = Tons of Oil Equivalent; **Sources:** https://npp.gov.in/dashBoard/cp-map-dashboard; https://ppac.gov.in/#snapshot-bg			

The PM's target of 500GW through renewable energy by 2030 is most likely to be achieved well before time, as 164GW is under construction (including by private sector) and 86GW is under bidding process. This is part of Modi's commitment to the world that India will be a NET ZERO nation by 2070 (have a zero-carbon footprint).

Foreign investment is flowing into the sector. For example, Spain's Zelestra is investing $5B in building 10GW of wind and solar capacity by 2030.

India is No.2 among the world's 10 largest countries in share of renewable energy in total power generation capacity, after Brazil, and No.4 among all countries.

The UJALA scheme was launched to save energy and reduce CO_2 emissions.

Saving Energy via UJALA Source: http://ujala.gov.in/	**Quantity**
Free LED Bulbs Distributed	**368.7M**
Free LED Tube Lights Distributed	**7.219M**
Free Energy Efficient Fans Distributed	**2.3593M**
Street Lights Replaced with LED under SLNP	**13.321M**
Energy Saved per year	**47,882M kWh**
CO2 Emissions Reduced per year	**45.38MT**
Cost Saved per year	**₹25,634Cr**
Peak Power Demand Reduction	**11,281MW**

Offshore wind energy projects of 7GW are planned along the Gujarat and Tamil Nadu coastline with viability-gap funding. Global bids have been invited for 4 blocks of 1GW each. The GoI plans to auction 37GW of offshore wind projects by FY30.

PM-KUSUM aims to add solar power capacity of 35.57GW by March 2026 with three components: (a) 10GW via small solar plants of 2MW each; (b) 2M standalone solar-powered agriculture pumps; and (c) Solarisation of 1.5M grid-connected agriculture pumps.

GoI is investing ₹75,021Cr on 'PM Surya Ghar Muft Bijli Yojana' in which 10M houses will install rooftop solar systems of 1–3KW with subsidies of ₹30,000–78,000. They can use 300 units/month free and sell surplus power to DISCOMs. Each household can save up to ₹18,000/year at current prices. Over 13M people registered in six months and over 685,000 installations were done by December 2024.

Modi is also making India a gas-based economy. A humongous sum of ₹5.56LCr is being invested to raise the share of natural gas in India's energy basket from 6.7 per cent in March 2024 to 15 per cent by 2030. The government has announced a phased program for mandatory blending of Compressed Natural Gas (CNG), Piped Natural Gas (PNG), and Compressed Bio Gas (CBG).

As of November 2024, 6,592 fuel stations sold CNG/LNG/CBG, and 19,317 had EV charging points.

Let's look at what Modi started in his first year in office.

Ethanol Blended Petrol (EBP)

TARGET	WHEN	Estimated Forex Saving per year	Estimated CO2 Reduction per year
10%	Achieved in FY22	₹15,000cr	68+MT
18%	December 2024	₹26,900cr	121+MT
20%	By May 2025	₹31,000cr	148+MT
30%	By FY30	₹49,400cr	232+MT

By 2024, India had already saved more than ₹1.09LCr in oil imports in 10.5 years.

Compared to around 380M litres in FY14, supplies of ethanol increased to 7,074M litres in FY24 (up by 1,761.6 per cent).

Over 17,400 fuel outlets offered E20 (20 per cent EBP) as of November 2024. To accelerate adoption, a revolutionary new fuel ETHANOL 100 was launched on 15 March 2024 and this was available at over 400 outlets by July 2024.

Four regassification terminals for LNG have come up since 2017 and eight are under construction.

India has 307,000MT of coal reserves. Around 80 per cent coal is used in thermal power plants. Coal gasification is a cleaner option compared to burning and has use for coal in other forms of energy.

It produces Syngas that makes Synthetic Natural Gas (SNG), ethanol and methanol, and ammonia for fertilizers and petrochemicals. 'National Coal Gasification Mission' was set up in 2021. Initially, 100MT coal gasification and liquefaction will be set up by 2030.

GoI is providing incentives of ₹8,500Cr to promote Coal/ Lignite Gasification Projects of PSEs and private companies.

Reliance has set up three CBG plants to convert surplus Agri-waste to various forms of bioenergy. Its target is to set up 2,000 CBG plants by 2030 by investing more than ₹2.6LCr, each producing 10–20MT/day of CBG. These will consume 110MT of Agri-residue and organic waste, help mitigate about 40MT of CO_2 emissions and produce 50MT of organic manure annually, resulting in reducing LNG imports by 14mtpa. Reliance has signed a MOU with the Government of Andhra Pradesh to set up 500 CBG plants in the state by 2028.

India is building 16 Pressurised Heavy Water Reactors of 700MW of nuclear power, which is also a clean source of energy. The first two have been commissioned at the Kakrapar Atomic Power Plant in Gujarat.

Modi Government has requested five corporate houses including Reliance, Tata, Adani, and Vedanta to invest ₹44,000Cr each for producing nuclear power of 11GW (combined). Currently the only nuclear power producer NPCIL (a PSE) produces 7.5GW and another 1.3GW is in the pipeline. If these five projects take off, it will increase India's nuclear power capacity by 125 per cent.

We have covered how Modi is encouraging EVs and plans to have a whopping 800,000 public e-Buses on Indian roads by 2030.

There are more than 3,350 registered startups engaged in the business of renewable energy.

Modi Government funded green projects and schemes of ₹39,247Cr in FY23 and FY24 alone and has a budget of ₹32,061Cr for FY25, almost 63.4 per cent higher than the average of the previous two years.

48

Railways on the Fast Track

The Indian Railways, despite being India's largest employer with 1.254M employees, was one of the sickest sectors in May 2014. Modi took the problem head-on, with a massive modernisation drive. This data says it all:

BIG LEAP in RAILWAYS	UPA	MODI	CHANGE
Total Expenditure on Railways	₹1.072 Lcr	₹10.017 Lcr	**▲ 834.4%**
Track Length Added	11,336 Rkm	33,470 Rkm	**▲ 195.3%**
Track Electrified	8,162 Rkm	41,655 Rkm	**▲ 410.4%**
Unmanned Railway Crossings	8,948	0	▼▼▼
Flyovers/Underpasses Built	4,148	11,686	**▲ 181.7%**
Electric Locomotives Made by PSEs	2,021	6,803	**▲ 236.6%**
LHB Coaches produced	2,584	32,662	**▲ 1164%**
Train Accidents	1,709	681	**▼ 60.2%**
CCTV Surveillance in Stations	117	827	**▲ 606.8%**
Foot Over Bridges Built per year	20.6	203	**▲ 885.4%**
Divyangjan-friendly (Accessible) Stations with Lifts/Escalators	118	1,165	**▲ 887.3%**
Cities with Metro Rail	5	23	**▲ 360.0%**
Metro Rail Network Length Added	189.3km	758.5km	**▲ 300.7%**

Almost 80% of India's total Metro Rail Network has been built in the Modi-era

SOURCES: GOI Budget; https://ga7a.short.gy/SAlpXS; https://ga7a.short.gy/px4gOY; https://ga7a.short.gy/m16ajI; pib.gov.in; https://ga7a.short.gy/7FvQPr; https://ga7a.short.gy/P65lgH; https://ga7a.short.gy/7EAg7m; https://ga7a.short.gy/xH8J22

Due to electrification, expenses on buying diesel to run train engines has been constantly coming down by 20–25 per cent per annum.

Around 4,300 more over/under bridges are being built.

Salient features of LHB (Linke Hofmann Busch) coaches include better ride quality, enhanced safety and anti-climbing features, axle-mounted disc brakes, sturdy/robust design to minimize damage and obviating capsizing of coaches in accidents, bio-toilets, more seating capacity, large panoramic windows, FRP panels in AC coaches, microprocessor-controlled ACs, etc.

Unmanned railway level crossings were a major reason for railway accidents. The Modi Government spent ₹1.27LCr on passenger safety. Almost 7,000km of worn-out tracks are being replaced annually.

Indigenously-designed Kavach Automatic Train Protection System has been deployed on 1,548 Rkm of tracks and track-side works have been completed on 1,081 Rkm as of October 2024. Kavach has also been provided in 381 stations and 480 locomotives. The target is to achieve 10,000 locos by 2029.

Electrical/Electronic Interlocking Systems with central operation of points and signals have been provided at 6,498 stations up to October 2024.

Over 110 Gati Shakti Multimodal Cargo Terminals have started, and 263 other locations have been identified.

A whopping ₹11LCr is being invested on 434 major economic rail corridors of 40,000km.

Semi-High-Speed Trains (SHSTs)

Four SHSTs were launched, with bio-vacuum toilets with soap dispensers, touch-less taps, hand dryers, odour-control, occupancy indicators, WiFi, GPS-based passenger information system, CCTV cameras, LED lights and displays, reading lights, charging sockets, tea/coffee vending machines, braille signage for the visually impaired, and a fire/smoke detection and suppression system.

Vande Bharat Express is an AC semi-high-speed (110—160kmph) Electric Multiple Unit; India's 1st engineless train) designed and Made-in-India—136 VBE trains were running as of 15 December 2024 (in <70 months). For faster turnaround, it has a driver coach at each end. There are two seating options—Regular (2+3) and Executive (2+2).

VBE is loved by passengers; even Opposition members of parliament have been regularly demanding routes to their constituencies. By 2028, 40,000 normal bogeys will be converted to VBE coaches.

Work has also started on exporting Vande Bharat trains, as almost 10 countries have shown interest in buying them.

Alstom of France is making coaches for 200 VBE sleeper trains in India—these started running in by January 2025.

Mahamana Express operates on six routes. It has LED indicators, under-seat/overhead luggage racks, ladders for upper berths, snack tables in seats, powered Venetian blinds, and catering from modular pantry with electric chimneys.

Humsafar Express is an AC 3-tier train that is operating on 68 routes.

Tejas Express runs on 16 routes. Eco-leather seats with LED TV, snack table, phone socket, digital display boards, and celebrity chef's local cuisine make it nothing less than flying on a plane.

Other Trains

In addition to the above four, Vistadome AC coaches have been added to 22 trains on scenic routes. These have large glass windows and roof, observation lounge, 180° rotatable reclining seats so that passengers can witness the locales, a mini-pantry and aircraft-type food trolleys.

Amrit Bharat Express is a non-AC sleeper-cum-unreserved class service, prioritising affordability for longer distances. The night trains connect cities that are over 800km apart or that take over 10 hours by existing trains. Despite being capable of high speeds, operational limitations such as track capacity, multiple stoppages, and traffic congestion confine speed to 110–130kmph. India will make 1,000 new Amrit Bharat trains that can run at speeds up to 250kmph.

Rajdhani and Shatabdi coaches now have attendant-call buttons, entertainment systems, night signage, ladders to upper berths, seats and berths with fire-resistant foam, roller blinds, and magazine and mobile pockets.

All trains now have bio-toilets with epoxy-coated commodes, stainless steel basins, 'auto janitor' systems, fast-dry floor mats, improved soap dispensers, and better-quality dustbins.

Suburban Rail in Metro Cities

The 148km Bengaluru Suburban Railway Project (local trains) with 48 stations was approved. The under construction project will connect Bengaluru with Electronic City, Kengeri, Devenhalli, and Chikabanvara.

Mumbai Suburban Rail got ₹65,000Cr for upgrades. Mumbaikars' long-awaited desire for an 'AC local train' became a reality in December 2017. All 2,400+ Mumbai locals will become AC trains by 2036. By November 2024, almost 180 AC trains were operating.

Railway Stations

The Amrit Bharat Station Scheme will transform 1,337 stations, making them airport-like travel hubs. Four are ready and work on 1,198 stations has started. All stations will have lifts, escalators (some will also have travelators), modern toilets, shopping zone, food court, children's play area with gaming zone, fancy waiting areas, including AC executive lounges, separate entry/exit gates, walls adorned with traditional folk art, roof plazas, vibrant lighting, multi-level parking, and facilities for PwDs. During the UPA-era, though an 'Adarsh' station scheme was announced, no real work happened.

Six stations have opened at Bhopal, Gandhinagar, Bangalore (SMVT), Lucknow (partial), Ayodhya and Cuttack. The Gandhinagar station in Gujarat's capital has a 5-star Leela Hotel above the rail tracks.

Metro Rail

As of December 2024, new Metro lines of over 1,050km were under construction in 19 cities, that will more than double the nation's Metro Rail network by 2030.

Now, when a contract is given for trainsets/coaches for Metro, the OEM (original equipment manufacturer) must also maintain them for 15 years. This reduces delays and headaches and saves costs. *The same thing is being done for Vande Bharat Express for 30 years.*

India's first under-river twin tunnels (520m long, 121.4ft deep), built by Modi Government for Kolkata Metro, are now open. They connect Kolkata to Howrah. A 115ft-deep metro station has been built under Howrah Station (India's busiest railway station). It is India's largest and deepest metro station. With a built-up area (BUA) of 581,000 square feet (SFT), larger than 90 per cent of India's airports, it was built to accommodate an hourly footfall of more than 50,000 passengers.

NamoBharat RRTS

See the chapter 'Delhi Capitals' in this book.

Dedicated Freight Corridors

In April 2005, Dr Singh announced an 1875km Eastern Dedicated Freight Corridor (EDFC) from Ludhiana to Dankuni (near Kolkata), and a 1506km Western Dedicated Freight Corridor (WDFC) from Dadri (near Delhi) to Jawaharlal Nehru Port Trust (JNPT) in Navi Mumbai.

The Dedicated Freight Corridor Corp of India was set up 18 months later. It took another 16 months for Cabinet approval. Another 19 months later the Cabinet approved a loan from Japan International Cooperation Agency (JICA). Then nothing happened till the UPA was voted out 56 months later.

Modi revived both projects in 2018. His government spent a ₹1.24LCr to make the EDFC 100 per cent operational (with a reduced length of 1,337km due to viability concerns) and the WDFC 93.23 per cent operational by March 2024.

Around 300 freight trains now run daily, including 1.5km long trains, 2-stack container trains, and heavy trains with 25MT axle load.

Other Passenger Conveniences

There is a remarkable improvement in cleanliness. Housekeeping is done regularly in stations as well as moving trains. You can also request cleaning services just on a call/SMS/tweet.

Any help during a train journey is now just a tweet away. Many passengers have been helped in a medical emergency or otherwise. Trains have made unscheduled stops to cater to a passenger in need. A 24x7 control room monitors

Indian Railway's twitter account and provides help to needy passengers. Passengers can get to know about their reservation status (confirmed or RAC, reservation against cancellation) with an SMS.

A mammoth discount of ₹4LCr has been given to citizens on railway tickets.

6,112 stations have free WiFi and 1,051 have CCTV.

All stations have LED lights, which has resulted in a reduction of power bills by ₹180Cr and CO_2 emissions by 60,000 tons/year. As of October 2023, solar power of 211.5MW and wind power of 103MW were installed at 1,498 stations.

Over 70,000 coaches (100%) and over 7,500 stations have been fitted with eco-friendly LED lights.

Over 7,200 ATVMs (Automated Ticket Vending Machines) have been installed in hundreds of stations.

Around 4,000 POS machines had been provided on more than 600 trains for on-board payments; and around 5,600 POS machines have been installed in stations.

IRCTC's ticket issuing capacity was increased from 2,000 tickets/minute in May 2014 to 25,000 (up 1,150 per cent) by December 2022 and this will further go up to 250,000 by end-2025 (up by 12,400 per cent in 11.5 years).

Rail Drishti portal is a one-stop-shop for interacting with the Indian Railways. From tenders to public complaints to rail tracking to accounts payable—several areas of Indian Railways' working have been exposed digitally.

The Railways have 12 Apps including Bhasha Sangam, Indian Railways PNR, National Train Enquiry System, IRCTC Air, IRCTC Rail Connect, Rail Madad, Rail Saarthi, Food on Track, PortRead, Satark, TMS-Nirikshan, and UTS.

49

Bullet Train Catches Speed

A feasibility study for a 650km Ahmedabad–Mumbai–Pune high-speed rail corridor ('Bullet Train') and 5 other corridors, commissioned by UPA in 2009, was completed in September 2012. The Ministry of Railways (MoR) signed a memorandum of Understanding (MoU) with SNCF (French national railways) for an 'Operations and Development Feasibility' (funded by France) in February 2013. Soon, India's Railway Board dropped the Mumbai–Pune section, as the Western Ghats section would escalate costs.

Government of Japan stepped in with better terms. JICA has provided grants and low-cost loans to more than 70 development projects in India, including the 2 DFCs and some Metro Rail lines in 5 cities. In May 2013, Japanese PM Shinzō Abe and Dr Singh in a Joint Statement had said that India and Japan would co-finance a joint feasibility study of Ahmedabad–Mumbai route, and an MoU was signed in October 2013. Traffic forecasting, alignment surveys, and a comparison between many high-speed rail technologies/systems used worldwide was done. While JICA researched technology, alignment and traffic-related aspects, SNCF worked on business projections. The pre-feasibility study proposed an elevated corridor. JICA's report recommended

63.3 per cent of the route to be slightly above ground, 28.3 per cent on stilts, 4.1 per cent underground, and 3 per cent through bridges or tunnels.

When Modi spoke about a Bullet Train in 2013–14, the Opposition said India is 'too poor to afford a bullet train', but the same people were executing the project at the time. What a dichotomy!

Modi greenlit the project within two days of becoming PM.

MoR announced India would use Japanese Shinkansen technology with technology transfer to support Make-in-India. In January 2016, National High Speed Rail Corp Ltd (NHSRCL) was set up. MoR, NHSRCL, and JICA signed an agreement in December 2016 to implement the project. Three Japanese companies were appointed to prepare design and bidding documents, technical specs and schedule.

The project includes India's first undersea tunnel of 7km under the Thane Creek in Greater Mumbai.

In September 2017, the 508km Ahmedabad–Mumbai High Speed Rail (HSR) project was expected to cost ₹1.08LCr, including 24 train sets.

Modi secured 81 per cent funding from JICA vide a 50-year loan at an interest of just 0.1 per cent, with repayments starting after 15 years, with the balance to be borne by the Government of Gujarat and the Government of Maharashtra. While 20 per cent components would be imported from Japan, 80 per cent would be Made-in-India. The project received all approvals by June 2019.

It got delayed by three years as the Uddhav Thackeray–Congress–Nationalist Congress Party (NCP) Government blocked land acquisition in Maharashtra.

Within six months of the Eknath Shinde Sena–BJP Government coming to power, 100 per cent of the 3435ac land was acquired.

Work is going on at a fast pace in the 348km section within Gujarat that will fully open in 2027, after the first 48km Surat–Bilimora line opens in August 2026.

By November 2024, over 243km of viaduct construction (52.3 per cent) was complete, along with 352km (75.7 per cent) of pier work and 362km (77.8 per cent) of pier foundation work. Bridges have been constructed across 13 rivers, and multiple railway lines and highways have been crossed through these bridges. One mountain tunnel using the New Austrian Tunnelling Method is complete, with 7 more progressing fast. The 12 stations in Gujarat and Maharashtra, designed with thematic elements and energy-efficient features, are also under rapid construction.

Feasibility studies for seven more corridors are underway, which will increase India's HSR network to 4,883km.

Detailed Project Reports (DPRs) for Delhi–Varanasi (801km), Delhi–Ahmedabad (841km), Mumbai–Nagpur (785km), and Mumbai–Hyderabad (693km) are ready; while Kolkata–Varanasi (618km), Chennai–Bengaluru–Mysuru (449km), and Pune–Nashik (188km) are under preparation.

Japan has had such trains for over 60 years, the US over 57 years, France over 55 years, Italy over 47 years, Germany over 33 years, China over 21 years—why shouldn't India?

50

Roads to Prosperity

America's GDP shot up from $93B in 1939, before it joined Allies in World War II, to $1,018B in 1969—14 years after the end of the war, primarily because it built many interstate highways to move military equipment and personnel from its east to west coasts, which helped develop hitherto unconnected semi-rural/small urban areas.

This exact same thing has made India richer in the last 10 years and will make us even more rich in the next 10–20 years, as many National Highways and expressways are still under development.

In May 2014, India had only about 53,500km of National Highways, built in 2,336 years since before the Maurya Empire, at 22.9km/year.

How did the Modi Government do?

A whopping 64.2 per cent of the total National Highways in the country as of March 2024 were built in 10 years by the Modi Government. Construction of more than 80,000km of NHs is underway for completion in FY25–FY27. Modi plans to make all National Highways at least 2.5-lane-wide in his 3rd term.

ROADS for PROSPERITY	UPA	MODI	CHANGE
Investment on Roads & Highways	₹1.57 LCr	₹13.02 LCr	▲ 729.3%
National Highways Built	25,718 km	96,087 km	▲ 273.6%
Highways with <2 lanes	27,517 km	13,000 km	▼▼ 52.8%
2-lane / 2-lane + Paved Shoulder	45,399 km	84,723 km	▲ 86.6%
4-lane and wider	18,371 km	48,422 km	▲ 163.6%
Number of Expressways Built	13	36	▲ 176.9%
Expressway Length Built	844 km	4,605 km	▲ 445.6%
State Highways Built	14,687 km	24,392 km	▲ 66.1%

SOURCES: 1) GOI Budget Documents and Economic Survey 2023-24; 2) https://bit.ly/NH-Modi; 3) Various media reports

Though the pace of building National Highways increased by almost 3.74 times in Modi's first 10 years, quality issues remain, and the Modi 3.0 government needs to work on this.

While Modi is building 12–16-lane wide highways, the UPA did not build a single road wider than 8 lanes.

The 8-lane 1,386km Delhi–Mumbai Expressway is India's longest, with land for 4 additional lanes in the median, so that greenery and wayside utilities on either side is not disturbed for widening. Three spurs include a 4-lane to Ujjain (Madhya Pradesh), a 4-lane to Jaipur, and a 6-lane to the Noida International Airport. Work started in May 2019—66.4 per cent was open by November 2024 despite Covid-induced shutdowns. It will be fully operational by end-2025, reducing travel time from 25 hours to under 16 hours.

At least 48 more expressways of almost 15,000km are under development. These will reduce travel time substantially, e.g., Chennai–Bangalore (7 to 3.7 hours), Delhi–Dehradun (5.2 to 2.5 hours), Meerut–Prayagraj (12.5 to 6.8 hours), and Varanasi–Kolkata (17 to 7 hours).

Way Side Amenities (WSAs) are coming up at approximately every 40km on most national highways. Each WSA will have a fuel station, food court, restaurants, dhabas, convenience stores, clean water, first-aid room, child-care room, area for local artisans, car/bus/truck parking, DronePort, Helipad, etc. By the middle of 2026, more than 600 WSAs will be developed. Of this, 55 WSAs are operational and over 300 other sites have been awarded as of October 2024.

To support the National Electric Bus Program, the GoI is working on a parallel plan to build EV-ready highways of about 6,000km along the Golden Quadrilateral by 2032. This will help reduce fuel consumption and logistics costs, apart from curbing emissions.

Hundreds of bridges and tunnels have been built across the country.

51

Fasten Your Seatbelts

UDAN (Ude Desh ka Aam Naagrik) was launched in April 2017 to make air travel affordable and widespread, and it has done wonders.

India now has 15 airlines, of which nine were started after Modi became PM, primarily due to the UDAN scheme.

FLYING HIGH	FY14	FY24	CHANGE	FY 2029 (estimates)
Total Airports	71	**158**	**▲ 122.5%**	375
Private Airports	6	**14**	**▲ 133.3%**	30-35
International Airports	28	**35**	**▲ 25%%**	55-65
Expanded/Modernised	23	**74**	**▲ 221.7%**	140
Capacity (million passengers p.a.)	122mppa	**580mppa**	**▲ 417.9%**	824mppa
No. of Civilian Aircraft	404	**834**	**▲ 106.4%**	2,750
Air Routes	581	**1,164**	**▲ 100.3%**	1,620
Domestic Passengers	60.67M	**307.84M**	**▲ 407.4%**	536M
International Passengers	43.08M	**72.255M**	**▲ 68.4%**	127.3M

Frequent flyers know that the ease of movement and cleanliness at private airports are way better than ones operated by the government-owned Airports Authority of India (AAI). Another 13 AAI airports—Trichy, Bhubaneswar, Indore,

Raipur, Amritsar, Varanasi, Kushinagar, Gaya, Hubbali, Aurangabad, Jabalpur, Tirupati, and Kangra (Himachal Pradesh) will be privatised by 2027.

A whopping 2,036 new aircraft have been ordered by India's civilian airlines since 2015.

It is projected that India will have 1.8767M daily passengers in 2042.

Keeping this in mind, the Indira Gandhi International Airport (IGIA) in New Delhi (India's largest airport) increased its capacity to 100 million passengers per annum (mppa), only one out of seven airports in the world with 100 million-plus capacities. By 2027, IGIA will further increase capacity to 130mppa, making it the world's 6th largest airport. Like dozens of airports around the world, IGIA is also planning a Terminal Train to connect its three terminals.

Together with Hindon (near Ghaziabad, UP) where domestic civilian flights are starting in March 2025 and Noida International Airport opening by July 2025 with an initial capacity of 12mppa the NCR will have a capacity of around 145mppa by 2027.

Other cities are also seeing action on the airports front. Mumbai will get a second airport in 2025 with an initial capacity of 20mppa, giving the city a total capacity of 70mppa. Bengaluru's airport is being expanded to handle 60mppa and together with a proposed airport at Hosur (Tamil Nadu) that is about 45 minutes from South Bengaluru, India's third largest city by population will have a capacity of 70mppa.

Adani Group, India's largest private sector airport operator that runs seven airports and handles 23 per cent of the country's passenger movement and 33 per cent of air cargo, is investing ₹1.75LCr in its airports business over the next 10 years.

In June 2024, India launched a Fast Track Immigration-Trusted Traveller Programme for registered flyers at seven major airports that will enable them to clear immigration much faster through e-gates and these opened in January 2025. The facility will be expanded to 21 airports.

Air traffic over Indian airspace and adjoining oceans (9.604M km^2) is controlled from 4 regional centres, which calls for tremendous coordination. Work has begun on a Central Air Traffic Control and Command Centre at Nagpur; 70–80 per cent of air traffic controllers will be based there. This will reduce controllers' stress/fatigue, reduce pilot's workloads, help determine the most optimal routes, facilitate planes to fly at higher altitudes, thus burning less fuel.

52

Ports, IWT, Oceans, and the Coast

India has a 7,500km coastline, 13 major ports and 205 minor ports, making it the 16th largest marine industry in the world. Of the total cargo handled at Indian ports, over 54 per cent is handled at the country's 13 major ports.

Port capacity more than doubled to 1,617.4MT in the Modi-era. In FY24, around 823MT cargo was handled.

The ₹5.8LCr Sagarmala flagship scheme was launched by Modi in April 2016. It has 839 projects divided into five pillars and 24 categories—Port-Led Industrialisation, Coastal Community Development, Coastal Shipping and Inland Water Transport (IWT), Port Modernisation, and Port Connectivity.

Out of this, 262 projects of ₹1.4044LCr were complete by March 2024 and 577 projects of ₹4.3836LCr were under various stages of development.

For the 'Holistic Development of Coastal Districts', 567 projects with an estimated cost of ₹58,000Cr have been identified.

To propel India to the forefront of the Global Maritime Sector, the Modi Government formulated Maritime India Vision 2030 (MIV 2030) in 2020—a blueprint to ensure coordinated and accelerated growth of the maritime sector, shipping and inland waterways, in consultation with more than 350 public and private sector stakeholders.

More than 250 brainstorming sessions, studies of over 100 global benchmarks and analysis of over 50 Acts and laws (including state and environmental) led to the development of MIV 2030.

MIV 2030 identified more than 150 initiatives across 10 themes and was a comprehensive effort to define India's national maritime objectives. It identified key interventions in 4 areas—Capacity Augmentation, Developing World-class Mega Ports, Developing a Transhipment Hub in South India, and Infrastructure Modernisation.

Building upon MIV 2030, the Maritime Amrit Kaal Vision 2047 (MAKV 2047) report with more than 300 initiatives/actionable points was prepared in 2022 as a more comprehensive roadmap for maritime transformation in the next 25 years. MAKV 2047 calls for a whopping investment of ₹75–80LCr.

India's Maritime Vision	Actual in 2020	MIV 2030 Targets	MAKV 2047 Aspirations	Achieved by FY24
Overall Capacity of all Ports	1800mtpa		8412mtpa	2605MT
Total Cargo Handled by All Ports	1307MT	2165MT	5468MT	~1555MT
Number of Major Ports	12		14	13
Number of Transshipment Hubs	1		3	1
Major Ports with LNG Bunkering facilities	1		8	3
Cargo Handled at PPP Berths of Major Ports	51%	>85%	100%	
No. of Hydrogen/Ammonia Hub Ports	0		14	Development of 04 ports started
Share of Renewable Energy at Major Ports	<10%	>60%		
Avg. Vessel Turnaround Time (Containers)	25hrs	<20hrs		21.5hrs
Average Container Dwell Time	55hrs	<40hrs		30.22hrs
Average Output per Ship Berthday	16,500 tons	>30,000 tons		18,829 tons
Number of Inland Waterways	22		50+	23
Cargo Volume Handled by Waterways	109MT		>500MT	134+MT
Global Rank in Ship Building	22	Top 10	Top 5	19
CRUISE SECTOR				
Annual Cruise Passengers	468,000	>1.5M	5M	>493,000
Passenger Volume Rank in Asia Pacific	No. 4		No. 1	
Ports in Top 20 for Cruise Services in A-Pac	1		4	
Number of Cruise Terminals	6		25	

Sources: https://ga7a.short.gy/0dihkD; https://ga7a.short.gy/WxSxWN

Six port clusters (Cochin–Vizhinjam cluster, Galathea South Bay Port, Chennai–Kamarajar–Cuddalore cluster, Paradip and other Non-Major Ports cluster, Deendayal–Tuna Tekra, and JNPT–Vadhavan) are being developed as mega ports by 2047.

To achieve the vision of becoming among the Top 10 shipbuilders in the world by 2030, the Modi Government is in the process of inviting global tenders for two mega shipbuilding parks, one each on the East and West coasts. Two more will be developed by 2037-2040.

The average Turn Around Time of cargo ships at major Indian ports is now only 0.9 days, against 1.5 days in the US and 1.7 days in Australia.

The average Container Dwell Time at 13 major ports was only 30.22 hours in FY24, compared with 4 days in countries like South Africa and the UAE, 7 days in the US, and 10 days in Germany.

India reached Rank 22 in international shipment category in the World Bank's Logistics Performance Index (LPI) Report 2023, compared with the 44th rank in 2014.

Vadhavan Port

A ₹76,220Cr major port is being developed by JNPT at Palghar district, about 122km north of Mumbai Airport, with DP World (Dubai), a company that operates in more than 70 countries and handles 9 per cent of the world's container throughput. DP World already operates five Port Container Terminals in India, including two at JNPT. With a capacity of 298MT, Vadhavan Port will become India's largest port.

In December 2024, Vadhavan Port awarded the contract for near-shore reclamation and shore protection to a company that has worked on all 13 major ports and most of the minor ports. This is a key step in building the core infrastructure for the project.

International Cruise Terminal, Mumbai

The first-of-its-kind iconic sea cruise terminal in India is moving towards completion at Ballard Pier Extension berth of Mumbai Port and is expected to open by June 2025. It has a capacity of 200 cruise ships and 700,000 passengers/year and can berth two cruise ships at a time, with a total BUA of 415,000 SFT, 22 elevators, 10 escalators, and multi-storied car parking for 300 cars. Around 61 per cent of the total project cost is being incurred by Mumbai Port Authority and the remaining by private operators.

Inland Water Transport

India has over 14,850km of rivers, canals and other waterways, and 121 notified National Waterways, but there is still huge untapped potential. IWT is popular worldwide for its fuel efficiency, cost effectiveness and environmental friendliness, especially for bulk goods, hazardous goods and over dimensional cargo.

Cargo tonnage went up from 18.07MT in FY14 to 132.89MT in FY24 (up 635.4 per cent) via 22 operational waterways. Another 14 waterways have been sanctioned.

Ocean Development

About 30 per cent of India's population lives on the coast and derives their livelihoods from the oceans.

The Modi Government established a state-of-the-art observation, data, modelling, and forecasting systems covering ocean, coast, and atmospheric domains to serve a broad spectrum of Blue Economy stakeholders, ranging from farmers to coastal fishermen.

Tsunami Early Warnings and other important ocean services related to coral bleaching, harmful algal blooms, high waves, swell surges, oil spill trajectories, marine search, and rescue information, etc., have been activated for India and 25 Indian Ocean Rim countries. Average errors reduced from 93km in 2013 to 74km in 2017 for 24-hour forecasts, and 201km in 2018 to 153km in 2022 for 72-hour forecasts.

A Comprehensive Records Database containing around 120,000 records of more than 6,500 marine species has already been created.

Innovative coastal engineering techniques are being implemented to restore the various beaches lost due to erosion in Kerala, Odisha, Puducherry, and Tamil Nadu.

Coastal Regions

The Chandra Shekhar Government in 1991 made Coastal Regulation Zone (CRZ) rules to regulate activities up to 500m from seas/bays and up to 100m on banks of rivers/backwaters (excluding lakes).

In 2011, the UPA permitted forests, agriculture/horticulture, gardens, parks; notified special provisions for Greater Mumbai, Goa, Kerala; increased 100m to 200m for other water bodies and included lakes; froze the Floor Space Index (FSI) or Floor Area Ratio (FAR) (both are terms used for the BUA a building is permitted to have on a particular piece of land) in Urban CRZ areas to 1991 DCR levels; and retained all other curbs. The maze of regulations stifled development of 83 coastal districts, making it extremely difficult for communities in coastal regions.

In Dubai, Muscat, Hong Kong, New York City, Miami, and other coastal cities, there are buildings on the coastline. Sea-facing office and residential buildings enjoy premiums in rentals or sale prices.

In January 2019, the Modi Government amended the CRZ with a balance between environmental and developmental priorities, to promote sustainable development based on scientific principles.

The new rules permitted FSI/FAR as per 2018 DCR levels, permitted tourism infrastructure (such as shacks, toilet blocks, and changing rooms) on beaches, reduced the 200m restriction to 50m for densely populated areas (2161 persons/km^2 as per 2011 Census), and reduced the 'No Development Zone' to 20m for islands close to the mainland coast as well as backwater islands within the mainland.

Water Metro

India's first Water Metro started in Kochi (formerly Cochin, Kerala's largest city) in April 2023 with eight fast, electrical hybrid boats. When fully operational, it will connect Kochi's 10 island communities with the mainland through 78 electric hybrid boats (23 were operating by 2024), 38 terminals (nine operational) and 16 routes (four operational) spanning 76km. It has been planned for a daily ridership of 150,000 (average 5,850 in April–December 2024).

In November 2024, the GoI's Ministry of Ports, Shipping, and Waterways assigned Kochi Metro Rail Limited (KMRL) with the task of conducting a feasibility study to assess the potential for similar water metro systems in other parts of India. KMRL has already begun a feasibility study to explore the viability of water metro in Kollam (Kerala) and 17 locations in other states.

53

Namami Gange, Riverfronts, River Cruises

'It's my destiny to serve Maa Ganga,'[1] said PM Modi when he was elected in May 2014 to Parliament from Varanasi (Uttar Pradesh), India's spiritual capital, situated on the banks of the 'Holy Ganga'. He kept his word with the 'Namami Gange'—National Mission for Clean Ganga—to arrest the pollution and revive the river, not just because of its cultural importance but also because over 40 per cent of India's population resides in its catchment area. It was launched in June 2014 to rejuvenate Ganga and 15 tributaries.

The status of 488 projects as of December 2024 is as below:

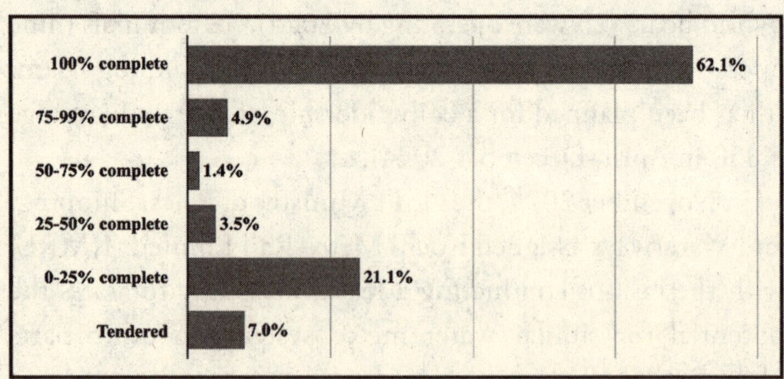

One of the most notable achievements is substantial enhancement in the water quality and rehabilitation of polluted sections. Increased sightings of endangered aquatic species prove the project is working. Over 9.3M Indian major carps and 90,000 Hilsa fish have been reintroduced into the Ganga Basin, bolstering the river's ecosystem.

Namami Gange was in the Top 10 'World Restoration Flagships' at UN Conference on Biological Diversity in Montreal in December 2022.

Clean Riverfronts

As the CM of Gujarat, Modi developed the 11.3km Sabarmati Riverfront in Ahmedabad with 20–60ft wide two-level Promenades with lifts/escalators, parking bays, cycle tracks, and 1,641 vendor platforms; pedestrian bridge connecting both banks; 14 washroom complexes, three ghats; 11ac Paldi Sports Park with five sports academies; 1.9ac Shahpur Sports Park; two water sports stations; event centre (stage, VIP lounge, and parking); six parks of 56ac; 12.5ac events ground for 50,000 people; and a 7-floor multi-level car parking for 1,000 cars, 700 two-wheelers and EV charging points. More than 135,000 trees have been planted. There is a floating restaurant and a riverfront cruise. A 2.32ac Dhobi (washer man/woman) campus has seven state-of-the-art blocks with wet areas, drying on terraces, water, electricity, drainage system, vehicle access, and dedicated parking. The Riverfront has hosted many world leaders including President Xi Jinping of China and Late PM Shinzo Abe of Japan. Over 25,000 people visit daily. The under development 260ac Phase 2 with a 5.5ac riverfront will have commercial and residential buildings apart from public spaces. On completion of all five phases, the 38.3km length will make it the world's longest riverfront.

In Jaipur, the 47.5km Dravyavati River has been cleaned and 3 gardens developed, including a bird park. Beautiful riverfronts have been developed in Srinagar, Guwahati, and many other places.

A 2.7km riverfront in Kota (Rajasthan) has been developed with 27 ghats represented by 27 unique architectural styles of Rajputana rulers.

River Cruises

Modi encouraged the concept of river cruises in India and several companies took the bait. There are three main cruise routes—Ganga River, Brahmaputra River, Pathsala River in Odisha, and the backwaters of Kerala, which have cruises of 3–50 nights each.

MV Ganga Vilas has the longest river cruise in the world. Covering 51 days across 2 countries, 5 states, and 27 river systems, it sails from Varanasi to Dibrugarh via Dhaka (Bangladesh).

Inland Waterways Development Council (set up in the Modi-era) has committed ₹45,000Cr for developing river cruise tourism.

54

River Interlinking

India is home to about 17.76 per cent of the world's human as well as livestock population, but just 4 per cent of the world's freshwater resources. Thanks to past governments and generations, we have the most unclean water resources—be it surface or underground water.

The average rainfall is about 4,000 billion cubic metres (BCM) per year, but about 75 per cent comes between June and September. The north and east get more rainfall than the south and west. India also has frequent floods in the north and east, and drought in the west and south. This geographical and time variance in the natural supply versus the year-round demand creates a gap that has been worsening with a rising population. As a result, only about 25 per cent of rainwater is used.

The per capita availability of fresh water has declined from 3,000m^3 to 1,450m^3 over the past 60 years. The global average is 6,000m^3.

India's water storage capacity of 257.8BCM equals only about 84 days of demand; developed nations store 900 days. We rely excessively (65 per cent) on groundwater to feed over 50 per cent of irrigated area with over 2.6Cr tube-wells. The situation is extremely critical, and India needs sustainable management of surface and groundwater.

The answer to India's water problem is to store abundant monsoon water in reservoirs and deliver it by using Interlinked Rivers to areas and over time periods when and where water becomes scarce. Beyond water security, the project also offers benefits to transport (shipping has a low-carbon footprint) and will broaden income sources in rural areas with fish farming.

With an increase of about 1.31Cr persons per year, there is rising demand for food, which needs adequate irrigation.

A National Perspective Plan for interlinking rivers was formulated in 1980 with a Himalayan Component and a Peninsular Component. Vajpayee proposed it in 2002, but lost the 2004 election.

Dr Singh initiated it in 2005, but the project was scrapped when Rahul Gandhi said interlinking rivers was dangerous.

In August 2017, Modi announced a ₹5.56LCr plan to connect over 60 rivers, with nearly 210BCM storage or about 68 days' requirement. This will take storage capacity to 152 days, enable irrigation of additional 8.65Cr acres land and add 40GW hydropower.

Though the project will take several years to implement, the benefits will be availed by crores of Indians for decades. ₹5,259Cr has been spent on various feasibility studies and DPRs for 15 projects.

Implementation of the Ken-Betwa Link Project, at an estimated cost of ₹44,605Cr has started. It will provide irrigation benefits to 9,081km^2 of farmers' lands, drinking water for 6.2M people, 103MW of hydropower and 27MW of solar power.

DPRs for six link canals, draft DPRs for two, and feasibility reports for five have been finalised.

Once consensus is reached among the states that will benefit from each of these links, the Modi Government will provide support for their implementation.

55

Delhi Capitals

The National Capital Region (NCR) is the world's largest defined metropolitan area by size (55,083km^2) and population (74.1M in end-2024). It includes 26 districts in Delhi, Uttar Pradesh, Haryana, and Rajasthan.

Several mega/large infrastructure projects have been completed in the past 10 years or are under development.

All railway lines in the NCR are planned to be widened to 4-track by 2030 and 6-track by 2040.

Delhi Development Authority (DDA) has identified 50ac along Urban Extension Road (UER)-II in Northwest Delhi for a cricket stadium, a 5-star hotel and a world-class hospital. It is also identifying other lands there to create infrastructure for football, hockey and other Olympic sports, to strengthen Delhi's claims to host the 2040 or 2044 Olympics and promote development in the area.

The NCR will have five ring roads: (1) Inner Ring Road; (2) Outer Ring Road; (3) 271km KGP+KMP; (4) UER-II + 56km FNG Expressway; (5) part of Dwarka Expressway, KMP, Gurgaon–Sohna Elevated Corridor, Sohna–Faridabad section of Delhi–Mumbai Expressway, and 47km Ghaziabad–Narela Expressway.

Developing NCR	Length	Status as of December 2024	Notes
RRTS = Regional Rapid Transit System (The Name Bharat trains run up to 160 kmph, twice the speed of Metro Rail. They have several new signalling technologies used for the first time in the world.); ORC = Orbital Rail Corridor			
Delhi-Ghaziabad-Meerut RRTS	82 km	55km is operational; balance to open by July 2025	
Delhi-Gurugram-SNB-Alwar RRTS	164 km	The Arvind Kejriwal Govt in Delhi was refusing to commit their financial share of the development cost of both projects. Now that Delhi's commuters have been praising the Delhi-Meerut RRTS, the AAP Govt should clear the project soon	
Delhi-Sonipat-Panipat RRTS	103 km		
Palwal-Sohna-Manesar-Kharkhoda-Harsana Kalan (near Sonipat) ORC	122 km	First 31.74km to start by Sept 2025 and 100% expected to start by August 2026	
Panipat-Rohtak-Rewari-Palwal-Khurja-Hapur-Meerut ORC	372 km	Expected to start by June 2031	
Sonipat-Sampla-Jhajjar-Gurgaon-Faridabad-Dadri ORC	157 km	Awaiting GOI approval	
6-lane KGP Expressway	135 km	Construction started Sep 2015; Completed May 2018	*Both projects were announced by UPA, but work did not start till Modi became PM.*
6-lane KMP Expressway	136 km	Construction started May 2016; Completed Nov 2018 *(it had been planned as a 4-lane road by the UPA)*	
16-lane Dwarka Expressway (DWE)	29.1 km	Mahipalpur (Delhi)-Kherki Daula Toll Plaza (Gurugram) connects with Delhi-Mumbai Expressway; 19km opened in March 2024; 10.1km expected to open by April 2025; a Metro Rail corridor has been planned alongside the Gurugram section	*Planned in 2006 by the UPA as a 6-lane 18km road, only 14km was completed in 7yrs*
Faridabad-Noida-Ghaziabad (FNG)	56 km	20km Noida section expected to open by July 2025; balance by September 2027	
12-lane Urban Extension Rd-II (UER-II)	75 km	38.8km main road starts near Splash Water Park in North Delhi and ends at Mahipalpur, where it meets DWE; There is a 29.6km Sonipat spur and a 7.3km Bahadurgarh spur; 9.6km opened inMar24; entire road to open by June 2025	
8-lane IGIA Airport Tunnel	5 km	This connects Dwarka Expressway and UER-II; Expected be ready by September 2025	
Phase-2 of UER-II	15 km	Rangpuri Bypass to Vasant Kunj; upgraded Nelson Mandela Marg to new interchange at Andheria Mor, Anuvrat Marg-Mehrauli-Badarpur Road intersection.	
Phase-3 of UER-II	155 km	Badarpur Interchange-Okhla Bird Sanctuary-DND Flyway; Chilla-Splash Water Park. Spurs include Burari-Ghaziabad-Okhla and Agraula-Jawli. Connects with the Delhi-Dehradun Expressway and the FNG Expressway.	
Circular Expressway-1 (planned)	~950 km	Karnal-Muzzafarnagar-Hapur-Aligarh-Mathura-Agra-Alwar-Bhiwani-Karnal	
Circular Expressway-2 (planned)	~570 km	Panipat-Rewari-Nuh-Jewar-Panipat	
Zonal Expressway-1 (planned)	Bareilly-Dehradun-Rishikesh-Nainital covers a catchment area of ~106,000km2		
Zonal Expressway-2 (planned)	Hisar-Agra-Hathras-Sambhal-Moradabad-Amroha-Bijnor-Roorkee-Kurukshetra; Catchment Area of around 125,000km2		
Zonal Expressway-3 (planned)	Agroha-Patiala-Chandigarh-Haridwar-Bareilly-Firozabad-Jaipur Catchment Area of around 220,000km2		

Noida International Airport (aka Jewar Airport) is being developed by Zürich Airport of Switzerland. Phase 1 will have 1 runway and 12mppa capacity and is expected to open by July 2025. Once all phases are completed by 2050, it will span 48.6km^2 with 8 runways and a capacity of 70mppa. This airport was proposed by then Uttar Pradesh CM Rajnath Singh in 2001 and approved by the Vajpayee

Government in April 2003, but like most other projects, the UPA put it on hold. Modi re-approved it within 13 months of becoming PM. The airport will have several transportation linkages including Delhi Metro, Delhi–Mumbai Expressway and with the existing Indira Gandhi International Airport (IGIA) in Delhi, the world's 9th busiest airport.

By March 2025, Air India Express is also starting domestic flights from the civil terminal of the Hindon Air Force base near Ghaziabad (UP), which currently has a civilian passenger capacity of 2.6mppa.

With three airports, the NCR will have a capacity of 144.6mppa by 2027, overtaking New York City (seven airports, 133mppa). As of December 2024, London has the highest capacity of 222mppa with six airports, Beijing has 176mppa with two airports and Shanghai 121mppa with two airports. Dubai has planned a capacity of 350mppa with two airports by 2030, which will make it the largest air passenger hub in the world.

56

Central Vista Remake

By 2026, the GoI will have infrastructure that is more modern than any other nation's capital. The Central Vista Project (CVP) involves a massive redevelopment of the 919ac that abuts the 2.9km Kartavya Path (earlier Rajpath) from Rashtrapati Bhavan to India Gate.

Designed by the British using exemplary planning practices, the area underwent multiple changes after 1947. A cross street and node was added due to traffic. Public spaces and pedestrian paths degraded over time. Road junctions were dangerous, there was haphazard parking, and no proper vendor facilities. Green spaces became fading landscapes, with dry canals. Increased land use, waste generation, and crowding resulted in extensive pollution.

North and South Block, which have the PMO, the four CCS ministries, and offices of the NSA and the Cabinet Secretariat, have undergone various extensions and alterations. Corridors have pigeon poop and files stored in ugly steel racks due to lack of storage space. Most of the offices (except ministers and senior officers) are overcrowded. The toilets leak and smell. Rats run around.

Other ministry buildings, mostly built between the 1950s and 1970s, have no symmetry or standardisation. There are too many 'closed' rooms (which makes corruption easier) instead of contemporary 'open floor plan' culture. There is inadequate parking.

The GoI has more than 100 rented buildings spread across Delhi. Tens of thousands of employees find it difficult to travel from one building to another in heavy traffic. The government pays over ₹1100Cr/year as rent and estimated ₹360Cr/year on unnecessary security/transport costs.

Most of the old buildings in the Central Vista with total BUA of about 4.94msft have or are being demolished. All 51 ministries will move to 11 eight-storeyed Common Central Secretariat buildings, with a combined BUA of about 13msft, of which 3 are expected to be ready by August 2025.

54,000 persons will work at these 11 buildings in modern 'open floor' layouts with standard designs, so that an officer transferred to a new ministry can adapt easily. Red and yellow sandstone facades match British-era buildings. Large central courtyards increase the natural light to help well-being and productivity, apart from saving costs. Transport and service cores at all corners make movement and maintenance easy. Basements have 6,500 parking spaces. Underground automatic people-movers (like Dubai, Bangkok, Singapore, and other airports) will connect to Delhi Metro and overground e-Shuttles to the Delhi Transport Corporation (DTC) bus network.

The 16.4ac VP Enclave (BUA 0.253msft) with residence, guesthouse, secretariat, and ancillary buildings is complete and the Vice President of India now lives there.

The 20.2ac Executive Enclave (0.99msft) will have the PM's residence, a 4-storeyed PMO (0.51msft), buildings for the SPG that provides security to the PM, National Security Council Secretariat, Cabinet Secretariat, a two-storeyed Bharat Bhavan for the PM to host VVIPs (93,000 SFT), and ancillary buildings. It is expected to be ready by May 2026. Indian PMs currently host visiting world leaders at Hyderabad House (5.4km away). The security convoy is a nuisance for citizens.

The revamped Kartavya Path that was opened for public use in January 2023, has modern/sustainable/upgradeable facilities, parking for 1,116 cars and 40 buses, dedicated spaces for social gatherings/vendor areas, underpasses, camouflaged toilets, and modern way-finding signage. A 'sunken' enclave for media outside broadcasting vans ensures that their satellite dishes are not eyesores.

Environmental Sustainability

No trees were cut due to the CVP. 3,753 trees were planted in the Central Vista, 3,230 transplanted to the 884ac Eco-Park at Badarpur (Asia's largest). The Central Vista has gained 563 trees. In Delhi, 40,573 trees have been/will be planted, including 36,820 in the Eco-Park.

A National Biodiversity Arboretum is planned on the west side of the President's estate (that includes Rashtrapati Bhavan), to showcase endangered plants of India in high-tech greenhouses set amidst indigenous forestations.

By extending the Rashtrapati Bhavan—India Gate axis by 2.24km east to the banks of the Yamuna, a 30ac Nav Bharat Udyan comprises an 'iconic' museum, gardens, and public spaces.

India Gate and National War Museum

India Gate now has a statue of Netaji Subhash Chandra Bose in the empty umbrella where once stood the statue of King George V.

Amar Jawan Jyoti, previously engraved with names of soldiers who fought for the British, has been replaced by a

National War Museum to honour soldiers who died while fighting for India, a long-time demand of the armed forces that was not honoured by past governments.

National Museum

The world's largest museum, the Yuge Yugeen Bharat national museum with a BUA of 1.26msft (950 rooms) that will be built in the North and South Block buildings, will replace the old 0.376mst National Museum and will showcase India's culture spanning over 5,000 years. A Central Plaza will have installations, performances, and public events with options for visitors to enjoy even after museum hours. Giving the 'Raisina Hill' back to the people is a tremendous gesture that reflects Modi's faith in our dynamic democracy and places 'people' at the centre of it.

National Archives of India (NAI)

NAI's buildings have obsolete infrastructure. Chambers lack proper temperature/moisture control, putting priceless documents at risk. Almost all facilities/utilities malfunction. The layout is not suitable for proper document processing/storage. They are being renovated and a new purpose-built facility being created alongside.

Indira Gandhi National Centre for the Arts (IGNCA)

All departments are crammed into just one structure. Water penetration has harmed the floors and the roof. There have been various expansions/adjustments for services such as air-conditioning and cabling throughout the years. A 1986 prize-winning plan by an American architect envisaged a reference library, research wing, tribal/folk arts centre, exhibition galleries, 2,000-seat concert hall, 1,200-seat national theatre, 400-seat Indian theatre, offices, and a residential block. Only the library was built—the rest was never executed. A larger, purpose-built IGNCA facility is being built opposite Hyderabad House, with modern, sustainable facilities and upgradeable infrastructure.

Not Being Built for Modi

There has been a lot of criticism of the CVP, especially the new PM's residence, by Opposition leaders (especially Rahul Gandhi), self-appointed historians who support the Congress mindset, and leftist journalists. Most of the criticism used inflated project costs and blamed Modi for 'building a grand palace for himself'.[2]

The Executive Enclave is built to last for at least 150 years. It is not a 'Modi Palace', but a permanent residence-cum-office for whoever is the 'elected' Prime Minister of India at any given time.

Modi will occupy it for maximum 3 years. Nothing stops Opposition parties from occupying it for the next 147 years if they keep winning the general elections.

Nehru lived in 'Teen Murti Bhavan', but Shastri chose '10 Janpath' (now Sonia Gandhi's residence). Indira Gandhi resided at '1 Safdarjung Road', but Rajiv Gandhi chose '7 Race Course Road' (renamed by Modi as '7 Lok Kalyan Marg'), which is the PM's current residence. No PM in the past created a 'permanent' residence-cum-office.

57

Parliament of the Future

The old Parliament House, now renamed Samvidhan Sadan (Constitution House), was designed as the 'Council House' for 405 members (260 and 145) of British India's Imperial Legislative Council and built between 1921 and 1927.

Despite adding two floors in 1956 and many other modifications over the years, the building was struggling to accommodate 790 MPs (545 in the LS in a hall designed for 260, and 245 in the Rajya Sabha or RS in a hall designed for 145). Very few MPs had offices and almost all parties regularly complained about this over the years. For those MPs who had offices, there was no space for their staff.

India's population went up about 4.28 times since 1947, but LS MPs only went up from 489 to 543.

One Indian LS MP represents 2.685M persons, against 0.107M in the UK on which Nehru modelled our Parliament. Among other parliamentary democracies, it is 0.115M in Germany and 0.265M in Japan.

With 'delimitation' exercises based on population, LS MPs went up from 489 to 494 in 1952, 522 in 1963, and 543 in 1976. Delimitation was suspended for 25 years twice (to 2001 and 2026), as states in the south felt they will get punished for controlling population growth while northern states like Uttar Pradesh and Bihar will get rewarded. The delimitation is unlikely to be postponed in 2026, and the strength of the LS is expected to increase to 750–850. The 99-year-old old Parliament House could not hold even 50 more MPs, leave alone 205–305.

'If UK can have 650 parliamentarians, Canada 443, and the US 535, why can't we have 1,000?' asked President Pranab Mukherjee in December 2019, one of the senior-most Congress leaders for decades.

In July 2012, LS Speaker Meira Kumar's office sent a letter to the housing ministry stating that the Speaker has approved construction of a new Parliament building as the old one is showing signs of distress at various places.

The letter said that the number of MPs may go up after 2026 and this issue should be given 'top priority'.

'We badly need a Parliament building. This one simply isn't functional and is outdated,'[3] said Jairam Ramesh, then a UPA cabinet minister and today one of Rahul Gandhi's top advisors.

Even the new Parliament building has been criticised. Their MPs wanted it, top ministers wanted it, the Speaker wanted it, even their nominee for the post of President of India wanted it, but how could they allow Modi to build it?

In any case, as with so many other projects—some of which we have covered in the book—the UPA slept on it.

Modi took up the construction of Sansad Bhavan (new Parliament House) on a war-footing, wanting to make it ready by the 75th anniversary of India's Independence on 15 August 2022. Fate did not allow this as COVID-19 delayed construction. The Sansad Bhavan was ready in May 2023, and a 'special session' of Parliament was held in it on

19 September 2023. 'If the [old Parliament House] gave direction to post-Independence India, the new building would become a witness to the creation of AatmaNirbhar Bharat,' Modi said.

The 4-storeyed Sansad Bhavan has a BUA of about 0.7msft, about three times the size of the old Parliament House. It has 1,100 car parking spaces. The design takes reference from the old Parliament House and other historical buildings of the Central Vista. Built using green construction techniques, Sansad Bhavan reduces electricity consumption by 30 per cent compared to the old Parliament House. A 3-stage air filtration system with ultraviolet lamps ensures clean and fresh indoor air. Ultrasonic humidifiers maintain desired relative humidity inside. Built to last for at least 150 years, the building is earthquake safe.

The architectural ornamentation of Sansad Bhavan reflects the classical, folk and tribal arts and crafts of India. A 21ft-high bronze sculpture of the National Emblem of India crowns the new building.

The LS Hall has 888 seats, but can accommodate 1,272 in a 'joint session' of the Parliament, which used to be held in a 'central hall' in the old Parliament House. The RS Hall has 384 seats.

Along with offices of the PM and PMO staff, 72 ministers, the entire Ministry of Parliamentary Affairs, LS and RS Secretariats, Sansad Bhavan also has publicly accessible galleries and exhibits. The Constitution Hall and Gallery showcase the Constitution of India and other artefacts of India's heritage for public viewing, symbolically and physically putting people at the heart of the Indian democracy. There is a dining hall for MPs, a library, and six committee rooms (there were only three in the old Parliament House).

Features in the LS and RS halls include a desk in every MP's seat (the old Parliament House had these only in the front rows) and enough space behind seats for free movement. Each bench has only two seats, so no MP has to cross another to move in or out.

There are smart displays, a touchscreen-based Digital Voting System with dual authentication using biometrics, intuitive Multilingual Graphical User Interface, digital language interpretation, programmable microphones, and recording infrastructure to produce real-time metadata.

The old Parliament House will be suitably retrofitted as per heritage conservation standards and refurbished to be earthquake-proof, safe from fire risks and fit for use. It will continue to be used for parliamentary functions including offices of MPs and their staff.

Myths were spread that the triangular shape of Sansad Bhavan is against the principles of 'Vastu'. The endpoints of the 'triangle' have been cut to create angles on all sides. The resultant shape creates BG3 energies that have been used in lakhs of temples, mosques, and churches built in the last 4,650 years. BG3 energies are very beneficial for all of us at all levels of consciousness—physical, emotional, mental, and spiritual.

58

Maximum City

Mumbai Metropolitan Region is the world's 6th largest by area (6328km^2) and 5th by population (26M).

Mumbai @ Maximum	Length	Status	Benefits
A Congress-NCP Government was in power in Maharashtra from Oct 1999 to Sept 2014 —— MMRDA (Mumbai Metropolitan Region Development Authority) was controlled by Congress and MSRDC (Maharashtra State Road Development Corporation) by NCP			
6-lane Atal Setu (Mumbai Trans Harbour Link) MSRDC invited bids in 2004, 2005, and 2008, but project did not move due to fights with MMRDA; Govt of Maharashtra gave MMRDA the authority; Bids invited in 2011; Project cleared by CM in October 2012 and the GOI cleared it in January 2013. No contractor submitted bids as they were unhappy with Congress's policies (was it KICKBACKS?)	21.8 km	Construction started in April 2018 after the BJP came to power in the Centre and the state; India's longest sea bridge connects the island city to the rest of India via Navi Mumbai **Opened in Jan2024**	Labour and material are coming to South Mumbai via Atal Setu instead of via Thane and beyond, thus helping businesses. Annual savings of 10cr litres' fuel are estimated due to the shorter distance
4-lane Sewri-Worli Elevated Connector (SWEC)	4.5 km	Late 2026	Connects Atal Setu with Worli Seaface
Shivaji Nagar-Ulwe Interchange		2025	Together will connect Atal Setu with NMIA Airport and JNPT Port
6-lane Ulwe Coastal Road (UCR), Navi Mumbai	5.8 km	2026	
4-lane Khargar Coastal Rd (KCR), Navi Mumbai	9.6 km	2027	Will connect Kharghar to CBD Belapur.
6-lane Orange Gate to Marine Drive Tunnel (10.5ft wide each)	4.46 km	Late 2026	Connect Marine Drive at the southern end of MCR with Orange Gate near the southern end of Eastern Freeway
Chirle-Palaspe (two 6-lane elevated roads)		2027	Chirle to Gavhan Phata; Palaspe to Mumbai-Pune Expressway
8-lane Mumbai Coastal Road (MCR) **Phase-1** (including 02 BRTS lanes)	10.58 km	Partly Opened in March 2024; Will be fully operational by May 2025	Has reduced the travel time between Marine Drive and Worli by 33-66%
8-lane Mumbai Coastal Road (MCR) **Phase-2** (02 BRTS) — length includes 12.57km VBCR	19.22 km	Awaiting VBCR to be completed as the 19.22km includes the 12.57km of VBCR	Will reduce travel time between Bandra and Kandivali by 33-66%
8-lane Versova-Bandra Coastal Road (VBCR) (including 02 BRTS lanes)	12.57 km	Work started October 2018 but <3% was done till January 2022 when one of the contractors pulled out due to financial trouble and was replaced; Only ~25% work is complete	Apart from the main 12.57km sea bridge, there is a 6-lane, 1.8km Carter Road Connector and a 4-lane, 2.8km Juhu-Koliwada Connector
Pre-feasibility studies for 2 Coastal Roads (MCR & VBCR) were done in 2007-08; Congress-NCP Govt only approved them in Jan 2014			
6-lane Thane Borivali Twin Tunnel (TBTT)	11.84 km	Will run under Sanjay Gandhi National Park (SGNP); Travel time will reduce by 63-80%; Expected completion by 2028	
10-lane Goregaon Mulund Link Road (GMLR)	12.2 km	4.7km 6-lane twin tunnels under SNGP; Travel time will reduce by 33-75%; Expected completion by 2030	
Versova-Dahisar Coastal Road (VDCR)	22.93 km	Includes 4.46km connector to GMLR; Work started Feb 2024; Expected late 2028	
8-lane Versova-Virar Sea Link (VVSL)	79.11 km	Will start from VBC;. Length includes four 6-lane connectors of 35.36km; New consultant has to do Peer Review of DPR prepared by Pentacle-Cemosa JV	
6-lane VVSL Extension to Palghar	26.3 km	Consultant to be appointed for preparing the DPR	
6-lane Airoli-Katai Naka Freeway (AKNF)	13.7 km	About 7.4km will be completed by May 2025; When fully complete, the AKNF will benefit those traveling between Mumbai, Kalyan and Badlapur Industrial Estate	
SOURCES: https://bit.ly/TMRG and Various Media Reports			

Suketu Mehta's book *Maximum City* talks about the ills of Bombay (now Mumbai). The Table on the previous page shows you what all the Modi Government has done and is continuing to do to make the city well.

Phase-1 of Adani's 20mppa Navi Mumbai International Airport (NMIA) is expected to open by August–September 2025. Once all four phases are complete by 2036, it will have two runways and 90mppa capacity.

Redevelopment of Dharavi Slum

Featured in the multiple-Oscar-winning film Slumdog Millionaire, the 590.6ac slum (with an established population 0.9–1M with 58,000–80,000 families and about 12,000 commercial establishments) is one of the world's most densely populated areas.

Starting in the 1950s, there were many redevelopment proposals, but all failed due to lack of proper financial backing or political support.

In November 2022, the Adani Group won a bid to redevelop Dharavi, with 20 per cent stake of Government of Maharashtra. The estimated cost is ₹23,000Cr and timeline 7–10 years.

Under current byelaws, almost 110msft can be built.

Before June 2025, Adani is expected to submit a detailed master plan with designated areas for rehab/free-sale buildings, playgrounds, parks, schools, hospitals, etc. The Government of Maharashtra will take a final call on the plan and suggest changes, if any.

Adani has committed new flats of 350SFT with kitchen and toilet, about 11 per cent bigger than current slum rehab housing.

Residents not eligible for free rehab homes within Dharavi will be offered subsidised homes within a 10km radius. The Government of Maharashtra will identify land parcels, Adani will buy the lands, construct the homes, and transfer free ownership to the Government of Maharashtra, which will then decide the price and sell them to ineligible residents who wish to buy them.

A Third Mumbai

After Mumbai and Navi Mumbai, MMRDA is working on a master plan to develop a smart city of 334km^2 named 'NAINA' with 100 per cent green energy near NMIA airport. It also abuts JNPT, Atal Setu, and Mumbai–Pune Expressway.

There will be a 1,000ac Tourism Zone with a mega amusement park and hotels in this zone.

59

New Tourist Havens

Apart from the 6 iconic religious destinations covered in Part X of this book, Modi has already created or is creating several other iconic tourist destinations that are not based on religion.

Statue of Unity (Sardar Sarovar Dam, Gujarat)

The world's tallest statue at 597ft (787.4ft with base) is built with 134.3 tons of iron donated by thousands of villagers. It is a testimonial to Former Deputy PM and Home Minister 'Sardar' Vallabhbhai Patel, known as 'the Iron Man of India', for his role in getting 562 'princely states' (about 48 per cent of independent India's land area) to join the Indian Union, after the British left without deciding their fate.

Many tourist attractions have been developed in the complex and a 3km radius around it.

There were 5.83M visitors in 2024 and over 23M in 74 months since the opening, despite 19 months being lost to COVID-19. This is significant because the Statue of Unity was subjected to a smear campaign by Modi-haters such as Dhruv Rathee, Deshbhakt and Ravish Kumar (former NDTV Hindi anchor), and others who said the project would be a grand failure.

Pradhanmantri Sangrahalaya (New Delhi)

This newly built museum at Teen Murti Estate (Nehru's residence) pays tribute to every PM since 1947. Holograms, augmented/virtual reality, multimedia, interactive kiosks, computerised kinetic sculptures, interactive screens, etc., make the experience highly interactive.

Panchteerth

Four places associated with Dr B.R. Ambedkar have been developed, apart from the memorial in Dr Ambedkar Nagar (formerly Mhow) in Madhya Pradesh—Ambedkar Memorial in London; Deeksha Bhoomi where he converted to Buddhism; Dr Ambedkar National Memorial at Mahaparininirvan Sthal in Delhi is shaped like an open Constitution amidst expansive landscaped gardens; and the 2-storey stupa-style structure at Chaitya Bhoomi in Mumbai, where he was laid to rest.

Mahatma Gandhi Sabarmati Ashram (Ahmedabad)

Mahatma Gandhi mostly lived at the 32ac Sabarmati Ashram (built in June 1917), when not travelling or not in prison. In March 1930, he led the Dandi March from there. The museum, built within the Ashram complex in 1964, and the Ashram itself have deteriorated over the decades and they do not befall the stature of the Mahatma.

In 2020, Modi came up with the idea to redevelop them and appointed his trusted architect Bimal Patel (famous for Sabarmati Riverfront in Ahmedabad, Kashi Vishwanath Corridor, Central Vista, and the new Parliament House) to redesign the complex.

The Ashram is being expanded as a 55ac attraction with 36 heritage properties, an amphitheatre, VIP lounge, a 2nd museum, food court, shops, etc., with about 322ac around it also being developed.

The project started three years late due to a Public Interest Litigation (PIL) by Tushar Gandhi (one of Mahatma's grandsons) who claimed the Ashram would lose its ethos if redeveloped. The PIL was junked twice by the Gujarat High Court, and the SCI did not interfere.

Jallianwala Bagh Memorial (Amritsar, Punjab)

About 1,500 civilians were killed and more than 1,200 injured in the Jallianwala Bagh massacre in April 1919, when Col. REH Dyer ordered British Indian Army soldiers to fire on a peaceful crowd protesting the arrest of pro-Independence activists and a draconian Act passed by the British Government. The memorial at the site was filthy and unbecoming.

The revamped Jallianwala Bagh Memorial complex (opened in August 2021) has a granite 'Jalkund', black granite pillars dedicated to the martyrs with quotes of famous freedom fighters, glass-panelled façade of the historic well where hundreds jumped to escape the firing, framed bullet marks, and the narrow entrance street walls embossed with murals depicting people who came to the protest. A 'light and sound show' depicts the events; a documentary showcases the history of the freedom struggle and WWI. Galleries showcase the freedom movement, history of all 10 Sikh Gurus and Sikh ruler Maharaja Ranjit Singh, and the ancient civilisation of Punjab.

60

Promoting Tourism

Swadesh Darshan Scheme was launched by the GoI in FY15 to provide financial support to state and UT governments to develop tourism infrastructure at various destinations, and 15 theme-based circuits were identified. Though 76 projects were sanctioned by FY18, only 66 were able to achieve 90–100 per cent completion in five years.

Due to shortcomings, in 2022, the scheme was revamped as Swadesh Darshan 2.0 in which 36 cities were identified. Swadesh Darshan 2.0 has compulsory benchmarks and standards which states must follow while planning and developing projects. The major themes are Eco-Tourism, Culture and Heritage Tourism, Adventure Tourism, Beach Tourism, Rural Tourism, Wellness Tourism, Cruises (Ocean and Inland), and MICE or Meetings, Incentives, Conferences, and Exhibitions. There are 2 sites each in 18 states/UTs, of which 11 did not have BJP governments. Comprehensive Master Plans have been developed for 15 cities and others are being developed.

Other Initiatives

Other than 36 cities under Swadesh Darshan 2.0, 15 sites are being developed as Iconic Tourist Destinations—Taj Mahal and Fatehpur Sikri in Agra, Uttar Pradesh; Kaziranga Wildlife Sanctuary in Assam; Mahabodhi Temple at Bodh Gaya in Bihar; Humayun's Tomb, Red Fort, and Qutub Minar in Delhi; Kevadia and Somnath in Gujarat; Amer Fort in Jaipur; Khajuraho in Madhya Pradesh; Ajanta and Ellora Caves in Maharashtra; Sun Temple in Konark, Odisha; and Golconda Fort in Hyderabad, Telangana.

Millions of people working in small hotels/dhabas/travel agencies, airports, monuments, railway/bus/police stations, or as guides, coolies, taxi/coach drivers, etc., encounter foreign tourists and the tourists' experiences with them influences their opinion of India. Any bad experience gets posted on social media channels and often gets amplified. A scheme was formulated to train these service providers to upgrade their behaviour and service skills.

Areas being covered include cleanliness, personal hygiene, basic service techniques, cooking techniques, garbage disposal, basic manners and etiquette, basic tourism awareness, communication skills, first aid, and client handling. The duration of the courses are 4–6 days.

Here are some more initiatives:

- The 12.44km Govindghat–Ghangharia–Hemkund Sahib Gurudwara ropeway will connect to the gateway of Valley of Flowers National Park and reduce travel time from 10–12 hours on the 19km steep and tough foot track to just 45–50 minutes.
- Another 17 ropeway projects are planned across India with the main purpose of cutting down travel time. An added benefit is that in most places, travellers get scenic views from high up.

- An Auli Development Authority is being set up to prepare a plan for developing the picturesque town in Chamoli district as a major skiing destination and implementing it.
- A National Maritime Heritage Complex is being set up on 400ac in Lothal, Gujarat.
- By opening the doors to India's captivating locales, vibrant rituals, rich gastronomy, and world-class infrastructure, the GoI is trying to change foreigners' perception about India being suitable only for royal, extravagant weddings through the Wed in India scheme. The objective is to enthral foreign couples and entice them to host their wedding in India.
- The tourism ministry, in collaboration with Indian embassies and consulates abroad, has been taking part in several travel/tourism exhibitions.

The tourism sector generated almost 285M direct and indirect jobs between FY20 and FY23.

As a result of the initiatives taken by the Modi Government to promote tourism and the booming economy, major global hotel chains have changed their expansion plans for India.

During 2019, the contribution of travel and tourism to the Indian economy was 6.8 per cent of GDP, or ₹13.68LCr.

Huge Expansion by Global Hotel Chains		Actual Mar 2024	Target by 2030	Growth
RADISSON	Radisson, Park Plaza, Park Inn, Country Inns & Suites	115	265	▲ 130.4%
MARRIOTT	Ritz Carlton, St. Regis, JW Marriott, W, Sheraton, Westin, Le Meridien, Renaissance, Courtyard by Marriott, Fairfield, Four Points by Sheraton, Aloft, Residence Inn by Marriott	150	250	▲ 66.7%
WYNDHAM	Ramada by Wyndham, Ramada Encore by Wyndham, Howard Johnson by Wyndham, Trademark Collection, etc.	59	140	▲ 137.3%
IHG	Six Senses, Intercontinental, Crowne Plaza, Holiday Inn, Holiday Inn Express	46	100	▲ 117.4%
HILTON	Waldorf Astoria, Conrad, Hilton, Doubletree, Hampton, Embassy Suites, Hilton Garden Inn, Homewood Suites	26	120	▲ 361.5%
HYATT	Park Hyatt, Andaz, Grand Hyatt, Hyatt Regency, Hyatt, Hyatt Place, Alila, Hyatt Centric, JdV by Hyatt	51	93-95	▲ 82-86%

Inbound foreign tourists went up from average 5.3M during 2004–13 to 9.671M during 2015–19 (up 82.5 per cent).

Forex earnings from tourism went up from $18.445B in 2013 to $30.058B in 2019 (up 63 per cent in 6 years).

After 2019, tourism was affected by COVID-19, the Russia-Ukraine war and Israel's conflicts with Hamas, Hezbollah, Palestine and Iran.

However, tourism did revive slightly in 2023 with 9.52M foreign tourists (total 18.89M international tourists including NRIs/OCIs) with Forex earnings of $27.7B, and the estimated number for 2024 is a record 9.92M with record Forex earnings of over $30.7B.

61

GIFT City

With a vision to become a leading global financial and FinTech hub, the 886ac GIFT City (Gujarat International Finance Tec-City) was set up in October 2015 along Sabarmati River between Ahmedabad and Gandhinagar. The idea was germinated by Modi as CM of Gujarat and GIFT City has become an integral part of India's growth story. Phase 2 of around 2,470ac is coming up along a 4.5km riverfront.

The 62msft of BUA includes a Domestic Tariff Area for businesses related to India, a Multipurpose SEZ (Special Economic Zone) with an International Financial Services Centre (IFSC) for export of financial services, and an area for export of non-financial services. IFSC is a deemed foreign jurisdiction where foreign universities/institutions are not subject to Indian law/rules.

Ranked 1st in the Global Financial Centres Index 28, the IFSC has an International Arbitration Centre that settles disputes under international law.

By March 2024, 680 entities were functional, including IndiaINX, NSE-IFSC International Exchange (NIIE), India International Bullion Exchange, 3 data centres, 12 foreign banks, 16 Indian banks, 3 infra finance companies, 82 fund managers, 41 FinTech companies, 31 insurance entities, 7 IT giants, 8 ship leasing and 5 aircraft/aviation equipment leasing companies (21 coming up), over 80 jewellers, and over 100 intermediaries. The ₹16,000Cr Immerso AI Park is India's first. Software Technology Parks of India has set up the FinGlobe Centre of Entrepreneurship.

Australia's Deakin University set up India's first foreign university campus, and two more Australian universities are coming up. University of San Diego from the US is setting up India's first American university campus. Education New Zealand has signed an Education Cooperation Arrangement. The 300-bed Lilavati Hospital at GIFT is tying up with USA's world-renowned Mayo Clinic.

GIFT City also has a 5-star hotel (two more coming up) and a club.

A world trade centre, a school, and 4,400 apartments are among 20 buildings being built as of March 2024.

A new 2.8msft complex will have workspaces for 20,000, an innovation and startup hub, and 3,500 parking spaces. Located just 500m from the residences, people can comfortably walk to work.

The Government of Gujarat is working on a Pod Taxi pilot project to operate on elevated corridors and provide connectivity between metro stations and various buildings within the city.

GIFT City has invited bids for a 20.5ac site adjacent to the riverfront to be developed as a 1.5msft of recreation, entertainment, retail, and F&B spaces, and a 518.4ft high GIFT Eye—a giant Ferris wheel (London Eye is 443ft high).

An underwater aquarium, an aqua park and water sports facilities will be developed by 2027.

Indian companies listed on local stock exchanges, as well as unlisted companies can list their shares on IndiaINX and NIIE. This will help them get access to a much larger pool of foreign capital and get global scale valuations.

Foreign investors pay no capital gains tax and can trade in foreign currencies. IIE and NIE have long trading hours for convenience of investors/traders based at world's different time zones.

Banking transactions of $714B have been done from GIFT City.

Being Gandhi's birthplace, Gujarat had introduced 'prohibition' in 1949, banning the sale and consumption of any type of alcohol (including beer and wine). In 2017, the Government of Gujarat made the liquor law stricter, with up to 10 years in prison and a fine of ₹5L for manufacturing/purchasing/selling/transporting liquor.

In December 2023, the Government of Gujarat lifted prohibition within GIFT City.

GIFT City was Narendra Modi's GIFT to Bharat even before he became the nation's *pradhan sewak*.

62

Dholera SIR

The ancient port-town of Dholera (62.3km from Bhavnagar; 106km from Ahmedabad) had a population of less than 3,500 persons in 2011.

'Twice the size of Mumbai, Dholera "smart city" is one of dozens planned in India but…it will…dispossess farmers. As investors pull out, will India's utopian experiment end in chaos?' wrote UK's Guardian in April 2014, when Modi was CM of Gujarat.[4]

'Modi's Dholera dream is a tale of delay and destruction,' wrote Hindustan Times in November 2017.[5]

Locals claimed it would destroy the lives, culture, and livelihood of 110,000 residents of the region. 'This is not a project for development but destruction,' Rahul Gandhi said,[6] promising them loss of their lands would be addressed if Congress came to power in Gujarat. But neither did the Congress come to power in 2017, nor in 2022, and nor is it likely to come to power in Gujarat in 2027 or 2032.

The 920km^2 Dholera Special Investment Region is now a reality. Many infrastructure works are complete/going on.

Construction of Dholera International Airport started in February 2024. Master planned to handle 50mppa and two runways, in Phase-1 to be completed by 2026, it can handle 1.5mmpa.

A 4-lane expressway (expandable to 6 lanes) from Ahmedabad to Dholera will cross the airport. It is expected to be ready by end of 2025. A Vande Metro or a monorail will be built alongside.

The Tata Group with Powerchip Semiconductor of Taiwan started building a ₹91,000Cr Giga fab in March 2024, and the plant will produce its first chip by the end of 2026.

The Government of Gujarat announced a 4,400MW Ultra-Mega Solar Park. Out of this, Tata Power has already commenced a 300MW solar power plant, which the company described as 'India's largest single-axis solar tracker system'. Another 700MW is under development.

The Vedanta Group is looking for Japanese partners to set up a semiconductor fab in Dholera.

ReNew Power has announced its intention to develop a 2GW solar cell and module factory.

Many other industrial projects are under discussion between the Government of India, the Government of Gujarat, and private sector companies (both foreign and Indian).

AJU Japanese Hotels, which already have 6 hotels in India, won a bid to develop the region's first 5-star hotel on a 130,191SFT plot of land auctioned by the state government.

Many real estate developers have already started developing apartments and villa projects.

63

IMEC Corridor

China's Belt and Road Initiative (BRI) aims to connect most of the world with land and maritime corridors with 21 China-controlled transport hubs, including 8 ports/multimodal transport hubs with majority Chinese ownership, 8 with minority/indirect ownership, and 5 railway hubs. China gives interest-free or low-interest loans to countries to build these hubs, which are then built by Chinese companies using Chinese labour, and China inflates project costs by 2–3 times, making the projects unviable. When most countries are unable to repay the loan, China acquires the assets.

The India–Middle East–Europe Economic Corridor (IMEC) was conceived by Modi as a counter to BRI. The sea and land corridor will start at 2–4 ports in Maharashtra and Gujarat and connect to Mina Jebel Ali Port in Dubai. Two alternate ports in the UAE are also being considered. In addition, India has plans to build a tunnel running on the seabed for high-speed freight trains to the UAE.

The Western DFC (see the 'Railways' chapter in this book) runs from near Delhi to JNPT Port in Navi Mumbai and has 15 terminals on the route.

From Dubai, a rail corridor will move containers to Al Ghuwaifat in UAE, then to Al-Hadithah via Riyadh (both in Saudi Arabia), and finally to the Adani-owned Haifa Port in Israel.

Around 62 per cent of this 2,915km rail line exists and 19 per cent is already being built by the UAE, so only around 19 per cent will have to be newly funded and constructed. From Haifa, there are many shipping routes for Europe, including Gioia Tauro (Italy), Piraeus Port (Greece), and Marseille (France).

All trade between India and Europe happens via the sea route passing through Suez Canal, controlled by Egypt. Cargo ships from India take 4–5 days to Jebel Ali, 14–16 days to Gioia Tauro, 15–17 days to Marseille, and 17–19 days to Piraeus. A freight train from Jebel Ali to Haifa will take just a day. Shipping from Haifa is 3 days to Piraeus, 5 days to Gioia Tauro, and 6 days to Marseille.

Indian products can reach Italy/France 4–6 days earlier (24–43 per cent time savings) and Greece 9–11 days earlier (47–65 per cent time savings).

This will ensure that not only will non-perishable goods producers get money faster but even some Indian perishable commodities can reach European supermarkets.

The IMEC MoU was signed at the G20 Summit in New Delhi by India, the US, Saudi Arabia, the UAE, the European Union, Italy, France, and Germany, in the presence of all their leaders.

For this ambitious multi-billion-dollar project, Modi worked for over six years in getting rulers of Abu Dhabi, Dubai, Jordan, and the Crown Prince of Saudi Arabia to agree for a rail line to go through their countries to Israel, as the Arab world does not have the best of relationships with Israel. US President Trump encouraged Modi to move ahead with the project. Former President Joe Biden said in no uncertain terms during the MoU signing ceremony that his country was very excited about the IMEC corridor.

In February 2024, India and UAE signed an agreement for establishing an intergovernmental framework on the IMEC.

64

More Business Infra

Modi has also created other global-scale business infrastructure.

Bharat Mandapam

Delhi's Pragati Maidan trade fair complex was redeveloped as the 'Bharat Mandapam' International Exhibition and Convention Centre (IECC). From 0.7msft exhibition space and zero convention space earlier, it now has 4.2msft space (up 500 per cent), including an iconic world-class elliptical-shaped convention centre that can hold 7,000 people in a single format, and 7 modern exhibition halls with an area of 1.5msft. It is the world's 4th largest IECC after Canton Fair Complex in Guangzhou (China), Hannover Messe in Germany and National Exhibition and Convention Center in Shanghai (China).

Parking for over 4,800 car units, two auditoriums with up to 900-seat capacity, and 24 tech-enabled meeting rooms are part of the complex. From the 4th floor, one can see the canopy of India Gate, the domes of Rashtrapati Bhavan and the Kartavya Path. A massive public canopy that connects all the exhibition halls provides protection from sun and rain and has landscaped food and beverage spaces with breakout areas and an amphitheatre. A 6-lane tunnel was built under Bharat Mandapam to decongest traffic.

As per the architect Sanjay Singh,

> The PM's brief was very clear that the building should be an iconic landmark which can compete with infrastructure globally and become a matter of pride for the country. The PMO was involved in almost all stages of the project. His personal secretaries and advisors frequently visited the site and interacted with us.

Yashobhoomi IICC

'Yashobhoomi' is the name given by Modi to the 11.2msft India International Convention and Expo Centre coming up on a 222ac site in Dwarka, which will be connected with an underpass to IGI Airport.

In three phases, there will be 2.6msft indoor exhibition space, 0.79msft convention centre (15 halls/rooms with 11,000-person capacity including a plenary hall for 6,000 persons), 2.54msft offices, hotels with about 3,500 keys, 1.65msft retail areas, and a 20,000-person multipurpose arena, totalling 11.2msft, making it the world's 2nd largest MICE facility after the Canton Fair Complex in China. Yashobhoomi will also have 76.4msft of outdoor fair ground and 34,800 parking spaces. A 1-km grand foyer will connect the 5 exhibition halls and convention centre with other buildings.

Transport linkages include a metro station below the complex, roads to the Dwarka Expressway and the UER-II.

Phase 1 that opened in September 2023 has 0.55msft of indoor exhibition area and the multipurpose arena.

Surat Diamond Bourse (SDB)

The SDB has about 6.7msft of BUA on 35.54ac, with 4,700 offices for manufacturers/traders of rough/polished diamonds and jewellery. When it opened in December 2023, the SDB surpassed the Pentagon (the US defence headquarters), making it the world's largest office complex. It is part of the upcoming 1,683ac Diamond Research and Mercantile (DREAM) City. The nine platinum green-rated towers have an auction house, a customs office, a jewellery mall, multipurpose banqueting and conference halls, bank branches, safe deposit vaults, restaurants, and parking for 6,100 car equivalents.

Unfortunately, the SDB has not taken off as per expectations due to a slump in Surat's diamond cutting and polishing industry, which has happened due to lesser demand from foreign buyers.

YEIDA Film City

YEIDA is developing a 1,000ac International Film City on the Yamuna Expressway, about 4km from the upcoming Noida International Airport. The first phase will cover 230ac (75ac industrial 155ac commercial). It will have multiple filmmaking studios, post-production facilities, a film institute, hotels, retail, food and beverage outlets, and media offices.

Bollywood film producer Boney Kapoor's Bayview Projects and real estate developer Bhutani Infra have won the bid to develop the project. The studio and film institute are expected to be ready by 2027 and the entire project by 2032.

Uttar Pradesh Defence Industrial Corridor (UPDIC)

The UPDIC is being set up with six nodes—Jhansi (7,467ac), Agra (2,450ac), Chitrakoot (1,236ac), Kanpur (538ac), Aligarh (131ac), and Lucknow (about 500ac).

Over 90 MoUs have been signed with public/private companies including Adani Defence and Aerospace, Bharat

Dynamics, Bharat Electronics, Bharat Forge, BrahMos Aerospace, HAL, SpiceJet, Tata Technologies, Texmaco Defence, and Triveni Engineering, with total investment commitments of ₹28,411Cr as of November 2024.

Around 1,850ac of land has been allotted to 41 companies that have already invested ₹3,767Cr as of November 2024.

Centres of Excellence are coming up in collaboration with Indian Institute of Technology (IIT), Banaras Hindu University (BHU) and IIT Kanpur. DRDO will set up a Defence Technology and Test Centre in the Lucknow node. New Technology Extension Centre is coming up at Jhansi in PPP mode.

Tamil Nadu Defence Corridor

A Defence Industrial Corridor has also come up in Tamil Nadu with five nodes—Chennai, Coimbatore, Hosur, Salem, and Trichy—36 companies are already operational. This has received investment commitments of ₹21,825Cr, of which ₹4,663Cr has already been invested up to November 2024.

65

Building Information Modelling (BIM)

According to the Online Computerised Monitoring System (OCMS) for Projects and Infrastructure Monitoring—initiative of the Project Monitoring Division in the Ministry of Statistics and Programme Implementation, about 27 per cent of projects witness cost overruns, whereas 45 per cent witness time overruns. One of the least digitalised sectors, it is estimated that 20 per cent of time is lost in searching relevant information in the infrastructure and construction sector.

It is estimated that for complex infrastructure projects in India, adopting BIM can reduce the average project delays of 39 months, reduce infrastructure construction costs up to 30 per cent, maintenance costs up to 20 per cent, information and systemic inefficiencies up to 20 per cent, construction sector related carbon emission up to 38 per cent, water consumption up to 10 per cent, and result in over 4M skilled professional employment and about 2.5M additional construction sector jobs by reinvesting savings in additional infrastructure.

The motto of BIM is to construct digitally before constructing physically. NITI Aayog (National Institution for Transforming India) has identified the challenges, solutions, and enablers related to BIM implementation. Relevant public/private and academic stakeholders have been identified and are being engaged. Based on a roadmap for creating an ecosystem towards faster adoption of BIM in India, guidance, and strategies are being provided to infrastructure projects, including Central Vista, New Parliament, and the Common Central Secretariat.

BIM is now being extensively utilised and leveraged by some ministries and departments like the National Capital Region Transport Corporation, all Metro Rail projects, select complex industrial and tourism projects, various airports, along with organisation-wise acceptance at Central Public Works Department and extensive digitalisation in the form of Data Lake across NHAI that is now being extended to the entire Ministry of Road Transport and Highways.

[illegible]

and [illegible]
[illegible]
[illegible]
[illegible]
[illegible]
including [illegible] and [illegible]
[illegible]

[illegible]
[illegible]
[illegible]
[illegible]
[illegible]
[illegible]
[illegible]
[illegible]

Part V

Healthcare for All

66

Free Hospital Treatment

Ayushman Bharat Pradhan Mantri Jan Arogya Yojana (PMJAY), literally 'Long Live India Prime Minister's People's Health Scheme', is the world's largest *free* health insurance scheme.

It targets to provide 549.04M 'means-tested' beneficiaries of 120.96M families in the lowest 40 per cent income strata an amount of up to ₹5L per family/year for hospitalisation. Means testing assesses if a person/family can pay for hospitalisation without government support.

In 2018 Modi said that every year, about 25 per cent of India's rural and 18 per cent of the urban population sinks into poverty and debt traps due to medical emergencies. The poor are often denied access to healthcare facilities/treatment due to lack of money. Despite various regional and national programs introduced by past governments, there was much more to be done.

The scheme had been launched in September 2018 and by 14 September 2024, almost 354.35M Ayushman Bharat Health Account (ABHA) cards with eKYC verification (64.5 per cent of target) had been created. The current pace is around 46,000 approvals/day.

Around 78M treatments worth ₹1.07LCr were done at ₹13,718 per treatment. As per an advertisement of the scheme, this resulted in a saving of ₹1.25LCr out-of-pocket expenditure for the poor people.

With an ABHA card, beneficiaries get cashless treatment at 30,510 empanelled hospitals (44.1 per cent of which are private hospitals) that get reimbursed by the GoI.

The scheme has been lauded by the World Bank, IMF, WHO, and more than 40 world leaders. Several countries have asked for India's help in introducing a similar scheme in their countries.

PMJAY was extended to ASHA and Anganwadi workers in 2024, and to all senior citizens aged 70 and above (estimated number about 60M), irrespective of their family income.

Delhi, Odisha, and West Bengal have their own schemes instead of PMJAY.

67

Free Health Services, Cheap Medicines

Apart from *free* hospital-based treatment under PMJAY, the Modi Government has started many more *free* or subsidised health programs.

Ayushman Arogya Mandirs

Ayushman Arogya Mandirs are being set up to deliver *free* primary health care closer to the communities. They deliver maternal and child health care, and include oral, eye, ENT, non-communicable diseases, rehabilitative, palliative, and mental health care, including free essential drugs and diagnostic services, plus first level care for emergencies and trauma. Between April 2018 and December 2024, the target of 150,000 was exceeded by over 17 per cent with 175,603 Ayushman Arogya Mandirs set up.

Free Dialysis

Every year, India adds about 220,000 end-stage renal disease patients, resulting in additional demand for 34.3M dialysis treatments/year at the rate of three sessions per week. Dialysis costs ₹2,250-8,000 per session, depending on the city/hospital, so the bare minimum annual cost is ₹3.5L. This leads to financial catastrophe for the family. The GoI launched the 'PM National Dialysis Program' in PPP mode in April 2016 at all district hospitals, to make dialysis accessible and affordable for BPL patients. In August 2024, there were 1,520 Namo Dialysis Centres with 10,605 Haemodialysis machines that provided 29.339M sessions to 2.49M patients. As is clear from this Table, when it comes to citizens' welfare, Modi clearly does not favour BJP/NDA-ruled states.

DIALYSIS MACHINES at NAMO DIALYSIS CENTRES (per Million persons)			
Top 7 Opposition States	Quantity	Top 7 NDA States	Quantity
Kerala	33.91	Gujarat	21.41
Telangana	15.54	Uttarakhand	14.08
Tamil Nadu	16.15	Assam	8.36
Himachal Pradesh	16.61	Haryana	8.05
Andhra Pradesh	11.19	Chhattisgarh	4.74
Karnataka	8.86	Madhya Pradesh	4.50
Odisha	8.51	Maharashtra	3.40
SOURCE: https://pmndp.mohfw.gov.in/en			

National Mobile Medical Units

National mobile medical units are a key strategy to facilitate access to public health care for people in remote, underserved, and unreached areas. The objective is to take healthcare to doorsteps. The vehicles meet the technical and service quality standards of a primary health centre by providing a package of services in 12 areas: maternal health; neonatal and infant health; child and adolescent health; reproductive health and contraception; dental; eye; ENT care; geriatric care; mental illness; emergency medicine; basic care for common non-communicable diseases; and basic care for chronic communicable diseases. Around 1,525 mobile medical units were deployed in 504 districts as of June 2023 and we could not find updated data.

Affordable Medicines, Equipment, and Consumables

Jan Aushadhi Yojana was launched by UPA in November 2008 to set up Janaushadhi Kendras (pharmacies) at affordable prices. Only 87 were functional when Modi became PM.

Modi re-launched it as the 'PM Bhartiya Janaushadhi Pariyojana' in September 2015. The targeted 10,000 Kendras were established by 2023 (within the deadline). By September 2024, there were 13,822 Kendras of which about 27 per cent were owned by women. From ₹7.45Cr in FY15, revenues crossed ₹1,460Cr in FY24 (up 19,497 per cent).

These Kendras sell 2,347 generic (unbranded) medicines, surgical equipment, and consumables at 50–90 per cent lower rates than branded ones in regular pharmacies, and this has resulted in total savings of more than ₹27,500Cr for consumers in nine years.

For example, a strip of 15 Paracetamol 650mg tablets sells at ₹15 at a PM Bhartiya Janaushadhi Pariyojana Kendra, whereas Dolo 650 is ₹28.90 on PharmEasy and ₹29.90 on Tata1mg, and Crocin 650 is ₹30.24 on PharmEasy and ₹33.60 on Tata1mg; a strip of 10 Pantoprazole 40mg sells at ₹22 at a Kendra whereas Pansec is ₹96.80 and Pantodac ₹137.00 on Tata1mg. Azithral 500 sells for ₹25.40 per tablet on Tata1mg against only ₹14 at a Kendra. A digital thermometer costs ₹100, a medical steam vaporizer ₹250, and a digital blood pressure monitor ₹1,000.

To ensure presence in all 806 districts (including 112 aspirational districts), there will be 25,000 Janaushadhi Kendras by FY29, including at railway stations.

Other Programs and Conclusion

Due to Modi's efforts, organ transplants went up from 6,916 in FY14 to 18,378 in 2023 (up 165.7 per cent). There were 212,892 registered donors as of 22 January 2025, which Modi wants to increase to 10M under the Angdaan Mahotsav launched in July 2023. A National Digital Organ Donor Register will maintain confidential records of prospective donors and is expected to be rolled out in 2025. As of December 2024–January 2025, an average of only 254 persons are registering daily but the numbers are showing a growth trajectory.

National Tele Mental Health Program was launched in October 2022 to improve access to quality mental health counselling/care services. As of June 2024, 52 Tele MANAS (Mental Health Assistance and Networking Across States) Cells and 23 Mentoring Institutes had been set up and over 1.38M calls had been handled on the helpline.

Under the Ayushman Bhav Campaign launched in September 2023, in the first 5 months alone, a whopping 343.9M people went through seven types of health screening, 29.07M had OPD consultations and 18.9M had tele-consultations, 65,094 major surgeries and 196,156 minor surgeries were performed, 8.21M mothers and 9.015M children availed of antenatal checkups and immunization, 116.4M persons got drugs, and 92.8M persons got diagnostics. Everything was *free* for the citizens.

The Modi Government runs over 35 other health-related programs.

The share of government health expenditure in total health expenditure of the country was just 28.6 per cent in FY14, but rose to 41.4 per cent by FY20, the last year for which data is available.

Government health expenditure (GHE) went up from 1.1429 per cent of GDP in FY14 to 1.9806 per cent in FY24 (up 73.3 per cent in percentage terms and 350.8 per cent in actual outflow).

The share of GHE in general government expenditure increased from 3.94 per cent in FY15 to 6.12 per cent in FY22 (up 55.3 per cent in seven years). The National Health Accounts data for FY23 had not been released when this book was finished.

In FY22, India's total health expenditure (including government and private expenditure) was estimated at ₹9.0446LCr, which was about 3.83 per cent of that year's GDP. This amounted to around ₹6,383 per person, of which patients and/or their families spent around 35.3 per cent out of their own means.

68

Health Insurance

As of July 2024, there were 453.6M (around 32 per cent of India's population) enrolments in PM Suraksha Bima Yojana (PMSBY) Personal Accident Insurance Scheme that has a premium of only ₹20 p.a., and 141,252 claims had been settled.

By the same month, 206.2M people were enrolled in PM Jeevan Jyoti Bima Yojana (PMJJBY), a Life Insurance Scheme with a subsidised premium of only ₹436 per annum, and 818,954 claims had been settled.

The Employees' State Insurance Corporation (ESIC) scheme has 48.93M insured persons as of August 2024, a network of 165 hospitals in 611 districts with 26,846 inpatient beds; and 1,574 dispensaries.

Atal Beemit Vyakti Kalyan Yojana (ABVKY) provides relief to unemployed persons equal to 50 per cent of the average daily earning in the last job. ESIC had approved 68,105 ABVKY claims from July 2018 to July 2024.

In 2021, around 514.75M Indians had health insurance—342.91M in government-sponsored schemes, 118.7M private employer-sponsored covers (excluding ESIC), and 53.14M self-pay individuals. As it was just 36.57 per cent of the population, the world was mocking India.

As of 15 September 2024, PMJAY has 354.02M insured persons, ESIC 48.93M, West Bengal's Swasthya Sathi 108M, Odisha's Biju Swasthya Kalyan Yojana 47.9M, and Delhi's Arogya Kosh an estimated 8.75M. There are a few other central/state government insurance schemes, mostly for government employees, and the coverage of all of these put together is estimated at 30M. Thus, the total coverage of all central and state government-sponsored schemes had gone up to 597.6M.

Assuming private sector employer-sponsored coverage went up at a CAGR of 12 per cent and self-pay by 9 per cent, we get 168.8M and 75.2M, respectively.

This gives us a total of 841.6M persons with health insurance (up 63.5 per cent since 2021) and means that 59.3 per cent of Indians had health insurance coverage.

Insurance Regulatory and Development Authority of India (IRDAI) is soon launching the 'Amazon of Insurance', that will be a game changer in the insurance sector. IRDAI's ambition is to make 'Bima Sugam' the largest online market for insurance products and services, something not available anywhere in the world. It will facilitate the comprehensive convergence of all stakeholders and insurance services in a single platform.

The salient features of Bima Sugam are: (a) It will connect all insurance stakeholders; (b) All insurance requirements, including life, health, motor, travel, etc., will be met; (4) The online platform, that will also have an App, will be backed by IRDAI, the Life Insurance Council, and the General Insurance Council, and allow individuals to fulfil all their insurance needs, from buying the policy to claim settlement and much more.

69

e-Healthcare

The free eSanjeevani National Telemedicine Service launched in November 2019 facilitates quick and easy access from smartphones to allopathic and Ayush doctors and specialists, or by visiting an Ayushman Bharat Health and Wellness Centre (AB-HWC). It gives the option of chat or video consultations on a real-time basis, has a multilingual interface and ABHA card integration.

The process for patient to doctor telemedicine is: (1) register and login on eSanjeevani; (2) book an appointment; (3) enter the eOPD; (4) consult doctor/specialist virtually; and (5) get ePrescription.

The process for assisted telemedicine is: (1) visit nearest HWC; (2) meet Community Health Officer (CHO); (3) The CHO will create a case in eSanjeevani; (4) consult doctor/specialist virtually; and (5) get ePrescription. Yes, it's really that simple!

By August 2024, over 220,000 doctors/specialists had been onboarded, 16,273 hubs established, 128,182 spokes operationalised, and more than 290.83M consultations had been done—and the scheme is getting more and more popular by the day.

As part of Digital India, the National Informatics Centre (NIC) developed the eHospital, eBloodBank, and Online Registration System Apps.

Data on e-Hospitals **Source:** https://dashboard.ehospital.gov.in/ehospitaldashboard/	**Quantity** (as on 22 Jan 2025)
Total Number of e-Hospitals	**1,416**
Patient Registrations	**470.163M**
Admissions	**36.708M**
Prescriptions	**8.014M**
Lab Reports	**18.152M**
Radiology Reports	**562,515**
Discharge Summaries	**15.166M**
ABHA Cards Created	**2.163M**
Health Record Link Requests	**27.470M**
Data on NextGen e-Hospitals **Source:** https://nextgen.ehospital.gov.in/dashboard/	**Quantity** (as on 22 Jan 2025)
OPD Transactions	**130.388M**
In-patient Admissions	**4.264M**
Prescriptions Generated	**2.355M**
Lab Reports	**475,499**
Radiology Reports	**2.400M**
Pharmacy and Medical Supply Transactions	**870,095**
ABHA Cards Created	**6.937M**
Billing Transactions	**1.822M**

70

More Medical Colleges, Hospitals, Doctors, and Nurses

In 2014, India had only 0.7575 doctors per 1,000 persons, 24.25 per cent less than the norm of 1:1000 recommended by the WHO.

There was an urgent need to create the infrastructure (medical colleges) to educate and add new doctors.

All India Institutes of Medical Sciences (AIIMS) are a chain of autonomous GoI-owned medical colleges and tertiary care hospitals, considered as India's best public sector hospitals.

AIIMS New Delhi started in 1956.

In 2014, there were 7 operational AIIMS and 1 was under construction. Only 8 were built or seeded in 58 years.

Under Modi, as of November 2024, 13 new AIIMS had started, 3 were under construction, and 2 more had been announced, which will take up the total to 25.

In March 2022, Modi announced that 50 per cent of students in private medical colleges would pay the same fees as government medical colleges.

Let's look at India's supply-side scenario.

HEALTH INFRASTRUCTURE	May 2014	May 2024	Increase
Medical Colleges	387 in 179yrs (since 1835)	783	▲ 102.3%
New Medical Colleges per year	2.162	39.6	▲ 1,732%
MBBS Seats	51,348	109,095	▲ 112.5%
PG Medical Seats	31,185	71,893	▲ 130.5%
Registered Allopathic Doctors	0.978M	1.363M	▲ 39.4%
AYUSH Doctors	686,319	815,423	▲ 18.8%
Doctors per 1000 persons	0.7575	1.535	▲ 102.6%
Registered Nurses	1.7913M	3.514M	▲ 96.2%
Nurses per 1000 persons	1.38	2.475	▲ 79.3%
Hospital Beds	1.4mn	2.54mn	▲ 81.4%
Beds per 1000 persons	1.084	1.778	▲ 64.0%

SOURCES: https://ga7a.short.gy/H8ETOP; https://ga7a.short.gy/xmxmc6; https://ga7a.short.gy/cg1fos; https://ga7a.short.gy/vWUB9O; https://ga7a.short.gy/7NmgRH
NOTE: Many of these figures are calculated by adding past growth figures to last published data as organisations such as National Medial Commission, Indian Nursing Council, etc., have not published updated information after Dec 2022 or Mar2023 on their websites / press releases.

Post-graduate seats will cross 80,000 by academic year 2025–26. This will ensure availability of substantially more 'specialist' doctors.

The PM has also announced the addition of 75,000 new MBBS seats by 2029.

As India had a 28–32 per cent shortage of nurses, in April 2023, the Modi Government approved 157 new Government Nursing Colleges to be co-located with Government Medical Colleges built after 2014 and laid out detailed plans and timelines for completing the projects by May 2026.

This will address the skewed availability of qualified nurses and resultant impact on delivery of healthcare in under-served areas.

Reforms are also planned in the policy for nursing education to meet emerging requirements in healthcare delivery. Co-location with medical colleges allows optimal use of infrastructure and faculty.

This unique initiative (in the Indian context) is expected to provide better clinical exposure to nursing students and result in better care and service for patients.

The table below shows the number of hospital beds (per 1,000 persons) in the 12 largest countries by population, as per the World Health Organization (WHO).

HOSPITAL BEDS per 1,000 persons	**Approx. Number**	**Which Year**
Japan	12.72	2020
Russian Federation	7.03	2021
China	5.00	2020
USA	2.74	2020
Vietnam	2.55	2017
Brazil	2.46	2021
India	1.78	2024
Mexico	1.02	2021
Philippines	0.96	2021
Bangladesh	0.88	2019
Pakistan	0.51	2019
Nigeria	0.50	2004
NOTE: More recent estimates from other sources vary from 0.44 to 0.9		

71

Yoga and AYUSH

Yoga was not new to the world, but Modi brought it the much-needed respectability, something no other Indian leader in the past had done. On 11 December 2014, Modi achieved an extraordinary feat when 193 members of the UN General Assembly and 173 co-sponsor countries approved a UN resolution to establish '21st June' as the International Day of Yoga (IDY). Since 2015, IDY is being celebrated every year across the globe with millions participating in thousands of activities.

Modi led the world in celebrating the IDY on 21 June 2023 from the iconic North Lawns of the UN headquarters building in New York City, USA, where participants from 135 nations set a Guinness World Record.

Ministry of AYUSH (Ayurveda, Yoga, Naturopathy, Unani, Siddha, and Homoeopathy) was set up in November 2014. Its budget went up from ₹1,272.2Cr in FY15 to ₹3,647.5Cr in FY24 (up 186.7 per cent). The traditional Himalayan medicine 'Sowa-Rigpa' was also added. The National Yoga and Naturopathy Promotion and Development Board was set up as a national advisory body.

Ayush initiatives include Ayush visas; over 3,100 hospitals that treat more than 165,000 inpatients and more than

4M outpatients/year; 137 Ayush hospitals; 848 colleges/institutes with Ayush courses; 19,000 HWCs; 37,000 Ayush dispensaries; 'Yoga for All' project to reach entire population in 5 years; 'Ayush Mark' for Ayush products; Ayush parks for research and manufacturing; AYUSH GIS for mapping of health facilities, practitioners, medical colleges, and students; AyuSoft to convert classical Ayurvedic texts into comprehensive, authentic, intelligent, and knowledge repositories; etc.

In collaboration with the WHO, the 'WHO Global Centre for Traditional Medicines' is coming up at Jamnagar.

Exports of Ayush and herbal products went up from $106M in FY20 to $649M in FY24 (up 512.3 per cent in four years).

Part VI

Women Empowerment

The mark of a progressive and inclusive nation is the respect and care the nation's leadership accords to women citizens. On this front, Modi will never disappoint. More than ₹13.6LCr has been spent on women's schemes in Modi's 10 years. That is an incredible ₹20,792 per woman per year.

'Today there is no area in the country in which the women power of the country has lagged behind. Other areas where women have demonstrated their leadership abilities is natural farming, water conservation and sanitation,' said Modi.[1]

72

Educating/Skilling Females

There is 43 per cent female enrolment in Science, Technology, Engineering, and Mathematics (STEM) courses now.

There are several programs for providing skills to women in both urban and rural India, so that they can get more satisfying and better paying jobs.

We have covered the Cybersecurity Ambassador training program in the Digital India section.

Here are some more.

Vigyan Jyoti

This program was started by the Department of Science and Technology (DST) in 2019 in Jawahar Navodaya Vidyalayas to motivate meritorious girl students studying in classes 9–12 to pursue higher education and careers in STEM, particularly in the areas where women are underrepresented. Over 54,000 girls have pursued higher education in STEM under this program in 200 districts.

Boeing Sukanya

The Boeing Sukanya Program at Bengaluru supports entry of more women into the aviation sector. It provides opportunities for girls and women to learn critical skills in STEM fields and train them for high-paying jobs. The Program will create STEM labs at 150 locations for young girls to spark an interest in STEM careers. It will also provide scholarships to women training to be pilots.

The 1996 female pilots constitute over 16.8 per cent of total civilian pilots in India, the highest percentage in the world. The aim is to take this up to 20 per cent and then at least 25 per cent. No other country has surpassed even the 11 per cent mark. Germany has less than 7 per cent female pilots, the US has less than 6 per cent, and the UK has less than 5 per cent.

Boeing already partners with seven incubators including four IITs to organise BUILD (Boeing University Innovation Leadership Development). These relationships will help the girls/women trained in the Boeing Sukanya Program to further develop their careers.

IBM STEM for Girls

IBM partners with Navodaya Vidyalaya Samiti to create a robust STEM ecosystem that creates critical thinkers, problem-solvers, and next-generation innovators through MANAK, to build 1M ideas rooted in science from school students, as an extension to IBM's flagship programme 'STEM for Girls' running in 14 states. The partnership aims at strengthening the Vigyan Jyoti program.

DST and IBM India aim to work together to further integrate and develop science and technology in the education ecosystem with short-term courses, workshops, mentoring, and online science content communication for teachers and students.

Women tech experts working at IBM India will interact with and inspire girl students to embark on a career in STEM under the program. This will act as a force multiplier to DST's ongoing initiatives to increase the number of women in technology fields.

Rural Livelihoods Mission

Deendayal Antyodaya Yojana National Rural Livelihoods Mission (DAY-NRLM) mobilises rural women into community SHGs and community federations like Village Organisations, Cluster Level Federations, Producer Groups, and Farmer Producer Organisations (FPOs) to provide diversified livelihood opportunities for their upliftment, empowerment and growth.

The program had reached about 729,000 villages in 742 districts by March 2024.

Almost 100M Mahila Kisans have been mobilised into about 9.05M SHGs of which more than 4.2M SHGs got revolving funds of ₹6298Cr, and over 3M SHGs got community investment funds of ₹21,000Cr.

There are more than 465,000 Village Organisations. Community institutions have cumulatively got over ₹5.83LCr bank credit and ₹19,750Cr capital support. During COVID-19, SHGs made about 1.69M masks, around 530,000 PPEs (Personal Protective Equipment) and more than 510,000 litres of sanitizers.

More than 116,000 villages are covered for farm livelihood interventions, in which over 310M Mahila Kisans are covered under Agro Ecological Practice interventions, over 2.184M Mahila Kisan households have Agri Nutri Gardens, and over 576,000 Mahila Kisans are organised into FPOs.

73

Caring for the Girl Child

Pre-Conception and Prenatal Diagnostic Techniques (Prohibition of Sex Selection) Act of February 2003 or PCPNDT replaced the Pre-Natal Diagnostic Techniques (PNDT) Act of 1994. It prohibits sex determination before or after conception. The basic change was the inclusion of ultrasound scans.

Any gynaecologist/doctor, lab owner, counselling centre, or clinic, or any person employed at such places who contravenes the Act can get jailed for three years with a ₹10,000 fine. This may increase to five years on subsequent conviction with a ₹50,000 fine. The State Medical Council can suspend the medical practitioner's registration and remove his/her name from the register of the Council.

If a person seeks the aid of any counselling centre, clinic or lab for sex determination, s/he can get jailed for five years with ₹50,000 fine. On subsequent conviction, the fine goes up to ₹1L. The punishments do not apply to women who are 'compelled' to undergo a diagnostic test for sex determination/selection, and the husband and her relatives are presumed to be liable for compelling a woman to undergo such a diagnosis.

National Population Policy (NPP), 2000, was made by the Vajpayee Government to achieve a gender-balanced population.

Despite the PCPNDT and the NPP, the child sex ratio, defined in India as the number of girls per 1,000 boys aged 0–6 years, which had already declined from 976 in 1961 to 945 in 1991, continued to decline unabated, to 918 in 2011.

Between 1991 and 2001, the child sex ratio declined from 875 to 798 in Punjab, 879 to 819 in Haryana, 951 to 896 in Himachal, and 915 to 868 in Delhi. Two of these four states are responsible for the farmer agitations—how chauvinistic!

This was extremely alarming—a major indicator of women disempowerment. It reflects pre-birth discrimination through sex selection, and post birth discrimination including infant genocide.

Beti Bachao Beti Padhao

Since well-coordinated efforts were needed to ensure the survival, protection, and empowerment of the girl child, Modi announced the 'Beti Bachao Beti Padhao' (BBBP) campaign in January 2015. 'Our mantra should be "Beta Beti, Ek Samaan". We should be equally proud of our daughters. I urge you to sow five plants when your daughter is born to celebrate the occasion,' Modi expressed.[2]

Apart from addressing the child sex ratio issue, BBBP took up issues relating to women's empowerment over a life-cycle continuum. Its key elements are proper enforcement of the PCPNDT Act, awareness and advocacy campaigns, and multi-sectoral action in 100 low-child sex ratio districts in the first phase.

There was a strong emphasis on mindset change through training, sensitization, raising awareness, and community mobilization. Modi was trying to bring about a transformational shift in the way our society looks at the girl child. The scheme also ensures that girls can inherit family property, are sent to a good quality school, and have access to better quality education.

In a 'Mann Ki Baat' address in June 2015, Modi lauded Sunil Jaglan, Sarpanch of Bibipur (Haryana), who started an innovative initiative named 'Selfie with Daughter'. The PM urged people to share selfies with their daughters and it became a global movement. Jaglan started the 'Selfie with Daughter Foundation' and launched a website on which he asked people to post their selfies. President Pranab Mukherjee launched a 'Selfie with Daughter App' in June 2017. Modi spoke about Selfie with Daughter in many of his radio addresses, for 3 years up to June 2018.

As per an Organisation for Economic Co-operation and Development (OECD) publication, the SDG communicator that focuses on WHO's SDGs, 'The website registered more than 100,000 pictures and 27,000 families participated in the 2019 contest alone'[3].

Compared to 918 in 2011, India's child sex ratio improved to 929 (924 in rural areas and 931 in urban areas) in the National Family Health Survey (NFHS-5) done in June 2019–April 2021 by International Institute for Population Sciences (IIPS). The child sex ratio further improved to 933 in December 2023 (there is regular monitoring now).

Opposition leaders and leftist journalists accused the Modi Government of doing a 'fake' survey, saying that such remarkable improvement is not possible in such a short time.

Let's look at some facts.

IIPS was set up in July 1956 (Nehru was the PM at the time) jointly by Sir Dorabji Tata Trust (Tata Group founder

Jamsetji Tata's son), the GoI, and the UN, and serves as the UN's Regional Centre for Training and Research in Population Studies for Asia-Pacific. It was declared a 'Deemed University' in August 1985 (Rajiv Gandhi was the PM). Students from many countries in Asia-Pacific, Africa, and North America have trained there. Its alumni are in prestigious posts at international organizations, universities, and reputed NGOs.

The NFHS was done by 17 agencies in 636,700 households by interviewing over 724,000 women and almost 102,000 men. Fact sheets for each district of India are available on the Reproductive and Child Health or RCH-IIPS website. IIPS conducted all five NFHSs starting 1992–93 when the Congress Government was in power. NFHS-3 was conducted in 2005–06 when the Sonia Gandhi-led UPA Government was in power.

Is any more proof needed about the authenticity of NFHS?

Epic Change in Adoptions

Hindus who did not have a child of their own and adopted a child, traditionally chose a male child due to a variety of reasons, including performance of last rites, which is still not done by girls. In 2021–23, data of 11 states (others did not furnish data despite the SCI's direction) shows that adoptive parents took home 61.2 per cent girls against 38.8 per cent boys. Surprisingly, Punjab, the state with the lowest child sex ratio, emerged as the leader, with as many as 66.25 per cent girls.

Sukanya Samriddhi Yojana (SSY)

The SSY is a small deposit scheme for girls. Launched by Modi simultaneously with the BBBP, the SSY scheme encourages parents to build a fund for the future education and marriage expenses of their girl child. The account can be opened by a parent or legal guardian of a girl below the age of 10 years. A family can open maximum two SSY accounts (for two girls). The minimum investment is ₹250/year and maximum ₹1.5L/year.

The maturity period is 21 years. Parents must contribute at least once a year for 15 years including the initial year. The maturity amount (including principal and interest) is 100 per cent tax-exempt.

Let's say you invested ₹3,000/month for 15 years starting from 2024 when your daughter is one year old. On maturity in 2045, when your daughter is 22, you will get an interest-free amount of ₹16,63,835 based on an interest rate of 8.2 per cent per annum (the interest rate changes quarterly).

As of August 2024, over 40.086M accounts had been opened under the scheme, with an amount of almost ₹2.555LCr in deposits.

Balika Samriddhi Yojana (BSY)

The BSY is a scheme to support girls in BPL families. It ensures the enrolment and retention of a girl child in primary and secondary schools. One of the motives of the scheme is to prevent a girl's infanticide and break the stigma related to a girl child's birth. BSY also aims at ensuring that no girl child becomes a victim of child marriage and attains the legal age of 18 before she is married off.

Every girl child registered under BSY is looked after and helped in getting trained in income-generating activities that make her financially independent.

At the time of birth, ₹500 is offered to the parents. When the child starts attending school, an amount ranging between ₹300 and ₹1,000 is offered as scholarship annually until the child graduates Class 10.

Anganwadi

Anganwadi Workers (AWWs) are women from poor families who staff almost 1.4M Anganwadi Centres (AWCs are a type of rural childcare centres). They are paid a fixed honorarium per month by the government. AWWs provide various health services for children, including regular health check-ups, simple medicine administration, weight recording, immunization, malnutrition management, diarrhoea treatment, and de-worming.

The AWWs' responsibilities include encouraging community participation, working with auxiliary nurse midwives (ANMs) to train ASHAs (an Accredited Social Health Activist is a community health worker who works as part of the National Rural Health Mission; ASHAs are selected by the community and work to improve the health of the community), motivating ASHAs to bring beneficiaries to the institution, bringing pregnant women to the ANM for check-ups, and bringing married couples to the ANM for counselling on family planning.

Poshan Tracker

'Poshan Tracker' is an App rolled out in March 2021 as a job-aid to the AWWs for efficient delivery of services, along with reflection of their efforts.

It enables real-time tracking and monitoring of all AWCs and beneficiaries on defined indicators. Tracking is done for services like take-home rations and hot cooked meals, vaccination for infants and pregnant women, at the click of a button. Nutritional indicators like stunting, wasting and underweight prevalence are measured as per WHO standards. It also has a home visit alert feature.

In remote and backward areas, it brings children aged 3–6 years together at an AWC, where different activities related to physical, cognitive, social, emotional, and creative development of children are facilitated by the AWWs.

As of August 2024, the total 99.88M eligible beneficiaries included 3.957M children aged <6 months, 40.52M children aged six months to three years, 44.2M children aged 3-6 years, 4.254M lactating mothers, and 6.942M pregnant women.

More than 2.3M adolescent girls are also enrolled at AWCs.

Cervical Cancer Vaccination

Around 5 per cent of women in the general population are believed to carry cervical Human papillomavirus or HPV-16/18 infection at any given time. Cervical cancer is the 4th most prevalent cancer among women worldwide; in India, it is the 2nd most common cancer among women.

Only 1 per cent of Indian women undergo screening compared with the recommendation of at least 70 per cent by the WHO; which says that cervical cancer can be eliminated (four or lesser cases per lakh women per year) by ensuring that 90 per cent of girls receive the HPV vaccine by age 15, aim for 70 per cent of women to undergo high-quality screening tests during age 35–45, and ensure that 90 per cent of women diagnosed with the cancer receive appropriate treatment.

Girls in the 9–14 age group will be vaccinated (primarily in schools) for prevention of cervical cancer. For girls absent on the vaccination day or those who do not go to a school, the vaccination drive will be conducted through community outreach and mobile teams.

The U-WIN App will be used for the registration, recording, and reporting of vaccination numbers.

74

₹1 Sanitary Pads

Roughly 120M menstruating girls and women in India experience menstrual dysfunctions, affecting their normal lives. Poor menstrual hygiene also causes cervical cancer and is the 5th largest killer of women globally. Keeping good hygiene is extremely important during menstrual cycles. But menstruation is such a taboo subject (especially in India) that many women are ashamed even to seek medical advice even if they are regularly facing health problems due to 'those 3–7 days' every 25–30 days.

India has made significant progress under Modi, who did many things to get the taboo removed. Arunachalam Muruganantham is a social entrepreneur from Coimbatore (Tamil Nadu), who invented a machine that makes sanitary pads at less than 1/3rd the cost of commercial pads and is credited for generating awareness about traditional unhygienic practices around menstruation. Modi got the famous filmmaker R Balki to make a film titled *Pad Man* in which the lead actor Akshay Kumar plays the role of Muruganantham. The film was watched by nearly 17.5M people in cinemas (excluding OTT).

Modi also took steps to make sanitary pads accessible and affordable in every corner of the country. Since inception in

June 2018 to June 2024, over 570M Jan Aushadhi Suvidha Sanitary Napkins had been sold at the Janaushadhi Kendras. The rural absorption of these sanitary napkins has increased from 11 per cent in June 2018 to over 52.3 per cent in FY24 (up 375.5 per cent in <6 years).

Initially launched at ₹2.50 per piece, prices were reduced to ₹1 per piece in August 2019. Market prices for similar (branded) pads range from ₹3.57 to ₹350 per piece.

An earlier scheme started by the UPA in 2011 in 107 districts in 17 states in which a pack of six sanitary pads called 'Freedays' was sold to rural adolescent girls for ₹6, was a complete failure.

75

Easy Pregnancy and Maternity

There are many schemes for pregnant women and new mothers.

Maternity Benefit (Amendment) Act, 2017

This increased paid maternity leave from 12 to 26 weeks for working women who had completed minimum 80 days' attendance at an organisation in 12 months prior to the expected delivery date of their child. Eight weeks' paid leave can precede the expected delivery date, compared with 6 weeks earlier. The period of 26 weeks is only for the first two children. Any deliveries beyond the 2nd child will get only 12 weeks' benefit and only six weeks can be availed before the date of expected delivery.

The Act is applicable to all establishments that employ 10 or more persons, including factories, offices, shops, plantations, government establishments, mines, or any others as notified by the GoI.

Every establishment or organisation with 50 or more employees now must mandatorily have a crèche in the premises, or within a maximum prescribed distance. The beneficiary woman is allowed four crèche visits per day, including resting intervals allowed to her.

Pradhan Mantri Matru Vandana Yojana (PMMVY)

PMMVY offers a cash incentive of ₹5,000 paid in three instalments directly in the bank/post office account of pregnant women and lactating mothers. As of August 2024, around 40.5M women had enrolled and almost 35.1M women had been paid a total of ₹15,698Cr. There is an additional benefit of ₹6,000 for a 2nd girl child.

Janani Suraksha Yojana (JSY)

The JSY is a safe motherhood intervention under the National Health Mission for reducing maternal and neonatal mortality by promoting institutional delivery among poor pregnant women in states with low institutional delivery—Assam, Bihar, Chhattisgarh, J&K, Jharkhand, Madhya Pradesh, Odisha, Rajasthan, Uttar Pradesh, and Uttarakhand.

Janani Shishu Suraksha Karyakram (JSSK)

Institutional deliveries increased substantially after the launch of JSY, but 25 per cent women still hesitated using health facilities for delivery due to out-of-pocket expenditures on drugs, food, diagnosis, arranging blood, etc. JSSK was launched basically to eliminate these expenditures. Essential care is provided to the mother and neonate within 48 hours. JSSK covers all antenatal and post-natal complications of pregnancy. All mothers and sick new-borns/infants (up to one year of age) have zero out-of-pocket expenditure at public health institutions.

Surakshit Matritva Aashwasan (SUMAN)

The SUMAN initiative was launched to provide assured, dignified, respectful, and quality healthcare at no cost and zero tolerance for denial of services or negligence.

There are 1.708M health workers (including 6,813 private doctors who have volunteered) providing various services related to RCH across 20,752 health facilities.

SUMAN guarantees free comprehensive and quality antenatal care on the 9th of every month; counselling and IEC including behavioural changes for safe motherhood; transport from home to health facility; at least four antenatal check-ups (ANC); elimination of mother to child transmission of HIV/HBV/syphilis; deliveries by trained midwife/skilled birth attendant; choice of delayed cord clamping beyond five minutes/up to delivery of placenta; birth registration certificates; zero dose vaccination; early initiation and support for breastfeeding; management of sick new-borns and infants; drop back from healthcare facility to home after due discharge (minimum 48 hours); free access for management and identification of maternal complications; six home-based new-born care visits by ASHA workers; conditional cash transfers or direct benefit transfers under various schemes; time bound redressal of grievances through a call centre/helpline; postpartum family planning counselling; and respect for women's autonomy, dignity, feelings, and choices.

Under SUMAN, there is zero tolerance for negligence by anyone employed throughout the healthcare delivery ecosystem.

What else could a pregnant lady or new mother ask for?

From inception till March 2024, almost 47.347M pregnant women had been examined, more than 265.4M couples had registered and 248.1M pregnant women had delivered over 216.8M babies.

As per data from NFHSs of over 630,000 families across India, conducted every four–five years, in 2019–20, as compared with 2015–16, (a) First trimester antenatal registrations increased from 58.6 per cent to 70 per cent; (b) Institutional deliveries increased from 78.9 per cent to 88.6 per cent; and (c) Skilled birth attendant deliveries increased from 81.4 per cent to 89.4 per cent.

There was a reduction in Maternal Mortality Ratio (MMR) from 130/lakh live births in 2014–16 to 97/lakh in 2018–20.

Upon achieving this, India has accomplished the National Health Policy target for MMR, less than 100/lakh live births, and is on the right track to achieve WHO's SDG target of MMR less than 70/lakh live births by 2030.

76

Banned Triple Talaq

The Muslim Women (Protection of Rights on Marriage) Act, 2019, was passed by the LS on 28 December 2017, and after a lengthy debate by the RS (where the BJP-led NDA did not have a majority) on 30 July 2019.

It criminalised the practice of *talaq al-bid'ah*, a form of Islamic divorce that was used by Indian Muslims, especially practitioners of Hanafi Sunni Islam.

Prior to the Act being passed, this inhuman practice allowed any Muslim man to 'legally' divorce his wife by using *talaq* (the Arabic word for 'divorce') three times in a row either in oral, written, or electronic form.

On 22 August 2017, the SCI had deemed the practice of *talaq al-bid'ah* to be unconstitutional.

Triple Talaq is not mentioned in the Quran. It is also largely disapproved by Muslim legal scholars—19 Islamic nations are among 23 countries that barred the practice, including Iran (99.5 per cent Muslim population), Türkiye (98 per cent), Pakistan (96.5 per cent), Egypt (95.3 per cent), Bangladesh (90.8 per cent), Indonesia (whose 87 per cent Muslim population is the world's largest), Iraq, Afghanistan, Saudi Arabia, Malaysia, Syria, Jordan, UAE, Kuwait, and Qatar.

77

Mission Shakti

Mission Shakti comprises two sub-schemes, and its approved outlay for the 5-year period FY22 to FY26 is ₹20,989Cr.

'Sambal' is for the safety and security of women and comprises:

- Nirbhaya Fund is a non-lapsable corpus specifically for projects that improve the safety and security of women, and ₹4,923Cr had been released for 42 Nirbhaya projects as of April 2023.
- One-stop centres provide support and assistance to women affected by violence and in distress (in private and public spaces) under one roof and facilitates immediate, emergency and non-emergency access to medical and legal services, temporary shelter, police assistance, and psychological counselling. There were 786 operational one-stop centres that assisted 957,631 women from April 2015 to April 2024.
- 34 women helplines registered 14.235M calls and helped 7.263M women from April 2016 to January 2024.
- Nari Adalats, comprising 7–11 committed and socially respected women members, provide an alternate grievance redressal mechanism for resolving petty cases

of harassment, subversion, curtailment of rights, or entitlements faced by rural women. This platform will also be used for engaging with the public for generating awareness and getting feedback to improve the schemes and for effective public delivery of services. As of November 2023, implementation of Nari Adalats had started in seven districts in Assam and two districts in J&K.

'**Samarthya**' is for women's empowerment and comprises:

- Palna National Crèche Scheme—up to November 2023, 2,249 crèches were opened and had been used by over 39,000 children.
- Shakti Sadans are homes for destitute, distressed, marginalized, victims of trafficking, etc., to provide care and support and daily needs and services—432 (with a capacity of 16,216) were open as of December 2023.
- Sakhi Niwas for working women away from their native place, provides a safe/secure place with accommodation, food, and day care for children—494 (with capacity of 40,303) were open as of September 2023.
- Hub for Empowerment of Women aims to facilitate inter-sectoral convergence of schemes and programs meant for women both at the central, state/UT and district levels to create an environment for women to realise their full potential. The Hubs will guide, link and handhold women for their empowerment and development, including equal access to healthcare, quality education, career and vocational counselling and training, financial inclusion, entrepreneurship, health and safety for workers, social security and digital literacy.

78

Women in the Forces

With Modi's guiding principle that our daughters are no less in valour than our sons, India has strategically evolved to ensure permanent commission of women in the Armed Forces.

Permanent commission is now being granted to women officers in 12 Arms and Services (in addition to Army Medical Corps, Army Dental Corps, and Military Nursing Service).

Indian Armed Forces have ensured parity between women officers and their male counterparts with a complete gender-neutral environment in the 12 Arms and Services they serve in.

As of March 2023, there were 1,733 women officers in the Army, 1,648 in the IAF, 748 in the Navy, 1,212 in Army Medical Corps, 168 in Army Dental Corps, and 3,841 in Military Nursing Service.

Entry of women was approved in the National Defence Academy, Khadakvasla, with 19 cadets joining every six months. The first batch of women cadets started training at the NDA from July 2022. Seats reserved for women in other institutions include 80/year in Officers Training Academy (Chennai), 20 in Indian Military Academy (Dehradun),

30 in Armed Forces Medical College (Pune), and 220 in the College of Nursing.

Women officers are now serving as pilots in the Corps of Army Aviation.

Enrolment of women in Corps of Military Police started in 2019, and 1,700 women will be inducted in a phased manner (about 100 per year).

Captain Shiva Chauhan became the first woman officer to be operationally deployed on Siachen Glacier (the world's highest battlefield) in January 2023. In December 2023, Captain Geetika Koul became the first woman medical officer to be deployed at Siachen. Days later, Captain Fatima Wasim became the first woman medical officer to be deployed on an operational post at the Siachen Glacier.

The induction of women officers in the Regiment of Artillery is under progress. Ten women officers were commissioned in 2023.

The IAF's experimental scheme to induct women officers in all combat roles, initiated in 2015, was regularised in 2022 into a permanent scheme.

The gender-neutral approach is facilitating employment of women officers of the IAF in all combat roles without any restrictions.

Women officers are also being appointed on board warships, and as Specialist Naval Air Operations officers on ship-borne helicopters.

Command of units by women officers has commenced.

When Group Captain Shaliza Dhami took over the command of a frontline combat unit in the western sector, she became the first woman to command any combat unit of the IAF.

Lt. Commander Prerna Deosthalee was the 1st woman officer to command an Indian Navy warship. Army Medical Corps Officer Colonel Sunita became the first woman officer to command Armed Forces Transfusion Centre, Delhi Cantonment, the largest blood transfusion centre of the Armed Forces.

Squadron Leader Manisha Padhi was named as India's first woman Aide-De-Camp (ADC) to a Governor.

Lt. Gen. Sadhna Saxena Nair became Director General Medical Services (Army). Vice Admiral (Surgeon) Kavita Sahai became Director General Medical Services (Navy).

In October 2024, Vice Admiral (Surgeon) Arti Sarin became the first woman officer to take over as the Director General, Armed Forces Medical Services (DGAFMS), the highest post for any medical officer in India's armed forces. The DGAFMS is directly responsible to the Ministry of Defence for overall medical policy matters which relate to the Armed Forces.

Maternity, childcare and child adoption leave rules for women soldiers, sailors, and air warriors in the Armed Forces were made at par with their officer counterparts.

79

Other Benefits for Women

Apart from the 40-odd benefits listed in the previous 5 chapters, Modi has also done more for women's empowerment, while Congress just kept talking about it but hardly did anything.

Nari Shakti Vandan Adhiniyam

In the 2024 LS elections, of the 543 MPs elected, only 74 were women, compared with 78 in 2019. Only 52 out of 192 countries globally, and just 10 out of 48 in Asia (6 with Muslim majority) have a lower percentage than India.

Nari Shakti Vandan Adhiniyam or Women's Reservation Bill was passed by Parliament in September 2023. It mandates reservation of 1/3rd seats (including seats reserved for women in SC/ST categories) in the LS and all state assemblies for women, for 15 years. It was the first bill to be considered and passed in the new Parliament building.

This happened after 6 failed attempts over 27 years, in 1996, 1997, 1998, 1999, 2008, and 2010. Mulayam Singh Yadav (then CM of Uttar Pradesh and father of Akhilesh Yadav) had suggested in 2010 that the bill should not be passed, as it would compel men to wolf-whistle at their female colleagues in Parliament.

PM Ujjwala Yojana (PMUY)

Before PMUY was launched, most rural women (121M as per Census 2011, or almost 42 per cent of rural women aged more than 15 years at the time) cooked by burning wood, kerosene, or coal. This led to smoke pollution causing lung diseases and resultant deaths. Under PMUY, up to 4 July 2024, 100 per cent free LPG gas connections (LPG stove and cylinder) have been given to more than 103.294M adult women in poor rural households—that translates to 53 per cent of current rural households.

PMUY beneficiaries get a subsidy of ₹300 per refill up to 12 refills of 14.2kg cylinders/year, or ₹106 per refill up to 34 refills of 5kg cylinders/year, and an option of 5kg double bottle connections and a swap option from 14.2kg to 5kg.

The Opposition and leftist media claim that the PMUY has failed as beneficiaries do not want to pay for refilling cylinders.

The fact is that the per capita consumption of LPG by PMUY beneficiaries rose from 4.274M kg/year in FY20 to about 9.25M kg in FY24; LPG distributors in rural India went up from 6,724 in April 2014 to 17,461 in March 2023 (up 160 per cent versus 10.5 per cent in urban India); more than 86 per cent of PMUY beneficiaries took refills in FY24; and more than 40M LPG refills were delivered to PMUY beneficiaries in October 2024 alone.

Yes, the Opposition and leftist media are spreading lies, just like they do in most of their accusations against Modi and his government.

Greater penetration and usage of LPG is estimated to have prevented at least 150,000 pollution-related deaths (down 13 per cent) and PMUY helped avoid at least

1.8MT of PM2.5 emissions in 2019, in a single year alone, according to the first independent assessment study by three researchers of World Resources Institute. Other surveys have shown that almost 97 per cent of rural women are happy not just due to the reduction in pollution, but also elimination of the exhausting and time-consuming task of having to collect firewood daily, and efforts involved in cooking by the old method.

Lakhpati Didi Yojana

Announced by Modi on 15 August 2023, this scheme helps in women's financial empowerment. Various types of skills training are provided to women SHGs such as Anganwadi *didi*, bank *wali didi* and medicine *wali didi*, offering them the tools that enable them to earn a sustainable income of at least ₹1L per annum per household and become a '*lakhpati didi*' (prosperous sister).

Lakhpati Didi Yojana also provides financial literacy workshops, credit facilities, insurance, financial incentives, and monetary inclusion. Less than 3M rural women earned ₹1L per annum when the scheme was launched.

In less than a year, about 8.3M SHGs had helped more than 10M women to become *lakhpati didis*. The initial target of 20M *lakhpati didis* was increased to 30M in February 2024.

Modi's Other Successes

About 336.5M PM Mudra Yojana loans have been disbursed to women entrepreneurs, which comprises about 71 per cent of all Mudra loans.

Over 60M mothers and children have been vaccinated under Mission Indradhanush.

There are 11,515 women help desks in police stations in the 18 large and medium states.

WOMEN EMPOWERMENT	FROM	TO	CHANGE	Source
Female Labour Force Participation Rate (all-India)	23.3% in FY17	41.6% in FY24	**▲ 78.5%** in 7yrs	1
Female Enrolment in Higher Education	15.7M in FY15	20.7M in FY22	**▲ 31.8%** in 7yrs	2
Women faculty/teachers	48.184% in 2013	56.671% in 2023	**▲ 17.6%** in 10yrs	3
Enrolment of women in IITs	8% in FY16	20% in FY22	**▲ 150%** in 6yrs	4
Increase in Income of Women Self Help Group (SHG) Members from FY19to FY24 (5yrs)				5
	OVERALL		**207%**	
	Urban India		**362%**	
	Semi-Urban India		**221%**	
	Rural India		**180%**	
	Age <28 years		**366%**	
	Age 28-42 years		**259%**	
	Age >42 years		**154%**	

Sources: 1) https://ga7a.short.gy/8XKfu8; 2) https://ga7a.short.gy/8fRNzk; 3) https://ga7a.short.gy/d5N3ax; 4) https://ga7a.short.gy/lSM9PP; 5) https://ga7a.short.gy/Hq1etd

Part VII

Education, Skilling, Jobs

More than 340M 'APAAR One Nation One Student IDs' have been created. APAAR ID links the 'Academic Bank of Credits' (ABC) of a student, storing all his/her academic learning, certificates, credentials, formal or informal credits earned from different sources to granular level of credits, including skilling credits or sports or social work, digitally verified by the agency awarding those credits. There are 2,312 higher education institutions registered on ABC.

Exam paper leaks have been a major problem plaguing India for decades. The Modi Government enacted the Public Examinations (Prevention of Unfair Means) Act 2024 to prevent paper leaks.

About 40-odd programs/schemes launched by the Modi government to improve the education sector have not been covered in this book, in order to reduce pages.

80

New Education Policy

In July 2020, a new National Education Policy (NEP) was approved by the Union Cabinet, after 34 years. Though the real benefits will only be known after 8–10 years, here are salient features of the most sweeping education sector reforms in India's history:

- The earlier 10+2 format (ages 6–18) is being replaced with a 5+3+3+4 structure (ages 3–18), consisting of (a) Foundational Stage with 3-year universal 'Early Childhood Care Education' via pre-school or Anganwadi plus two years of primary school (classes 1–2) with multilevel play/activity-based learning for ages 3–8; (b) Preparatory Stage (classes 3–5) with play, discovery, and activity-based and interactive classroom learning for ages 8–11; (c) Middle Stage (classes 6–8) with experiential learning in sciences, maths, arts, social sciences, and humanities for ages 11–14; and (d) Secondary Stage (classes 9–12) with multidisciplinary study with flexibility to choose subjects for ages 14–18, with an option to exit at the end of class 10 and re-enter later into class 11.
- School exams will be conducted in classes 3, 5, and 8, with a 360° progress card, which will include self/peer and teacher assessment, to reflect the uniqueness and

the progress of the student in the cognitive, affective, socio-emotional, and psychomotor domains. Progress in project-based and inquiry-based learning, quizzes, role-plays, group work, portfolios, etc., will be included. This 360° progress card will involve parents. AI-based software will be used to help track a child's growth and help him/her make optimal career choices. Results of exams will only be used for developmental purposes, and the continuous monitoring and improvement of the schooling system.

- The medium of instruction till class 5 (and preferably till class 8) will be in home/regional language/mother tongue. The 3-language policy to continue with two native languages.
- Classes 10 and 12 board exams will be easier, will test core competencies and will be offered twice a year. Students will have a wider choice of subjects and will be assessed on 'best-of-two' attempts.
- Students will have the flexibility to choose subjects across arts, science, humanities, extra-curricular, sports, and vocational streams.
- Beginning with maths, all subjects will be gradually offered at two levels (basic and advanced).
- Vocational education to start from class 6. Students to compulsorily have 10 bag-less days/year, during which they are exposed to an informal internship in a vocation of their choice.
- The curriculum in all subjects will be reduced to its core essentials. There will be focus on critical thinking, inquiry, discovery, discussion, and analysis-based teaching and learning methods for holistic education. Assessment will be done of core concepts and knowledge, higher-order skills and their application in real life.

- Questions from students to be encouraged.
- The undergraduate program under the NEP will be of 3/4 years for a bachelor's degree, with preference for a 4-year multidisciplinary program.
- A student can exit with a 'certificate' after completing one year in a discipline or field including vocational and professional subjects, or an 'advanced diploma' after completing two years.
- There will be an academic bank of credit with credit transfer facility to enable the student to leave at any time and re-join the same or another college at any time.
- Postgraduate college will be of 1 year or 2 years for a master's degree.
- Programs for an integrated 5-year bachelor's-cum-master's degree will be introduced.
- There will be extensive use of technology in teaching, learning, and assessment. Interactive teaching will be introduced with reduced dependency on textbooks. There will be emphasis on digital literacy, computational thinking and coding, and ethical and moral reasoning.
- Teachers must identify, recognise, and utilise the unique capabilities of each student.
- Critical thinking and creativity for logical decision-making and innovation will be encouraged.
- There will now be common norms for public and private institutions, as well as fee limits for private colleges/universities within a broad regulatory framework.
- There will be diversity and local context in all curricula, teaching and policy. Programs will focus on Indian culture and development of scientific temper and inculcation of knowledge and practice of human and constitutional values such as patriotism, sacrifice, non-violence, truth,

honesty, peace, etc. All kinds of Indian arts will be offered at all levels of education, starting with ages 3–6. There will be focus on literature and scientific vocabulary of Indian languages. Departments and programs will be set up for Indian languages, comparative literature, creative writing, arts, music, and philosophy.

- Over 15 years, colleges will get graded autonomy to grant degrees. They will have an independent board of governors. Affiliation with universities and deemed university status will end.
- By the year 2040, all higher education institutions must compulsorily become multidisciplinary.
- Top 100 foreign universities will be allowed to set up campuses in India. Top Indian institutes such as Indian Institute of Management (IIMs) and IITs to be encouraged to set-up campuses abroad.
- The Higher Education Commission of India (HECI) will replace the University Grants Commission (UGC), excluding medical and legal education. There were too many regulators earlier, and they were often at loggerheads with each other.
- New bodies to be set up include National Research Foundation, National Educational Technology Forum, and Indian Institute of Translation and Interpretation.
- A new National Mission on Foundational Literacy and Numeracy will be set up, so that all students up to class 3 can attain universal foundational literacy and numeracy.

The National Testing Agency (NTA) was set up in November 2017 as a specialist, autonomous, and self-sustained testing organisation for conducting efficient, transparent, and international standardised tests to assess the competency of candidates for admission to premier higher education institutions with a mission to improve equity and quality in education by developing and administering research-based valid, reliable, efficient, transparent, fair and global level assessments.

Before NEP came into being, NTA was already conducting the AISSEE, CMAT, GPAT, IIFTEE, JEE (Main), NCHM-JEE, NEET-UG, NET-CSIR, and several UGC-NET tests. It is now conducting the Common University Entrance Tests for Undergraduate and Postgraduate (CUET-UG and CUET-PG) programs into which separate entrance exams of BBAU, BHU, ICAR, and JNU have been merged.

The CUET was introduced for admission into all undergraduate programs in all central universities for the 2023–24 academic session. It provides a common platform and equal opportunities to candidates across India, especially those from rural/remote areas, and helps establish better connect with universities.

A single exam will enable candidates to cover a wide outreach and be part of the admissions process to various central universities.

The single biggest idea in the NEP is the emphasis on learning by conceptual understanding to prepare better for a competitive 'real world', rather than 'rote learning' or 'mugging' to pass exams.

Most reputed educationists, including the chancellors/directors of reputed institutions such as IIT Delhi, IIT Kanpur, Delhi University, JNU, Jamia Milia Islamia, used terms like 'positive step forward', 'transformative', 'long overdue', 'ground-breaking', etc.

Such a transformative policy will undoubtedly take a long time to get fully implemented and for substantial results to show, but a beginning has been made in the right direction.

We are 17.76 per cent of the world's population, but only 43 universities made it to the Top 1,000 and only one to the Top 500 in the 'Times Higher Education World University Rankings 2024'.

Why did governments before Modi not think of such reforms?

81

Temples of Higher Learning

Setting up of new 'institutes of national importance', universities and other institutes of higher learning is revolutionising the face of Indian education in the Modi-era.

HIGHER EDUCATION **Source:** Annual Reports of UGC	**UPA**	**MODI**	**Increase**
Universities	**348**	**504**	**▲ 44.8%**
AIIMS (All India Institute of Medical Sciences)	**6**	**13**	**▲ 116.7%**
Medical Colleges	**153**	**396**	**▲ 158.8%**
IIT (India Institute of Technology)	**9**	**7**	**▼ 22.2%**
IIIT (India Institute of Information Tech)	**7**	**16**	**▲ 128.6%**
IIM (Indian Institute of Management)	**6**	**8**	**▲ 33.3%**
NID (National Institute of Design)	**0**	**4**	∞
Gross Enrolment Ratio	23% (13-14)	28.3% (22-23)	**▲ 23%**
Enrolment in Higher Education	34.2mn (13-14)	44.7mn (22-23)	**▲ 30.7%**
Enrolment in PhD courses	117,000 (13-14)	231,000 (22-23)	**▲ 97.4%**
Enrolment of Females in PhD	48,000 (13-14)	109,700 (22-23)	**▲ 128.5%**

There are hundreds of more medical colleges and other institutes under development.

82

Schooling India

In March 2024, there were over 1.489M schools (82.9 per cent rural), 265.24M students (48 per cent girls), and 9.507M teachers (51.3 per cent female).

Samagra Shiksha covers all school education from pre-school to class 12. It has been aligned with NEP and aims to ensure that all children have access to quality education with an equitable and inclusive classroom environment, which takes care of their background, multilingual needs, and different academic abilities.

In September 2022, the PM SHRI (PM ScHools for Rising India) scheme was approved for developing over 14,500 schools as PM SHRI schools by strengthening select existing schools being managed by the GoI, state governments, and local bodies.

PM SHRI schools will showcase all components of the NEP, act as model schools and offer mentorship to other nearby schools. They will focus on cognitive development to create and nurture holistic and well-rounded youth equipped with key contemporary skills.

The scheme, that will run till 2026–27, aims for enrolment of over 2M students. The learnings will be scaled to other schools nationwide.

Over 10,000 Atal Tinkering Labs (ATLs) have been set up since 2016 inside schools. The objective is to foster curiosity, creativity and imagination; create scientific temper; nurture innovation; raise entrepreneurial spirit; and inculcate skills such as design mindset, computational thinking, adaptive learning, and physical computing. Around 60 per cent of the ATLs are in government or government-aided schools and about 96 per cent are either in girls' schools or co-ed schools.

More than 6,200 'Mentors of Change' have been engaged for mentoring students, and over 11M students are actively engaged in ATLs. More than 1.6M innovation projects have been created.

National Scholarships Portal is a one-stop solution for application receipt, processing, sanction, and disbursal of various scholarships to students.

83

Improvement in School Infrastructure

The numbers in the Table below say all that there is to say about the work that Modi and his team have done to improve the infrastructure of almost 1.472M schools spread across the country.

Status of School Infrastructure	FY13	FY24	Increase
	Source: https://dashboard.udiseplus.gov.in/#/home		
Girls' Toilet	88.1%	97.2%	▲ 10.3%
Boys' Toilet	67.2%	95.7%	▲ 42.4%
Hand Wash Facility	36.3%	94.7%	▲ 160.9%
Electricity	54.6%	91.8%	▲ 68.1%
Library / Reading Facility	69.2%	89.0%	▲ 28.6%
Annual Medical Check-ups	61.1%	75.2%	▲ 23.1%
Computer	22.2%	57.2%	▲ 157.7%
Internet	6.2%	53.9%	▲ 769.4%

84

Pariksha pe Charcha

Imagine an elder brother motivating a child during the most pressuring time—an exam. That's what Modi aims to achieve with '*Pariksha pe Charcha*', part of a larger movement called 'Exam Warriors' to create stress-free atmosphere for youngsters. It is a movement driven by Modi's efforts to bring together students, parents, teachers, and the society to foster an environment where the unique individuality of each child is allowed to express itself fully.

The inspiration is Modi's book *Exam Warriors*, in which knowledge gaining and holistic development of students are given primacy. The PM urges everyone to put exams in the right perspective, rather than making it a life-and-death situation punctuated by undue stress and pressure. The Namo App's *Exam Warriors* module adds an interactive tech element. It communicates the core messages of each mantra in the book. The module is not just for youngsters but also for parents and teachers. It also has thought provoking but enjoyable activities that help absorb concepts through practical means.

At the annual *Pariksha pe Charcha* events, Modi interacts with students appearing for forthcoming board exams and answers queries related to stress and other issues. 'Failures can become a bigger motivation; a temporary setback doesn't mean success is not waiting. In fact, a setback may mean the best is yet to come,' he said.[1]

As per him, a balance between studies and extracurricular activities with optimal time management is necessary. He cautions parents not to make extracurricular interests of their children a fashion statement or a calling card. He encourages curtailing usage of mobiles and tells students to stay at least an hour away from technology and spend time with family. He also suggested creating a room where there is 'no entry' for technology.

In 2023, 3.8M students registered for *Pariksha pe Charcha* and this number went up to a whopping 22.6M in 2024 (up 494.7 per cent in just one year).

85

Skilling India

Much before becoming PM, Modi recognised the limitations of the traditional education system in equipping youth with job-ready skills and thus created Ministry of Skill Development and Entrepreneurship in November 2014. No government of the past had thought about doing this.

National Skill Development Mission was launched in July 2015 to address the fragmented approach of UPA programs.

Skill India has 42,645 training centres offering more than 7,100 skill courses and runs more than 8.4L job exchanges.

Till 2024, 1.785M youth received apprenticeship training under National Apprenticeship Promotion Scheme (NAPS). The number of enrolments grew from 35,517 in FY19 to 932,358 in FY24 (up 2,525 per cent in 5 years).

Pradhan Mantri Kaushal Vikas Yojana (PMKVY) was launched in 2015 to promote skill development via free short duration skill training programs and incentivising this with monetary rewards for skill certification. As of 17 September 2024, there were 13,702 Skill Training Centres where over 15.52M persons have been trained and over 2.47MM placed in jobs.

There are 738 Pradhan Mantri Kaushal Kendras (model training centres) of 3,000–8,000SFT BUA each.

Entrepreneurship Skill Development Programme (ESDP) has 24,055 programs to help promote new enterprises and enable capacity building of MSMEs. It motivates SC/ST, women, PwDs, ex-servicemen, and BPL category persons to get trained to become self-employed. More than 1.105M persons have been trained.

Craftsman Training Scheme provides training for becoming a professional in 153 trades, including the most basic ones and up to high-tech contemporary professions. Crafts Instructor Training Scheme covers 51 trades.

More than 72.6M youth have been trained under different skilling schemes of the Modi Government in the past 10.5 years.

AatmaNirbhar Skilled Employee Employer Mapping (ASEEM) acts as a directory of skilled workforce. The objective is to provide a platform that matches supply of skilled workforce with the market demand, thereby facilitating better livelihood opportunities.

More than 2,250 startups are involved in skill development and skills assessment.

India's rank at the WorldSkills competition organized by WorldSkills International (Netherlands) improved from 16th in 2013 to 5th in 2022 (by total points scored).

86

Job Schemes

AatmaNirbhar Bharat Rojgar Yojana incentivises job creation by employers. In the 3-year period from its launch in December 2020 till December 2023, 152,517 establishments created 6.049M jobs.

Up to March 2022, 153,702 establishments created over 12.439M jobs under a similar incentive scheme called the PM Rojgar Protsahan Yojana.

Rozgar Melas are run by National Skills Development Corporation at the national level; PMKKs at the parliamentary constituency level; and Fee-based Model Training Partners, PMKVYs, and Sector Skill Councils at the district level; to provide job opportunities in the private sector to unemployed youth. These Melas cater to ages 18–35 who have passed minimum class 8 and are Industrial Training Institute (ITI) certificate holders.

Between October 2022 and December 2024, there were 14 editions of the National Rozgar Mela during which job appointment letters were issued to more than 930,000 youth.

PM National Apprenticeship Mela was launched in April 2022 to connect the youth with industry for apprenticeship training opportunities.

Since the implementation of mandatory Corporate Social Responsibility (CSR) spending under the Companies Act by the Modi Government in FY15, Indian corporates have spent more than ₹2.06LCr on CSR projects, including skilling and livelihood enhancement projects.

Under the PM's Internship Scheme announced in Budget 2025, the top 500 companies (private and PSEs) will offer one-year internships to 10M youth. On an average, each company is expected to hire 4,000 interns a year for 5 years, who will get a one-time aid of ₹6,000 and a monthly allowance of ₹5,000. The GoI will pay the one-time aid and 90 per cent of the monthly pay, while the companies will pay for the training costs and 10 per cent of the monthly allowance, from their CSR funds. The pilot project closed on 15 November 2024 with 650,000 applicants for 127,000 job opportunities.

NREGA was expanded from the Gram Panchayat-level to district level. Funds of ₹685,241Cr were released, compared with ₹244,805Cr by the UPA (up 179.9 per cent). The average NREGA wages went up from ₹155.54 in FY14 to ₹236.78 in FY24 (up 52.23 per cent).

Over 60 other programs of the Modi Government are oriented towards generating nation-wide job opportunities and self-employment.

Part VIII

Farmers, Backward Classes, and Special Groups

87

Jai Kisan

Prime Minister Modi refers to farmers as '*annadatas*' (food givers). His government spent a whopping ₹529.5LCr on the agriculture sector (including research and education, animal husbandry, dairying, fisheries) compared with ₹101.7LCr spent by UPA Government (up 421 per cent).

Institutional credit for the sector was increased from ₹7.3LCr in FY14 to ₹25.48LCr in FY24 (up 249 per cent).

Benefits of about ₹30,000/year are provided to 178M small farmers through multiple schemes.

PM-KISAN provides ₹6,000/year income support for an average of 101.3M eligible farmers—almost ₹3.46LCr has been given during December 2018–November 2024.

National Mission for Sustainable Agriculture (NMSA) aims to make farms more productive, sustainable, and climate resilient; help conserve resources; and optimise use of water resources.

A key component of NMSA is soil health management by:

- Judicious use of chemical fertilizers.
- Use of more organic manure/biofertilizers.
- Improving soil heath and productivity.
- Strengthening soil and fertilizer testing facilities.
- Providing recommendations for improving soil fertility.

Up to December 2024, more than 11,750 soil testing labs were set up, over 246.96M tests were completed, and an equal number of Soil Health Cards issued to farmers. Around 680,000 demonstrations, 93,781 farmer's training programs and 7,425 farmer's melas had been organised to educate farmers regarding proper use of fertilizers as per recommendation of Soil Health Card to improve soil quality.

National Agriculture Infra Financing Facility assists post-harvest management infrastructure and community farming assets through interest subvention and credit guarantee. Up to August 2024, ₹54,246Cr was sanctioned for 89,434 projects.

Up to December 2024, Agriculture Infrastructure Fund sanctioned ₹51,364Cr for 84,159 projects. The sanctioned projects mobilized ₹78,433Cr from private entities and generated 819,000 jobs.

Farmers get information/advisories by SMS in the mKisan App—up to July 2024, almost 7.46M SMSs were received from almost 5.31M farmers, and 108,783 advisories were given.

To provide 'Demand Based Tele Agriculture Advisories', the Indian Council of Agricultural Research and Digital India Corporation collaborated to launch the 'Kisan Sarathi' toll-free interactive voice response system (IVRS) in 13 languages with an App and Web portal on which Agri-related information can be pulled by farmers on their mobiles. Calls from farmers are received at a Central Command Centre and routed to a relevant Agri-expert. The farmer's data pops up on the expert's mobile/laptop/desktop on logging in and s/he can understand the farmer/field problem, access an extensive knowledge database available in the system, and facilitate an appropriate solution to the problem. Almost 25.1M farmers from 321,510 villages have registered.

Drones to Revolutionise Agriculture

Namo Drone Didi scheme helps 15,000 selected Women SHGs to buy drones for renting to farmers for application of fertilizers and pesticides. Financial assistance at 80 per cent of the cost of drone and accessories/ancillary charges up to ₹8L is provided to women SHGs. The scheme will provide sustainable livelihood support to SHGs, and they can earn additional income of at least ₹1L/year.

Up to November 2024, 27,099 drone demonstrations covered 302.35km^2 and benefited 351,856 farmers. 527 drones were given to farmers on subsidy and 1,595 drones to custom hiring centres (CHCs) for providing drone services to farmers on rental basis.

The SHGs will undergo training in drone operations and repairs. The integration of drones has the potential to revolutionise agriculture, enabling precision farming, crop monitoring, and pest control.

Some more schemes and their progress include:

- Pradhan Mantri Kisan Samriddhi Kendras (PMKSKs) converts existing village, block/taluk/district-level fertilizer shops into model shops for all agri-related inputs and services. Around 330,000 are to be established of which over 170,000 are operational.
- Participatory Guarantee System of India with two components (PGS-India Green and PGS-India Organic) is a quality assurance initiative. As of August 2024, it had 73,058 local groups and over 1.9M farmers as participants, and 177,358 certificates had been issued covering 2.9144M acres of farmland.
- Jaivik Kheti portal is a one-stop solution for facilitating organic farmers to sell organic produce and for promoting organic farming and its benefits. As of July 2024, it catered

to 19,011 local groups, 622,686 individual farmers, 8,605 buyers, and 89 input suppliers.

- By November 2024, 9,180 FPOs were registered. They get financial assistance up to ₹18L per FPO for 3 years.
- As of March 2024, 77.5M Kisan Credit Cards (KCCs) had been distributed and loans worth over ₹9LCr had been given to farmers.
- Between FY16 and FY24, farmland under sprinkler irrigation went up from 204,650ha to 664,244ha (up 224.6 per cent), and through drip irrigation from 346,936ha to 477,194ha (up 37.5 per cent) through the Pradhan Mantri Krishi Sinchayee Yojana.
- In 8.5 years since the launch of the PM Fasal Bima Yojana crop insurance scheme in February 2016, the government settled claims of over ₹1.7LCr (more than five times the premium amount paid by farmers).
- The eNAM (Electronic National Agriculture Market) connects 17.845M farmers with 1,410 *mandis*, 4,289 FPOs, 262,754 traders, and 114,612 commission agents. Trading volume has crossed ₹4LCr.
- An Agri Accelerator Fund is being set up.
- Kisan Suvidha is a one-stop App with 17 subjects in agriculture and five in animal husbandry.
- The GoI will set up agri storage units in 65,000 villages. 48,512 storage infrastructure projects with 940MT capacity had been sanctioned by June 2024.
- Over 99.8% Fair Price Shops have been automated using electronic Point of Sale devices for transparent and ensured distribution of subsidised food grains.
- Kisan Call Centres helped almost 6.6M farmers (5.532M in agriculture, 1.025M in horticulture, 33,920 in animal husbandry, and 6,205 in fisheries) in 2022 and 2023 alone.

- Over 2.4M farmers have enrolled in the Pradhan Mantri Kisan Maandhan Yojana (PMKMY) old age pension scheme for farmers.
- From May 2014 to November 2024, 1.91M agricultural machines have been distributed to farmers.
- 26,637 CHCs, 609 Hi-Tech Hubs, and 24,176 Farm Machinery Banks have been established.
- From FY16 to December 2024, 95,000 km^2 of farm lands have been covered under the Per Drop More Crop (PDMC) scheme. An evaluation in 2020-21 found PDMC improved water use efficiency by 30–70% and increased farmer income by 10–69%.
- 53.23M trees were planted on 1210km^2 and 1,061 nurseries established, benefiting about 186,000 farmers.
- Under the Mission for Integrated Development of Horticulture, 13,960km^2 of horticulture crops were expanded; 1,520km^2 orchards rejuvenated; 525km^2 covered under organic farming; 3,080km^2 covered under protected cultivation; 55,347 water-harvesting structures created, and 1.645M bee colonies distributed. The scheme also provided 274,000 horticulture machines, established 129,000 post-harvest units, set up 15,973 market infrastructures, and trained 977,000 farmers.

Sugarcane Sector

The Modi Government gave ₹1.2LCr to sugar and bio-energy manufacturers to help sugarcane farmers invest in R&D to improve cane yield and sugar content, reduce water wastage, and improve soil health, and achieving 20 per cent ethanol blending by 2025. As a result, 50M farmers are getting timely payments (against delayed payments in UPA-era), offering cheaper sugar to consumers as of March 2024.

88

AH, D, and F

Modi created a Ministry for Animal Husbandry, Dairying, and Fisheries (AHD&F) in May 2019.

An interest subvention scheme gives short-term loans of up to ₹3L at 7 per cent interest for one year to farmers engaged in crop husbandry and AHD&F, with 3 per cent subvention for prompt repayment, thus reducing the effective rate to 4 per cent per annum. As of December 2023, more than 46.54M applicants were sanctioned almost ₹5.7LCr.

Animal Husbandry Infrastructure Development Fund (AHIDF) motivates investments in dairying, breed multiplication, meat processing, animal feeds, veterinary drugs, vaccines, and conversion of animal waste to wealth, with funding up to 90 per cent of project cost. The GoI gives 3 per cent interest subvention for eight years including two years' moratorium on repayment, and credit guarantee of up to the 25 per cent of loans from the credit guarantee fund. AHIDF has helped in adding 141L litres/day of milk processing, 7.924MT of feed processing, and 0.91MT of meat processing capacity (2–4 per cent output increases). It will help in creating 3.5M direct and indirect jobs and in increasing livestock farmers' wealth. It has already benefitted about 150,000 farmers.

Contribution of livestock in total agriculture and allied sector gross value added increased from 24.38 per cent in FY15 to 30.23 per cent in FY24. Under Rashtriya Gokul Mission, 621M animals are covered, 79.6M artificial inseminations done, and more than 40M farmers benefitted.

The Modi Government invested ₹38,572Cr in the fisheries sector in 10.5 years, compared with only ₹3,682Cr invested in 66.8 years since independence (66.7 times higher average annual investment).

Fisheries and Aquaculture Infrastructure Development Fund (FIDF) has ₹8,462Cr with similar interest subvention as AHIDF. Till FY23, about 121 infra projects of ₹5,589Cr were approved. The 27 completed projects provide safe landing/berthing facilities for 8,100 fishing vessels, enhance fish landing of 109,000 tons, benefitted about 330,000 fishers/other stakeholders, and helped create over 250,000 direct and indirect jobs.

Pradhan Mantri Matysa Sampada Yojana (PMMSY) was launched in 2020 to bring a 'Blue Revolution' via sustainable and responsible development of fisheries with estimated outlay of ₹20,050Cr; and 677,462 fishers' families get livelihood and nutritional support during the fishing ban and lean period. Till December 2023, projects of over ₹18,500Cr had been sanctioned with an estimated 1.6M direct and indirect beneficiaries.

A sub-scheme called Pradhan Mantri Matsya Kisan Samridhi Sah Yojana (PMMKSSY) was granted ₹6,000Cr for FY24–27 to support 640,000 MSEs and 5,500 fisheries cooperatives. The program focuses on improving value chain efficiency and ensuring safe, quality fish. It is projected to create 170,000 new jobs (including 75,000 women) and create 540,000 continued job opportunities in the MSE value chain.

Five integrated aqua parks are being set up by the GoI.

Group accident insurance coverage per fisher went up from ₹1L to ₹5L, benefitting 26.78M fishers. There was priority sector lending of ₹34,332Cr compared to zero in FY14.

Around 160,000 KCCs were issued to AHD&F farmers after the scheme was extended to them in 2019.

WHAT	FY14	FY23	Increase
Milk production	137.69MT	230.58MT	**▲ 67.5%**
Egg production	74.75B eggs	138.38B eggs	**▲ 82.9%**
Meat production	6.24MT	9.77MT	**▲ 56.6%**
Fish production	9.579MT	17.4MT	**▲ 81.6%**
Inland & Aquaculture production	6.136MT	13.137MT	**▲ 114.1%**
Shrimp production	0.322MT	1.184MT	**▲ 267.7%**
Seafood Exports	₹30,213Cr	₹63,960Cr	**▲ 111.7%**
Shrimp Exports	₹19,368Cr	₹43,135Cr	**▲ 122.7%**
Sources: https://ga7a.short.gy/4bxkz3; https://ga7a.short.gy/vS7Gdb			

89

Farm Reforms Derailed

In September 2020, the Modi Government made path-breaking changes in major laws in the agriculture sector to not just increase farmers' incomes but also reduce consumers' costs. These were based on many reports over the years, the most notable by Bharat Ratna Dr MS Swaminathan, and came after due consultation with thousands of stakeholders and subject experts over six years.

In northern Europe, the gap between the farmers' selling price and the consumers' buying price is 10–20 per cent; in Indonesia it is 20–30 per cent—in India, it is a colossal 70–100 per cent. This is due to various British-era laws, most notable being the Essential Commodities Act and the Agriculture Produce Marketing Committee Act (APMC Act)—the latter has been amended from time to time by various states.

Farmers are forced to sell produce through 'commission agents' at market yards (*mandis*) regulated by states under their APMC laws. The agents earn 1.5–7.5 per cent of sale value for cleaning, sorting, displaying, and auctioning the crop, while states earn an 'APMC cess'. Government agencies buy the crop at minimum support price (MSP) and then private traders buy the produce through commission agents at market price.

The *mandis* are based on geographical restrictions. Imagine that they are based on pin codes. So, you could be a farmer at pin code 110011, but you cannot sell to your neighbour because s/he lives in pin code 110012. Isn't this ridiculous in the era of free markets?

Modi said that 'powerful gangs' have been exploiting India's poor farmers, especially the landless.

Farmers are not free to sell their produce anywhere they like. They are forced to sell below MSP if government procurement is delayed. *Mandi* cartels fix prices. Commission agents buy crops at low rates, store them and sell at MSP in the next procurement season, so the MSP goes to them instead of farmers for whom it is meant.

The 'gangs' have survived for decades by 'feeding' state politicians and bureaucrats.

What Were the September 2020 Reforms?

Under the Farmers' Produce Trade and Commerce (Promotion and Facilitation) Act, a farmer could sell to anyone, anywhere and at any price. Transactions outside *mandis* would not be charged the APMC cess. Farmers would benefit from direct market linkages and better supply chains. This would increase their incomes.

Under the Farmers (Empowerment and Protection) Agreement of Price Assurance and Farm Services Act, farmers could do 'contract farming' with large buyers at mutually agreed prices. They could grow tomatoes for Pizza Hut, potatoes for Lay's, onions for McDonalds, rice for MTR, and so on. The buyer had to pay the market rate if it was higher than the contract rate. Farmers could withdraw from the contract at any stage without penalty, but the buyer had to pay the agreed price and a penalty for breaching a contract. 10,000 FPOs would be set up to enable small farmers to deal with corporates (9,180 were set up by November 2024). McDonalds and Pizza Hut already have dozens of contract farmers in India for many years and they have all become super rich. Corporates like Amul and Nestlé have benefitted lakhs of milk farmers for decades.

Under the Essential Commodities (Amendment) Act, the GoI could remove cereals, pulses, potato, onion, oilseeds, and oils from the list of essential commodities, and regulate their supply and prices only during war, famine, extraordinary price rises, or natural calamities; and regulation could only be imposed if prices of horticultural produce rise 100 per cent and non-perishables 50 per cent. This would allow traders, wholesalers, retailers, and exporters to keep stocks without penalty. It would attract domestic and foreign private investment in supply chain and logistics operations including cold storages, as it would remove fears of excessive regulatory interference. Supply chain improvements would bring price stability, transparency and timeliness, and reduced wastage. Consumers would also benefit as a more efficient and quicker supply chain reduces prices since fewer intermediaries are involved.

In Punjab and Haryana, state governments do about 75 per cent procurement and large farmers are incentivised to grow only certain crops. This creates a surplus, which is stored in dysfunctional godowns where it rots.

The UN's Food and Agriculture Organization says that more than ₹70,000Cr of fresh fruit/vegetables perish annually in India; and that wheat grain of over ₹53,000Cr/year rot because of improper storage by the FCI.

Mohinder Gulati, former energy advisor to The World Bank says that India wastes 67MT of food worth over ₹1.125LCr per year, which could feed 100M people.

Most sections of the industry and stakeholders in agriculture trade said that the Acts were 'progressive and visionary'.

Soon after the Acts were introduced, farmer unions began protests. After two months of protests, the unions—mainly from Punjab and Haryana—began a movement named *Dilli Chalo* in which lakhs of their members marched towards the nation's capital. These states provide 70–90 per cent of wheat and 28–44 per cent of rice for India's PDS. Some protestors came in cars such as Toyota Fortuner and Range Rover, many others had Toyota Innova. Most could be seen using expensive phones like iPhone or Samsung Galaxy.

There were 11 rounds of inconclusive talks between the GoI (led by three senior ministers) and farm unions in October 2020–January 2021.

On 21 January 2021, the SCI 'stayed' the new farm laws, meaning they could not be implemented without the apex court removing the stay.

Five days later, on Republic Day 2021, tens of thousands of these 'poor farmers' drove into Delhi and held a parade with a large convoy of tractors. They deviated from Delhi Police's pre-approved routes, and clashes with police ensued. Thousands reached the Red Fort, where they installed flags of farmer unions and the Sikh 'Nishan Sahib'.

It was widely known that the protestors were funded by 'Khalistan' factions in Canada and the UK, and funding was being routed via the Aam Aadmi Party. AAP supported the protests, which led to it winning the Punjab Assembly election and forming the government there in March 2022.

Opponents to the reforms say that the freedom to hoard commodities means that corporates can beat down crop prices and hurt farmers. In reality, corporates would compete like in any other open market and farmers would get the best prices. Free trade would co-exist with *mandis*, and competition would compel *mandis* to reinvent their role. Isn't that the essence of a free market?

The reforms would drastically increase farmers' profits. As in any other industry, once profit is earned, it is reinvested back for generating better quality and higher quantities. The reforms were particularly beneficial for small and marginal farmers who own less than 2ac land but comprise about 80 per cent of farmer population. Supply chain efficiencies such as better demand–supply matching, lower price volatility, and superior cold storage are big desires of smaller farmers. They were not the ones protesting. Farmers from Andhra or Telangana, Maharashtra, Assam, Kerala, or Tamil Nadu were also not protesting, as they have moved with the times.

CONSUMPTION HABITS HAVE CHANGED			
Market Share in Value Terms	**2007**	**2022**	**CHANGE**
Livestock Produce (Milk, Eggs, Meat, etc.)	25.6%	36.9%	▲ 44.1%
Fruits and Vegetables	17.4%	24.3%	▲ 39.7%
Cereals (Rice, Wheat, etc.)	23.3%	16.7%	▼ 28.3%
Oilseeds	8.2%	5.2%	▼ 36.6%
Annualised Increase in Prices	**2014**	**2023**	**CHANGE**
Fish	No MSP support, No Input Subsidy		▲ 9.0%
Dairy and Other Livestock Products	Cooperative Marketing of Milk, No Subsidy		▲ 5.8%
Fruits and Vegetables	No MSP, but High Subsidies		▲ 5.8%
Coarse Cereals, Pulses, Oilseeds	Some produce has MSP. Small Subsidies		▲ 2.4%
Rice, Wheat, Sugarcane, Cotton	Strong MSP & Procurement Support; High Subsidies		▲ 1.4%
Production of Horticulture Crops is ▲ at a 12yr-CAGR of 3.3%, compared with only 2.52% in Food Grains			
The 355.3MT of Horticulture Crop is almost exclusively produced by Non-Protesting States			

Only 6 per cent of Indian farmers sell on MSP. Should the welfare of 94 per cent be sacrificed for this 6 per cent?

Mark Kahn, Managing Partner of agritech-focused venture capital firm Omnivore said,

> Do we really want to pay farmers to grow more rice to rot in FCI godowns? India is a grain-surplus country and is today … eating more *subzi*, fruits, dairy and animal protein. The fear of middlemen being eliminated seems naïve because farmers depend on them as moneylenders.[1]

Then why such aggressive opposition? Because Modi was removing yet another source of corruption. Commission agents' fat profits would have become history, and state governments (especially Punjab and Haryana) would lose sizeable revenue from *mandi* fees. These 'interest groups' convinced many uneducated/gullible farmers that the new laws would end the government's MSP support and thus harm them.

In a rebuttal to the extortionist farmers, the Modi Government made several 'legal' decisions to achieve the key goals of the 'SCI-stayed' agri-reforms.

A Ministry of Cooperation was created under Amit Shah, Modi's toughest Cabinet colleague, who has effectively dealt with terrorists. As of June 2024, there were 809,303 cooperative societies with over 296M members (imagine, there was no ministry for them), including around 102,000 PACS (Primary Agricultural Credit Societies), around 142,000 primary dairy cooperatives, and around 25,000 primary fishery cooperatives.

PACS became multifunctional entities; 200,000 new multipurpose PACS/dairy/fishery cooperative societies are being set up. They were allotted 2,100 FPOs, made eligible for LPG distributorships, given priority in fuel retailing, among other benfits. 41,075 PACS were functioning as CSCs by November 2024, with thousands more in process, and 36,180 PACS were upgraded to PMKSKs.

Four PSEs were established as umbrella organisations:

- National Federation of Urban Cooperative Banks and Credit Societies Limited to provide necessary IT infrastructure and operational support to about 1,500 Urban Cooperative Banks.
- National Cooperative Exports Limited to promote exports.
- Bhartiya Beej Sahakari Samiti Limited for cultivation, production, and distribution of high-quality seeds under a common brand name.
- National Cooperative Organics Limited to supervise production, marketing, and distribution of certified organic products. In November 2023, Amit Shah launched the 'Bharat Organics' brand. Six organic products—tur dal, chana dal, sugar, rajma, basmati rice, and Sonamasoori rice—are sold through Mother Dairy Safal outlets and online platforms, and a nationwide network of retail outlets is being created; 20 products were added in January–February 2024. Initially, NCOL is selling in India and later it will start exports. About 50 per cent of profits from sale through NCOL are transferred directly to member farmers.
- National Cooperative Development Corporation is a development-funding organisation for cooperatives like PFC/REC in the power sector, IRFC in railways and similar PSEs in various sectors. It disbursed credit/financial assistance of more than ₹1.25LCr during FY22–24.

India has 17.76 per cent of world population, but only 11.6 per cent of cultivable land (1.6M km^2), 34.7 per cent lower than the world average. Food grain production in FY24 was 332.3MT, but storage capacity only 145MT (43.6 per cent of production), resulting in wastage and losses to farmers. The US has 161 per cent capacity, Brazil 149 per cent and China 107 per cent.

In February 2024, Modi launched the world's largest decentralised grain storage program costing ₹1.25LCr, to create storage infrastructure at the PACS level for 70MT by 2027, encompassing warehouses, custom hiring centres (comprising farm machinery, implements and equipment for hiring), processing units, fair price shops, etc. Apart from addressing storage infrastructure shortage, the program will empower PACS to act as procurement centres, function as fair price shops, and create common processing units for sorting, grading, etc. By October 2024, godowns had started in 11 PACS, foundation stones laid for 500, and 1,275 identified for the next phase.

The GoI is building storage silos of 10MT capacity in PPP mode. To assist FCI in building infrastructure, the Modi Government increased its authorised capital from ₹10,000Cr to ₹21,000Cr.

On 9 August 2023, the Modi Government launched Bharat Dal chana dal at subsidised rates of ₹60/kg/₹55/kg for 1kg/30kg packs; and onions at ₹29/kg. On 6 November 2023, Bharat Atta wheat flour was launched at a subsidised rate of ₹27.50/kg—275,936MT Bharat Atta, 296,802MT Bharat Dal and 30.44Mkg onions were sold till 6 February 2024. On that day, Bharat Rice was launched at ₹29/kg in 5kg/10kg packs. Due to excellent response, supply of Bharat Atta and Bharat Rice were doubled to 650,000MT/month from April 2024 onwards.

By reducing import duties, retail prices of refined sunflower oil, soybean oil, and Palm Olein fell by 29.04 per cent, 18.98 per cent, and 25.43 per cent, respectively, from 2021 to 2022. India imports about 17MT of palm oil annually. GoI aims to increase domestic production from 0.35MT to 1MT by 2030 via the ₹11,040Cr National Palm Oil Mission by adding plantation of minimum 100,000 hectares/year for 5–6 years.

To prevent hoarding and black-marketing, the Modi Government imposed stock limits on wheat in all states/UTs from June 2023—1000MT for traders/wholesalers, 5MT/outlet for retailers, and 70 per cent of monthly installed capacity multiplied by remaining months for processors. There is a Wheat Stock Portal on which 20,456 registered entities declared stocks of 6.543MT. They upload stock positions every Friday, failing which they can be banned.

On 13 February 2024, farmers from Punjab once again landed up in Delhi. Though fewer in number, there were more luxury cars and phones compared to 2020–21. They had 21 demands. The most hilarious one was 'better integration with agri-industry to bypass intermediaries and secure direct market access and establishment of FPOs, enabling collective bargaining power, fair pricing, and reduced dependency on middlemen'.

Isn't that what the 2020 reforms were all about?

90

Housing for All

Under Pradhan Mantri Awas Yojana-Urban, 11.864M affordable homes were sanctioned for city dwellers (including slum dwellers) with committed GoI assistance of ₹2LCr.

Ownership is in the name of a female member or in a joint name. Preference is given to single women, PwDs, senior citizens, minorities, SC/ST/OBCs, minorities, transgender, and other vulnerable sections of the society.

Of the average cost of ₹683,600/home, 60 per cent is borne by the owner, 25 per cent by the GoI and 15 per cent by the state government.

Construction started in June 2015 and 9.001M homes (75.9 per cent) were delivered by December 2024 @ 78,956 per month, compared to 804,000 by UPA under Jawaharlal Nehru National Urban Renewal Mission (JNNURM) at 6,700 per month (up 1,078.4 per cent). Another 2.33M are under construction.

83,534 vacant houses were made available to be used as Affordable Renting Housing Complexes (ARHCs) and 5,648 were converted to ARHCs as of March 2024. Another 7,413 were in process. An additional 70,473 ARHC units have been sanctioned in 13 states/UTs.

The Real Estate (Regulation and Development) Act or RERA was enacted in 2016 to bring transparency in the real estate sector. More than 127,500 projects and over 75,000 real estate agents have been registered.

More than 1,900 all-weather permanent shelters have been created for almost 140,000 homeless persons in urban areas.

UPA built 21.05M houses under Indira Awaas Yojana in rural India at 175,400/month. By December 2024, under PM Awaas Yojana-Gramin, the Modi Government had built over 26.863M houses at 218,400/month (up 24.5 per cent) and over 4.5M were under construction.

The Modi 3.0 Government will build an additional 20M rural houses by 2029.

91

EWS Reservations

The Constitution (103rd Amendment) Act, 2019, enabled 10 per cent reservation for Economically Weaker Sections (EWS) of the society for admission to GoI-run and private educational institutions (except minority institutions), and for employment in central government jobs.

Modi called it a 'landmark moment in our nation's history'.[2]

The Amendment did not make such reservations mandatory in state government-run institutions or state government jobs. However, some states have chosen to implement the 10 per cent EWS reservation.

There existed 22.5 per cent reservations for SCs/STs (introduced in 1937 by the British, adopted in the Constitution in 1950, and specified as 15 per cent for SCs and 7.5 per cent for STs in 1982) and 27 per cent for OBCs (enacted in 1990). The reservation for EWS was above 49.5 per cent, so it ensured that existing reservations were not affected.

In 1992, a 9-judge bench of the SCI had ruled that there could be no reservation solely on economic criteria, as it was unconstitutional. The 103rd Amendment introduced enabling provisions for GoI to make special provisions for 'any EWS of citizens' other than those for 'socially/educationally backward classes' and SCs/STs. Two Articles were changed to allow special provisions and reservations for the EWS category, subject to a maximum of 10 per cent.

Anyone with an annual family income below ₹8 lakh from all sources in the preceding financial year is EWS for reservation purposes. Those with 5ac agricultural land, or residential flat of 1,000 SFT, or residential plot of over 100 square yards in notified municipalities, or over 200 square yards in other areas are excluded.

EWS students can qualify for quota in about 428,000 college seats, including 20,000 engineering seats and 10,900 MBBS seats.

In November 2022, the SCI upheld the validity of the Act by a 3:2 majority.

92

Uplifting EWS, SC/ST, and OBCs

Modi understands the pains and pangs of poverty and decades of neglect of people from marginalised communities. He comes from humble means and believes everyone should feel included, valued, and respected. He has been tirelessly working on alleviation and eventual elimination of poverty on the one hand, and bestowing dignity to the hitherto marginalised, on the other.

Criteria for Economically Backward Classes (EBCs) differ from state to state but are the same as EWS in most states.

Free Food Grains and Sugar Subsidy

Modi Government is providing free food grains to 813.5M poor persons (almost 57 per cent of India's population) for five years from January 2024 at a cost of ₹11.8LCr under Pradhan Mantri Garib Kalyan Anna Yojana.

The scheme was launched during COVID-19. Phases 1–2 were open in the period April–November 2020. After a gap of five months, it was relaunched in the second wave and was extended five more times. Phases 3–8 operated in May 2021–December 2023.

About ₹5.88LCr were spent on average 790M beneficiaries till December 2023.

Sugar subsidy facilitates access of sugar to the poor and adds energy to their diet so that their health improves. The GoI gives subsidy of ₹18.50 per kg per month of sugar to 18.9M families.

PM-DAKSH

This scheme provides skilling to marginalised persons—all SCs, OBCs/EBCs with family income below ₹300,000, DNTs (De-notified Nomadic and Semi-Nomadic Tribes), the transgender community, *safai karamcharis* (including waste pickers) and their dependants, and geriatric caregivers. Modi wants to skill around 271,000 of these people during FY22–26.

Scholarships and Loans

Scholarships for Higher Education for Young Achievers Scheme (SHREYAS) provides 1,000 junior research fellowships per year for MPhil/PhD programs for students from SC/ST/OBC communities, over and above GoI's normal reservation policy for UGC fellowships. After 2 years, if progress is satisfactory, his/her tenure is extended for 3 years as senior research fellow. Total period of award of junior and senior research fellowships cannot exceed 5 years.

Loans of about ₹57,758Cr have been given to about 255,893 SC/ST persons and women to start new businesses under Stand-Up India scheme up to December 2024.

National Backward Classes Finance and Development Corporation (NBCFDC) has disbursed loans of ₹7,409Cr to 3.269M entrepreneurs in marginalised classes for skill development. It also gives educational loans to students of

BPL families for courses/training at graduate and higher levels of up to ₹10L for studies in India, and up to ₹20L for foreign studies, at subsidised interest of 4 per cent per annum for boys and 3.5 per cent per annum for girls. Loans had been given to 171,496 students up to FY23.

Welfare of SCs and STs

Apart from various schemes, the Modi Government under its umbrella programs for development spends over ₹11,000Cr/year on SCs and STs.

Venture Capital Fund for SCs (VCF-SC) and Venture Capital Fund for STs (VCF-ST) were launched to help scheduled castes and tribals in setting up various kinds of businesses. Beneficiaries can avail investments of ₹10L to ₹5Cr for up to 10 years at concessional rate of interest of only 4 per cent per annum (3.75 per cent for women and PwDs).

Assistance of more than ₹11,700Cr was given to over 2.5M SCs, EWS, and sanitation workers to promote entrepreneurship.

211 exclusive special courts and 145 police stations have been set up for prevention of atrocities towards SCs and STs.

Ambedkar Social Innovation Incubation Mission (ASIIM) was set up to encourage innovative SC students to take to innovation and entrepreneurship without seeking jobs—1,000 initiatives of SC youth are being identified to give them equity funding up to ₹30L in a 3-year period.

Under the e-Utthaan Development Action Plan for SCs, a humongous amount of almost ₹7.056LCr has been spent in 6.8 years till December 2024.

Post-matric scholarships of ₹24,296Cr were granted to 29.108M SC students and pre-matric scholarships of ₹4,074Cr were granted to 21.471M SC students in 6 years from FY19 to FY24. Scholarships of crores have also been given to students from the OBC, EBC and DNT (denotified tribes) communities.

See the successes of the Modi Government in the education of SC/ST/OBC students:

Enrolment of SC/ST/OBC Students in Higher Education Courses	FY15	FY22	Increase
	Source: https://ga7a.short.gy/CxyTxV		
SC Students	4.607M	6.623M	▲ 43.8%
Female SC Students	2.102M	3.171M	▲ 50.9%
ST Students	1.641M	2.71M	▲ 65.1%
Female ST Students	0.747M	1.346M	▲ 80.2%
OBC Students	113M	163M	▲ 44.2%
Female OBC Students	5.236M	7.819M	▲ 49.3%

Dr Ambedkar Young Entrepreneurs League (AYE Mentor) program has been established to create an ecosystem to nurture and help grow entrepreneurial efforts of SC youth.

National Scheduled Caste Finance and Development Corporation released ₹5,552.40Cr to 838,227 beneficiaries (about 64 per cent women) in Modi's 10 years.

Pradhan Mantri Adarsh Gram Yojana is developing 29,851 villages with majority SC population, comprising 7.006M households, with total population of almost 48.76M persons and SC population of almost 26.29M. Out of 254,536 works identified, 38,246 were complete by December 2024. 10,672 villages have been declared as 'Adarsh Gram'.

The ₹79,156Cr PM Janjatiya Unnat Gram Abhiyan will benefit more than 5Cr tribal people in around 63,000 villages, who will get pucca houses with tap water and electricity, and also get the ABHA Cards under PMJAY.

The ₹24,104Cr PM Janman Yojana aims to saturate 22,000 Particularly Vulnerable Tribal Groups (PVTG) and their families and majority tribal habitations, by making them aware about their entitlements. This will cover every PVTG household that has remained unreached because of distance, lack of road, and digital connectivity. The campaign started initially in 100 districts, covering about 15,000 PVTG habitations in 18 states and A&N. Phase-2 will cover balance districts.

By July 2024, the government had set up 405 Eklavya Model Residential Schools for tribal (ST) students distributed over 30M scholarships to these students.

Ten Tribal Freedom Fighter Museums are being set up.

Expenditure of the tribal affairs ministry went up from ₹1,691.4Cr in FY14 to ₹7,605Cr in FY24 (up 349.6 per cent).

93

Improved Lives of PwDs

Persons with disabilities or 'PwDs' is the globally accepted term for disabled people and Modi also refers to them as '*Divyangjan*'. PwDs accounted for about 2.215 per cent of India's population in 2011. Assuming the same percentage, India is home to around 31.64M PwDs currently.

The Modi Government's commitment and pioneering efforts in providing PwDs with inclusive socio-economic opportunities is an eye-opener.

One example is the 2-day 'International Purple Fest' that was held in Goa in January 2024. It was India's first-of-its-kind inclusive festival that embraced and celebrated PwDs.

In 2015, the government launched the National Action Plan (NAP) for skill development of PwDs.

In 2016, it got the 'Scheme for Implementation of Rights of Persons with Disability Act 2016' (SIPDA) passed by the Parliament.

Department of Empowerment of Persons with Disabilities (DEPwD) supervises three statutory bodies, two PSEs, and nine institutions, and has 16 schemes for the welfare of PwDs.

A 'Unique Disability Identification' (UDID) project is undergoing implementation across India to create a national database of PwDs, and almost 11.633M UDIDs had been issued till December 2024.

The PM Daksh–DEPwD Portal is a one-stop digital destination for PwDs, skill training organisations and employers of PwDs from across India to be a part of the NAP. Included in this are a 70-hour English program 'Employability Skills for PwDs', 70 hours of Indian sign language videos of employability skills for PwDs, and 60 hours of interactive digital content of employability skills.

Till FY24, the Modi Government had assisted 2.865M PwDs in purchasing assistive aids and appliances; provided scholarships to 257,596 students with disabilities; supported more than 6,330 NGOs with aid grants, which has impacted over 590,000 beneficiaries; and provided skill training to 91,978 PwDs.

The GoI has built the Atal Bihari Vajpayee Training Centre for Disability Sports at Gwalior (Madhya Pradesh).

India participated in the Summer Paralympic Games in 1968 and 1972 but skipped the next two. It started participation again in 1984. This means India had participated in total 10 Summer Paralympics till Modi became PM. Cumulatively, 76 Indian athletes had taken part (average 7.6 per Paralympic) and India had won total eight medals (average 0.8 medals per Paralympic).

In the 2020 Tokyo Paralympics, India won 19 medals. In the 2024 Paris event, India won 29 medals!

If this is not one obvious criterion for measuring Modi's success in empowering PwDs, then what else can be?

94

Other Special Groups

Modi does not just think about the lower castes but also many other special groups of people who had been neglected for 66.8 years.

Senior Citizens

Elderly persons (aged over 60 years) in India increased from 19.8M in 1951 (5.48 per cent of total population) to 76.62M in 2001 (7.45 per cent) and 156.67M in 2024 (10.8 per cent). It is projected that India will have 228.49M seniors by 2035 (14.574 per cent) and 321.727M by 2047 (19.42 per cent).

Atal Vayo Abhyuday Yojana (AVYAY) provides basic facilities such as shelter, food, medical care, and entertainment opportunities, and encourages productive and active ageing by supporting state/UT governments, local bodies, NGOs, and the community at large to build capacities.

Senior Citizens Welfare Fund has a budget of ₹980Cr.

Elder Line 14567 is a national helpline for senior citizens that started on 26 January 2021. It's open from 8:00am to 8:00pm and provides free information, guidance, emotional support, field intervention in cases of abuse, rescues, and reunion of elderly homeless persons. Till March 2024, the

Elder Line had served almost 264,000 elderly persons through more than 2.4M calls.

Under the Integrated Program for Senior Citizens, more than 150,000 senior citizens have been supported and grants had been provided to more than 750 Senior Citizen Homes.

More than 90 new Senior Citizen Homes have come up.

From April 2017 to October 2024, 387,589 seniors received over 1.554M *free* assistive devices under the Rashtriya Vayoshri Yojana

Safai Karamcharis or Sanitation Workers

National Safai Karmacharis Finance and Development Corporation (NSKFDC) has disbursed capital subsidies for the training of 16,444 *safai karamcharis*. It also has nine loan schemes that provide various types of loans ranging from a minimum of ₹1L to a maximum of ₹25L, as well as job fairs, awareness camps, and workshops.

NAMSTE (National Action for Mechanised Sanitation Ecosystem) aims to ensure the safety and dignity of sewer/septic tank workers, provide access to entitlements, livelihood support, instil behaviour change for safe sanitation services, and convert to mechanised cleaning. Sanitation workers get free health insurance, PPEs, safety devices, occupational safety training, and capital subsidy of up to ₹5L plus interest to buy vehicles/equipment. There is also a NAMASTE App. The objectives are increased awareness among citizens, no direct contact with human faecal matter, and zero fatalities.

Hotline 14420 is for customers to call a registered sanitation worker for cleaning a septic tank or maintenance hole.

Street Vendors

Under PM Street Vendor's AtmaNirbhar Nidhi (PM SVANidhi), term loans of ₹11,232Cr have been given to almost 6.344M street vendors.

Transgenders

Modi Government allocated ₹365Cr for SMILE (Support for Marginalised Individuals for Livelihood and Enterprise) for FY22–26.

A National Portal for Transgender Persons was launched in 2020 through which any transgender applicant can obtain a certificate of identity. The certificate and ID card are nationally recognised. Till December 2024, the portal had over 6.3M visitors and around 24,500 ID certificates have been issued.

Under the Ayushman Bharat TG Plus, each transgender will receive ₹5L insurance cover.

Under the National Social Assistance Program, 3384 transgenders are provided monthly pension. All GoI ministries and departments have included transgenders as a separate category in exams and application forms for all Central Government jobs.

A new Transgender and Beggary Division was created by the National Institute of Social Defence in FY22 and this division conducted 907 programs with 49,801 participants in the first 3 years.

Eighteen Garima Greh shelter homes have been built for transgenders.

Nineteen Transgender Welfare Boards and 11 Transgender Protection Cells have been set up by States/UTs under the guidance of the GoI.

Part IX

Duniya se Dosti

Modi's foreign policy is focused on three objectives—attracting foreign direct investment (FDI), engaging with the 32.3M Indian diaspora, and raising the profile of India's role in multilateral and regional forums.

India's foreign policy, and its relationship with other countries and with their political leaders has been championed and contoured by the nation's most prolific global brand ambassador, Modi himself.

95

Vaccine *Maitri*, First HADR Responder

Due to a global shortage of vaccines during COVID-19, especially for nations that could not afford expensive Western ones, India donated 15.127M doses to 52 countries starting in January 2021 with eight countries in India's extended neighbourhood. Other recipients included three countries each in the Middle East and Southeast Asia, 22 in Africa, and 14 in the Caribbean—that were much closer to the US (who had extra stock of vaccines) than they were to India.

We also sold about 286M vaccine doses to 76 countries including Australia, Brazil, Canada, Netherlands, UAE, UK, and the US. This included over 5.9M doses of the Made-in-India Covaxin vaccine.

In March 2020, with less than 150 cases combined in the eight SAARC nations, Modi proposed a SAARC COVID-19 Emergency Fund, which collected $21.8M including $10M from India. Modi also sent teams of Indian military doctors to Maldives, Nepal, and Kuwait to help them draw up plans to combat the pandemic.

India Supplied COVID-19 Related Medical and Other Assistance to over 150 Countries during the Pandemic

With this 'Vaccine *Maitri*' (friendship) diplomacy, India not only enhanced its credibility as a leading vaccine producer in the new world order but also a genuine 'friend' that the world can depend on in a humanitarian crisis for as long as Modi is in power.

Leading American scientist Dr Peter Hotez, Dean of the School of Tropical Medicine at Baylor College of Medicine (USA) said that India's vaccines 'rescued the world' and India's contributions must not be underestimated. It is 'India's gift' to the world.[1]

Canadian businessman Patrick Brauckmann said, 'Important for Canadians and the world not to forget that almost half the vaccines Canada has administered were given by India because Canada couldn't source enough.'[2]

Australian Cricketer Matthew Hayden said,[3]

> The world media has spared no time in lambasting a country of 1.4B where the sheer numbers make the implementation of any public scheme a challenge. My heart bleeds … for the bad press that has been hurled at it by those who I am not sure spend any time here to understand India. I have always had the highest respect for the leaders who are entrusted with the task of running such a vast country … India has already vaccinated six times the entire population of Australia.

First HADR Responder

Under Modi, India has emerged as the 'First Responder' in HADR (Humanitarian Assistance and Disaster Relief) at a global level and gives about ₹6,300Cr humanitarian assistance per annum to foreign nations.

India hosts HADR exercises with various countries and multilateral organisations such as PANEX 21 for BIMSTEC (Bay of Bengal Initiative for Multi-Sectoral Technical and Economic Cooperation) members at Pune in 2021, and SMANVAY 22 for ASEAN members at Agra in 2022.

In the first 43 days of the ongoing Israel–Hamas conflict, India sent 70.5MT of aid to Palestine. India also contributed $5M to a UN Agency to support its programs for Palestinian refugees.

After a huge earthquake struck Türkiye and Syria in 2023, under 'Operation Dost', Modi sent seven of the IAF's C-17 heavy-lift aircraft with teams from the National Disaster Response Force (NDRF) and the Military Hospital Agra and about 190 MTs of material, dog squads trained for search and rescue, reconnaissance drones, and supply drones. The first C-17 was among the earliest relief planes to land in Adana. Indians set up a 30-bed field hospital in less than three days and stayed for two weeks to run it. Modi sent this even though President Erdoğan of Türkiye supports Pakistan in all international forums.

Regardless of sanctions on Syria by the US and its allies, India sent five C-130J aircraft to Syria with NDRF/medical personnel and about 29MT of relief material.

India's humanitarian assistance to Afghanistan in 2022 and 2023 includes 67,500MT wheat, 213MT medicine and medical supplies, winter clothing, as well as assistance for drug addicts.

India sent relief materials in four naval ships to Myanmar for people affected by a powerful Mocha cyclone in 2023.

Despite having to balance our friendship with Russia (our biggest arms supplier) in the ongoing Russia–Ukraine War, India sent over 120MT humanitarian assistance to Ukraine in 14 batches.

Following the earthquake in Nepal in 2015, India was the first to respond with its largest-ever disaster relief operation abroad, 'Operation *Maitri*'. India also gave Nepal ₹6360Cr as long-term assistance for rebuilding houses and infrastructure.

The Modi Government aided Sri Lanka in the 2016 cyclone, Indonesia in the 2018 earthquake, Madagascar in the January 2020 flooding, Mauritius in its 2020 oil spill, and Myanmar in the 2023 cyclone.

Indian Navy ships rescued more than 120 Pakistani hostages from hijacked ships between 2018 and 2023.

In an operation that lasted for 40 hours in March 2024, the Navy also rescued seven Bulgarians from a Maltese-flagged ship that had been hijacked for three months by Somali pirates.

96

e-Visas, Weighty Passports, OCI Cards

In November 2014, the Modi Government launched e-Visas for tourists from 43 countries. They could arrive at nine designated airports. The scheme was extended from time to time and categories such as business and conference visitors, medical and Ayush visitors and their attendants, were included. Currently, e-Visas are valid for passport holders of 171 countries and territories at 31 entry airports, 36 exit airports, and five seaports.

How India's e-Visas are Growing Source: https://meadashboard.gov.in/indicators/2

Fiscal Year ending	e-Visas	Regular Visas	Total Visas	Share of e-Visas
2015	516,510	3,994,603	4,511,113	11.4%
2016	1,180,933	4,015,592	5,196,525	22.7%
2017	1,901,419	3,922,971	5,824,390	32.6%
2018	2,470,272	3,511,829	5,982,101	41.3%
2019	2,887,220	3,185,354	6,072,574	47.5%
2020	697,719	708,600	1,406,319	49.6%
2021	134,757	653,343	788,100	17.1%
2022	1,357,701	2,116,450	3,474,151	39.1%
2023	2,660,283	2,185,147	4,845,430	54.9%
2024	3,018,730	1,610,040	4,628,770	65.2%

The 484.4 per cent increase in the number of e-Visas and the 471.9 per cent increase in share of e-Visas out of total visas in 9 years shows how Modi made a smart move by introducing e-Visas.

There is also a Visa-on-Arrival facility for passport holders of Japan, South Korea, and the UAE. However, for those from the UAE, there are restrictions if they are of Pakistan origin.

In a major benefit to foreign tourists, the GoI has brought a new relaxation that foreign nationals who fall sick during their stay in India can now avail medical treatment without converting their Visa into a Medical Visa. This takes care of sudden medical emergencies.

Overseas Citizenship of India (OCI) Cards

The Modi Government announced in 2015 that Persons of Indian Origin (PIO) cardholders must apply for an OCI card to continue to preserve their travel rights but has regularly extended the deadline to ease the transition.

Apart from other benefits, an OCI card allows a multi-purpose multi-entry, life-long Visa to a foreign national of Indian origin. In a recent development, families that shifted from India four generations back are also eligible. OCI cardholders do not have to report to police anymore when they are in India. An e-portal called Madad has been started to assist OCI cardholders with all their needs. An e-Migrate portal does away with the need to go to an Immigration Office.

From April 2014 till December 2024, India issued over 3.57M OCI cards.

97

Carrousel de Louvre

Just 10.5 months after becoming PM, Modi demonstrated his vision at a PIO event in Carrousel de Louvre, Paris, on 11 April 2015. He said,[4]

> I have come with a dream that sometime India may be ahead of France. In World War I, 75,000 Indian soldiers laid down their lives, 9000 in France. I went to pay my tributes at a memorial erected in their honour. I wanted to send a message that the global community should understand India and change its perceptions. What a country India is! It sacrifices not for itself but others and that too in such huge numbers. India is the largest contributor to UN peacekeeping forces. The world owes a lot to India, but it has yet to get its due recognition. A nation that works for world peace and whose soldiers are ready to die for peace is still yearning for a permanent seat in the UN Security Council. Those days are long gone where India would beg. This nation demands its right. Sometimes when we leave behind our land, after a few centuries future generations find problems in getting associated. They fail to understand who they are and why no one accepts them. If you write to the Indian Government, if you send a letter on my website, I will make all efforts to connect you to India or any of its States based on your

language or traditions. When last year's election results came, you burst crackers and distributed sweets, because all of you had expectations. I assure you the expectations with which citizens of India have chosen us to govern, in my experience of 10 months, I can say that we will fulfil all those. We can tackle the challenges. There is no reason for India to be poor. I am running a campaign called 'Make in India'. The French President talks about 'Make in India'. We are opening railways for 100 per cent FDI. I visited the Airbus plant and saw most of the workers were Indians. India has ample opportunities and the best in the world should also be on Indian soil. I believe railways have the power not just to connect India but to drive India forward. But first railways have to be modernised. We need to upgrade technology, increase speed, and expand.

France has the expertise. Yesterday I invited railway officials saying India has several opportunities, our rail lines pass through the heart of the city and cross the most premium land. The train can run on tracks, and you do construction above it. Erect seven storied buildings. There can be malls and hotels above. We have 20km long stations. A whole city can be built on Indian stations. I told them our railways are so huge that at any point passengers equivalent to 20 per cent French population are travelling in a go. The world is still not aware of the enormity of India, leave apart its potential. I am sure that day is not far when they will know us and acknowledge us. We are making efforts. The world is saying the Indian economy is the world's fastest moving. You can see data of World Bank or IMF. Every single parameter indicates that India is fastest moving economy. Then I ask the world what are you waiting for? The opportunities are ripe. Come, we will give opportunities to all. There should be factories in railways, warships and submarines should be made in India, and equipment for healthcare sector too. We want to do all this work in India because I wish that Indians find jobs on Indian soil, according to their capabilities and potential. I don't want Indian youth to leave their aged parents or villages for a job. We want to create a country where we achieve welfare of the poorest of the poor. Development should focus on employing the youth. I was telling company owners here that you might be getting huge incentives all over the world to establish factories, but after 20 years you will not find any labour. The entire world is ageing. India is the youngest nation in the world, 65 per cent population is below 35. After 20 years India will be the only place to meet global workforce requirements. The world's biggest industrialists, whichever corner they establish a plant in, the day is not far when they will have to come to India scouting for their workforce. So, I am explaining that instead of coming 20 years down the line, why not come now? Our Indian brethren living all over the world, their potential needs to be capitalised. We will have to use our clout meticulously to enhance their prestige. We are working in that direction.

We got two lakh crores by auction of just 20 coal mines out of 204. If any government achieved this in its entire tenure, the country would have given the reigns for next 25 years. This money is not with central government as it has been passed onto the states. They have been told to utilise it to create infrastructure to fight poverty. Industries have to be established, improvement in education and access to better healthcare have to be pursued by the states. They are being pressurised to do these tasks. Which states got money? Gujarat does not have coal mines. If I gave it money, newspapers would write that I am giving money to states because Gujarat has coal mines. The money is going to Bihar, Jharkhand, Odisha, and West Bengal, which have potential but are currently lacking behind. I have to bring them forward. If you see India's east coast, you will realise its backward.

The west coast—Goa, Karnataka, Maharashtra, Rajasthan, Gujarat—things are happening here. My first intention is to develop eastern coast. The east will march ahead of the west, it has such a potential. The entire natural resource reserves are in the east. If they start on the developmental journey, there is no stopping them. We started Pradhan Mantri Jan Dhan Yojana on 15th August and wanted it to finish by 26th January. The poorest of the poor should have a bank account. I can say with immense pride that in just 75 days almost 14 crore new accounts were opened—probably more than the population of France. If we decide, anything can be accomplished. Next, we focused on gas cylinders on subsidy given by the government. We decided to transfer this subsidy directly into the bank accounts, because earlier it would get siphoned. It is the largest event in the world, the transfer of subsidy in accounts of 13 crore people. There are no middlemen now, leakages have stopped, there is no corruption, and the common man has benefitted. The world is worried about climate change. The solutions are here itself. Deforestation will stop when people stop using wood to cook. Then we can develop smoke free systems. Decisions taken in past few months have all been proven to be right. Based on this I say that in front of your very own eyes you will see India of your dreams.

98

Connect with OCIs and PIOs

From US to Australia, UAE to Italy, Rwanda to Myanmar, Modi makes it a point to meet with the Indian diaspora.

First Indian Rockstar at MSG New York

In September 2014, Modi addressed over 18,500 PIOs (who had come from across the US and Canada) at New York's famous arena Madison Square Gardens. 'Modi, Modi'—the audience chanted, drowning out the announcer trying to introduce a man who needed no introduction. The PM brought the roof down when he said India sent a spacecraft to Mars for ₹7/km when an autorickshaw ride costs ₹10/km in Ahmedabad. Modi announced that those who come to India for long stays will not have to periodically report at police stations as was required in the UPA-era. For the more than 40,000 who could not make it due to a maximum capacity of 20,000, Super Modi parties were organised in dozens of American and Canadian cities. Over 15 global TV networks telecast the event live.

Sydney SuperDome, November 2014

Modi charmed a packed audience of 18,000. Like New York 2 months earlier, there were chants of 'Modi, Modi'.

'He represents change from the status quo in India', said banker Amrita Burman, 'The old Indian leaders were quite elitist. He's more grounded.' Nirav Trivedi summed up the man's appeal in a few words: 'He's a magician. His work, his achievements, his dedication, his efforts. What he imagines, he does. The work that used to be done in 20 years; he can do in two years.'

Canada, April 2015

Canadian PM Stephen Harper introduced Modi to more than 9,300 PIOs at Ricoh Coliseum, Toronto. Many MPs and ministers were present. In a 66-minute address, the audience cheered Modi 64 times! Some of the fascinating anecdotes went something like this:

> Ten months back only the government changed but today mindsets have also changed. There was a time when you went to open a bank account, the officer would not even look at you, now they went house-to-house to open 14 crore accounts in 75 days. I told poor people to open 'zero balance' accounts, but look at their 'ameeri', they deposited ₹14,000 crores. A new belief is born. When you travelled to India you would complain that airports were dirty—those who dirtied them left, but we cleaned them. Every day news comes about some bankers or college students or *pujaris* or an MLA or MP or sports personality cleaning public places. Sachin Tendulkar adopted a long footpath, would go at 4:00am daily for a full month with his friends, they not only cleaned it, but made it a park. I said we should build toilets for the girl child in schools and people asked if this is a PM's job. I said this is a different PM. Just like an ocean is made of drops, the face of India will change with these small works. One day

I thought—is it graceful for people who pay ₹15–20,000 for restaurant dinners to take gas subsidy of ₹400? I said it casually to some friends and the message spread so fast, in two months, four lakh people voluntarily gave up gas subsidies. Mindsets have truly changed. We are using the money saved to give free cylinders to poor village women. By not using wood, they will breathe easier, and forests will be saved. Let me share a surprising thing. A newspaper owner wrote a letter saying they have made a policy to print only positive news once a week—I did not give this thought to them, it was 100 per cent voluntary. I guarantee that the dreams you have for India will see light of day in front of your eyes.

Dubai International Stadium, August 2015

There were 26,000 PIOs. As Dubai has a large population from Kerela, Modi spoke a sentence in Malayalam. The Crown Prince of Abu Dhabi, many Arabs, Indian Muslims, and international diplomats attended. The crowd cheered 77 times in Modi's 74-minute speech. They cheered the loudest when he said the Crown Prince has conferred with India's views about terrorism.

Silicon Valley SAPped, September 2018

In a visit to the Bay Area in the US (home to most large tech companies), Modi visited Tesla, Facebook, and Google. No Indian PM had visited the Silicon Valley, despite 580,000 PIOs living there. Modi had a televised 'Town Hall' event with Mark Zuckerberg. He met the CEOs of Adobe, Apple, and Microsoft. This resulted in these companies and their suppliers investing tens of billions of dollars in India. Several US and California State senators and MPs were present at SAP Centre, San Jose. Modi said to the crowd of more than 18,000 people: 'For a few months, people are no longer saying the 21st century is Asia's century, they are saying it is India's century.' There was very loud cheering when he said, 'They made 100 crores, the son made 250 crores, the daughter earned 500 crores and the son-in-law 1000 crores.'

Modi was cheered 71 times in 62 minutes.

Stealing Another PM's Dream in the UK

As a college student, UK PM David Cameron dreamed of taking Britain's most famous stage to address a crowd of tens of thousands. In November 2015, Cameron had that opportunity in London's famous Wembley Stadium, cheered by 60,000 people in a reception unlike anything a British politician had experienced before. Unfortunately, the cheers were not for him but for his Indian counterpart, for whom Cameron was just a brief warm-up act. Modi got a huge applause for his pledge to make India 'a country on the same level as any other'. He said: 'We don't just want charity from others. What we are looking for is equality.'

Singapore Expo Convention Centre, November 2015

Modi had the crowd of more than 6,000 people in ruptures when he said media persons are intelligent and cunning, but in his case assumed that a leader of a midsize state (Gujarat) won't even have policies for the whole of India, forget diplomacy; so, when he was campaigning, they kept asking him about his foreign policy. Modi said,

> What foreign policy could I talk about during a domestic election, but they would think that this guy is weak on foreign policy and went round and round to the same topic. So, I only used to say, listen, when I get the responsibility to handle foreign policy, I will see, but I guarantee that neither will India lower our eyes to speak with another country, nor will we show our eyes, we will speak with the world by meeting them eye-to-eye.

'Friends of India', Moscow, December 2015

Addressing 30,000 people at Moscow's Expocentre, Modi said, 'Every Indian must ensure at least five Russian families visit India every year. Earlier they used to talk about European Union and ASEAN. The day is not far when they start talking about Eurasia.'

Lunch with Workers in Riyadh, April 2016

Modi shook hands and had *pakoras* (an Indian snack) with 300 L&T workers building the Metro Rail in Saudi Arabia's capital. Asking them to download the Narendra Modi App, he said, 'If you download the App, I will always be in your pocket ...what else do you want?'

TicketPro Dome, Johannesburg, July 2016

To an audience of 20,000, Modi said,

> We may be in different time zones, our nationality may be different, we may support different cricket teams but are still connected in hearts and minds. We want our youth to meet the global need of skilled manpower. The mindset of our people is changing. Credit for this does not go to Modi but to 1.25 billion people of India.

Sultan Qabool Sports Complex, Muscat, February 2018

To a massive crowd of 36,000, Modi said,

> In the changed India, poor people are not being insultingly turned back from the banks. In the changed India, the government is coming home to provide gas connection, to provide electricity connection. Now, decisions are not delayed; now challenges are being confronted. The projects are being completed on time by setting the target. This is an example of changing work culture. It's an example of a New India.

300,000 Indians and Nepalese

In May 2018, at a reception in Barah Bigha Maidan in Jankpuri (Nepal), a crowd of over 300,000 came from different districts of Nepal and Bihar. Modi spoke about the contributions of philosopher King Janak in the spiritual and cultural life of India.

A Nepalese minister rightly said that the city of Janakpur had become *Modimaya*.

Bahrain National Stadium, August 2018

Addressing 23,000 PIOs, Modi said,

> Our goals are high, but when you have the arms of 130 crore people, you get encouragement. India is moving forward not only with the efforts of the government, but with the participation of crores of Indians. Government is at the steering only; it is the people who are pressing the accelerator.

'Howdy, Modi', Houston, Texas, USA September 2019

Modi was accorded a rousing welcome by 55,000 people at the NRG Stadium, where he jointly addressed the PIOs with

US President Donald Trump. Also attending were as many as 24 American lawmakers, the largest-ever American gathering with a foreign political leader.

'From Australia to Canada, from the United Kingdom to the US, from Dubai to Israel, no foreign leader has courted his country's diaspora as assiduously as Modi,' wrote *The Washington Post*, which is normally critical of Modi and his policies.[5]

Modi said 'All is well in India' in 9 Indian languages without reading, which drew a thunderous applause.

G7 Summit, Elmau, Germany, June 2022

Chants of 'Modi, Modi' and '*Bharat Mata ki Jai*' are common wherever Modi goes, but at Elmau a small crowd of PIOs had gathered outside the resort where the G7 summit was being held and were saying: '*Modiji humari jaan hain, Bharat ki shaan hain*' (Modi is our life, he is the pride of India).

Qudos Bank Arena, Sydney, May 2023

Many Australian MPs were present. Australian PM Anthony Albanese told the crowd of 22,500:

> I said to my friend the prime minister [Modi] before, the last time I saw someone on the stage here was Bruce Springsteen, and he didn't get the welcome that PM Modi has got. PM Modi is the boss. But tonight, as Prime Minister of Australia, I want to say thank you [to Modi]. You have brought the spirit of the world's biggest democracy to Australia, and you have helped make our democracy stronger and more inclusive.

La Seine Musicale, Paris, July 2023

The tightly packed crowd of more than 6,000 people at the small venue erupted when Modi said:

Namashkar, *Bonsoir*, *Vanakkam*, *Sat Sri Akaal*, *Kem Cho*? Wherever we go, we create a mini-India. Footballer Kylian Mbappe probably has more fans in India than in France; 46 per cent of real-time digital transactions globally are happening in India. When you come to India, there is no need to carry cash. Just download the UPI App on your phone. India and France have signed a pact on UPI and Indian tourists can soon pay in rupees when they visit the iconic Eiffel Tower.

'Ahlan Modi', Abu Dhabi, February 2024

Modi shared his vision with more than 40,000 PIOs at Zayed Stadium. He spoke of India's progress in the last 10 years, expressing confidence that India will become the third largest economy by 2030 on its way to becoming a developed country or '*Viksit Bharat*' by 2047. He also spoke of India being recognised as a '*Vishwabandhu*' (friend of the world).

THE AFTER EFFECT

Modi participated in more than 60 PIO events in 77 country visits in his first 10 years as PM. Inward foreign remittances from OCIs/PIOs increased from $65.5B in FY14 to $120B in FY24 (up 83.2 per cent). OCIs/PIOs remitted a whopping $750.267bn to India in 10 years.

99

Leaders' Visits

These two tables show the PIOs in different countries, visits by PM Modi to those countries, and visits of their heads of government to India during Modi's tenure. Dr Manmohan Singh's visits are added to compare their relative priorities.

Country	No. of PIOs	Visits by Modi	First Indian PM to visit in how long	Visits by Dr Singh	Visits by their Head of Govt during Modi's premiership
SOURCES: https://ga7a.short.gy/dbpxrT; https://ga7a.short.gy/nPGF9B					
USA	5,409,062	9		10	3
France	119,000	7		4	3
Japan	47,810	7		5	4
UAE	3,568,848	7	34 years	-	6
Germany	260,864	6		5	5
Russia	62,825	6		9	3
China	8,460	5	28 years	4	2
Nepal	700,004	5	17 years	-	6
Singapore	650,000	5		2	3
Bhutan	60,000	3		2	6
Indonesia	134,817	3		3	2
South Africa	1,700,000	3		4	2
Sri Lanka	1,607,500	3		1	12
UK	1,864,318	3		4	4
Uzbekistan	6,000	3		1	1
Afghanistan	0	2		2	5
Australia	976,000	2	28 years	-	3
Bangladesh	3,100	2		2	4
Brazil	4,048	2		3	4
Kazhakstan	10,235	2		1	-
Kyrgyzstan	16,598	2	20 years	-	2
Malaysia	2,914,127	2		2	2
Maldives	27,200	2		1	4
Myanmar	2,002,660	2		2	1
Qatar	836,784	2		1	1
Saudi Arabia	2,463,509	2		1	3

Country	No. of PIOs	Visits by Modi	First Indian PM to visit in how long	Visits by Dr Singh	Visits by their Head of Govt during Modi's premiership
South Korea	17,001	2		2	2
Switzerand	26,055	2		-	-
Thailand	150,000	2		3	2
Argentina	2,678	1		-	2
Austria	32,500	1	41 years	-	-
Bahrain	327,807	1	First in History	-	-
Belgium	28,834	1		1	-
Brunei	15,211	1	First in History	-	-
Canada	2875954	1		1	2
Denmark	No Info	1	20 years	1	1
Egypt	3,533	1	26 years	1	3
Fiji	316,081	1	33 years	-	1
Greece	35,000	1	40 years	-	1
Guyana	321,500	1	56 years	-	1
Iran	10,765	1		1	1
Ireland	61,386	1	59 years	-	-
Israel	105,000	1	First in History	-	1
Italy	206,503	1		1	4
Jordan	17,050	1		-	1
Kenya	80,000	1	35 years	-	2
Kuwait	995,528	1	43 years	-	-
Laos	700	1		1	1
Mauritius	894,848	1		1	5
Mexico	10,650	1		1	1
Mongolia	109	1	First in History	-	1
Mozambique	28,262	1	34 years	-	1
Netherlands	228,787	1		1	3
Nigeria	51,800	1		1	-
Oman	686,635	1		1	3
Pakistan	0	1		-	-
Papua New Guinea	4,062	1	First in History	-	-
Palestine	13	1	First in History	1	1
Philippines	150,010	1		2	1
Poland	24,200	1	45 years	-	-
Portugal	103,682	1	First in History	-	2
Rwanda	3,000	1	First in History	-	1
Seychelles	13,238	1	33 years	-	2
Spain	67,592	1	29 years	-	-
Sweden	60,000	1	30 years	-	1
Tajikistan	1,800	1		-	1
Tanzania	55,000	1		-	2
Türkiye	3,306	1		-	1
Turkmenistan	109	1	20 years	-	-
Uganda	37,660	1	21 years	1	1
Ukraine	3,336	1	45 years	-	-
Vatican City	0	1	First in History	-	
Vietnam	8,012	1		2	2

100

Love Thy Neighbour

Modi has tried to befriend all neighbours of India in the BIMSTEC region, plus some others, and is actively engaging with them to try and counter China. His first swearing-in ceremony in May 2014 was attended by heads of government of Afghanistan, Bhutan, the Maldives, Mauritius, Nepal, Sri Lanka, as well as Pakistan. Bangladesh sent the Speaker of their Parliament.

Retired IAS officer Nripendra Misra, Principal Secretary to Prime Minister Modi from May 2014 to August 2019, wrote in *The Times of India*,[6]

> To the surprise of [Ministry for External Affairs] foreign affairs mandarins who viewed him as a novice in foreign affairs, Modi was at his best while conveying the message of good neighbourly relations. A loud message went out right at the outset that he didn't approve of being captive to the wisdom lying in files … the baggage of the last 70 years was unwelcome, and no dogma would guide his foreign policy initiatives [which] was solely geared to achieve peace without compromise of sovereignty and his commitment to development goals for the betterment of 1.3B Indians.

Modi's 2nd swearing-in ceremony in May 2019 was attended by the Presidents of Bangladesh, Kyrgyzstan, Myanmar, and Sri Lanka, and the PMs of Bhutan, Mauritius, and Nepal.

Bangladesh: Train services started from Kolkata to Khulna (Bangladesh), New Jalpaiguri (West Bengal) to Dhaka, and Agartala (Tripura) to Akhaura (Bangladesh). Five bus routes have also opened. India can now use Bangladesh's Chittagong and Mongla ports. Two inland waterways and cruises have also started. India extended four lines of credit of $8B as well as grants for them to create infrastructure. India is also negotiating taking over the management of Mongla port.

Bhutan: Modi addressed their Parliament and opened their Supreme Court building (funded by India). In August 2019, the two PMs inaugurated the 720MW Mangdechhu Hydroelectric plant that increased joint projects to 2GW. RuPay cards were also launched.

Mauritius: Modi was the guest of honour at their National Day Parade in 2015. India extended lines of credit of $990M and grants of $388M for infrastructure and social projects.

Myanmar: India and Myanmar share a 1,643km land border. India gave grants of more than $1.75B and extended several lines of credit. Almost 97 per cent of a 1,260km, 4-lane India–Myanmar–Thailand Trilateral Highway is complete. Development economists say it will add an estimated $70B/year to GDP and create 20M jobs by 2025. By adding existing roads from Manipur to Delhi via Guwahati, this Highway will become a 4,780km Delhi–Bangkok Highway. Modi wants to extend it to Cambodia, Laos, and Vietnam. By linking an existing Bangkok–Vietnam corridor, the Highway will become a 6-nation highway of 5,930km. The 1,813km road from Imphal (Manipur) to Bangkok via Mandalay (Myanmar's 2nd largest city) is in good condition, but India is widening a 101km stretch to four lanes. Kaladan Multimodal Transit Project will connect Kolkata with Sittwe (Myanmar) by sea, link to Paletwa (Myanmar) via an inland waterway, and then by road to Mizoram, and further to Assam. This will fulfil a long-time dream of over 52M people of the Northeast region as transportation time and cost from Kolkata to Mizoram and Tripura will be halved. Apart from reducing road traffic, marine transport will reduce carbon emission. An Indian cargo ship was docked at Sittwe Port in May 2023. The current political situation in Myanmar has hampered the rest of the work. There will also be a link from Sittwe to Tripura via Bangladesh.

Nepal: Nearly 8M Nepalese persons work in India. Modi was the first foreign leader to address Nepal's Federal Parliament. In May 2018, he inaugurated Ayodhya–Janakpur bus service. India provides major financial/technical assistance for large infrastructure/connectivity projects, and high-impact community development projects. In February 2021, 13 Terai Road packages of ₹400Cr were completed and handed to Nepal. Indian cargo train operators can carry Nepal's containers/other freight, including private operators. India handed over the 34.9km cross-border rail link from Jayanagar (Bihar) to Kurtha (Nepal) to Nepal, and the countries signed an MoU for a final survey for Kathmandu–Raxaul broad gauge. Discussions are on for four multi-modal routes using Indian inland waterways. India is giving a grant for a bridge across Mahakali River connecting Dharchula (India) with Darchula (Nepal). Four cross-border transmission lines of 884kV were completed in 2016–21. About 600MW power is supplied by India to Nepal. Export/import of electricity has started. GoI permitted Nepal Electricity Authority to sell its surplus energy. In the first phase, 63MW power produced by

Nepal Electricity Authority was permitted for trading in the Indian Energy Exchange.

Sri Lanka: Modi addressed Sri Lanka's Parliament and went to Tamil-majority cities Talaimannar and Jaffna to hand over houses built by India under a $350M project for Tamilians in Sri Lanka's tea gardens. India is building 62,500 houses (83.3 per cent are complete) in Tamil areas for ₹1933Cr—one of GoI's largest projects abroad. Modi was chief guest at Vesak (Buddha Purnima) festival, opened a ₹150Cr super-speciality hospital built with Indian assistance in Dickoya, home to many Tamilians. In June 2019, Modi went to express solidarity after Easter Sunday attacks and paid tributes at St Anthony's Church. In August 2020, India gave a $15M grant to promote Buddhist ties and an inaugural flight carrying Sri Lankan pilgrims to Kushinagar. Indian pledges of more than $3.5B to Sri Lanka include grants of about $570M. Lines of credit of $913.3M are funding several infrastructure and other projects in the country. The first ever pilgrimage to Bodh Gaya for 160 Sri Lankan Armed Forces personnel and their families by a special IAF aircraft was organised in June 2018. The 2nd visit was in June 2019 for Sri Lankan Forces and their families, and for the 1st time, an Indian Military contingent went to visit Sri Lanka's sites. During Modi's visit in May 2017, he announced direct Air India flights between Varanasi and Colombo that started in August 2017. In October 2019, Jaffna International Airport was inaugurated by President Sirisena and an Alliance Air flight from Chennai landed there. In November 2019, Alliance Air started regular Chennai–Jaffna flights.

101

Indo-Pacific Region

BIMSTEC, which is part of the Indo Pacific, has been covered earlier.

Since 1947, China has had designs on India's Northeast region. Through local recruits of their foreign spy agency MSS (Ministry of State Security) in the Northeast region, China is trying to convince the people of the region (and of Ladakh) that they are not Indians, just like Pakistan has been doing in Kashmir. Indians in the Northeast region are told that their facial contours, food habits and culture is more like China than those of India. China has been funding scores of separatist and militant groups in the Northeast region.

With constant military moves in the East China Sea and South China Sea, China is also showing aggression against Japan, South Korea, the Philippines and Vietnam, and Indonesia to some extent, and all these countries are strengthening ties with India, which they see as the only counterbalance to China. Through its Belt and Road Initiative (BRI), China also has eyes on Bangladesh, the Maldives, and Sri Lanka.

Modi rejigged India's 1991 'Look East Policy' to 'Act East Policy'. The Policy was launched at the 12th ASEAN–India Summit at Myanmar in November 2014. The Policy aims to boost India's economic, strategic, and cultural ties not just with ASEAN but also with the huge Asia-Pacific region overall.

Indian Ocean Rim Association has 23 members including India, Australia, France, Indonesia, Kenya, Malaysia, Singapore, Thailand, Iran, Oman, South Africa, Sri Lanka, Tanzania, UAE, and Yemen.

Mekong–Ganga Cooperation has India, Cambodia, Myanmar, Laos, Thailand, and Vietnam.

India is actively engaging with these forums in order to counter China.

In a brilliant move by Modi, the heads of states/governments of all 10 ASEAN nations were joint chief guests at India's 2018 Republic Day parade—the first time in Indian history when more than one foreign leader was invited.

Modi has a grand plan to create transport linkages from the Northeast region to ASEAN, and ultimately to Japan. This helps increase economic activity, and India can be the driver. India offered a $1B lines of credit for India–ASEAN connectivity projects. These have been covered in the previous chapter.

Defence cooperation has increased with ASEAN and East Asian nations. The Indian Navy has regular joint exercises with navies of ASEAN and East Asian nations, as well as Australia and Japan. About 47 per cent of India's defence exports between 2015 and 2021 went to Myanmar. In January 2022, the Philippines placed a $375M order for three batteries of BrahMos missiles, which have been delivered. Deals of $700M with Vietnam and $450M with Indonesia are being negotiated for India's BrahMos missiles. India gifted a missile corvette to Vietnam's Navy and trains their military on operating submarines and fighter jets.

Modi convinced BRICS leaders to let Indonesia become a full partner of this global grouping.

India has undertaken 'Quick Impact Projects' in Cambodia, Laos, Myanmar, and Vietnam for development assistance to grassroot-level communities in education, healthcare, and water resources.

Modi has also forged robust relations with Australia, Fiji, Japan, Papua New Guinea, South Korea, and Taiwan (30,680 PIOs).

In 2017, Japan invited Australia, India, and the US to Manila for a joint foreign ministers meeting. The Quad group of the four nations, abandoned in 2009, was revived. Since then, Quad foreign ministers have met over 12 times. A Quad Leaders' Summit started in March 2021 and heads of government have met six times. In the first Summit, the Quad leaders described 'a shared vision for a Free and Open Indo-Pacific', and a 'rules-based maritime order in the East China and South China seas', which they stated are needed to counter Chinese maritime claims.

Modi was the first Indian PM to address a joint session of the Australian Parliament. Australia has the world's highest lithium deposits (needed for EV batteries) and the world's 4th largest producer of rare earths.

In 2023, the Australia–India Critical Minerals Investment Partnership was signed, and Australia identified five target projects—two for lithium and three for cobalt—for Indian companies to invest in.

India engages with Pacific Ocean Island nations through initiatives like the Forum for India–Pacific Islands Cooperation. Modi visited Fiji in November 2014, when he was the first Indian PM to address their Parliament, and Papua New Guinea in May 2023. In Papua New Guinea, the PM received Modi at the airport and touched his feet as respect for helping his country during COVID-19. In August

2023, two Indian ships made a call at Port Moresby (Papua New Guinea) to enhance maritime cooperation.

India and France agreed on a roadmap for the Indo-Pacific region in which they asserted the need for more cooperative initiatives in the Pacific.

Out of India's total global trade in 2023, India–ASEAN trade accounted for 8.425 per cent; Japan, South Korea, and Taiwan 4.21 per cent; and Oceania almost 1.81 per cent.

In 2014, Japan agreed to invest $33.5B in Indian companies and this was achieved by March 2023. South Korean FDI to India has steadily increased in recent years, crossing $8B in June 2023, whereas Indian companies have invested $5.2B in South Korea.

In February 2024, an MoU was signed to send over 40,000 Indian workers to semiconductor hubs in Taiwan. Only around 2,700 Indians work currently in Taiwan, predominantly in the high-tech sector.

Clearly, Modi is not going to let China win the battle for dominance of the Indo-Pacific easily.

102

The Arab Connect

Despite being accused of being anti-Muslim, Modi made 17 trips to the Middle East in his first 10 years as PM.

Dr Singh made only seven visits, and his first was almost 4.5 years after becoming the PM in May 2004. In contrast, Modi's first visit was 1.2 years after becoming the PM.

Indian Navy has excellent ties with the navies of Egypt, Kuwait, Oman, Qatar, Saudi Arabia, and the UAE—most of them established in the Modi-era—and joint naval exercises are held regularly.

The friendship Modi established with many Arab leaders and Egypt helps dilute Pakistan's anti-India agenda in the Organisation of Islamic Cooperation is the world's 2nd largest organisation after the UN, with 57 member states, 48 with Muslim majority).

Six Gulf Cooperation Council (GCC) countries—Bahrain, Kuwait, Oman, Qatar, Saudi Arabia, and the UAE—host about 8.92M PIOs, who comprise around 14.5 per cent of GCC's estimated 61.5M population and about 27.6 per cent of the total 32.29M PIOs worldwide.

With $68B, Indian expats in GCC accounted for 54.4 per cent of the $125B total remittances received by India in 2023.

The GCC is India's largest trading partner and about 60 per cent of India's oil needs come from the GCC countries, plus Iraq.

Bahrain: Indians comprise the 2nd largest expat group in the Kingdom. Trade with Bahrain in 2023 was about 0.114 per cent of India's global trade. Modi launched a $4.2M project to redevelop the Shrinathji temple complex at Manama.

Kuwait: Kuwait has a population of 4.35M of which PIOs comprise over 995,500 (about 22.9%), the largest expat community. Kuwait is a source for 3–4 per cent of India's oil imports. Kuwait Investment Authority had investments of ₹9812Cr in 14 listed Indian companies as of December 2023. Modi was the first Indian PM to visit in 43 years, and was conferred with Kuwait's highest national honour.

Oman: PIOs are the 2nd largest expat community in this Sultanate. Trade in 2023 was around 0.66 per cent of India's total global trade. The IAF has a base in Oman and is allowed to use Omani airbases. Indian Navy has a base and berthing privileges at Muscat Naval Base. Oman is the first Gulf country with which all three military services hold joint exercises. In January 2024, an MoU was signed for defence collaboration, including Oman buying Made-in-India equipment.

Around 6,000 India–Oman join ventures have invested over $7.5B in Oman. In October 2022, the Central Bank of Oman signed an MoU with NPCI to link the digital payment systems of the two countries.

Qatar: PIOs are the largest expat community in Qatar that provides about 10 per cent of India's oil, 48 per cent of LNG, and 28 per cent of LPG imports. In February 2024, India signed a $78B deal with QatarEnergy to buy 7.5mtpa of LNG till 2048. A deep-sea Qatar–India gas pipeline is under discussion. Since January 2019 alone, Qatar Investment Authority has invested about $4.86B in Indian companies.

In the chapter '*Jai Jawan*', we wrote how Modi negotiated the release of eight former Indian Navy personnel imprisoned in Qatar and sentenced to death.

Saudi Arabia: PIOs are the largest expat community in Saudi Arabia that accounts for 17–22 per cent of India's oil imports (3rd largest source). Trade with Saudi Arabia in 2023 was about 3.11 per cent of India's global trade. There were 2,783 Indian companies registered in the Kingdom as joint ventures or 100 per cent Indian-owned entities with investments worth about $2B in January 2022, and Indian corporate groups such as L&T, Tata, Wipro, Shapoorji Pallonji, etc., now have a strong presence there. The Saudi Public Investment Fund has invested around $7.85B in Indian listed companies and startups. A proposed mega investment is a $44B refinery-cum-petrochemicals complex in Maharashtra, to be jointly built by Saudi Aramco and three Indian PSEs.

In 2018, India awarded a Padma Shri to Nouf al-Marwaai, a Saudi, in recognition for her efforts to popularise Yoga.

The UAE: The United Arab Emirates is a federation of seven Emirates including Abu Dhabi and Dubai. PIOs (about 35.5 per cent of UAE's population) are the largest expat group followed by Pakistanis at 16.7 per cent.

Total trade with the UAE in 2023 was about 5.5 per cent of India's global trade. The UAE has invested about $21B in India. It was India's 4th biggest FDI investor in FY23 and has additionally committed $75B in Indian infrastructure. In 2023, a historic MoU was signed between the RBI and Central Bank of UAE to establish a Local Currency Settlement System to promote the use of Indian rupee and UAE Dirham for cross-border transactions in gold, crude oil, food products, etc.; and this system is already functional.

A 1.08msft Bharat Mart retail and logistics complex will open in 2025 at Jebel Ali Free Trade Zone in Dubai, being built to boost exports by Indian MSMEs.

Sheikh Mohammed bin Zayed, President of the UAE and Ruler of Abu Dhabi was chief guest at India's Republic Day parade in 2017 and at the Vibrant Gujarat Summit in 2024.

In July 2021, India, the UAE, Israel, and the US formed the I2U2 intergovernmental economic cooperation forum In February 2023, India, France, and the UAE created a trilateral cooperation initiative for solar and nuclear energy to combat climate change, and joint production of military hardware.

In February 2024, Modi did the '*Pran Pratishtha*' (consecration ceremony) of the BAPS Hindu Mandir at Abu Dhabi, the largest Hindu temple in the Middle East on a 27ac plot gifted by Mohammed bin Zayed.

An average of 6,740 Indian tourists per day stayed at least a night in Dubai in 2023, compared with the previous high of 5,397 in 2019 (pre-pandemic). For the first time, the UAE has introduced 5-year multiple entry Visas for Indians, with length of stay up to 90 days per visit. The UAE has also started issuing visas on arrival to Indians with a US visa that is valid for at least 6 months from their date of arrival in the UAE.

Let's come to some non-GCC middle-eastern and northern African countries with whom Modi has established good relationships.

Egypt: Only about 4,300 PIOs live in Egypt, a country with over 113.4M people. India's total trade with Egypt in 2023 was about 0.4 per cent of India's global trade. Around 50 Indian companies have invested over $3.25B in Egypt. Investments by Egyptian companies in India are under $50M.

Iran: The countries signed an MoU in 2015 to jointly develop Chabahar Port in Iran. In May 2024, India signed a 10-year deal to operate the port. India will invest around $120M in the port and around $250M in credit to reinforce India's connectivity to Central Asia, Afghanistan, the South Caucasus, and the greater Eurasian region. The agreement will provide India with much-needed access and the right to transit across Eurasia for economic growth and give India significant leverage over the China—Pakistan alliance and China's BRI. The project also helps India circumvent Pakistan to gain connectivity to Eurasia.

Iraq: A little more than 18,000 PIOs live in Iraq, a country with 46.15M people. Iraq is India's 2nd largest source of oil imports, accounting for almost 21 per cent. It was the largest supplier from FY18 to FY22 after which Russia became India's largest supplier. Total trade with Iraq in 2023 was about 1.7 per cent of India's global trade. A bust of Mahatma Gandhi was unveiled in the largest public park, Hawary Shar of Sulaymaniyah, on 9 April 2022.

103

Rest of the World

Under Modi, India is also constantly improving its relationship with the rest of the world.

India and the US

Remittances from PIOs in the US account for 23.4 per cent of India's total. Modi met US presidents a record 29 times. Barack Obama became the first US president to attend India's Republic Day parade in 2015, Modi's first Republic Day as PM. For 66.8 years, no other Indian PM was able to get the most powerful leader on earth to attend the parade.

Modi addressed a joint session of both houses of the US Congress (their Parliament) twice, becoming one in five individuals to get this rare honour, and one of the only two since 1994.

As India's largest trade partner, the US accounts for 17.924 per cent of India's exports and 6.35 per cent of imports. Bilateral trade went up from $48.478B in 2016 to $119.494B in 2023 (up 146.5 per cent in seven years), as India's exports grew 139.9 per cent. US was the 3rd largest source of FDI inflows with $47.843B during FY15–23.

There are over 30 treaties between India and the world's largest economy (as well as the most powerful nation) on various subjects, including defence, terrorism, space, narcotics, investments, hydrocarbons, energy, climate, information and communications technology, health, education, science and technology, etc.—many of which were signed in the Modi-era.

India and European Union

The 27 European Union (EU) nations have about 1.454M PIOs. Bilateral trade went up from $56.203B in 2016 to $90.758B in 2023 (up 61.5 per cent). India's exports grew 120.9 per cent, thus changing the balance of payments in India's favour.

India and the EU cooperate on climate neutrality, wastewater management, recycling of EV batteries, plastic litter/waste-to-hydrogen conversion, etc. Modi made 21 visits to 11 EU nations.

There were 21 visits to India, including visits by the President of Cyprus and the PMs of Finland and Latvia, apart from those in the two tables in the chapter 'Leaders' Visits').

India and the UK

PIOs comprise about 2.9 per cent of UK's population. Bilateral trade went up from $9.154B in 2016 to $20.256B in 2023 (up 121.3 per cent) and is now in India's favour.

In November 2015, Modi addressed their parliament. He was also the first Indian PM to be invited for the rare honour of an overnight stay at 'Chequers', the official country home of UK's PM.

India and EFTA

After nearly 16 years of negotiations, in March 2024, India signed a trade agreement with the European Free Trade Association or EFTA (Iceland, Liechtenstein, Norway, and Switzerland), under which EFTA committed $100B investments in 15 years (from $10.7B cumulative in 2022), in addition to investments by Norway's sovereign and climate funds that have invested $25B and will continue investing.

India and Russia

Russia was India's 'best friend' in the Nehru and Indira eras. Though this started changing from the Rajiv-era, it was Vajpayee who befriended the West more, and Modi has continued his policy, while at the same time he has refrained from doing anything to offend President Vladimir Putin.

Refer to the chapter 'Modernised the Armed Forces' in this book to see how arms imports from Russia have reduced.

Bilateral trade is heavily skewed in Russia's favour and went up from $5.175B in 2016 to $64.969B in 2023 (up 1,155 per cent primarily due to oil imports from Russia). India's oil and gas PSEs have investments in Russia.

The countries cooperate in nuclear energy, space, counterterrorism, science and technology, etc.

Latin America/Caribbean Islands

Latin America and the Caribbean Islands (aka the West Indies) are home to more than 1.04M PIOs.

Bilateral trade is in Latin America's favour due to oil imports from Venezuela and Brazil. It went up from $17.958B in 2016 to $34.67B in 2023 (up 93.1 per cent), but trade balance reduced by 29.7 per cent in India's favour. President Bolsonaro of Brazil was the chief guest at the 2020 Republic Day parade.

Indian oil and gas PSEs have invested over $3.6B in exploration and production assets in Brazil.

India and Africa

Africa has over 2.85M PIOs. Bilateral trade is in Africa's favour due to oil imports from Nigeria and gold from South Africa. It went up from $32.26B in 2016 to $69.938B in 2023 (up 116.8 per cent).

Modi was the first Indian PM to address the Ugandan Parliament. NTPC secured contracts to develop solar parks in Mali and Togo, and is looking to invest in Gambia, Malawi, Mozambique, Sudan, and other African countries. In 2021, the Modi Government pledged $2B in concessional credit to solar power projects in Africa.

Modi managed a huge diplomatic coup in September 2023 by convincing G20 leaders to accept the African Union as a full member of the global grouping.

India and Central Asia

In July 2015, Modi visited all five Central Asian 'stans'. Alongside agreements on defence, trade, tourism, and culture, he signed an agreement with Kazakhstan to purchase uranium—this now accounts for about 80 per cent of India's uranium imports.

Bilateral trade with the five nations went up from $570M in 2016 to $936M in 2023 (up 64.2 per cent). From a negative trade balance of $101M in 2016, India was able to have a positive balance of $551M in 2023.

104

Over 2,040 Stolen Artefacts

Modi has accorded high priority to conserving our heritage, and over 2,040 invaluable antiques/artefacts originally stolen from India were brought back by December 2024 at an average of 192/year, compared with only 13 antiques since Independence at average 0.194/year (up 989.7 times in the Modi-era). The process of bringing more antiques/artefacts continues on a fast track.

As many as 1,981 of the 2,040+ (around 97%) antiques/artefacts came back from the US. Others were brought back from the UK, Scotland, Singapore, Switzerland, Canada, Germany, and Australia.

Among the antiques brought back are metal idols of Ram, Sita, Laxman and Ganesha, stone sculptures of Nataraj, Brahma and Brahamani, a Bodhisattva head, a 'Dancing Shiva', and a Sri Devi antique from the Chola period, Ardhanariswara artefact, Parrot Lady artefact, Mahisamardini, and Uma Parameshwari.

In 2021, the Metropolitan Museum of Art, New York, returned 15 artefacts. These included a ceramic pot from Chandraketugarh (West Bengal) belonging to the 1st Century BCE, a stone bust of Kamadeva (the God of Love) from the 8th Century CE, and a Svetambara enthroned Jina, with attendant Yaksha and Yakshi from the 11th Century CE. As many as 157 came back from the US in 2021.

In 2022, Scotland returned seven, including a ceremonial Indo-Persian sword from the 14th century and an 11th-century carved stone door jamb seized from a temple in Kanpur.

In 2023, an ancient idol of Lord Hanuman (14th–15th century) stolen from a temple in Tamil Nadu, was traced and returned by Australia.

In 2024, the US returned around 1,700 artefacts or antiques, including around 1,404 valued at nearly $10M that were trafficked by criminal networks linked to alleged antiquities trafficker Subhash Kapoor and convicted trafficker Nancy Wiener.

The stolen antiquities include a sandstone sculpture of a Celestial Dancer, stolen from a temple in Madhya Pradesh in the early 1980s. It was looted and divided into two to make it easier to smuggle and sell. Professionally reassembled, the sculpture was later donated to the Metropolitan Museum of Art in New York City (the 'Met') by one of Kapoor's clients. The Celestial Dancer remained on display at the Met until it was seized by the Manhattan District Attorney's Antiquities Trafficking Unit (ATU) in 2023, in collaboration with Homeland Security Investigations (HIS), a part of U.S. Immigration and Customs Enforcement.

Indian LEAs assisted in the investigations and India's extradition request for Kapoor is pending with U.S. authorities.

105

Global Leadership

In Morning Consult's Tracker that measures the public approval of 25 global leaders (they started with 10) in their home countries, Modi has continuously been No.1 from August 2019, when the Tracker started.

We wrote about how Modi got the American and Chinese presidents to intervene when Pakistan captivated an IAF pilot in 2019.

Awards and Honours

Afghanistan, Barbados, Bhutan, Egypt, Fiji, France, Greece, Kuwait, Maldives, Palestine, Papua New Guinea, Russia, Saudi Arabia, and the UAE have bestowed Narendra Modi with their highest civilian honours, and Bahrain bestowed it's 3rd highest honour.

Apart from these, Modi has received the highest US military award for foreign heads of states/governments, Champions of the Earth Award (highest environmental award of the UN), Seoul Peace Prize, and the Global Goalkeepers Award.

International Solar Alliance (ISA)

In the COP21 UN Climate Conference held in November 2015 at Paris, Modi proposed the ISA, now a UN-recognised intergovernmental organisation with 120 signatory nations, most of which lie fully or partly between the tropics of Cancer and Capricorn, and thus considered 'sunshine countries'. ISA's primary objective is to work for the efficient consumption of solar energy to reduce dependence on fossil fuels.

With its headquarters at Gurugram (Haryana), ISA is guided by its 'Towards 1,000' strategy of mobilising $1,000B of investments in solar energy solutions by 2030, delivering clean energy solutions to 1,000M people and resulting in installation of 1,000GW of solar energy capacity. This would help mitigate global solar emissions to the tune of 1,000MT of CO_2 every year.

Modi came up with the idea for 'One Sun One World One Grid' (OSOWOG) in October 2018, and in November 2021, Modi and the PM of UK launched the Green Grids Initiative-OSOWOG, the first global network of interconnected solar power grids. 'Solar energy is only available at daytime and is dependent on the weather. OSOWOG is the solution. Through a worldwide grid, clean energy can be transmitted to anywhere and anytime,' Modi said.[7]

This is a brilliant idea, as when it is 6am in Los Angeles (USA), it is midnight in Brisbane (Australia).

ISA's Global Solar Atlas is a map-based App that displays annual average solar power potential anywhere in the world and identifies potential sites for solar power generation, helping governments save millions of dollars on research and providing solar developers with an easily accessible and uniform platform to compare resource potential between sites in a region or across multiple countries.

International Big Cat Alliance (IBCA)

On Modi's urging, 96 countries have agreed to become members of the IBCA that will have its headquarters in India.

The IBCA will serve as a platform and centralised repository of successful practices for conservation of seven big cats—tiger, lion, leopard, snow leopard, cheetah, jaguar, and puma.

Path-setting G20 Presidency

The G20 is a forum of nations that plays a critical role in steering the global economy, represents 85 per cent of global GDP and over 80 per cent of population, and includes the US, China, Germany, Japan, India, 15 other nations, and the 27-member EU. It was set up in 1999 as an alternative to G8 (the eight largest economies) to expand the number of countries whose leaders could discuss global issues and take decisions on multilateral initiatives that would impact humanity, such as climate change and sustainable development. G20 is now more prominent and effective than the G8.

India's G20 presidency in 2023 was unlike any other. Modi got G20 members to agree to admit the 55-member African Union, establishing India as the undisputed leader of the 'Global South' (all countries except those in North and Central America and Europe). This was remarkable as even US President Obama, who is of African descent, could not do this when the US had the G20 presidency in 2009.

India secured a consensus on over 100 issues, including the contentious Russia–Ukraine war, as G20 leaders adopted an action-oriented, ambitious and decisive 'Leaders' Declaration', a reflection of India's growing global influence and the impact Modi has had on important world leaders.

With over 200 meetings in 60 cities in 36 states/UTs, the size, scale and scope of India's G20 presidency was unprecedented. Never in the previous 17 presidencies had meetings been organised in more than two cities.

Other Leadership Initiatives

The UN International Year of Millets at India's initiative brought *Shree Anna* into the global discourse.

Coalition for Disaster Resilient Infrastructure (CDRI), with its headquarters in Delhi promotes rapid development of resilient infrastructure to respond to the SDGs' imperatives of expanding universal access to basic services. It has 40 member nations plus the EU, and six member organisations.

Modi also launched a One Future Alliance that aims to shape digital DPI of the future, as an accelerator of the SDGs. It has been recognised by the UNDP.

Other Leaders' Initiatives

Part X

Modi and *Sanãtan Dharma*

'Mughal architecture is so amazing. They always build an ancient Hindu temple in the basement first' is the pinned tweet on Kamal Vedā's timeline on 'X' (formerly Twitter), obviously referring to how the Archaeological Survey of India and others keep discovering the ruins of temples beneath mosques, like in the case of Babri Masjid.

The Modi Government and several BJP state governments have changed names of around 25 cities, roads, etc., that were named after Mughal rulers, to Hindu/Indian names. For example, the Mughal Gardens in the Rashtrapati Bhavan complex were renamed as 'Amrit Udyan' and these gardens were opened to the public. A few more examples are Allahabad to Prayagraj, Aurangabad to Chattrapati Sambhajinagar, Hoshangabad to Narmadapuram, and Ahmednagar to Ahilyanagar.

106

New Ayodhya Nagri

Ayodhya town had a population of around 95,000 and Ayodhya district around 2.7M in 2023. The district is undergoing a huge transformation. Of the 134km^2 area being developed, a core city area of about 32 km^2 is complete.

- An old airstrip of 178ac has become Maharishi Valmiki International Airport of over 821ac. The 1mppa capacity will go up to 4–5mppa over 3–7 years.
- A new 3-storey station, 10 times the size of the old one has been built at Ayodhya Dham junction, with a 4-lane approach road.
- Many rail lines have been doubled and electrified.
- Several highways and bypass roads leading to Ayodhya have been widened and strengthened.
- A 67.5km 4/6-lane Ayodhya bypass has been built.
- Old, narrow, dilapidated, pothole-ridden city roads have been revamped.
- Four main roads have been developed based on the four Vedas and four eras, with concrete carriageways and dividers with greenery.
- The 13km Ram Path and the 2km Dharma Path are now 4-lane wide.
- A huge Veena has been installed at Lata Mangeshkar Chowk.

- By removing encroachments, the 742m Bhakti Path has been widened to four lanes, and the 580m Janmabhoomi Path to two lanes.
- Gates have been built at six entry points.
- Bus shelters have been built at around 25 locations.
- An Intelligent Traffic Management System has been installed at 22 intersections, where traffic lights with more than 500 CCTV cameras streamline vehicle movement. Public address systems at 15 places address commuters, and a monitoring room gives warnings in case of a traffic violation.
- Emergency call boxes have been placed at more than 20 key locations.
- Most public buses and commercial vehicles are now EVs or run on CNG.
- Three parking lots of 35ac, 25ac, and 10ac have been developed. Three MLCP-cum-commercial complexes have been built. Parking spaces for up to 40,000 vehicles have been or are being built.
- Ayodhya now boasts of the world's largest 'solar-powered streetlights line' with 470 LED-based solar streetlights spread over 10.2km stretch.
- Façade lighting, Victorian solar tail lamps, arc lamps, pebble stone pavements, mural painting, mosaic art on the walls, legacy *stambhs* (specially designed pillars), sculptures, and other design elements themed on the Ramayana greet visitors in Ayodhya now.
- Bhimrao Ambedkar International Sports Complex is almost ready. It has a cricket stadium, swimming pool, and many other facilities.
- Around 3,500 structures in the old city are have been given a facelift. Shutters of shops and other road-fronting buildings have been designed to maintain consistency with the overall theme.

- Work is underway at a rapid pace for renovation of the path from Ram ki Paidi to Raj Ghat to the Ram Mandir with a visitor gallery, new concrete ghats between Guptar Ghat and Raj Ghat, rehabilitation of existing ghats, and beautification of four historic entrance gates.
- Apart from seven temples inside the Ram Mandir complex, nine more temples will come up—dedicated to Goddess Annapurna; Maharishis Agastya, Gautam, Valmiki, Vashisht, and Vishwamitra; Mata Shabri; Nishad Raj; and the huge bird Jatayu.
- Ayodhya now has 5G WiFi.
- A new medical college has opened.
- Upcoming projects include a 40MW solar power plant, a branch of CIPET (Central Institute of Petrochemicals Engineering and Technology), solid waste, sewage, and common effluent treatment plants.
- All electrical cables are being shifted underground.
- A 70ac 'Vashishtha Kunj' residential project, with high-, middle- and low-income group plots, will be developed on the Lucknow–Ayodhya Road.
- Uttar Pradesh Housing and Development Board (UPHDB) is developing a 1407ac township 'New Ayodhya City', a river-centric project with a focus on sustainability—653ac by 2028 and balance 754ac in the future. Work on infrastructure is underway on 318ac.
- Twelve private real estate developers have taken land from Ayodhya Development Authority and have received approvals to develop townships.
- A Mumbai-based firm is developing a 100-room palatial Leela Hotel on the banks of Sarayu River as part of its 51ac project, which has villas, apartments, and plots.
- Ayodhya has around 150 hotels. More than 240 more hotels are in the pipeline including 150 by OYO (which

already has 51 hotels in Ayodhya), four by the Taj Group, two by Radisson, and one each by ITC, Oberoi, Marriott, Wyndham, Trident, Sarovar, Ramada, and EaseMyTrip. Around 65 were under construction as of December 2024.

- MakeMyTrip has a charter train package with live *bhajan mandalis* and VIP *darshan* assistance at the Ram Mandir.
- Tata Group is developing a ₹650Cr 'Museum of Temples'.

Land prices are up 250-350 per cent since the Supreme Court verdict of 9 November 2019. The volume of transactions has more than trebled since April 2022.

AYODHYA Tourists	Average Daily Tourists	Increase from previous year
2022	55,616	NA
2023	82,192	▲ 47.8%
2024 (first half)	604,245	▲ 635.2%
2025-29 (projected)	300,000+	NA
SOURCES: https://ga7a.short.gy/ApKhxv; https://bit.ly/Ayodhya_2024		

About 150,000 jobs have been created since 2022. Leading staffing companies project 350,000 new jobs in 2–4 years. More than 35,000 local traders have seen their incomes triple. Small businesses reported ₹5.2LCr trade in January–April 2024. It is not surprising that even the city's Muslims are happy that Ram Mandir has been built.

But Rahul Gandhi, Mamata Banerjee, Akhilesh Yadav, and other Opposition leaders (most of them Hindus) have been continuously saying that the Ram Mandir is a waste of the nation's resources.

107

Somnath Temple Restored

The Somnath Temple located on the coastline in Gujarat is one of the most sacred Hindu temples. It was destroyed four times by Muslim invaders between 1026 CE and 1665 CE and rebuilt each time. The present temple was reconstructed in 1951.

Despite an imposing 154ft-high spire with a 37ft-high flag post, the view from the main road was unclear due to unplanned structures, irregular hoardings and encroachments.

In December 2019, Modi appointed an architect to develop a master plan and detailed designs to enhance access, redevelop the temple precinct, and upgrade public amenities and infrastructure in the more than 350ac temple influence area.

The design proposed a grand axis from the temple down a straight road and relocating some defunct structures, resulting in a clear view of the temple. Somnath has Z+ security as it can be easily attacked by terrorists via sea from Pakistan, so security and crowd control systems in the entire complex were compulsory.

A grand entry gateway and state-of-the-art visitor plaza was built; roads and streets leading to the temple, Somnath Beach (0.75km from the temple) and Bhidiya Beach (1.1km) were upgraded; the beaches were cleaned; and edges of the Hiran River and the sea were improved with a 1.49km landscaped promenade.

An exhibition centre with dismantled parts of the old Somnath Temple, many eateries, and a larger parking lot have been built, and the bus stand has been relocated. The old Somnath Temple precinct has been rebuilt and Prabhas Patan Museum upgraded. To integrate the local community with tourism, an 'Ecohaat' and a craft village were built, and the cave museum was adapted into a cultural village.

A Shree Parvati Temple is also being developed.

Kalika Mata Temple

Shree Kalika Mata temple at Pavagadh Hill (54km from Vadodara) in Gujarat has also been redeveloped.

108

The KKK

Kashi Vishwanath Corridor

Kashi Vishwanath Corridor was built to ensure easy movement of pilgrims and tourists between the Kashi Vishwanath Temple and several ghats along the Holy Ganga. Varanasi is not just Modi's LS constituency since he was elected from there in 2014, 2019 and 2024, but also the spiritual capital of India.

Earlier, pilgrims had to pass through congested streets. With the new wide vistas and a magnificent temple square, more than 22,000 people can gather in the 12.6ac corridor (70 per cent has a green cover), compared to less than 600 earlier.

New developments include grand gateways, ornamental arches, stone sculptures of Adi Shankaracharya, Ahilyabai and Bharat Mata, tourist facilitation centre, *Vedic kendra*, *bhojshala*, Varanasi Museum, viewing gallery, auditorium, food court, etc. A hi-tech command and control centre keeps a watchful eye 24x7 via cameras in every nook and corner. The history of the Kashi Vishwanath Temple and the 84 ghats is showcased on smart signages. LED screens display information on the history and architecture of Kashi and show the *Ganga aarti* and temple *aarti*.

More than 40 ancient temples were discovered during excavation. As these were in ruins, all were rebuilt.

Namo Ghat has an Open-Air Theatre and a food court, among other things, and is connected with Rajghat via spacious walkways and ramps. Other ghats and most of the riverfront has been developed with benches, gazebos, shops for local artefacts, statues, sculptures, murals, etc. Well-lit jetties with signages have been built to get on/off boats.

Kashi now has an international airport. The Kashi–Tamil Sangamam train links with Kanyakumari. Several roads leading to Varanasi (Kashi) were upgraded. A 1,200-seat Shivling-shaped convention centre has been built.

A 3.8km ropeway connecting the Varanasi Cantonment railway station to the Godowlia Chowk (about 400m from the temple) is under construction and is expected to reduce congestion on the roads once it opens by end-2025.

A 30,000-seat cricket stadium will be ready by 2026.

Hindus from across India are descending in droves to see the new marvel created by Modi. People who have been to Varanasi earlier gawk in awe at the transformation.

Over 46.116M persons visited Varanasi in the first half of 2024, making it one of India's top pilgrimage destinations. Compare it with only 8M annual tourists before the revamp project.

Kamakhya Corridor

Shakti Peeth Kamakhya is an ancient hilltop shrine overlooking the Brahmaputra River in Guwahati, the capital of Assam. A major revamp project is underway on the lines of the Kashi Vishwanath Corridor.

The temple's surrounding area will expand from only 3,000 SFT to about 100,000 SFT on three levels, and the access corridor will widen from 8–10ft to 27–30ft. Space is being created for 8,000 to 10,000 pilgrims to ease the crowd during major festivals like Ambubachi Mela.

Six major temples in the complex, which are currently hidden from the larger public view, would be restored to their original glory.

Kartarpur Sahib Corridor

The 6.9km Sri Kartarpur Sahib Corridor connecting Gurdwara Dera Baba Nanak in India's Punjab state to Gurdwara Darbar Sahib in Katarpur in Pakistan's Punjab province was operationalised for the first time since Independence.

Kartarpur, located on the bank of Ravi River, was where Guru Nanak ji spent his last 18 years.

For the convenience of Sikh pilgrims wanting to visit the Pakistani Gurdwara for over 70 years, the Modi Sarkar built a 4-lane highway on the 4.1km Indian stretch of this corridor along with a state-of-the-art iconic passenger terminal building at the international border.

109

Badrinath and Kedarnath

An 825km 2-lane all-weather highway is under construction (76 per cent complete as of 2024) to connect Rishikesh, Badrinath, Kedarnath, Gangotri, and Yamunotri. The extremely complex project has 132 bridges, 13 elevated corridors, and two tunnels. Over 5.6M people undertook the Char Dham Yatra in 2023, despite weak connectivity.

Badrinath Redevelopment Project

In 30 years, tourists to Badrinath went up over 10 times. Unchecked and unplanned construction led to decaying parking and public infrastructure. Streets were congested and dirty. Haphazard clutter blocked the beautifully carved coloured temple's visibility.

A 210ac area around the temple is being developed with larger spaces, pathways on either side of an elevated platform atop which the temple sits (with ramps for PwDs), expanse of landscape behind the temple, beautification of the river front and the ghats, and a foot bridge to the temple. A path will go through the town and a plaza to Sheshnetra Lake, around which a landscaped park will come up. Another landscaped pedestrian path will connect this park to another major lake park to create a large green zone. Ample parking spaces are being created; water supply, sanitation and waste disposal overhauled; the river edge being made resilient to flooding and erosion; and transport links between important pilgrim spots within Badrinath and outside the town strengthened.

All structures in a 246ft radius around the temple were removed to make its grandeur better visible.

A Badrinath bypass, a one-way loop road into the town, an arrival plaza, a civic amenity centre, and arks around Sheshnetra and Badrish lakes are complete, while other works are ongoing.

For those who have been there prior to 2020, if you visit again after 2025, you will see a brand new Badrinath.

Kedarnath Redevelopment Project

At 11,657ft above sea level, Kedarnath is one of the most scenic and ethereal places on earth. When Kedarpuri town was ravaged in 2013 by unprecedented flooding of the Mandakini and Saraswati rivers, the disaster caused massive devastation of life, property, and the environment. This ecologically sensitive area already had unsafe imbalances after being regularly plagued by misguided development and unchecked construction in the past several decades.

The Uttarakhand Government initiated a redevelopment plan not just for the town's revival but also protection from future harm. The stretch from the arrival plaza to the temple (with homes and shops on both sides) was designed as a non-vehicular zone, with vehicles only on the periphery. Buildings were planned as clusters on raised plinths to guard against floods. But there was hardly any progress because the Congress CM was too busy managing political trouble and saving his chair due to rebellion within his own party.

The BJP came to power in the state in March 2017. In October of the same year, Modi laid the foundation stone for the project. In five years, Modi visited Kedarnath six times to personally supervise the work.

Completed projects include a 35-ton Adi Shankaracharya statue at a *samadhi sthal*, a 840ft x 70ft concrete road connecting the temple with Kedarpuri, 3-tier retaining walls, *aastha paths* and ghats along Saraswati and Mandakini, a bridge over Mandakini, Sangam Ghat at the confluence of the rivers, tourist facilitation centre, police station, helipad, and a command centre. Guest houses, cottages, dormitories, and tent colonies have been built by different entities.

Ongoing projects include a hospital and 120 pilgrim cottages in Kedarnath, augmentation of Sitapur Bus Terminal, dormitory and public conveniences at Rampur, and a tourist reception complex with shopping and parking in Sonprayag.

A 9.7km ropeway planned from Gaurikund will help pilgrims reach Kedarnath in 30–35 minutes versus the much longer jouney of 6–8 hours at present.

Around 1.57M devotees visited Kedarnath in 2022 and over 2.55M in 2023.

110

Shri Mahakal Mahalok

The 290-year-old Mahakaleshwar Temple and its influence area in Ujjain (Madhya Pradesh) was expanded, decongested, and beautified. The area increased from 7ac to 116ac with the 42ac Rudrasagar Lake becoming part of it. The visitor plaza has a capacity of 20,000 pilgrims, and a 900m corridor (with 128 shops, eateries and convenience points) connects it to the temple.

Decentralised parking has been provided at various entry points and vehicular movement into the expanded temple area has been restricted.

A parking lot for 650 vehicles, dining halls for 6,000 pilgrims per hour, waiting halls, smart road, murals depicting Ujjain's history, Avantika Haat, control room with a 700-camera AI-based CCTV surveillance, heritage *dharamshala,* 7ac city forest, and restored Chhota Rudra Sagar Lake are complete.

Various other areas of Ujjain, such as Maharajwada, are being redeveloped. A Kumbh Museum will also be built.

As average visitors went up from about 25,000 to about 130,000–180,000/day after Phase-1 was completed, a 250m underground tunnel that can evacuate about 800,000 people/day is being built and will open near the sanctum sanctorum.

III

More Spiritual Tourism

Around 250M people went for the Kumbh Mela at Prayagraj in 2019 and 450M are expected in 2025. Work done in the 4,000km^2 Mahakumbh Nagar includes a tent city, a dome city, 29 beautified temples, 201 widened and strengthened roads, 8km riverfront roads, 12km ghats, 400+km temporary roads with 30 pontoon bridges, 14 flyovers, 150,000 toilets, 102 parking lots for 550,000 vehicles, 69,000 LED/solar street lights, thousands of water ATMs, food courts, 2,700 CCTV cameras and drones, customised Google Maps and a Kumbh App, etc.

Shri Ramayana Express trains run on a 17-day journey from Delhi to Rameswaram via Ayodhya, Sitamarhi (with road trip to Janakpuri in Nepal), Varanasi (road trip to Prayag, Shringverpur and Chitrakoot), Nashik, and Hampi.

Other pilgrimage trains include Puri GangaSagar, Baidyanath GangaSagar and 12 Jyotirlinga Yatras; and the Ambedkar Circuit, Bharat Darshan and Bharat Gaurav.

The National Mission on Manuscripts has been undertaken to digitise and disseminate the knowledge enshrined in over 300,000 manuscripts.

Renovation of the 17.5msft Angkor Vat in Cambodia, the world's largest Hindu temple is being done by India.

Part XI

Modi Has Done So Much More

112

Many Firsts

As prime minister, Modi did several things that were not done for 34–496 years. Here are some:

WHAT DID MODI DO	PENDING FOR
Ram Mandir at Ayodhya	496 years
Modernising the Indian Penal Code, 1860 (IPC)	163 years
Modernising the Indian Evidence Act, 1872	151 years
Modernising the Criminal Procedure Code, 1898 (CrPC)	125 years
2nd Railway Station in Nagaland	100 years
Connected many Cities in the Northeast Region with Railway Lines; Connected Kashmir with the rest of India by Rail Line	77 years
New Parliament Building	76 years
Created post of Chief of Defence Staff; Started Bullet Train Project	72.4 years
1st Prime Minister to visit Bahrain, Brunei, Israel, Mongolia, Palestine, Papua New Guinea, Portugal, Rwanda, and Vatican City	72 years
Created Ministries of AYUSH; North East Region; Skill Development and Entrepreneurship	67 years
First IITs in Andhra Pradesh, Chhattisgarh, Goa, J&K, Jharkhand, Karnataka and Kerala	65–66 years
National War Memorial	65 years
First AIIMS in Andhra Pradesh, Assam, Gujarat, Himachal, J&K, Jharkhand, Maharashtra, Punjab, Uttar Pradesh, and West Bengal	62–64 years
1st Prime Minister to visit Guyana and Ireland	56–59 years
Phased Removal of Armed Forces Special Powers Act from North East Region	57 years
First IIMs in Andhra Pradesh, Bihar, Himachal, J&K, Maharashtra, Odisha, and Punjab	54–55 years
Amendment of Unlawful Activities Prevention Act	52 years
One Rank One Pension for Armed Services	42 years
1st Prime Minister to visit Austria, Greece, Kenya, Kuwait, Mozambique, Poland, UAE, and Ukraine	34–45 years
New National Education Policy; National Police Memorial	34 years

113

India Conquers Space

The Indian Space Research Organisation (ISRO), India's national space agency, was founded on 15 August 1969.

ISRO in a new Orbit	UPA	MODI	Increase
Launch Missions	24	54	▲ 125%
Spacecraft Missions	31	55	▲ 77.4%
Foreign Satellite Launches	31	397	▲ 1181%
Mass of Foreign Satellites	2014kg	13,640kg	▲ 577.3%

Satellites of 34 countries have been launched including 36 of the US—launches of American satellites only started in September 2015.

ISRO has developed GSAT-N2 satellite for better Internet in remote areas. It is too heavy for ISRO's existing rockets. Elon Musk-owned SpaceX's Falcon-9 will launch this.

India became the 4th country to soft land on the Moon when 'Chandrayaan-3' mission's lunar lander 'Vikram' touched down on the moon's South Pole in August 2023. The Modi Government has approved 'Chandrayaan-4', which will bring lunar samples back to Earth.

In September 2023, ISRO launched a solar mission, 'Aditya-L1'. The satellite reached the target point within the expected 4 months.

The inexpensive reusable space platform POEM-3 completed all objectives within 4 weeks of being launched on 1 January 2024.

NISAR is an observatory being jointly developed by USA's NASA and ISRO. It will map the entire earth in 12 days and provide data to understand changes in earth's ecosystems, ice mass, vegetation biomass, sea level rise, ground water and earthquakes, tsunamis, etc.

People say that these are achievements of ISRO's scientists and engineers, not of Modi. Of course, they are and hats off to them, but can any government organisation work properly without the PM's support?

As Modi wanted Indians in space, ISRO planned the Gaganyaan Mission, and set up a Human Space Flight Centre in January 2019. A crew of three will go 400km above the earth for a 3-day mission and come back to Indian waters in the 3rd quarter of 2025. An Astronaut Training Facility was set up in Bengaluru. Four IAF pilots will be India's first astronauts ('Gaganauts'). Three will go on Gaganyaan and the 4th will go on a NASA mission to the International Space Station (ISS) in December 2024. Before starting training at the Astronaut Training Facility, they got trained at the famous Yuri Gagarin Cosmonaut Training Center in Russia for 14 months.

The ISS is the largest space station ever built. It is operated by the US, Russia, Europe, Japan, and Canada. The US and Russia had their own space stations in the past, but only China has one now.

ISRO plans to build Bharatiya Antariksh Station, India's own space station, smaller than the ISS, weighing just 20 tons.

A powerful Next Generation Launch Vehicle (NGLV), the 'Soorya' rocket, will carry parts to build the BAS and can also launch bigger satellites. It will also be used on a mission to take Indians to the Moon. A 3-stage rocket powered by green fuel, Soorya will be able to carry up to 30MT, three times more than India's current biggest rocket, LMV3. A crucial goal is making NGLV reusable, with recoverable components that can be re-flown to save costs. ISRO's chairman aims for NGLV to have a launch cost of around ₹160,000/kg, compared to around ₹252,000 for a throwaway configuration, ₹630,000–700,000 for Chinese or Russian rockets, and ₹15–17L for Western ones. After several months of planning and finalising the designs and architecture, ISRO selected a team to build the Soorya rocket. The first part of the BAS will be built using LMV3 and ISRO expects Soorya to be ready by 2034–35. As Soorya's configuration differs from ISRO's existing rockets, a 3rd launchpad will be built at Sriharikota.

Realising India had less than 2 per cent share of the $360B global space economy and wanting to have at least 9 per cent by 2030, Modi took a historic decision to allow non-government entities (NGEs) in the space sector.

IN-SPACe was created in June 2020 as a single-window, independent agency to promote NGEs. It also authorises use of ISRO facilities by private companies and launch of launch vehicles developed by NGEs.

The government had already set up New Space India Ltd in March 2019 as ISRO's commercial arm. Its revenues increased 12.3 times in four years. India had 16 successful NGE space missions since June 2022, and seven more are scheduled up to March 2025. Awais Ahmed, cofounder of Google-funded startup Pixxel, said[1]:

> We wanted to use ISRO rockets to launch a satellite but were told there was no procedure to launch Indian satellites, but if you are a foreign company, then yes, ISRO has a process. This didn't make sense. We had to hire SpaceX to launch our first two satellites.

Of course, a Congress-era policy didn't make sense!

After successful pilots at IIT Bombay and IIT Madras, IN-SPACe is enlisting three IITs and 3–4 non-IITs to start BTech/MTech courses. It also offers 10 different week-long skill development courses.

In April 2024, SpaceX launched India's first military-grade spy satellite made by Tata Advanced Systems Limited (TASL). The ground control centre is in India for secrecy of coordinates required to be monitored by the armed forces. In the past, exact coordinates and monitoring timings had to be shared with foreign vendors. TASL can produce 25 such satellites annually and has also received export enquiries.

Three space-tech startups launched their high-tech satellites to monitor earth and space objects aboard theTransporter-12 mission of SpaceX.

India has 93 space-tech startups and over ₹5,000Cr has been invested by venture capitalists in these companies.

Up to 74 per cent FDI is now automatically allowed for satellite operations, manufacturing, data products, etc., and up to 49 per cent for launch vehicles and associated systems, and creation of spaceports for launching and receiving spacecraft. Beyond these limits, GoI approval is needed.

Investments are going up by over 75 per cent year-on-year since Modi ignited private sector rockets in June 2020.

114

Khelo India, *Jeeto* India

Modi has played a pivotal role in the overall growth, development, and success of Indian sportspersons. Sports is now a part of the main curriculum in the NEP.

The first Khelo India Youth Games 2018 had 3,507 athletes. In the 2024 Khelo India Youth Games, 5,600 athletes (51 per cent females) took part in over 275 events. In Khelo India Para Games, 1,002 athletes (71 per cent females) took part in 2023. Overall, more than 40,600 females have participated in 17 disciplines and over 340 events with ₹4.59Cr of prize money.

Thirty-six Khelo India Centres of Sports Excellence were set up, one in each state/UT; 1041 Khelo India Centres opened in 756 districts, covering all states/UTs.

There are 209 other national sports training centres, including 23 national centres of excellence; 67 Sports Authority of India (SAI) training centres; 20 special area games training centres for training sports persons from tribal, rural, hilly, and coastal region communities; 30 extension of SAI and special area games training centres; 10 national sports talent contest regular schools, 10 centres for indigenous games and martial arts, and 49 *akharas*.

The expenditure on sports infrastructure went up from ₹419Cr during UPA to ₹2,704Cr in the Modi-era (up 545.3 per cent).

Modi Government provides scholarships of ₹628,000/year to more than 2,800 athletes for training, boarding, lodging, and out-of-pocket expenses.

India successfully got cricket included in the Olympics.

A reflection of Modi's personal touch is clearly visible during his interactions with Indian athletes. Here are a few examples:

- Asked Mary Kom how she takes care of her family and practices sport.
- Spoke with Elavenil Valarivan in Gujarati (she was raised in Ahmedabad), while he greeted her parents in Tamil.
- Told Dutee Chand her name means 'brightness'.
- Asked P.V. Sandhu about the practice court her father built at home.
- Praised Manika Batra for training poor children in sport and remarked about her wearing the tricolour in her hand while playing.
- Asked Vinesh Phogat how she copes with high expectations due to her legacy. Asked her father how he groomed such illustrious daughters.
- Asked Saina Mirza for her advice for younger aspirants.
- Inquired about Neeraj Chopra's experience with the Indian Army.
- Praised Ashish Kumar for not wavering despite the loss of his father.
- Asked Sharath Kamal about how different Olympic venues are.
- Aked Sajan Prakash how he overcame a grave injury.

- When India lost the Cricket World Cup final in November 2023, Modi spent a good 15 minutes in the players' dressing room, consoling them and saying—'there is always a next time'. He hugged Mohammed Shami who was upset as he had performed quite badly.

Every time an Indian sportsperson wins an international event, Modi is among the first to tweet his congratulations.

He takes out time from his gruelling schedule to meet sportspersons returning home, and sometimes even before they leave. You will find over 200 photos of Modi with sportspeople on Google. With the PM's encouragement, Indians are bound to keep climbing the podium across the world more and more with each passing year.

Do you remember any PM in the past encouraging sportspersons so much and spending so much time with them?

115

Olympics and F1 in India

One mega, one large and one smaller sports venue are being built in Ahmedabad, which is bidding for the 2036 Summer Olympic Games, competing with Nusantra (Indonesia) and Istanbul (Türkiye).

OLYMPIC Venues being built in Ahmedabad (1)	
₹4000Cr Sardar Vallabhbhai Patel Sports Enclave — 236 acres on 2km Riverfront Total area of OLYMPIC DISTRICT — 500-650 acres	
110,000-seat Narendra Modi Stadium that already opened in the year 2020	
15,000-seat Indoor Arena	10,000-seat Multi Sports Stadium
12,000-seat Aquatics Centre	10,000-seat Volleyball Arena
10,000-seat Tennis Centre	6000-seat Basketball Arena
3000-seat Velodrome	3000-seat Climbing Arena
Ring of Unity of 492ft dia. will host diverse art/cultural activities, with Lookout Deck facing Sabarmati River	
4-acre Open Plaza (capacity 5000), with temporary structures for 12,000 additional persons when required	
3000-apartment Games Village to house 12,000 athletes	
Existing Mahatma Mandir Convention Centre will be used as the International Broadcast Centre	

OLYMPIC Venues being built in Ahmedabad	
₹1200Cr Karai Sports Hub — 114 acres — Opening 2030 7.5km from SVP Sports Enclave	
35,000-seat Athletics and Soccer Stadium (expandable to 50,000 seats for larger events)	
Indoor Stadium (Swimming, Badminton, TT, Billiards)	Equestrian Sports Complex
Professional Shooting Complex	Tennis and Volleyball Courts
₹632Cr Naranpura Sports Enclave — 20.4 acres — Opening 2025 7.2km from SVP Sports Enclave	
5200-seat Indoor Multi-Sports Arena (16 badminton or 04 basketball/volleyball courts, plus gymnastics/kabaddi/wrestling mats)	
Indoor Community Sports Centre — 06 badminton & 06 TT courts, 10 billiards/snooker tables, 09 chess tables	
Centre for Sports Excellence — 02 Halls of 138ft x 79ft — 02 basketball/01 volleyball/08 badminton courts	
Multi Sports Hall that can hold either 04 kabaddi/taekwondo/wrestling mats or 12 TT tables	
1500-seat Aquatic Complex with 01 Olympic-size Pool and 01 Diving Pool	
Outdoor Tennis Courts	

The Metro and Bus Rapid Transit System (BRTS) will be extended to all the three enclaves.

The Government of Gujarat has incorporated Gujarat Olympic Planning and Infrastructure Corporation Limited to oversee Ahmedabad's Olympic bid and the development of Sardar Vallabhbhai Patel Sports Enclave, as well as the Karai Sports Hub. India already submitted an official 'Letter of Intent' to the International Olympics Association on 1 October 2024.

With the under-construction bullet train from Mumbai and the planned bullet train from Delhi, sports fans from both megacities can reach Ahmedabad in in 2.1 hours and 3.7 hours, respectively, and return home the same night, thus eliminating the need to stay in expensive hotel rooms. As the trains will stop at other large cities, fans can reach in 27 minutes from Vadodara, 1.1 hours from Surat, and 2.6 hours from Jaipur.

Delhi is also considering a bid for the 2040 or 2044 Summer Olympic Games. If Ahmedabad wins the bid for the 2036 Games (which is very likely with Modi's personal diplomacy and PR), it is unlikely that another Indian city will get a chance for at least 12-16 years.

F1 Motor Racing Circuit

GIFT city Ahmedabad (see the chapter 'GIFT city' in this book) is building an F1 circuit for over ₹10,000Cr.

It will probably be designed by Germany's Hermann Tilke, a former F1 race driver who has designed F1 circuits in Austin and Las Vegas (US), Abu Dhabi, and Shanghai.

'This is likely to be more of a street circuit like Singapore. Not just a purpose-built facility but one that can be available 365 days,' said Narain Karthikeyan, the first Indian to drive in an F1 race.[2]

However, not much movement has taken place since six teams of renowned global race track designers made presentations to the GIFT City management and representatives of the Gujarat Government in March 2024.

Sports Universities

National Sports University opened on a 168ac campus in Imphal, Manipur, in January 2019. A new 326ac, ₹900Cr campus is under construction and some media reports suggest that it is about 45% complete.

The ₹700Cr Major Dhyan Chand Sports University is coming up on a 90ac site in Meerut (Uttar Pradesh). Construction started in January 2024 and is expected to be completed by mid-2027.

116

RIP Article 370

In August 1947, J&K was a 'princely state', neither part of India, nor Pakistan. Under attack by Pakistan Army soldiers disguised as peasants, Maharaja Hari Singh requested India's help, and in exchange, 'acceded' to India in October 1947.

In May 1949, rulers/CMs of all 562 princely states told the GoI that they did not need separate constitutions and accepted the Indian Constitution as their own. Some suggested amendments that the GoI accepted and incorporated. The position of all princely states became the same as the rest of India.

J&K requested that only provisions of the Indian Constitution that concurred with the instrument of accession (defence, foreign affairs, communications) should apply to J&K and other matters to be decided by J&K's Constituent Assembly (JKCA) when formed. The GoI agreed and Article 370 was incorporated into the Indian Constitution, which stipulated that other articles that gave powers to the GoI would be applied to J&K only with concurrence of JKCA. The heading of Article 370 was 'Temporary provisions with respect to the state of Jammu and Kashmir' as it was only intended to last till adoption of J&K's Constitution. It was adopted in November 1956 and came into effect on 26 January 1957 and JKCA was dissolved the same day.

Only two articles of the Indian Constitution fully applied to J&K, not gender equality or caste-based reservations. Hindus and Sikhs who migrated from PoJK/Pakistan could not vote in J&K elections, though they could in LS elections. Other articles/provisions of the Indian Constitution would apply with exceptions or modifications specified by the President of India via presidential orders (POs) with concurrence of Government of J&K. From January 1950 to February 1994, 52 POs extended 260 of the 395 articles of the Indian Constitution to J&K. Power was with Congress or its dependent central government 94.7 per cent of the time. All POs were issued with concurrence of Government of J&K, without a JKCA. Some were issued with J&K under 'president's rule', with no state government, with concurrence of the governor, appointee of the GoI then in power.

Home Minister Gulzarilal Nanda opined that J&K's 'special status' included a 'very simple process to amend by a presidential order', whereas powers of all other states could only be amended by the tough process of a Constitutional Amendment, and Article 370 was the way of taking the Indian Constitution into J&K.[3] His successors interpreted Article 370 in the same manner.

Article 35A, added to the Indian Constitution through a PO in 1954, empowered the J&K legislature to define 'permanent residents' and provide them special rights and privileges—the right to purchase immovable property, vote/contest elections, seek government jobs, free healthcare, etc. Non-permanent residents, even if Indian citizens (including companies and firms registered outside J&K) were not entitled to these privileges.

On 5 August 2019, Amit Shah announced in parliament that the president had issued 'The Constitution (Application to Jammu and Kashmir) Order' superseding the 1954 PO and thereby removing all restrictions on the applicability of the entire Indian Constitution on J&K. Shah also introduced a bill to convert J&K into two UTs (with Ladakh separated). The RS passed the bill with 67.2 per cent majority and the LS with 84.1 per cent majority. Shah moved a resolution recommending that the president issue a PO to make Article 370 inoperative. After both the LS and RS adopted this, the president issued a PO due to which, Articles 370 and 35A both became inoperative.

This meant that 260,000–380,000 Kashmiri Pandits (Hindu) and Sikhs, who had been forced to leave the Kashmir Valley after December 1989 due to Islamic jihadist attacks (with the support of Pakistan's ISI), could reclaim their properties, and would have the same rights as J&K's erstwhile permanent residents.

NIA had already taken into custody thousands of separatists and their supporters. There were no phones or Internet. Three former CMs, Farooq Abdullah, his son Omar and Mehbooba Mufti, who have all taken pro-Pakistan/pro-separatist stands, were under house arrest. Kashmiris could only react to Shah's announcement in disbelief. They were not able to organise protests. Militants couldn't use social media to provoke people. The Valley had been tamed.

Who Benefitted from Articles 370 and 35A?

- Pakistan, as it helped them convince J&K's Muslims that they are different from 'Indians' and have a 'special status'.
- Radical Islamists/separatists who want J&K to separate from India. They usurped lands/properties of Kashmiri Pandits and Sikhs.

- The Abdullahs (ruled for 24.3 years) and the Muftis (ruled for over six years). They allegedly amassed lakhs of crores by siphoning funds sent by GoI (Congress party would have probably received its share). J&K received about 8 per cent of total central funds until FY15, for only 0.94 per cent of population—around ₹6.5LCr. Yet there was hardly any development.
- Separatists amassed enormous wealth and lived in lavish bungalows in central Srinagar, that too with security provided by the governments of India/J&K, with our (taxpayer) money.
- Normal Kashmiri Muslims did not benefit in any way.

J&K was amongst India's top 5 tourist destinations until 1988, with 722,000 tourists that year. This fell to just 6,287 in 1991. Goa gets its major income from tourism. Its per capita income in FY20 was ₹520,031. In comparison, J&K's ₹121,972 was 76.55 per cent lower.

Investments from companies from outside J&K nosedived after the violence of 1989–1995. No one wanted to build a facility on leased land (they were not allowed to buy), or have their staff face regular violence against non-Kashmiris. In the next chapter you will read how things have changed.

In December 2023, a 5-judge Supreme Court Constitution Bench headed by the Chief Justice of India (CJI) unanimously upheld GoI's decision to abrogate Article 370.

In nine *India Today* polls (January 2020–February 2024), average 15.78 per cent people voted that revocation of Article 370 is Modi's biggest achievement.

117

Developing J&K

There is no better proof of Modi's commitment to J&K than the fact that he visited J&K a record 24 times in 9.87 years—more than any other PM.

There is rapid work with the GoI-controlled J&K administration becoming proactive since Articles 370 and 35A were scrapped.

- In May 2020, the J&K administration started issuing 'domicile certificates' to permanent residents, as well as to non-permanent residents who have resided in J&K for minimum 15 years. Over 6.2M certificates have been issued. This was a big victory for the Valmiki Samaj who came from Punjab in 1957 on J&K government's invite due to a strike by the local sweepers' union that led to a sanitation crisis. The CM promised rehabilitation, saying the permanent resident clause would be relaxed; but they were treated like slaves and denied fundamental rights. For 63 years, Valmikis struggled to get a domicile certificate. Some even had PhD degrees but could only get sanitation worker/sweeper jobs. Apart from domicile certificates they now have SC status.
- Local Kashmiri tribes like Paddari, Pahari, Gadda Brahman, and Koli have got ST status.

- New land laws enable any person/entity from outside J&K to buy non-agricultural land.
- Agricultural land can now be purchased by an Indian person/entity subject to conditions.
- Over 4,500 Kashmiri Pandits and Sikhs have returned (over 620 have got their properties back) and over 150,000 more have registered to return.

J&K got 10.9M tourists in 2013. Tourist inflow started increasing under Modi—13.31M, 12.66M, 14.45M, 16.88M, and 16.22M tourists visited from 2015 to 2019. The arrivals were low in 2020 and 2021 due to COVID-19. J&K got 18.88M tourists in 2022 and a record 21.125M in 2023. Clearly, people now consider it safe to visit.

There's a lot more happening:

- In September 2022 a 3-screen 524-seat INOX multiplex, built by a Pandit family, opened in Srinagar. Kashmir's first cinema in 32 years has a 17,000SFT e-gaming zone.
- Jammu has a 2-screen 505-seat PVR multiplex.
- Multipurpose cinemas (usable for meetings and/or functions) of 100 seats each opened at seven places and will open in every district.
- Restaurants in Srinagar's earlier troubled Lal Chowk area now open till 9:30pm.
- Ola, Swiggy, and Zomato started operating in Kashmir.
- A 5-star hotel project to be built on a 7ac site in Gulmarg, abandoned in 1989, is being revived.
- The GoI is developing Ambharan, Kameshwar Purmandal, Uttar Behni, and Shiv Khori for religious tourism.
- In 2022, the tourism department introduced a homestay program to promote border tourism, which is benefitting

local families and providing jobs to the youth. There are over 1500 homestays with more than 3200 rooms.

- Some popular skiing trainers are earning as much as ₹104,000 per month.
- J&K has started attracting foreign investors' attention. The ₹500Cr Mall of Srinagar is being built by Dubai's real estate giant Emaar in a JV with an Indian builder, in which the UAE-based LuLu Group (with over 265 hypermarkets in 26 countries) will set up a hypermarket.
- In January 2024, horticulture startup Qul Fruitwall Farm received a ₹60Cr foreign institutional investment for research to modernise the sector. The Sopore *mandi* (Asia's 2nd largest fruit market) does business of around ₹7,000Cr per year. About 60 per cent of J&K's apple trade takes place in the Sopore *mandi* and residents of Bandipora, Baramulla, Budgam, and Kupwara districts in north Kashmir largely depend on it.
- Sri Lankan cricketer Muttiah Muralitharan's Ceylon Beverages is investing ₹1,600Cr for setting up a plant to make aluminium cans and filling beverages.
- Notable projects by Indian entities include a ₹1,100Cr pet bottling plant by Kandhari Beverages, Welspun Group's ₹850Cr plastic water tank manufacturing plant, and Haldiram's ₹585Cr snacks unit.
- By June 2024, J&K received investment proposals of ₹1.23LCr (₹81,595Cr in Jammu and ₹41,633Cr in Kashmir), including the above projects.
- National Buildings Construction Corporation (a PSE) is developing a 406ac township with an investment of ₹15,000Cr, located just 8km from Srinagar's city centre.

On 1 April 2021, the GoI announced a new central sector scheme with many incentives worth ₹28,400Cr to foster industrial development in J&K.

J&K's first electric train started on 185.7km Baramulla (Kashmir) to Sangaldan (Jammu) route with 19 stations and a 12.7km tunnel. The 272km Udhampur–Srinagar–Baramulla line has connected Kashmir with the rest of India 51 years after it was announced by Indira Gandhi. The 1.32km Chenab Bridge (world's highest rail arch bridge) is on this line; 38 tunnels and 927 bridges were completed. A centrally heated Vande Bharat sleeper train has started on the 800+km New Delhi–Srinagar route.

Other projects that have started include a centrally-heated Vande Bharat chair car on the Katra-Baramulla route, J&K's 2nd IIT, first IIM, and a 720-bed, 227ac AIIMS Jammu (2nd AIIMS in J&K) was about 61 per cent complete by 15 January 2025. Medical colleges in J&K have gone up from 4 in 2014 to 12 as of February 2024 (up 300 per cent).

Currently under construction are projects of ₹32,000Cr including Phase 2 of the 4-lane 61km Srinagar Ring Road the 58km, 4/6-lane Jammu Ring Road, new Jammu Airport terminal, upgrade of 161km Srinagar–Baramulla–Uri National Highway, and bypass roads for Kulgam and Pulwama. Some other projects are listed in the chapter 'Strengthened Border Infrastructure' in this book.

'We will develop so much infrastructure in Kashmir that people will forget Switzerland,' said Modi.[4]

118

Developing Ladakh

There has been unprecedented development in the most scenic UT of Ladakh:

- A 255km Darbuk–Shyok–Daulat Beg Oldie Road from Leh to Daulat Beg Oldie (DBO) military post on the LAC reduced travel time from 2 days to 6 hours.
- DBO has the world's highest transport aircraft airfield at an altitude of 16,730ft above mean sea level.
- Nyoma Airfield is the highest fighter aircraft landing strip in the world at 13,700ft.
- The 1,134ft-long Shyok River Bridge has been built at a height of 15,300ft.
- The 9km Atal Tunnel on Manali–Leh highway reduced travel time by 4–5 hours.
- UmlingLa, the highest motorable pass in the world, is situated at 19,024ft.
- The 298km Nimmu–Padam–Darcha Road links Manali directly with Leh.
- The widened and strengthened 2-lane Kargil–Zanskar Road was open throughout the winter of 2020–21—first time in history.
- The 64km-long Likaru-Mig La-Fukche road is the world's highest motorable road, touching about 19,400ft at a point.

- Fourteen roads and bridges of more than 680km have been completed.
- More than 40 other roads and bridges are being built.
- Many rural roads have been built under Ladakh Gramin Sadak Yojana and many are under construction.
- The 14.2km Zoji La tunnel between Sonmarg (J&K) and Drass in Kargil (Ladakh) on the Srinagar–Leh highway, which remains closed for over seven months due to heavy snowfall, will open by 2029 for year-long movement on the highway. This will provide connectivity to Amarnath Yatra base camp at Baltal, Kargil and other places in Ladakh, giving a boost to tourism.
- By 2027, the 4.1km Shinkun La tunnel will be the world's highest tunnel at 15,855ft and provide all-weather access to border areas.
- The 228km Srinagar–Leh power transmission line was commissioned with 92 distribution transformers.
- GoI approved an intra-state transmission project for grid connectivity to far-flung villages.
- Leh now has more than 60,500 smart meters.
- Modi wants to make Ladakh India's first carbon-neutral region and work is on at a rapid pace.
- A 10GW energy park is coming up on 20,000ac land.
- A solar power project of 7.5GW is being built.
- Solar Energy Corp of India initiated a 50MW solar storage plant.
- An MoU has been signed with Convergence Energy Services for solar power.
- About 2,200 solar streetlights have been installed.
- An MoU has been signed with ONGC for a geothermal field with 200MW potential.

- Mini-hydel projects of 550KW will complete in Drass, Matayen and Turtuk.
- Eight hydro-power projects of 144MW have been sanctioned.
- In February 2024, the GoI sanctioned the 'Green Energy Corridor Phase-II' project for 13GW of renewable energy, with a total cost of ₹20,774Cr.
- E-buses have been introduced.
- A pilot batch of EVs specially customised for Ladakh have been procured for offices of Ladakh administration.
- DG sets have been phased out in over 30 villages and are being completely phased out from Ladakh.
- Sindhu Central University at Khalatse now has a temporary campus. Construction of a permanent campus started in late-2024.
- A medical college (with a 100-student intake) is coming up at Spituk Pharka.
- A 30-bed hospital is coming up at Tangste.
- A government engineering college is coming up at Kargil.
- A Centre of Excellence has been established by the Indian Army and Hindustan Petroleum to prepare youth for medical and engineering exams.
- Under Samagra Shiksha Scheme, more than 100 ICT labs and smart classrooms have been established in polytechnics.
- Rewa scheme gives financial assistance to meritorious students of classes 10 and 12 to take up coaching for exams like NEET, JEE, NDA, CSE, IES, IFoS, etc.
- Astronomy labs have been established at Kendriya Vidyalayas in Leh and Kargil in collaboration with the office of the principal scientific advisor, GoI, and 20 more such labs are being established.

- Career counselling sessions are held in all government high schools and government higher secondary schools.
- Over 12,500 'YounTab' tablets pre-loaded with educational content have been distributed to students of classes 6–12.
- Various skill development programs are ongoing.
- Ladakh Incubation Centre was set up to accelerate growth of startups.
- Mission Organic Development Initiative was launched to make Ladakh 100 per cent organic. Polycarbonate greenhouses were provided to farmers at subsidised rates; bio-fertilizers were provided to 64 villages as a pilot; 120 packing/sorting/grading houses were established on 50 per cent subsidy to reduce post-harvest losses; 360 solar dryer-cum-space heating systems were commissioned in villages on 90 per cent subsidy.
- Thirty-six new helipads were built.
- Helicopter service has been started for essential commodities and citizens, particularly patients, and students residing in areas that remain disconnected during winters.
- Home stay policy has been launched to promote responsible and sustainable tourism practices and boost the rural economy.
- Dark Sky Park is coming up to promote astro-tourism.
- Several year-round tourism festivals are held regularly.
- Tourism development at Leh and Kargil is happening under Swadesh Darshan 2.0.
- Tourist facilities are being developed at Zanskar–Padum.
- VSAT has been installed in 186 sites for network connectivity to rural areas.

- About 96 per cent households had tap water connections as of December 2024.
- Many multipurpose indoor stadiums and ice hockey rinks have been built.
- Synthetic tracks and astroturf has been installed at the open stadium in Leh.
- The Modi Government is considering a ₹3,500Cr scheme for boosting industry and jobs.

Ladakh's budget has gone up by 5.25 times since FY19.

In calendar year 2023, the UT of Ladakh attracted around 525,000 tourists, including 36,315 foreign tourists.

119

Developing the Northeast

The day after being sworn in as PM, Modi created the Ministry of Development of North Eastern Region (MDoNER), a historical first.

His commitment to the Northeast region can be measured from the fact that he visited it 71 times in 9.87 years—more than the total visits by all previous PMs put together, while his ministers cumulatively visited the region more than 690 times (yes, that's right!).

Expenditure on Development of Northeast Region				
FISCAL YEAR	MDoNER	Other Ministries or Departments	NLCPR Scheme	TOTAL
2014-15	₹1719.13cr	₹24,819.18cr	₹605.90cr	**₹27,144.21cr**
2015-16	₹1986.79cr	₹28,673.73cr	₹645.00cr	**₹31,305.52cr**
2016-17	₹2495.84cr	₹29,367.90cr	₹837.29cr	**₹32,701.03cr**
2017-18	₹2519.05cr	₹39,753.44cr	₹862.42cr	**₹43,134.91cr**
2018-19	₹1962.62cr	₹46,054.80cr	₹526.55cr	**₹48,543.97cr**
2019-20	₹2657.87cr	₹48,533.80cr	₹576.59cr	**₹51,768.26cr**
2020-21	₹1853.66cr	₹48,563.82cr	₹341.84cr	**₹50,759.32cr**
2021-22	₹2519.66cr	₹70,874.32cr	₹137.81cr	**₹73,531.79cr**
2022-23	₹984.98cr	₹82,690.87cr	₹128.73cr	**₹83,804.58cr**
2023-24	₹5892.00cr	₹98,466.71cr		**₹104,358.71cr**
SOURCES: https://mdoner.gov.in/dashboard/; GOI Budget Documents				

Yes, the Modi government spent a whopping amount of more than ₹5.47LCr on the Northeast region in 10 years.

In addition, ₹11,540Cr was spent under Northeast Special Infrastructure Development Scheme and ₹6600Cr under the PM-DeviNE scheme.

Infra Projects by Modi Govt in North East Region — 1	
ROADS, BRIDGES, and TUNNELS	**Length or Amount**
Total Amount Invested on Roads, Bridges, and Tunnels	**₹297,000cr+**
New Roads including 5470+km National Highways	**27,600+ Km**
Widening, Strengthening, and otherwise Improving Existing Roads	**5300+ Km**
Amount Spent on Rural Roads	**₹26,140cr+**
Sela Tunnel Dirang–Tawang in Arunachal (height ~13,000ft), India's highest Himalayan tunnel	**12.04 Km**
Construction of Bagrakote–Pakyong 2-lane National Highway in Sikkim	**152 Km**
4-laning of Nagaon Bypass to Holongi in Arunachal	**167 Km**
4-laning of Dimapur–Kohima Road in Nagaland	**62.9 Km**
4-laning of Imphal–Moreh section of National Highway in Manipur	**20 Km**
2-laning of Aizawl–Tuipang National Highway in Mizoram	**351 Km**
2-laning of National Highway in Manipur	**75.2 Km**
Manipur's capital Imphal, Nagaland's capital Kohima, and Nagaland's 2nd largest city Dimapur got connected with the rest of India via Guwahati **for the first time in history**	
Aizawl Bypass with 2-lane twin tunnels of 2.5km length (under construction)	**34.5 Km**
6-lane Guwahati Bypass Road	**16.45 Km**
6-lane Road to New Airport Terminal Building at Guwahati	**12.6 Km**
6-lane Guwahati Ring Road including Narengi–Kuruwa Bridge across Brahmaputra	**₹4500cr**
6-lane Road from Khanapara (Guwahati, Assam) to Jorabat (Meghalaya)	**8.2 Km**
38 Km Elevated Corridor in Kaziranga National Park	**₹6000cr**
Roads currently under construction or construction to begin soon	**~7715 Km**
Jorhat–Majuli Bridge	**17 Km**
Bogeebil Rail Road Bridge opened in Dec2018 *The design and shortlisting of agencies was completed in 2004, but actual work only in 2011 and only around 10-15% was complete when Modi became PM. His Govt expedited the work and completed it in under 04 years.*	**4.94 Km**
Bhupen Hazarika Bridge connecting Dhola–Sadiya in Assam's Tinsukia district (opened May2017) *First connection between Northern Assam and Eastern Arunachal;* ***Bridge designed to handle Tanks of 60MT***	**9.15 Km**
Dhubri (Assam) to Phulbari (Meghalaya) bridge will reduce distance by 250km (opening 2028)	**18.4 Km**
4-lane Palashbari–Sualkuchi Bridge in Guwahati (opening 2028)	**12.2 Km**
6-lane Guwahati North Guwahati Bridge (opening December 2024)	**8.4 Km**

Infra Projects by Modi Govt in North East Region — 2	
AIRPORTS, ROPEWAYS, RAILWAYS, and WATERWAYS	**Quantity**
New Airports in Assam — Jorhat, Lilabari, Rupsi (Dhubri), and Tezpur	**4**
New Airports in Arunachal Pradesh — Hollongi (Itanagar), Pasighat, and Tezu	**3**
New Airports in Other States — Shillong (barapani), Meghalaya; Pakyyong, Sikkim; Dimapur, Nagaland	**3**
Overall Increase in Number of Airports in 10 years (from 09 to 19)	**▲ 111.1%**
Guwahati Airport New Terminal Building	**10 mppa**
New Air Routes Started	**69**
Increase in Air Passenger Traffic in 10 years	**▲ 135.2%**
Five (05) Ropeways in Assam (under development0	**₹2100cr**
Total Amount Invested on Railways by UPA Govt (₹21,219cr) vs. by Modi Govt (₹65,022cr)	**▲ 206.4%**
Railways Line Sections Commissioned during UPA Govt (562.7 Km) vs. during Modi Govt (1807.2 Km)	**▲ 221.2%**
110.6 Km Jiribam–Imphal Rail Line built by Modi Govt to connect Manipur by Rail with the rest of India	
39.12km Belonia–Sabroom Rail Line provides easy access to South Tripura and Chattogram Port in Bangladesh	
Broad-Gauge Railway Network through the entire North East Region has been **100% electrified** by the Modi Govt	
2nd Railway Station built in Nagaland **after 100 years**	
12.24km Agartala (Tripura) to Akhaura (Bangladesh) Rail Line is the first rail connection between the countries. Built at a cost of ₹1101cr, it has reduced Agartala–Kolkata Distance from 1600 Km to 500 Km and Travel Time from 31 hours to 11 hours	
National Waterways up from 01 in May 2014 to 10 now; another 02 being developed for ₹6000cr	**▲ 1100%**

Here is some more work done by the Modi government:

- Access to clean drinking water has gone up 16 times since September 2020.
- Over 7,000 villages achieved 100 per cent tap connections. All households in Arunachal and Mizoram have tap water, whereas the progress is almost 90 per cent each in Sikkim and Nagaland, 85 per cent in Tripura, 81.3 per cent each in Assam and Meghalaya, and almost 80 per cent in Manipur as of December 2024.
- Arunachal, Assam, Sikkim, and Tripura are almost 100 per cent open defecation free.
- The 600MW Kameng and 110MW Pare hydropower projects in Arunachal, and 60MW Tuirial hydropower

project in Mizoram, have made these states power surplus. Tuirial was on hold for 17 years.

- The 69.755MW gas-based Lakhwa replacement power project in Assam went online in February 2018.
- Almost 2.615M households were electrified. No household in the Northeast is without power anymore.
- The 1,656km Indradhanush gas grid will connect all the 8 states, provide clean energy and boost industrial growth without pollution.
- Over ₹36,000Cr has been spent on healthcare.
- As of December 2024, there were 353 Jan Aushadhi Kendras in the region.
- The Northeast got India's first-ever 'air dispensary' that operates inside a helicopter.
- Modi spent ₹14,009Cr till FY24 to promote higher education in the region.

Infra Projects by Modi Govt in North East Region — 3

HEALTHCARE, EDUCATION, and SPORTS	Quantity
First AIIMS (All India Institute of Medical Sciences) in the North East Region opened at Guwahati in April 2023	
19 Cancer Institutes Approved for Assam — the State will have South Asia's Largest Cancer Hospital Network	
Integrated New Building for Gauhati Medical College & Hospital (to be built by 2027)	₹3250cr
New Karimganj Medical College & Hospital (to be built by 2027)	₹578cr
New Educational Institutes already set up, including 03 IIITs	191
Increase in Number of Universities since May 2014	▲ 39%
Increase in Central Institutions of Higher Education	▲ 40%
Barak Hostel inside the JNU campus in New Delhi, built exclusively for North-East Students, can accommodate 446 students	
5.5-acre Hostel in Bangalore University exclusively for Girl Students from the North East Region, can accommodate 2000 residents	
National Sports University opened on a 168-acre campus in Imphal, Manipur, in Jan2019. A 326-acre ₹900cr campus is under construction.	
62-year-old Nehru Stadium getting a FIFA-standard Upgrade and expanded Capacity of 30,000 seats	₹831cr
Multi-Sport Complex being built at Chandrapur, Guwahati	₹300cr
Amingaon Sports Complex, Guwahati	₹320cr
National Centre of Excellence for Badminton, Amingaon, Guwahati (16 courts, 3335 seats) opened Aug2023	₹93cr

Industrial Development

- Tata Group is setting up a ₹27,000Cr outsourced semiconductor assembly and testing (OSAT) unit in Morigaon, Assam.
- The SAMPADA scheme grants aid on concessional terms for entrepreneurs to set up mega food parks, integrated cold chain, and value-added infrastructure in the Northeast region.
- North East Business Process Outsourcing (BPO) promotion scheme attracts investments in BPO units.
- Over 1.6M persons got skilled and 900,000 got MSME benefits from the North East Development Finance Corp Ltd (NEDFi).
- The Northeast region has over 4,600 registered startups and 25 active incubators.
- NEDFi set up a dedicated venture capital fund for the Northeast region with a corpus of ₹100Cr—67 startups got ₹98.18Cr up to November 2023.
- The ₹3,000Cr North East Industrial Development Scheme gives incentives to new industrial units. It has 5 components: (1) CCIIAC subsidises 30 per cent of the investment in plant and machinery with a cap of ₹5Cr; (2) Central Interest Incentive of 3 per cent on working capital loan is available for five years from commencement of production; (3) Central Comprehensive Insurance Incentive reimburses 100 per cent premium on insurance of building and plant and machinery for five years from commencement of production; (4) GST reimbursement of GoI's share of CGST and IGST for five years from commencement of production; (5) Incentive up to 20 per cent of the

transport cost of finished goods by rail or inland waterways, and 30 per cent for transport of perishable goods by air freight from the airport nearest to the place of production to any airport within India.

Miscellaneous Projects

- A 125ft 'Statue of Valour', the world's tallest statue of General Lachit Barphukan (who saved Assam from Mughal rule) was built in Jorhat, including a museum and a 500-seat auditorium.
- North Eastern Cultural and Social Institute (with a 1,000-seat auditorium, two seminar halls, library, art gallery, exhibition hall, research centre, sales outlets, guest house, food court, and a banquet hall, etc.) is being built in Dwarka, near IGI Airport, Delhi. It was almost 30 per cent complete as of August 2024.
- With 1,550km^2 of land utilised for organic farming, Modi's push for smart and sustainable agriculture in the Northeast region has seen effective real-time governance and monitoring in 562 projects across 1,664 locations being geo-tagged.
- In 2018, Sikkim became the first fully organic state.
- Centre for Agriculture was set up in Mizoram in 2018 with Israeli collaboration, for processing of citrus fruits.
- National Bamboo Mission was announced in February 2018 with a budget of ₹1290Cr. The 90-year-old 'Indian Forest Act of 1927' was amended to exempt bamboo grown in non-forest land from the Act.
- Cane and Bamboo Tech Park opened in 2019 at Burnihat, Assam.
- A 55ac Zoram mega food park opened in Mizoram.

- A ₹10,000Cr fishery fund benefits people in the Northeast.

Efforts for Peace

One of the most significant decisions has been the removal of the contentious Armed Forces Special Protection Act (AFSPA). It has been completely removed from Tripura and Meghalaya, and majorly removed from Assam, Nagaland, Manipur, and Arunachal Pradesh, barring some areas. Peace agreements have been signed with 13 separatist and militant groups in the region. More than 10,000 youth of the Northeast have laid down arms and pledged to stand shoulder to shoulder in the country's development.

Tourism Success

- Amenities have been created at Nathu La in Sikkim for acclimatisation of pilgrims undertaking Mansarover Yatra.
- Tourist facilities have been developed at the popular tourist hub Majuli Island in Assam. A 12.7km Ro-Ro service between Neamati and Kamlabari (Majuli Island) became operational in October 2018. Tourists had to earlier take a 410km road journey that could take between 8–10 hours.
- An MoU has been signed between Airbnb, North East Council, and North East Tourism Development Corp to facilitate homestays in the Northeast region.
- MoUs have been signed for strategic partnerships by the North East Rural Livelihood Project and the North Eastern Region Community Resource Management Project with Airbnb to generate tech-enabled livelihood opportunities in tourism and hospitality for micro-entrepreneurs in the region.

Tourist arrivals in Northeast region went up from 7.471M in 2015 to 12.3M in 2023 (up 65 per cent in 8 years).

It is debatable whether J&K and Ladakh were more neglected by successive governments for 66.8 years before Modi, or did the Northeast face a more step-fatherly treatment, but given the fact that the population of the eight Northeast states was almost 3.71 times that of J&K state (which included Ladakh) in 2011, it was perhaps much more important to pay attention to this region's development, especially considering that China has designs on it.

It took a man from Gujarat to give it the attention it deserved. That too, despite Dr Manmohan Singh being an MP from Assam continuously for almost 28 years.

120

Andaman & Nicobar and Lakshadweep Islands

Modi is developing the Andaman and Nicobar Islands (A&NI) and the Lakshadweep Islands as per the Maritime India Vision 2030 plan we wrote about earlier, with a focus on job creation through tourism and export of local seafood and coconut-based products.

A total of 26 islands have been shortlisted. Phase-1 includes four islands in A&NI and five in Lakshadweep. In the 2nd phase, 12 more islands in A&NI and five more in Lakshadweep will be covered.

Projects included are eco-tourism facilities, ship repair, seaplane building and repair, maritime training institute, free trade zones, and bunkering terminals—58 projects worth ₹7,622Cr are being developed under the Sagarmala program.

Andaman and Nicobar Islands

The A&NI are located between the Bay of Bengal and the Andaman Sea, and are closer in distance to Myanmar and Thailand, than to India. They had 332,644 tourist arrivals in 2023. The first nine months of 2024 had 395,729 tourists (up 81.2 per cent compared with the first nine months of 2023).

The UPA government's budget for the islands in 10 years was ₹24,500Cr, the Modi government spent around ₹1.33LCr (up 443 per cent).

- The Modi government has approved a huge cargo transhipment terminal at Great Nicobar Island costing ₹43,700Cr. This hub is on the route from eastern India, the Northeast region, Bangladesh, and Myanmar to east and southeast Asia, Australia, and New Zealand. This will have a 450MW LNG-based power plant.
- Humphrey Strait Creek Bridge is now open to public.
- Middle Strait Bridge will be operational by early 2025.
- Veer Savarkar International Airport got a brand new terminal building.
- Two greenfield airports are in the pipeline, including one in Port Blair apart from the existing Veer Savarkar International Airport, and another in Great Nicobar.
- As of November 2023, submarine (underwater) optical fibre cables of 2313km have been laid between Chennai and A&NI. Eight islands have been connected through these cables.
- Everyone in A&NI now has a bank account.
- All have 'One Nation One Ration Card'.
- On 15 August 2019, 33,490 households in Andaman and Nicobar Islands had piped water connections (465/year), and the Modi government provided connections to 28,547 households in 4.125 years 6,899/year, up 1,384 per cent). All households in the islands now have functioning tap connections.
- The Andaman and Nicobar administration plans to allow tourists to visit the charming Aves Island in the North and Middle Andaman district.

- The administration also plans to create a 5-star eco-tourism resort through PPP to turn Aves into a popular tourist destination.

Lakshadweep Islands

The 36 islands located 222–389km off the coast of Kerala in the Arabian Sea have a total land area of 32km^2. Lakshadweep received 8,489 tourists in FY20, negligible in FY21 due to COVID-19, less than 42,000 in FY22, and 54,127 in FY23. There is an increased focus since Modi visited in January 2024, with the number of tourists visiting the islands going up by over 45% in the first half of 2024 compared with the same period of 2023.

As an initial step, the GoI is investing ₹3,600Cr for 13 tourism infrastructure projects including ports in 3 islands and beachfront roads on 3 islands.

HDFC Bank opened the first private bank branch on the island in April 2024.

The Taj Group of Hotels is building hotels in Kadmat and Suheli Islands by 2026 and many major hotel chains are scouting for land.

A dual-use airport for civilian and military purposes is coming up at Minicoy, and the 1.2km runway at Agatti will be expanded to accommodate Airbus 320s and Boeing 737 aircraft (today, only small turboprops of under 75 seats can operate there).

121

No Indians Stranded Abroad

The Modi government is working for the Indians in India and for Indian citizens outside of India too, especially in times of global distress.

Name of Op	When	Evacuated from Where	Mode	What was the need	Indians Evacuated	Foreigners Evacuated
Rahat	2015	**Yemen**	Indian Navy	War between Govt and Houthi Rebels	**4748**	964 (30 counties)
04 pregnant women, 01 cancer and 01 renal failure patients, and 02 malnourished children were provided medical aid onboard the ships						
Sankat Mochan	July 2016	**South Sudan**	Air	Hostilities between political groups	**152**	02 (Nepal)
Samudra Setu	05May-29Jun 2020 (55 days)	**Iran, Maldives, And Sri Lanka**	Navy Ships sailed 23,000km	Covid19 pandemic	**3992**	—
Vande Bharat	2020-2022	**30+ cities**	217,000 flights of IAF and Private Airlines	Covid19 pandemic	**18.3mn**	—
The longest flights of the Vande Bharat Operation were to Vancouver on the southwest coast of Canada (14:45hrs flying time from Delhi) and San Francisco on the US west coast (15:50hrs)						
Devi Shakti	August and December 2021	**Afghanistan**	IAF and Air India	Taliban takeover	**886**	206 (Afghans)
Ganga	01Feb-11Mar 2022	**Ukraine, Romania, Hungary, Poland, and Slovakia**	14 IAF flights, 76 by 06 Private Airlines	Russia-Ukraine War	**18,282**	—
Kaveri	24Apr-06May 2023	**Sudan**	IAF and Indian Navy	Civil War	**3961**	136
Ajay	12-22Oct 2023	Israel	06 flights of IAF	Hamas attack on Israel	**1327**	20 (Nepal)

Air fare for all these operations was borne entirely by the GoI.

During COVID-19, Indian missions and posts abroad assisted 173,618 stranded Indian nationals.

Excluding the COVID-19-related evacuations, the Modi government evacuated total 34,819 persons (including 1,328 foreign nationals).

The UPA government evacuated about 17,350 Indians in two operations.

122

Don't Dare Bully India Now

India is no longer a slave of a dynasty that is strongly influenced by a colonial mindset. Under Modi, India is acting on the stage of global geopolitics based on the principle of 'what is good for India'.

No More 'White Man' Pressure

The US and Europe exerted pressure on India to stop importing Russian oil and arms after Russia attacked Ukraine. India increased oil imports from Russia as India's Middle Eastern suppliers diverted large quantities to Europe for higher prices. As Europe reduced imports from Russia, the latter offered its excess stockpiles to India at very low prices. Foreign Minister Dr Jaishankar sternly rebutted European accusations in Brussels (Belgium)[5]:

> If you're looking at energy purchases from Russia, I'd suggest your attention should be on Europe. We buy some energy necessary for our energy security. But looking at figures, our purchases in a month would be less than what Europe does in an afternoon. You do what's good for you, I will do what's good for India.

When the Israel–Hamas war started, there was pressure from the West on India to support Israel, but India did not take sides despite the Modi–Netanyahu friendship. India voted for a UN resolution for 'an immediate humanitarian ceasefire' and immediate unconditional release of all hostages by Hamas. India also sent aid to Palestine.

Support for Khalistani Separatists by Canada, UK, USA

Thousands of Sikhs, especially in Canada, Pakistan, and the UK want to carve out an independent nation (Khalistan) by usurping the whole of Punjab and parts of Haryana and Himachal Pradesh. This has long been a source of tension in Indo-Canadian relationship.

Punjab-born Hardeep Singh Nijjar moved to Canada and became a vocal advocate for Khalistan. In 2016, the GoI reported its concerns to Canadian authorities.

Since 2019, India requested Canada 26 times to extradite people from Canada. In 2020, India accused Nijjar of being 'actively involved in operationalizing, training, and financing' Khalistan Tiger Force members, and running training camps for Sikhs to attack India.[6] He was associated with SFJ (Sikhs for Justice, a US-based pro-Khalistan group) and spearheaded its Khalistan Referendum 2020 campaign. The GoI banned SFJ in July 2019. In July 2022, the NIA announced a $1.2M reward for any information on Nijjar.

In June 2023, Nijjar was killed by 2 gunmen outside a gurdwara in Vancouver. In September, Canadian PM Justin Trudeau alleged that 'agents of the Indian Govt' were involved.[7] India firmly denied any involvement and called Trudeau's allegations 'absurd and motivated'.[8] The countries announced tit-for-tat expulsions of diplomats. India temporarily suspended issuing visas to Canadians and asked Canada to downsize diplomatic staff. India had 20 diplomats in Canada and said there should be 20 Canadian diplomats in India. On 20 October, Canada recalled 41 diplomats and their families. Canada's Foreign Minister Mélanie Joly said they were 'in danger of having immunity stripped on an arbitrary date' and that would 'put their personal safety at risk'.[9]

On 21 October, the US and the UK backed Canada. They are part of a 'Five Eyes' intelligence alliance with Canada, Australia, and New Zealand. Foreign Minister Dr Jaishankar said: 'We invoked parity due to concerns about continuous interference in our affairs. We haven't made much public. Over time more stuff will come out and people will understand why we had the kind of discomfort.'[10]

No concrete evidence was provided by Canada about India's alleged involvement in the Nijjar killing. India resumed visas in restricted categories. Visas for tourists, employment, students, journalists, film, and missionaries remain suspended. Free trade agreement discussions halted, a move that will hurt Canada more than India.

Nine wanted Khalistani terrorists had unnatural deaths since 2018. Six were top leaders of separatist groups.

India will not be bullied by Canada or its big brother, the US.

Stern with the US

Gurpatwant Singh Pannun, a dual citizen of the US and Canada, is a legal advisor and spokesperson of SFJ, and a top leader of the Khalistan movement. In July 2020, India declared Pannun as a terrorist. He has claimed responsibility for various terror incidents in India. In April 2023, he issued a video threat to Modi. He regularly threatens Indian politicians, diplomats, and intelligence officers. Pannun urged Sikhs in a video message of 5 November 2023 not to travel Air India on 19 November (Indira Gandhi's birthday), as 'their lives would be in danger'. He also said IGIA airport would be permanently shut on that day.

On 23 November 2023, the US said that it has 'thwarted a conspiracy to assassinate' Pannun on American soil and 'issued a warning to the Indian government over concerns it was involved in the plot'.[11] India said it takes US inputs on security 'seriously' and 'issues' in this context were being examined. The MEA immediately set up a 'high-level' committee of enquiry to investigate the allegations.

In February 2024, while on a visit to India, US deputy secretary of state (same as minister of state in India's MEA) Richard Verma said, 'We raised our concerns with the Government of India. There is a committee of inquiry looking into the matter. We look forward to their findings. They've taken it very seriously. And we're grateful for that.'[12]

In November 2023, Nikhil Gupta, a 52-year-old Indian national was charged by the US in the alleged plot to kill Pannun. The prosecutors alleged that Gupta, acting on the instructions of an unnamed Indian official, contacted a person whom he believed to be a criminal associate for help in killing Pannun on American soil.

The committee of inquiry found that at least one person directly involved in the alleged attempted assassination was a former RAW employee and had 'gone rogue'. India informed US authorities about the findings.

When the US State Department (their foreign ministry) made unfounded comments about CAA, the MEA retorted: 'Lectures by those with limited understanding of India's pluralistic traditions and our region's post-Partition history are best not attempted. The American view is misplaced, misinformed and unwarranted. CAA is about giving citizenship, not taking it away.'[13]

On Arvind Kejriwal's arrest, the US State Department remarked that rule of law must apply in agency investigations and any trial in courts. The MEA told their embassy's No. 2 in Delhi: 'In diplomacy, states [nations] are expected to respect the internal affairs of others, or it could end up setting unhealthy precedents. Casting aspersions on India's judiciary is unwarranted.'[14]

The next day, the US State Department said that the US encouraged 'Fair, transparent, timely legal processes and no one should object to that. We continue to follow closely, including the arrest of the Delhi CM.'[15]

The Americans added, 'We are also aware of the Congress party's allegations that tax authorities have frozen some of their bank accounts in a manner that will make it challenging to effectively campaign in the upcoming elections.'[16] Didn't Rahul Gandhi ask for exactly this? Interference by the US and UK in India's internal affairs.

The income tax department had frozen bank accounts of Congress as it had not paid taxes that were due on its rental income, claiming that political parties are exempt from income tax. As per India's tax laws (made by a Congress government), political parties are exempt from paying income tax on political donations they receive, and any business income (such as rent from property) is NOT exempt.

The MEA retorted: 'Any such external imputation on our electoral and legal and legal processes is completely unacceptable. India is proud of its independent and robust democratic institutions and are committed to protect them from any form of external influences.'[17]

Stern with Germany

On Kejriwal's arrest, Germany also interfered and said it expected that standards regarding judicial independence and basic principles of democracy would apply in the case. India lodged a 'strong protest' with Germany accusing it of undermining the independence of India's judiciary with its 'biased assumptions' and interfering in India's internal matter.

Stern with China

In late March 2024, China's ministry of foreign affairs said it has noted the reported US allegation that India plotted a murder-for-hire to assassinate a US Sikh leader: 'We hope relevant countries will observe international law and basic norms governing international relations.' The MEA retorted that India and the US, as two countries adhering to the rule of law are dealing with many issues between them, and that there was no role for speculative comments and gratuitous advice by unrelated parties.

Other Issues

In February 2024 at Munich (Germany), Dr Jaishankar was asked how India was balancing its growing bilateral ties with the US while continuing to trade with Russia, and responded, 'Why should that be a problem? If I am smart enough to have multiple options, you should be admiring me. In the contemporary word, it's very hard to have unidimensional relationships.'[18]

We already covered: (1) The issue about Wing Commander Abhinandan in the chapter 'Lifted the Morale of Soldiers' in this book, (2) Securing release of eight former Indian Navy personnel sentenced to death in Qatar; and (3) Acting against Chinese companies and Apps.

This is Modi's 'New India'.

123

Connected with Citizens

On 31 December 2023, Modi interacted with the public through his radio show '*Mann Ki Baat*' ('inner voice') for the 108th time.

His message was emotional, warm, and spiritual.

> My dear countrymen. Namaskar. '*Mann ki Baat*' means an auspicious opportunity to meet you, and when you meet your family members, it is so pleasing … so satisfying. Today is the 108th episode of our shared journey. For us the importance of the number 108 and its sanctity is a subject of deep study; 108 beads in a rosary, chanting 108 times, 108 divine sites, 108 stairs in temples, it is associated with immense faith. That is why the 108th episode of '*Mann ki Baat*' has become even more special for me. After reaching this milestone, we must resolve to move forward afresh, with new energy and at a faster pace. Best wishes to all of you for 2024.

Modi has never positioned himself as a 'ruler' but rather as someone who has come to serve the nation.

'*Mann ki Baat*' has opened doors of communication directly with the people rather than relying on media interviews or press conferences. He also ensured that he reached different corners of the country and touched the lives of millions of

Indians who have contributed to nation building in their own unique way by talking about their service to the nation.

Nearly 96 per cent of the population is aware of '*Mann Ki Baat*'. Over 800M people have listened to the program at least once.

As per a study by IIM Rohtak, about 230M people tune in regularly while another 410M are an occasional audience.

Apart from 22 Indian languages and 29 dialects, '*Mann Ki Baat*' is broadcast in 11 foreign languages, namely Arabic, Baluchi, Burmese, Chinese (Mandarin), Dari, French, Indonesian, Pashtu, Persian, Swahili, and Tibetan.

The program has become a key pillar of Modi's citizen-outreach program, addressing multiple social groups such as women, youth and farmers, and has spurred community action.

It is successful because it speaks directly to people, celebrates grassroot-level change-makers and achievements of people, and has influenced people towards positive actions.

The Narendra Modi App (over 12.6M downloads) is a one-stop destination for knowing all about his latest day-to-day activities. With one click, the interactive App allows the user to connect with the PM. It provides a unique opportunity to receive messages and emails directly from him. It allows users to contribute and earn badges through to-do tasks. One can log in, listen to all editions of '*Mann ki Baat*', read his blogs and know about him in the biography section. It lets users know about Modi's style of 'good governance', and the initiatives of his government. A dedicated section highlights the PM's efforts to augment India's global reputation. Infographics show how governance is improving the lives of people.

With over 105M followers on 'X' (formerly Twitter) Modi is the 7th most followed person in the world, the 4th most followed person who is not a singer, and the 2nd most followed politician after former US President Barack Obama (more than 131M).

He has 92.3M Instagram followers (making him the 4th most followed Indian), 50M Facebook followers and 26.5M YouTube subscribers.

Modi is one of the most tech-savvy leaders in the world and has always encouraged e-governance and m-governance from even before he became PM. In fact, he used Twitter (at that time) extensively for his 2013–14 election campaign.

124

Pension Schemes

Under the Old Pension Scheme (OPS), no corpus was created. The government paid pensions based on its current revenues, resulting in a huge burden to the exchequer every year. In FY91, the GoI's pension cost was 3.9 per cent of net revenue and rose at a CAGR of 21 per cent in the 1990s. It was 5.8 per cent in FY04. By FY21, the pension bill had jumped 58 times in 30 years. In FY23, the OPS liabilities for existing retirees were a huge 9.84 per cent of net revenue.

The Vajpayee government issued an ordinance to abolish the OPS for all GoI employees who join after 1 January 2004. As UPA came to power soon thereafter, it got the Pension Fund Regulatory and Development Authority (PFRDA) Bill passed in 2005 to replace the ordinance. A National Pension System (NPS) was introduced and an NPS Trust was set up to manage the system. The scheme was initially for government employees, but in 2009 it was expanded to include any citizen of 18 to 60 years.

The Pension Fund Managers (PFMs) offer investment schemes; and Points of Presence (PoPs) distribute these and service the subscribers. All major banks and brokerages are PoPs, and you can choose any PFM and any PoP.

In NPS, you contribute 10 per cent of your basic salary + dearness allowance, and your employer can contribute the same amount or higher.

People employed in the unorganised sector can invest as little as ₹500/month.

Tier I products have a tax deduction on your contribution up to ₹2L per annum and tax deduction on your employer's contribution up to 10 per cent of your basic salary + dearness allowance, subject to maximum ₹75,000 in a year, but you cannot make a withdrawal until retirement. Tier II offers more flexibility, including unrestricted withdrawals at any time without lock-in period, but does not offer a tax advantage.

MODI'S PENSION REFORMS and the RESULTS

WHAT	UPA	MODI	Increase
GOI Contribution for Central and State Govt Employees	10% of Basic + DA	14% of Basic + DA	▲ 40%
Tax Exemption for Self-Employed Persons	10% of Gross Income contributed to NPS	20% of Gross Income contributed to NPS	▲ 100%
Number of Annuity Providers	08	15	▲ 87.5%
Number of Pension Fund Managers	7	11	▲ 57.1%
Taxation on Withdrawal of 60% of Corpus	40% Tax-Free 20% taxable	Entire 60% Tax-Free	▲ 50%
Partial / Premature Withdrawal	NOT allowed	25% of your contribution can be withdrawn Tax-Free	✔✔✔
Number of Schemes	03	05	▲ 66.7%
Universal Pension coverage with auto enrolment for job mobility	NO	YES	✔✔✔
Opening of NPS Account	Physical Forms	Completely Online with Aadhaar-based e-Sign	✔✔✔
Pension Adalats to resolve complaints	NO	YES	✔✔✔
Centralised Pension Grievance Registration & Monitoring System	NO	YES	✔✔✔
Mobile App for Pensions	NO	YES	✔✔✔
Subscribers of Atal Pension Yojana (APY) and Swavalamban schemes	2.816mn	58.657mn	▲ 1983%
AUM of APY and Swavalamban	₹839cr	₹32,776cr	▲ 3807%
Number of NPS Subscribers (excluding APY and Swavlamban)	6.506mn	73.56mn	▲ 1031%
AUM of NPS Subscribers	₹0.481Lcr	₹11.283Lcr	▲ 2246%
Beneficiaries of NSAP (Central & State)	3.64mn	47.79mn	▲ 1213%

On maturity, 40 per cent of your corpus (contribution plus earnings) had to be used to buy an annuity plan and 60 per cent could be withdrawn in one go or by a systematic withdrawal plan.

Earlier you could invest in different schemes only through one PFM; now different PFMs are allowed for different products—this gives you flexibility and prevents PoPs from mis-selling.

State government employees' funds comprise 51.2 per cent and GoI employees 28.57 per cent in the total Assets Under Management (AUM) of PFMs.

NSAP (National Social Assistance Program) has five schemes.

APY (Atal Pension Yojana) is a social security scheme launched in 2015 to provide a guaranteed pension of up to ₹5,000 after the age of 60 years. There was a similar scheme in UPA-era called Swavalamban, which still exists, although enrolment is dropping every year.

By separating the NPS Trust from PFRDA, Modi has enabled a pension trust to be established by private sector employees. The NPS Trust was also removed as a nodal point and restricted to coordinate only the functions of withdrawals and exits with PFMs, trustee banks, custodian, and central recordkeeping agencies.

Several states are reintroducing the OPS. Political leaders, economists, and subject matter experts have criticised this. Finance Minister Nirmala Sitharaman commented,

> We should look at a reasonable balance and what we are leaving for generations to come. Unless we have a complete understanding of the fiscal health of the State, for not just today but future decades, the rush to a conclusion may not be good.

Axis Bank Chief Economist Saugata Bhattacharya termed the move as 'a ticking fiscal time bomb' and said,

> The problem with OPS is it is benefitting a bunch of people on the top. Calculating all the expenditure, you have some 10–15 per cent of your receipts for development. Commitment to OPS is going to affect development commitments. This is not sustainable in the longer run.

To resolve the debate between OPS and NPS, in August 2024, a new guaranteed pension scheme—the Unified Pension Scheme (UPS)—was announced by the Modi 3.0 Government under which the GOI's contribution to the pension of 2.65M Central and 6.7M State Government employees was increased from 14 per cent to 18.5 per cent. The UPS has an assured pension of 50 per cent of the last year's average basic pay for those who have completed 25 years of service, or ₹10,000 per month (indexed to inflation) for those who have completed 10 years.

PM-SYM was started by the Modi government to give pension of ₹3,000/month to unorganised sector workers after the age of 60. This is a contributory pension scheme on a 50:50 basis where the prescribed contribution is made by the subscriber and the GoI matches it. Around 4.998M workers were enrolled in PM-SYM as of March 2024.

125

PM CARES Fund

In the wake of the COVID-19 pandemic, Modi set up the PM CARES Fund to provide relief for Indian citizens affected by the coronavirus and similar emergencies that might occur in the future.

The Fund's main objective is to provide support to common people dealing with medical emergencies, natural calamities, manmade disasters, and epidemics, as well as funding for pharmaceutical drug processing and medical equipment.

The Fund got donations of ₹12,156Cr from India and ₹535.44Cr from foreign donors during COVID-19. Corporate contributions included ₹500Cr each by Reliance and Tata, ₹400Cr by Aditya Birla, and ₹175Cr collectively by ICICI, HDFC, and Kotak Mahindra banks.

During COVID-19, the Fund donated ₹7,692.5Cr including ₹2,146.6Cr for 50,000 ventilators, ₹1,905Cr for 1,224 pressure swing adsorption oxygen plants, ₹1,393Cr for 6.6Cr vaccines, ₹1,000Cr transfer to states/UTs for welfare of migrants, ₹500Cr for 99,986 oxygen concentrators, ₹322.5Cr for 150,000 oxygen saturation-based control systems with non-rebreather masks, ₹199.6Cr for six hospitals, and ₹20.42Cr for 18 labs.

PM Cares for Children gives financial support of ₹10L to a child who has lost both parents/surviving parent/legal guardian due to COVID-19, including school fees, boarding and lodging, scholarships of ₹20,000/year for children of classes 1–12, free health insurance of ₹5L, and loans for higher education. As of August 2024, 4,543 applications had been approved.

Mission Vatsalaya gives ₹4,000/month for children staying with relatives, with provision for admission in the nearest Kendriya Vidyalaya Sangathan/Kasturba Gandhi Balika Vidyalaya or private schools. Further, scholarships of ₹20,000 were provided to all school going children of classes 1–12. Children are also assisted in obtaining education loan for professional courses/higher education.

126

People's Padma

Gone are the days when political influence and patronage got you a 'Padma Award'. In the Modi-era, Padmas are only awarded to a deserving nation-builder based on meritorious work in her/his field, sacrifices and social relevance. Most praiseworthy is the fact that the awards are now given to ordinary citizens in almost all cases. Modi has transformed Padma Awards to 'People's Padma Awards'.

Departing from the decades-old Congress-era/UPA-era approach where 'select' persons recommended the nominees, the process has become broad-based, with nominations opened to the public. The Padma Awards have become a people's movement.

Here are some of Modi's awardees:

- Tulsi Gowda (aka Encyclopaedia of the Forest), an environmentalist from Karnataka's Hakkali tribe planted more than 30,000 saplings.
- Trinity Saioo of Meghalaya (aka Turmeric Trinity) developed women-owned sustainable organic farming.
- Harekala Hajabba, an orange vendor in Mangaluru (Karnataka), saved money from his earnings and built a school in his village.

- Dulari Devi of Madhubani (Bihar) rose from being an ordinary *dai* (maid) to an acclaimed Maithili painter against all adversity.
- Acharya M.K. Kunjol of Kerala fought to ensure justice for Dalits (SCs).
- Centenarian Nanda Prusty of Odisha is a rural teacher who has been instrumental in providing free education to thousands of children.
- Birubala Rabha of Goalpara (Assam) has crusaded against witch-hunting across the Northeast region for decades, with grave risk to her own life.
- Transgender folk dancer Manjamma Jogati rose from a life of abject poverty and hardship.
- A 66-year-old retired government doctor from Andamans, Ratan Chandra Kar (aka Jarawa ke Jeevandata), brought back Jarawa tribals from near-extinction in the 1999 measles epidemic, helping increase their population from 76 to 270.
- Through many Balwadis founded by her, Hirabai Lobi (aka Siddi ni Shakti) educates children of the Siddi tribe.
- A 76-year-old Naga social worker, Ramkuiwangbe Newme, has dedicated his life for the conservation and preservation of the Heraka religion.
- The 98-year-old Tularam Apreti has been practising organic farming with traditional methods for 61 years before the Sikkim government formed the Sikkim Organic Mission.
- Despite lacking any formal training, Dhaniram Toto of Totopara village in West Bengal is the first to write a novel in Toto (Dengka) language, a dying language listed as 'highly endangered' by UNESCO. He is the architect of the script that now has 37 alphabets.

Visit https://www.padmaawards.gov.in/ to see what kind of people were getting the Padma awards during the UPA regime.

Bharat Ratna

PM Modi chose 10 recipients for India's highest civilian honour, but not himself, as he is not like the Congress dynasts, as you will see below. Rather, 3 of 10 of Modi's choices are Congress leaders—Pandit Madan Mohan Malaviya, Pranab Mukherjee, P.V. Narasimha Rao, Karpoori Thakur of Janata Party, and 'Chaudhary' Charan Singh of Lok Dal.

Modi's other choices include three BJP leaders—Atal Bihari Vajpayee (former PM), his deputy L.K. Advani, and Nanaji Deshmukh (RSS volunteer and politician). Other choices include Assamese/Hindi lyricist, singer and music director Bhupen Hazarika, and agri-scientist Dr M.S. Swaminathan (recipient of several awards/honours).

Pandit Madan Mohan Malviya was a freedom fighter, an eminent educationist and a 4-time president of Congress; Pranab Mukherjee was a senior cabinet minister for decades and ended his career as President of India; P.V. Narasimha Rao was PM for five years and the father of India's economic reforms; freedom fighter Karpoori Thakur introduced reservations for SCs/STs as CM of Bihar; 'Chaudhary' Charan Singh was a tall leader of farmers and Jats who became PM.

Atal Bihari Vajpayee made India a declared nuclear weapons state; introduced the Prevention of Terrorism Act, the NSC, Debt Recovery Tribunals, and unlimited competition in telephony; built the 'Golden Quadrilateral' highways; launched PM Gram Sadak Yojana; and had the lowest inflation for any PM in India's history.

L.K. Advani was an MP for 47 years and was the political face of the Ram Mandir movement (BJP became

India's 2nd largest party in 1991 after his 1990 Rath Yatra). Nanaji Deshmukh was a social reformer who worked against poverty, and for rural health/education and improved the living standards of more than 650 villages. Bhupen Hazarika worked against casteism. His songs were based on the themes of communal amity, universal justice, and empathy.

Dr Swaminathan was the chief architect of India's green revolution; he introduced high-yielding varieties of wheat and rice that brought food security to India; his efforts led to a mass movement that saved India and Pakistan from famine-like conditions in the 1960s.

Jawaharlal Nehru had 13 recipients in 17 years, including himself. His daughter Indira Gandhi chose six in 16 years, including herself. Her son Rajiv Gandhi nominated two in five years. P.V. Narasimha Rao chose six in five years (including Rajiv Gandhi). Dr Singh decided to confer only three Bharat Ratnas in 10 years.

Among the non-Congress PMs, V.P. Singh chose two in 11 months, H.D. Deve Gowda three in 10.5 months, IK Gujral two in 11 months, and AB Vajpayee six in 6.2 years.

Modi gave 1,132 Padma Awards (10 Bharat Ratna, 62 Padma Vibhushan, 136 Padma Bhushan, and 924 Padma Shri) in his first 10 years, of which 739 were People's Padma given to the most ordinary citizens. None of the 4,108 recipients before Modi were ordinary citizens.

Part XII

Myths vs Reality

More than 60 per cent of opposition leaders and their party spokespersons are shameless liars. In the eight chapters of this section, we will bust many of their lies.

127

Adani–Modi Friendship

Adani Group's initial growth came from Adani Ports and Special Economic Zone Ltd (APSEZ)—its largest revenue generator is Mundra Port, approved by Congress's Government of Gujarat in 1993. Revenue was ₹88.84Cr for the 12-month period of April 2003–March 2004 (pro-rated from ₹111.044Cr in January 2003–March 2004) and went up to ₹4830Cr in FY14 (up 5,337 per cent). Revenue for FY24 was ₹26,711Cr (up 453 per cent). Yes, APSEZ grew 11.8 times more in the UPA-era.

Adani Group paid ₹18,184Cr in direct taxes and ₹127,358Cr interest to banks/institutions in the last 12 years. It employs more than 46,000 persons directly and over 70,000 others indirectly. It has plans to invest ₹9.5LCr in the next 5–6 years—that will create at least 125,000 more direct jobs. The group spends over ₹940Cr per year (2 per cent of total profit) on social initiatives through the Adani Foundation that is operating in 6,769 villages in 19 states and impacting around 9.1M lives each year.

As large corporates contribute to economic growth and create jobs, they are supported by the governments of most countries and states. Leaders of France, Israel, Russia, the UK, the US, etc., have lobbied the Indian government for years to sell arms, or even civilian aircraft. Donald Trump even lobbied for Harley Davidson motorcycles.

So, if Modi does help Adani (and that is a big "IF"), the PM directly helps the Indian economy—and that's one of the main jobs of any PM of India.

Because PMs of the past did not do this job properly, we had so much poverty, unemployment, low health outcomes, and were called a 'sleeping elephant'. Today, the world is calling us a 'roaring tiger' that is taking on the Chinese dragon.

128

Not Anti-Lower Castes

Compared to 2014, in the 2019 elections BJP had gained 39.6 per cent votes from the SC category, 15.8 per cent from STs, 36.7 per cent from upper OBCs, and 14.3 per cent votes from lower OBCs.

Of the 303 BJP LS MPs elected in 2019, there were 113 OBCs, 53 SCs and 43 STs—a total of 209 (69 per cent) of BJP's MPs belonged to the lower castes. In fact, 94.2 per cent of all OBC, 61.6 per cent of all SC, and 82.7 per cent of all ST MPs were from the BJP.

That's why the opposition believed that winning back 'caste votes' was crucial to maintain their electoral relevance in the 2024 LS elections. The Congress and most other opposition parties played the 'caste card'. They alleged that Modi is anti-lower castes.

'Prime Minister ji, the underprivileged need political and economic power, not empty words,' Rahul Gandhi tweeted on 17 April 2023. 'Take these three steps: Make the 2011 Census figures public, tell how many OBCs are there in the country and remove the 50 per cent cap on reservations. Give reservation to Dalits and tribals according to their population.'[1] He had started his demand in February 2023.

In 1990, to counter his ally BJP's consolidation of Hindu votes with Ram mandir politics, VP Singh had announced 27 per cent reservations for seats in government-run higher education institutions and government jobs for some OBC categories based on the 'Mandal Commission' report. As 22.5 per cent reservation for SCs/STs existed, it meant a total of 49.5 per cent reservation. Singh had to resign due to violent nationwide protests by students from the unreserved or 'general' category and his party was decimated in the 1991 election, winning just 59/543 seats.

Congress came up with a slogan *'Jitni abaadi, utna haq'* (rights as per population).

In 1992, the SCI ruled that reservations could not exceed 50 per cent as that would violate the constitution. Modi's 10 per cent reservations for EWS in 2019 did not violate the SCI order as it was not caste-based, and the SCI upheld its validity in a November 2022 judgment.

Since 1951, the decadal Indian censuses have been counting SCs and STs. Rahul wants OBCs also to be counted separately.

Jawaharlal Nehru opposed a caste census in 1951.

The Mandal Commission report on caste-based reservations was submitted in 1980 to Indira Gandhi, but she ignored it. She even coined an anti-caste slogan: *'Na jaat par na paat par, mohar lagegi haath par'* (vote for Congress, not on caste and community lines).

Rajiv Gandhi also ignored the Mandal report.

What was no good for great-grandfather, grandmother, and dad is good for Rahul Gandhi?

In an earlier chapter, we have demonstrated what Modi has done for the lower castes and covered some of the outcomes.

Modi himself belongs to an OBC community—a fact that Rahul Gandhi challenges. He has said dozens of times that Modi was not born an OBC, and that his 'Ghanchi' caste was included in the OBC list during the BJP government's tenure in Gujarat. Official documents reveal that the 2M strong 'Modh Vanik' community (aka Ghanchi in some parts of Gujarat) to which the PM belongs, was included in the OBC list in July 1994 (8 months before the first-ever BJP government got power in Gujarat, and 7 years before Modi became Gujarat's CM).

Rahul Gandhi keeps saying that less than 5 per cent of GoI's joint secretaries are from lower castes. Joint secretaries are aged 42–50 years, so they were recruited during 1974–1982 and Rahul Gandhi's grandmother Indira Gandhi was PM for 72 per cent of this period.

As a counter to Rahul's demand for additional quotas, Modi said that his government only works for four castes—GYAN or *Garib, Yuva, Annadata*, and *Nari* (poor, youth, farmer, and women), which if you have read the whole book, will agree is 100 per cent true.

Almost all PMs before Modi have added communities or groups to the SC/ST or OBC lists for the sake of vote bank politics. Modi resisted demands for including Gujjars in Rajasthan, Patels in Gujarat, and Jats in Haryana in the OBC list.

The opposition also alleges that crimes against SCs/STs increased under Modi. In reality, crimes increased much more in the UPA-era from 32,422 in 2004 to 58,515 in 2014 (up 80.5 per cent). In the Modi-era, crimes against SCs/STs went up to 67,481 in 2022 (only up 15.3 per cent). Data for 2023 has not yet been published by the NCRB.

The growing household expenditure is an example of rising incomes due to a rising economy. Let us look at the numbers from the Household Consumption Expenditure Survey (HCES) 2022–23.

Rising Incomes of Lower Castes			
Monthly Per Capita Expense	**2011-12**	**2022-23**	**INCREASE**
SCs in Urban India	₹ 2040	₹ 5310	▲ 160.3%
SCs in Rural India	₹ 1260	₹ 3480	▲ 176.2%
STs in Urban India	₹ 2190	₹ 5400	▲ 146.7%
STs in Rural India	₹ 1110	₹ 3030	▲ 173.0%
OBCs in Urban India	₹ 2280	₹ 6180	▲ 171.1%
OBCs in Rural India	₹ 1440	₹ 3840	▲ 166.7%

Modi has ensured that the incomes of lower castes has gone up by 146.7 per cent–176.2 per cent. This is *Sabka Saath, Sabka Vikas!*

129

No Farmer Distress

Congress MP Randeep Surjewala alleged that: (1) 75M farmers were kept out of the PM-KISAN scheme as only 80M out of 146M got the 15th instalment; (2) 161,000 farmers died by suicide between 2014 and 2022 (citing NCRB data); (3) daily incomes are only ₹27/day; (4) they have a total debt of ₹27,000Cr; (5) government has not kept its promise of giving MSP, that is 50 per cent more than the input cost and land rent. Let's examine these numbers.

(1) Surjewala needs to go back to junior school to learn math, as 146M minus 80M is 66M, not 75M. Firstly, 90.8M farmers got the 15th instalment of PM-KISAN, not 80M, compared to over 113M who got the 11th instalment. Why did the numbers fall? To plug leakages, GoI mandated farmers to feed their land details in the portal, link it with Aadhaar, have a Jan Dhan DBT account, and complete eKYC; and only 90.8M had complied. Over 115.4M farmers got the 16th instalment.

(2) Like his 'supreme leader' Rahul Gandhi, Surjewala too is a liar, as NCRB data in this link gives the truth—in 2014–22, farmer suicides were 100,474, not 161,000 as alleged by him (average 11,164/year), despite COVID-19 for 19 months. During the UPA-era (2004–2013), the average

was 15,983/year, which was 43.2 per cent higher. See https://ncrb.gov.in/accidental-deaths-suicides-in-india-adsi.html for more.

(3) As per the Household Consumption Expenditure Survey, regular wage-earning farm families spent ₹120/day in FY23, and casual farm labour spent ₹109/day. As expenditure is less than 90 per cent of income in their case, estimated income is ₹127/day—4.7 times Surjewala's imaginary figure. Average per capita expenditure for the poorest persons in rural areas is ₹46/day (up 170.6 per cent from FY12) and even this is 1.7 times Surjewala's imagination. These are FY23 numbers, the FY24 numbers will be 9.22 per cent higher.

(4) Assuming he is correct on ₹27,000Cr debt, this equals ₹1,849 per farmer family. Is that high for Congress leaders' IQ levels?

(5) Let's come to his last allegation about the MSP promise. Here is the actual data (based on PIB Press Releases), not Surjewala's lies:

Increase in MSPs paid to farmers by Modi Govt

Per Quintal (100kg)	2014	2024	INCREASE
Common Grade Paddy	₹ 1310	₹ 2300	▲ 75.7%
Grade-A Paddy	₹ 1345	₹ 2320	▲ 72.5%
Wheat	₹ 1400	₹ 2425	▲ 73.2%
Ragi	₹ 1500	₹ 4290	▲ 186.0%
Bajra	₹ 1250	₹ 2625	▲ 110.0%
Jowar (Hybrid)	₹ 1200	₹ 3371	▲ 180.9%
Jowar (Malandi)	₹ 1500	₹ 3421	▲ 128.1%
Maize	₹ 1310	₹ 2225	▲ 69.8%

Increase in MSPs paid to farmers by Modi Govt			
Per Quintal (100kg)	**2014**	**2024**	**INCREASE**
Barley	₹ 1100	₹ 1980	▲ 80.0%
Lentil (Masur)	₹ 2950	₹ 6700	▲ 127.1%
Arhar (Tur)	₹ 4300	₹ 7550	▲ 75.2%
Moong	₹ 4500	₹ 8682	▲ 92.9%
Urad	₹ 4300	₹ 7400	▲ 72.1%
Gram	₹ 3100	₹ 5650	▲ 82.3%
Soyabeen (yellow)	₹ 2560	₹ 4892	▲ 91.1%
Sunflower Seed	₹ 3700	₹ 7280	▲ 96.8%
Sesamum	₹ 4500	₹ 9267	▲ 105.9%
Nigerseed	₹ 3500	₹ 8717	▲ 149.1%

There are eight more items with similar price increases, but we think you've got the point.

130

No North–South Divide

The opposition accuses the BJP of being unfair to southern states in sharing tax money and says that the BJP is trying to impose Hindi on southern states.

Finance Minister Nirmala Sitharaman was born and brought up in Tamil Nadu and is married to a Telugu gentleman. External Affairs Minister Dr S Jaishankar is also a Tamilian. From 1947, these ministries have been two of the four most important/powerful ministries of India.

Thirteen out of 72 members (18.1 per cent) in the Modi government are South Indians despite the NDA only having 16.7 per cent LS MPs from the southern states.

In 9.87 years, Modi visited the South 149 times, including Tamil Nadu 39 times, Karnataka 42, Telangana 24, Kerala 23, Andhra Pradesh 16, Puducherry 3 times, and Lakshadweep 2 times. This is more than four times the visits by Dr Singh to the south when he was UPA's PM, despite the UPA having eight south-based parties as its constituents.

Most Apps like Aarogya Setu, DigiLocker, mAadhaar, Poshan Tracker, UMANG, etc., have 10–24 regional languages. Kisan Sarathi IVRS System is also available in 13 languages. Rapid Assessment System has all four southern languages.

For the first time in India's history, in February–March 2024, question papers for recruitment exams for CAPF constables included 13 regional languages including all the four southern languages. The JEE-Main exam papers are now available in 13 languages.

Why did governments before Modi not do this? Leaders of four southern parties were ministers in the UPA government.

Karnataka Deputy CM DK Shivakumar's brother and then Congress Lok Sabha MP DK Suresh said that there wasn't enough money allocated to southern states in the 2024 Interim Budget and that they should separate from India to form a new nation.

Tax transfer from the GoI to Karnataka under UPA was ₹81,795Cr and under Modi was ₹2,85,452Cr (up 249 per cent).

'Congress is speaking the language of separatism … and running a false narrative by making false monetary claims,' Sitharaman said.[2]

Kerala and Tamil Nadu also made similar accusations.

In January 2024, the GoI offered Kerala a loan of ₹5000Cr for helping in its financial troubles, but Kerala demanded ₹10,000Cr and has even filed a case against the GoI in the Supreme Court on this dispute.

From 2014 to 2023 the GoI received ₹6.23LCr as direct tax from Tamil Nadu but gave ₹6.96LCr to the state. About ₹57,557Cr came as cess and surcharge and 100 per cent was disbursed to Tamil Nadu to construct roads, PMAY, and 'Samagra Shiksha' school program. Of the ₹36,353Cr state GST from Tamil Nadu in FY23, the GoI released the entire sum and additionally gave 41 per cent from the ₹27,360Cr Central GST collection.

Modi took a decision to adopt the sacred Sengol from Tamil Nadu as a national symbol of India's 'Amrit Kaal' (2022–47).

The PM prostrated before the Sengol and sought blessings from high priests of various *adheenams* (*maths*) in Tamil Nadu with the holy sceptre in his hand. Modi then carried the Sengol in a procession amid tunes of *nadaswaram* and chanting of Vedic mantras to the new Parliament House and installed it in a special enclosure next to the Speaker's chair in the LS chamber.

The Sengol had been gifted to Jawaharlal Nehru on the night of 14 August 1947 as a symbol of transfer of power to India in the presence of several leaders but was lying in a museum for 76 years without even 100 persons in the whole country knowing its history and significance.

The Modi government is setting up Thiruvalluvar Cultural Centres across the globe to showcase India's rich culture and offer training in yoga, Ayurveda, *Bharatiya* languages, classical music, etc.

131

Sabka Saath, Sabka Vikas

To facilitate 'Ease of Doing Haj', the Modi government simplified registrations and visits with the Haj Suvidha App, with SIM cards linked to ensure Haj pilgrims get latest information about Haj immediately.

E-MASIHA online system helps pilgrims in Makkah and Madinah to manage their health. E-luggage pre-tagging enables them to provide their information on accommodation and transportation in Makkah–Madinah before leaving India.

The http://haj.nic.in/pto/ portal has all details relating to Haj group organisers, their packages, etc., ensuring transparency and better facilities for pilgrims.

Improvement in Education & Literacy of Indian Muslims				
CATEGORY	FROM	TO	Increase	Period
Female Minority Students	1.07mn in 2014-15	1.5983mn in 2022-23	▲ 49.37%	8 years
Enrolment of Muslim children in Primary Classes % of all students	14.2% in 2013-14	15.62% in 2021-22	▲ 10.0%	9 years
Muslim students in Higher Secondary as a % of all students	8.27% in 2012-13	10.76% in 2021-22	▲ 30.1%	9 years
Muslim students in Higher Educational Institutions	4.319% in 2012-13	4.872% in 2021-22	▲ 12.8%	9 years
Literacy Rate of Muslim Women	50.7% in 2015-16	73.6% in 2023-23	▲ 45.17%	7 years
WOULD THESE CHANGES HAVE HAPPENED IF MODI WAS ANTI-MUSLIM?				

From FY15 to FY22, the following scholarships were given to minority students:

- Almost 44.351M pre-matric scholarships (52.2 per cent females)
- More than 5.706M post-matric scholarships (55.9 per cent females)
- Over 1.002M merit-cum-means based scholarships (37.8 per cent females).

Modi visited the Vatican in October 2021 and had a 90-minute private audience with His Holiness Pope Francis. The pontiff spoke a full sentence in Hindi when he gave a gift specially prepared for the PM.

Special trains take Jain pilgrims from Mumbai and Ahmedabad to Pavapuri, Kundalpur, Guniyaji, Lacchuar, Rajgir, Parasnath, Rujuwalika, and Sammed Shikharji.

Buddhist circuits were developed in 12 places, including a 2,000-seat Mahabodhi Convention Centre at Bodh Gaya.

Buddhist Conclave is organised every alternate year to promote India as a Buddhist destination in major Buddhist countries.

The minority affairs ministry trained over 0.963M underprivileged minority persons under the PM VIKAS scheme.

National Minorities Development and Finance Corporation (NMDFC) promotes the socio-economic development of backward sections among minority communities:

National Minorities Development & Finance Corp			
PARAMETER	UPA-era	Modi-era	CHANGE
Total Loans Disbursed	₹2033.35cr	₹6215.64cr	▲ 205.7%
No. of Beneficiaries	7,74,848	14,09,270	▲ 81.9%
More than 85% of the beneficiaries are women			
Average Loan Size	₹26,242	₹44,105	▲ 68.1%

In 2023, NMDFC launched MILAN software to digitise the loan accounting processes between applicants, agents and banks, and it integrated data of 1.2M beneficiaries. There is a MILAN App too.

Under Pradhan Mantri Jan Vikas Karyakram (PMJVK), community infrastructure and basic amenities are created in areas with minority concentration, with skill development and women-oriented projects being a priority. Up to March 2023, almost 597,000 projects worth over ₹24,030Cr had been undertaken.

Pilgrimage Rejuvenation and Spiritual Augmentation Drive (PRASHAD) provides funds to states/UTs to develop infrastructure at temples, mosques, churches, and gurdwaras. Some religious places being refurbished and improved under PRASHAD include:

- The famous Hazratbal shrine in Srinagar is being restored at a cost of ₹40.5Cr. The key components comprise site development of the entire area, including the construction of a boundary wall; illumination of the shrine's precinct; improvement of ghats and devri paths; installation of signages; construction of MLCP, tourist facilitation centre, Sufi interpretation centre, public convenience block, and entrance gateway.
- Gurdwara Nada Sahib at Panchkula (Haryana) is getting new amenities for ₹25Cr, including a facelift to its gate, MLCP, façade illumination, toilet block, boundary wall, sewage treatment plant, reinforced cement concrete bridge, retaining wall, pathways, structural and tensile roofing, benches, signages, solar photo voltaic power generation system, and drinking water coolers.
- Nongsawlia Presbyterian Church at Cherrapunji (Meghalaya), one of the oldest churches in the Northeast region, will get new pilgrim amenities.

- At the congregation centre at Chite Veng, Aizawl City (Mizoram), ₹9.78Cr has been disbursed for site development of pilgrimage and heritage tourism facilitation.
- Sümi Baptist Akukuhou Küqhakulu Nito Mount Mission Centre, Zunheboto (Nagaland) got ₹18.2Cr for illumination with renewable, eco-friendly transport, first aid centre, drinking water, waiting rooms, toilets, parking, craft bazaar, souvenir shops, cafeteria, rain shelters, and WiFi.
- The famous Basilica of Bom Jesus in Old Goa (that holds the mortal remains of St Francis Xavier, after whom the St Xavier's schools and St Xavier's colleges in India are named) got ₹46Cr for a heritage interpretation centre with wayside amenities, safety and surveillance systems with CCTV cameras, WiFi, MLCP, universal pathway, street lights, e-Autos, power substation, façade lighting, etc.
- At the Four Patron Saints, Yuksom (Sikkim), ₹33.3Cr has been disbursed for a new Buddhist pilgrimage facility site near the helipad, pilgrimage stopover facility at Rimbi and coronation throne of Norbugang.
- Two Buddhism projects are scheduled in Varanasi—₹7.34Cr sound and light show at Dhamek Stupa, and ₹2.2Cr Buddha theme park at Sarnath.

CyberGram Yojana enables students of classes 6–10 belonging to minority communities in 710 blocks of 66 towns in 26 states to acquire basic ICT skills that empower them to become digitally literate; actively participate in knowledge-based activities; access financial, social and government services; use internet for communications. The beneficiaries get free internet access for up to a total of 30 hours to reinforce their learning.

For example, 23 per cent–34 per cent of the beneficiaries of Ayushman Bharat Pradhan Mantri Jan Arogya Yojana (PMJAY), Pradhan Mantri Jan Dhan Yojana (PMJDY), Jal Jeevan Mission, Mudra Yojana, PM-KISAN, Skill India Mission, Ujjwala Yojana, and Swachh Bharat Mission belong to the weaker and backward minorities.

Minorities have got proportionate share (and higher in some cases) in more than 350 of the 450-odd welfare schemes of Modi government.

Don't Muslims and Christians take subsidised UDAN flights or use the 82 new airports? Don't they use the cleaner platforms or the new trains or modernised trains? Do they not travel on highways? Minorities also benefit from the massive infrastructure that has been developed in the Modi-era.

In 2019 LS elections, NDA won 16/52 Muslim-dominated seats and 10/11 seats in the non-Assam Christian-dominated Northeast region.

For the 2024 LS elections, the BJP did not give 'tickets' to as many as 14 sitting MPs as they had made anti-Muslim remarks.

132

Not Anti-Middle Class

As per one of the world's leading management consultant Bain & Company of the US, about 29.8 per cent of Indians are upper middle-class (with an annual household income [AHHI] of ₹7.2–36L), and about 33.5 per cent are lower middle-class (AHHI of ₹3.6–7.2L). Many other studies have said that around 53–55 per cent of Indians have an AHHI of ₹6–30L.

We have heard hundreds of people say that Modi does not care for the middle-class. This is a myth spread by the opposition. How can a PM of any country ignore 53–55 per cent of his/her country's population?

Let us share what all Modi Government has done:

- Average time for processing tax returns and issuing refunds has reduced from 93 days to just 9–10 days. In FY24, over 1.66Cr ITRs were processed in a day. Complaints against the ITD have reduced by over 60 per cent.
- Apartment dwellers in multi-storey buildings can now choose what type of electrical connection they want (regular or rooftop solar). There will be separate billing for common areas and diesel generators in residential societies. Power distribution companies must install meters to check consumer complaints within 5 days.

- Twelve small finance banks and 6 payments banks have made banking more accessible for the middle class.
- UPI is available on more than 70 Apps of banks and fintech companies.
- Health insurance companies now have to approve cashless claims within 1 hour and provide final authorisation for discharge from a hospital within 3 hours. Insurers also need to provide a grace period of one month for annual renewal of health policies. A Customer Information Sheet has to be included with every policy document, explaining in simple terms the sum insured, coverage details, exclusions, sub-limits, deductibles, and waiting periods.
- More than 9M affordable middle-income group homes (average cost ₹6.84L) have been delivered in urban India and 2.33M are under construction.
- A scheme is starting soon to help middle-income group citizens living in rented houses, slums, chawls, etc., to buy or build their own houses.
- Under SWAMIH investment fund, ₹18,576Cr was provided to real estate developers to help them complete 116,572 apartments in 204 stranded projects.
- Reduced interest on home loans to 7.5–8.5 per cent, compared to over 10.5 per cent during the UPA regime.
- Out of 8,075 Smart City projects, 7,380 (91.4 per cent) costing ₹147,704Cr are complete and the balance are all ongoing.
- Out of 5,999 AMRUT (Atal Mission for Rejuvenation and Urban Transformation) urban development projects worth ₹83,327Cr that have been awarded, 5,304 projects were complete as of March 2024.

- mPassport Seva App has made it easy to apply for fresh passports, renewals/re-issues, and schedule an appointment to visit a passport kendra for document verification.
- A citizen with Aadhaar card and one more ID proof gets a new passport in 2–3 days (10 days minimum in 2014) for tatkal applicants and 5-7 days otherwise (16–22 days in 2014). No bribes need to be paid now.
- mPassport Police App has expedited the police verification process, which now takes 48 hours from the time your passport reaches you for tatkal applicants and 5–6 days for others.
- Passport Seva Kendras went up from 57 in 2014 to 521 by May 2022 (up 814 per cent).
- A pilot program issued e-passports to 20,000 officials and diplomats. Soon it will be available for all citizens.
- An annualised 15.16 per cent increase in income taxes paid by citizens in 10 years shows how incomes of citizens have risen.
- Modi has given the middle class a mammoth discount of ₹4LCr on train tickets.
- Cancelled rail tickets are now refunded within 72 hours in most cases.
- Automated seat/berth allocation on trains, doing away with one of the most corrupt practices of the past.
- Modi did away with the need to fix baggage tags and stamping of boarding passes at airports, as well as emigration and arrival cards for Indians at airports.
- One of his best moves has been to do away with having to get a 'gazetted officer' affix his seal and sign documents (the erstwhile cumbersome and, again, corrupt practice of notarization) and trusting citizens with 'self-attestation'. 'If I cannot trust my fellow citizens, who can I trust,' Modi said when he did away with the rule.

- As he promised, Modi repealed over 1,500 archaic laws. One such law required you to get a license to own a radio or a VCR; in another hilarious law, one had to get a pilot's license to fly a kite.
- To reduce the number of financial scams through spam phone calls, the Modi Government is introducing a '160' prefix to phone numbers of banks, insurance companies, and other financial institutions that serve citizens. All such organisations will have a '160ABCDXXX' number where ABC will be the STD code (e.g., 011 for Delhi, 080 for Bengaluru) and D will be the telephone operator's code (e.g., 1 for BSNL, 2 for Airtel, and so on).
- Due to the new criminal justice laws, every citizen has to get justice within a maximum of 3 years, compared with no time limit earlier.
- Terrorism-related deaths of civilians came down from 792 per year during the UPA-era to 189 per year in the Modi-era (down 76.1 per cent). In fact, in the last 6 years till 2024, the average further dropped to 130.8 per year, primarily due to reduction of terror incidents in J&K and the Northeast region. *Surely, your life, and the lives of your friends and family are your most important gift that Modi has given to you.*

The opposition has been spreading a narrative that petrol/diesel prices have shot up in the Modi-era. What is the truth?

Petrol per litre [Delhi]	Start Price	End Price	Increase
UPA (Sonia Gandhi) Govt	₹33.71	₹71.41	▲ 111.8%
Modi Government	₹71.41	₹94.72	▲ 32.6%
Modi-era increase is 70.8% lower than the increase in the UPA-era			

Petrol prices were reduced 8.24 per cent in May 2022 and again 2.07 per cent in March 2024. Diesel prices were reduced 7.29 per cent and 2.23 per cent.

The middle-class has also benefitted from at least 175 of the over 450 schemes introduced by the Modi government for helping in the welfare and development of citizens.

You equally benefit from the massive infrastructure and services that have been developed in the last 10 years—airways, highways, railways, waterways—everything has improved significantly.

There is so much more he has done for the middle-class that we could write an entire book on this subject alone.

133

The Name Is Bond

Regardless of the country, political parties and candidates will always be funded by corporates and wealthy individuals. This is happening since the year 1788 and will happen till the year 2288, until a better method can be found (highly unlikely!).

In most of the Western world, such funding is legalised (paid by bank transfer or cheque). In the US, one method is donating to a candidate via a Political Action Committee.

There are electoral trusts in most countries. Even India has Prudent, Progressive, AB General, New Democratic, Samaj, Triumph, Janta Nirvachak, People's Electoral Trust, and Janhit. However, very little money came through these trusts. Parties or candidates were getting 75–90 per cent funding via cash (black money).

To reduce the role of black money in election funding, Modi government introduced 'Electoral Bonds', and this was approved by the Parliament in February 2017. The corporates and the wealthy did not have to 'generate' black money and could even write-off the donations from their taxable income. It was a win-win situation for everybody.

Seven years later, on 15 February 2024, wise men perched behind high benches in the SCI made a huge error of judgment in striking down the electoral bond scheme as 'unconstitutional'. After all, they are not Martians or Gods, but human beings like us.

When electoral bonds were introduced, it was announced that the donations would be anonymous, so it is completely unfair for SCI to get the names disclosed. People will lose faith in the Parliament and leaders elected by us.

Unelected people who wear black coats are not supreme, WE THE PEOPLE ARE SUPREME.

BJP says it will bring back electoral bonds via a constitutional amendment. In the meantime, SBI disclosed data on donors and recipients on the Supreme Court's order. When this data came out, it opened a Pandora's box.

Which parties got disproportionate Electoral Bonds?

PARTY	LS MPs and MLAs	Amount Encashed	% of Total Legislators	% of Total Amount	Amount per Legislator
BRS	47	₹1408.2cr	1.04%	8.546%	**₹29.96cr**
TDP	20	₹320.7cr	0.44%	1.946%	**₹16.04cr**
BJD	123	₹1019.5cr	2.72%	6.187%	**₹8.29cr**
TMC	243	₹1716.8cr	5.38%	10.418%	**₹7.07cr**
BJP	1775	₹8250.7cr	39.3%	50.069%	**₹4.65cr**
DMK	163	₹656.5cr	3.61%	3.984%	**₹4.03cr**
YSRCP	162	₹499.8cr	3.59%	3.033%	**₹3.09cr**
Congress	696	₹1951.7cr	15.4%	11.843%	**₹2.80cr**

Others who got over ₹5cr were Shiv Sena, JDS, RJD, AAP, NCP, SKM, JDU, Jana Sena, SP, JMM, SAD, AIADMK, SDF

Total electoral bonds of ₹16,478.6Cr equal to ₹3.65Cr per legislator. Bharat Rashtra Samithi is 8.2 times the average and Telugu Desam Party 4.4 times, while BJP just 1.27 times.

'It is the world's biggest corruption scandal and extortion racket, and the PM is doing it,' said Rahul Gandhi.[3] Mallikarjun Kharge said BJP got half the donations while 'the principal opposition party got only 11 per cent'. He sought a SCI-led investigation into the 'saga of corruption'.[4]

First, a party that got ₹1,952Cr cannot call others corrupt. Second, donors decide who gets what, not the ruling party. Third, donors are smart and know we are headed towards 'Congress-*mukt* Bharat' or Congress-free India. Fourth, Congress is crying as it got the lowest share per legislator.

Last but not the least, if BJP's ₹8,250.7Cr is a scam, how is it the world's largest? The amount equals less than 0.18 per cent of UPA's scams, as you will see in a later chapter.

134

Other Lies Busted

We have already busted the opposition's lies about Modi's so-called 'friendship' with Adani, about him being anti-lower castes, about farmer distress, about North–South divide, about Modi being anti-minorities, and about him being anti-middle-class.

Let's do a fact check on 11 other allegations of opposition parties and leaders.

Congress Black Paper

A 'white paper' was tabled by the Modi government in the Parliament on 10 years of UPA misrule. The Congress came out with its own 'black paper' on the Modi-era, which said that Modi destroyed the economy and the agriculture sector, and aggravated unemployment.

We have already busted two of these lies and employment will be covered in the 'Top 10 Reasons' section in this book.

Congress says Modi government abetted crimes against women—though this a state subject and does not come under the Central government, it is important to mention that rapes went up from 15,847 in 2003 to 36,735 in 2014 (up 131.8 per cent) but came down to 31,982 in 2022 (down 12.9 per cent). Data for 2023 had not been published by NCRB.

EVMs Are Rigged

The 2004 and 2009 LS elections had 100 per cent Electronic Voting Machines (EVMs). But the BJP did not win these elections. Since Modi became PM in May 2014, the BJP has won 28 and lost 37 State Assembly elections. *In whose favour are EVMs rigged?*

Every Indian's Bank Account Will Have ₹15L

Opposition leaders say that Modi promised ₹15L in every Indian's bank account in the 2013–14-election campaign. This is a *senseless lie* because that would be 10.6 times India's average GDP of the last 10 years and even 1.37 times the average GDP of the US, so even Biden or Trump couldn't put that much money in American's pockets.

CBI, ED, and ITD Are BJP's Tools

The opposition says that the Modi government uses agencies to falsely prosecute opposition leaders, including CMs of many states.

The truth: Under Modi, the ED has a 96 per cent conviction rate in courts, which means that 96 per cent of the people that it files chargesheets against are sent to jail. *Are the courts in Modi's pocket?* Besides, most cases that are progressing now started in the UPA-era, since investigation, prosecution, hearing, and disposal takes years in India. As of August 2024, there were 51.284M pending cases, including 83,822 in the SCI, 6.02M in high courts, and 45.182M in district/taluka courts. Courts also grant too many 'stays'.

In 2023, the ITD found undisclosed cash and jewellery of ₹354Cr in a raid on Congress MP Dhiraj Sahu. He revised his income tax returns and paid tax on ₹150Cr undisclosed income. As Sahu admitted his crime, can Rahul Gandhi explain if the ITD was a 'BJP tool' in this case?

Modi Sold National Assets

Rahul Gandhi said in September 2021: 'The Congress has always been a building block for the country and all our hard work of 70 years has been sold by the BJP in mere seven years.'[5]

The fact: There were 234 PSEs in 2014, there are 254 now.

Six airports (Ahmedabad, Guwahati, Jaipur, Lucknow, Mangalore, and Thiruvananthapuram) were given on operational leases to a private entity and Air India was sold. The UPA (Congress) government leased out India's four largest airports by passenger traffic—Delhi, Mumbai, Bangalore, and Hyderabad, with a combined traffic of 108.3M in FY15, whereas it was 16.5M for the six leased by Modi. So, the Congress 'sold' 6.564 times more. Was any harm done by either government? Passengers flying in and out of the private airports are much happier compared to their experience with airports run by the AAI. By FY23, GoI's revenues went up 168 per cent from Guwahati airport, 155 per cent from Jaipur, 151 per cent from Ahmedabad, 148 per cent from Lucknow, 48 per cent from Mangalore, and 12.5 per cent from Thiruvananthapuram airport.

Let's discuss Air India. The Tatas started the airline in 1932 and by 1947, passenger surveys ranked it in the Top 3 airlines in the world. The Nehru government acquired 49 per cent stake in 1948, and 100 per cent in 1953. The Vajpayee government tried selling 40 per cent in 2000 but failed to find a buyer.

Modi tried in 2018 but failed as only 76 per cent was put up for sale. Air India has been making losses since 2007 and had accumulated losses of over ₹35,000Cr by FY22. It was losing about ₹22.5Cr per day. Once the terms were changed by offering 100 per cent stake, Tata Group bought Air India in October 2021 for ₹18,000Cr, and took control on 27 January 2022. This did not include the iconic Air India building facing the sea on Marine Drive in Mumbai that has been bought by the Government of Maharashtra from the GoI for ₹1,899.42Cr. Effectively, the Modi government not only got ₹19,899.42Cr from the buyers but also saved ₹18,480Cr in potential losses up to April 2024.

Air India—under Tata management—is now well on its way to become a world-class airline, the way it used to be before Nehru nationalised it in 1953. Since June 2023, Air India has placed orders for 570 aircraft to modernise its fleet. With India poised to become the world's 3rd largest aviation market, Air India's orders will contribute to India's journey of claiming its rightful place on the world aviation stage. *Could the old GoI-owned Air India do this?*

Mahua Moitra Was Targeted and Mistreated

Trinamool Congress' former MP Mahua Moitra was disqualified from the LS for 'unethical conduct' and 'serious misdemeanours'. She gave the password of her official MP account to Dubai-based Darshan Hiranandani, Adani's business rival, to post questions she could ask about Adani in Parliament. Hiranandani said that he gave her favours of monetary value. Moitra is being investigated by the CBI on those charges and by the ED on foreign currency transactions that are potential Foreign Exchange Management Act (FEMA) violations. Her supporters say she was targeted as she asked uncomfortable questions to Modi.

She does not know the PM. When we spent 27 minutes with him, we asked many uncomfortable questions. He answered all without flinching or batting an eyelid.

Other Narratives

Fuel prices shot up during Modi's reign: See table in the chapter 'NOT Anti-Middle-Class' in this book.

Modi wins elections due to good marketing: Did marketing add unprecedented infrastructure? Did marketing strategise, launch and execute over 450 welfare schemes? Did marketing ensure a terror-free India? Was India among the 3–4 best managers of the pandemic among the 20 largest countries due to marketing? In fact, we told the PM his government's marketing [communications] was terrible, and he said, '*Main aapse sehmat hoon, ji*' (I agree with you).

Modi's achievements are not his, but because India is the world's most populous nation, and this offers a huge market to investors and industries. Didn't India already have the 2nd largest population on 15 August 1947? So, what happened for 66.8 years before Modi?

Modi is too authoritative: Of course he is, how else would he achieve so much?

No press conferences: Modi knows the Lutyens media will ask him stupid questions. Why does he need to answer them when he already speaks to the citizens of India directly through '*Mann ki Baat*', 'X' (Twitter), Facebook, Instagram, and the Narendra Modi App?

'Rahul is an activist, not a politician. He is India's biggest fault finder. He finds faults with every good thing the Modi government has done, and they have done a lot of good, whether Rahul likes it or not,' says brand marketing guru, theatre actor, and TV panellist Suhel Seth.

Part XIII

Top 10 Reasons Why We Wrote This Book

144

The 10th: Managed the Pandemic

In May 2020, the GoI announced the AtmaNirbhar Bharat package to help people from hardships during the pandemic. Later in the year, it rolled out two more AtmaNirbhar Bharat packages.

The GoI provided free ration to 800M citizens under the Pradhan Mantri Garib Kalyan Anna Yojana (PMGKAY) scheme.

Total outlay of all three packages and measures by the RBI was about ₹27.1LCr in under nine months, more than 13 per cent of the then GDP.

Modi was leading the 'War on Covid' directly by managing the crisis with a single-minded determination to save lives and save India.

He did not let criticism tie him down, he just surged on, doing the best India needed in those moments of despair and an uncertain future.

He ensured that over 1979.4M vaccines were given free of cost in just 18 months, in the world's largest immunisation drive.

There was no discrimination of any kind by caste, creed, religion, economic status, or the state where the person lived (whether BJP-ruled or not)—every Indian who wanted the vaccines, got the vaccines.

Such a massive quantity of vaccines were administered in such a short time despite Rahul Gandhi, Arvind Kejriwal, Akhilesh Yadav, Jairam Ramesh (now Rahul's right-hand man), Shashi Tharoor, and others asking people not to take the 'Made-in-India' Covaxin, insisting on importing Pfizer vaccines that would cost more than ₹2,025/dose as we proved in our bestseller book, *Modi Stole My Mask*.

Author Chetan Bhagat was also gunning for Pfizer. Supreme Court lawyer and terrorist-supporter Prashant Bhushan, Kashmir-separatism supporter Arundhati Roy, Bajaj Auto's Rajiv Bajaj, and cartoonist Satish Acharya were among those who were discouraging vaccination in general, and Covaxin in particular.

Leftist media such as *Scroll*, *Quartz India*, *The Quint*, and *The Print* were not far behind.

India needed more than 1.9B doses to vaccinate everyone twice. It was impossible to do this before the onset of the 2nd wave on 10 March 2021 as the whole world had only given 330.17M jabs by then.

On 17 March, Modi set up a panel to ramp up vaccine production from 60M doses/month to 336M doses/month by November 2021.

By 2 June 2021, over 175.5M Indians got 1 jab. This was 20 per cent of the global number, more than India's 17.7 per cent share of world population.

India faced a huge oxygen shortage and demand shot up from just 900MTPD (metric tons per day) before the 2nd wave to over 7,000MTPD by 28 April 2021 (up 677.8 per cent).

PM CARES Fund between January–May 2021 sanctioned ₹1,905Cr for 1,224 pressure swing adsorption oxygen generation plants, including 7 years' maintenance.

It also funded ₹5,788Cr for hospitals, labs, ventilators, concentrators, vaccines, migrant welfare, etc. (see the chapter 'PM Cares Fund' in this book).

In a record 129 days, 3,846 pressure swing adsorption oxygen generation plants with a capacity of 5,126MT per day were commissioned in 736 districts.

Customs duty and health cess was removed on oxygen and oxygen-related equipment.

Modi directed all major ports to waive all charges for ships carrying oxygen-related equipment.

On 21 April 2020, India had 62,458 oxygen-supported hospital beds; this increased to 255,168 by 9 April 2021 (up 308.5 per cent in less than a year).

ICU beds increased from 27,360 to 75,867 (up 177.3 per cent) during the same period.

Around 70,000 isolation beds were made available by Indian Railways in more than 4,400 Covid-care coaches in 17 locations in 7 states. DRDO and HAL added over 7,000 beds in temporarily built/existing hospitals in 50 days.

The IAF was mobilised for airlifting cryogenic tankers from the UAE, Singapore, and other countries. They also airlifted tankers within India. Till 27 May 2021, the IAF carried out 168 international sorties and 1,443 domestic sorties.

Modi's rapport with leaders of different countries helped in getting assistance from abroad.

Among the items received by India between 15 April 2021 and 15 May 2021 alone were 19 oxygen generation plants, 11,058 oxygen concentrators, 13,496 oxygen cylinders, 7,365 ventilators, 530,000 Remdesivir vials, and over 25,000 rapid antigen test kits.

How did the Modi government manage the pandemic in comparison with other large countries?

Beta can lie, data cannot.

How badly did India manage Covid19?						
Per Million People	India	USA	Brazil	Russia	Germany	UK
Max Cases in 1 week	1962	5380	2423	1388	2149	6114
Cumulative Cases	15,445	1,00,315	70,819	33,257	41,500	64,947
Cumulative Deaths (Official Figures)	168	1786	1951	769	1010	1871
The Institute of Health Metrics and Evaluation (IHME) at the University of Washington School of Medicine suggested that Covid19 deaths were significantly underreported in almost every country, including the US. The IHME published underreporting data, given below:						
Correction Ratio as per IHME	2.96	1.58	1.46	5.43	1.45	1.39
Deaths as per IHME	497	2822	2848	4176	1465	2601
Case Fatality Rate as per IHME	3.22%	2.81%	4.06%	12.55%	3.53%	4.00%
Total Vaccine Doses as of 31Aug22	2130 million	613.39 million	470.48 million	175.09 million	184.88 million	151.22 million
People with 2 doses as of 31Aug22	942.5 million	225.3 million	171.7 million	76.44 million	63.47 million	50.73 million
% of Population	66.51%	67.86%	79.75%	52.82%	76.13%	75.15%
Healthcare Expense per person in US$	$ 275	$ 10,624	$ 1531	$ 1488	$ 6098	$ 4620

It is amply clear that despite India's per capita health expenditure being just 2.6 per cent to 18.5 per cent of other large countries, the Modi government was able to manage the pandemic very well.

In eight *India Today* polls from August 2020 to February 2024, average 17.75 per cent people voted that handling COVID-19 was the biggest achievement of Modi government. Among all topics, this got the highest approval rating.

136

The 9th: Return from 496-year *Vanvaas*

Babur conquered India in 1526 CE and founded the Mughal Empire. It is believed that in 1528, one of his generals built the Babri Masjid in Ayodhya, after destroying an ancient Ram Temple.

In 1853 and 1883, Hindus tried to forcible occupy the Masjid site but were stopped by the British government. In 1883, they filed a case that was dismissed by a lower court in 1885 and a higher court in 1886. In 1949, some Hindus placed Ram and Sita idols inside the building and claimed they appeared miraculously. As thousands of Hindus started visiting the place, the Congress government declared it a 'disputed site' and locked the gates. In 1950, a Hindu filed a 'title suit' in the Allahabad High Court seeking to do *puja* (prayer). In 1959, Nirmohi Akhara filed another title suit in Allahabad High Court seeking possession. In 1961, a countersuit was filed by Uttar Pradesh Sunni Central Waqf Board (UPSCWB).

In 1976, an ASI team surveyed the building and concluded that 12 of its pillars were made from remains of a temple. In the 1980s, Vishva Hindu Parishad (VHP) started a movement to build a mandir for *Ram Lalla* (infant Ram). In 1986, a district judge ruled that the gates would reopen, and Hindus will be allowed to worship.

In 1989, a suit was filed on behalf of *Sri Ram Lalla Virajman* (seated infant Ram) and *Asthan Sri Ram Janmabhoomi* (birthplace of Ram) by an individual seeking to represent the deity. In the same year, all the suits were transferred to the Lucknow Bench of the Allahabad High Court.

On 25 September 1990, BJP leader LK Advani started a *rath yatra* from Somnath to Ayodhya. There were Hindu–Muslim riots across India in which more than 500 people were killed. On the inkling of VHP and BJP, 40,000–60,000 *kar sevaks* (volunteers) moved towards Ayodhya. On 23 October, VP Singh (his government had BJP support) ordered Bihar CM Lalu Yadav to arrest Advani. Simultaneously, 150,000 BJP supporters were arrested by the government of Uttar Pradesh. On 30 Oct, 28,000 personnel of the state's armed constabulary were deployed in Ayodhya.

Police stopped all buses and trains, barricaded the 1.5km pathway to the 'masjid' and imposed a curfew. Only around 10,000 *kar sevaks* reached Ayodhya, mostly by foot. A large group headed towards the site. Police did a *lathi* charge, wounding some people. This resulted in a mob frenzy and open clashes between the police and civilians. About 5,000 *sevaks* entered the masjid. Some climbed on top and planted a saffron flag. Others attempted to tear down the building with axes and hammers. Uttar Pradesh CM Mulayam Singh Yadav ordered police firing in which several *kar sevaks* died. On 2 November, *sevaks* proceeded to the masjid again. Police used tear gas and *lathi* charge, but some managed to reach the structure and partially damaged it. Police opened firing for a second time in 72 hours. They chased *sevaks* through the alleys of Ayodhya and killed many. Though records show

17 deaths, many believe up to 150 *sevaks* were killed. The BJP withdrew support to the VP Singh government, which collapsed.

In September 1991, Congress got 'The Places of Worship Act' passed in the Parliament—it said the character of any place of worship must remain the way it was on 15 August 1947. This was done to appease Muslims, as Congress knew that thousands of mosques were built by Mughal rulers by demolishing temples. In July 2022, a SCI bench headed by Justice DY Chandrachud accepted a petition challenging the Act's constitutional validity. Its decision will shape the course for multiple challenges on the true nature of masjids pending before many courts. Hindu groups want temples to be built in Mathura (Krishna Janmabhoomi) and Kashi (Varanasi), among others, which were allegedly destroyed by Mughals to build masjids.

On 6 December 1992, VHP and BJP held a rally of about 150,000 *kar sevaks* near the site. Many senior BJP leaders made speeches. The crowd grew restive and stormed the 'masjid'. A police cordon was heavily outnumbered. The structure was attacked with improvised tools and brought down in a few hours. This provoked months of Hindu–Muslim riots across India. Around 2,000 people were killed. Several BJP leaders were arrested and the VHP was banned briefly.

A 2-member Allahabad High Court bench began hearing the case in April 2002. On its order, in January 2003, a more than 50-member ASI team did a 2nd evacuation and found over 50 pillars, hinting a Hindu temple stood below the masjid. On 30 September 2010 (after 8½ years), a 3-member bench ruled that the 2.77ac disputed land be divided into three parts, with 1/3rd each going to *Ram Lalla*'s representatives, the UPSCWB, and the Nirmohi Akhara.

The judgment affirmed that the site was Ram's birthplace as per Hindu faith and belief, Babri Masjid was built after demolishing a temple, and it was not built as per the tenets of Islam. All three parties appealed before the Supreme Court against the division of the land.

During his 2013–14 election campaign, Modi said if he becomes the PM, the BJP and its affiliates would not take any action to build a Ram Mandir until a final SCI verdict. As the Government of Uttar Pradesh was a party in the Supreme Court case but the GoI was not, Modi waited for a BJP government to be elected in the state. Once Yogi Adityanath became CM of Uttar Pradesh in February 2017, his government pushed for an early hearing. The SCI scheduled the hearing of 14 appeals in the title dispute on 5 December 2017 and told the government of Uttar Pradesh to translate oral evidence within 10 weeks. Displaying its eagerness to hurry the case pending for 134 years, including 7 years in the SCI, the Government of Uttar Pradesh said it needs just 4 weeks for translation, and the parties can translate documents they wish to use on their own.

UPSCWB's lawyer, senior Congress leader Kapil Sibal, strongly objected and said translations must be finalised before hearings start. The SCI bench asked the parties what they were doing for 7 years, as these documents had already been produced in the Allahabad High Court. It ordered the parties to complete the translations in 10 weeks. On 5 December 2017, when the SCI's hearings began, Sibal argued for deferment till the 2019 general elections were over. Modi unleashed a tirade against Sibal and the Congress. The UPSCWB chairman disowned Sibal's remarks and said the matter should be disposed of promptly. On 8 January 2019,

CJI Ranjan Gogoi assigned the case to a 5-judge constitutional bench of the SCI. On 8 March, the SCI ordered the main parties to attempt mediation for 3 weeks and appointed a 3-member mediation panel.

Mediation proceedings began on 13 March. On 6 August, the SCI began to hear final arguments in daily hearings. It first heard the Hindu parties, followed by the UPSCWB. On 16 October, the mediation panel submitted its report to the SCI. On the same day, the Court concluded its 40-day continuous hearings, the second longest in its history.

On 9 November 2019, the Supreme Court of India passed its final verdict. The Court ordered the GoI to create a trust and appoint a board of trustees within 3 months. The land would be owned by the GoI and handed over to the trust after its formation, to build a temple. It also ordered the Government of Uttar Pradesh to give 5ac of separate land to the UPSCWB to build a mosque.

The Supreme Court ruled that:

- The Allahabad High Court's decision to divide the land into 3 parts was incorrect.
- The demolition of Babri Masjid was illegal.
- Archaeological evidence from ASI shows that the Babri Masjid was constructed on a 'structure' with distinctly indigenous and non-Islamic architecture.
- All 4 biographies of Guru Nanak say in detail that he went to Ayodhya and offered prayers in the Ram Temple in 1510–11 CE.
- Muslim parties failed to establish exclusive possession of the land. The Hindu parties furnished better evidence to prove Hindus worshipped continuously inside the mosque, believing it to be Ram's birthplace.

Millions of Hindus celebrated the Supreme Court's verdict throughout the country and thousands of NRIs and PIOs also celebrated worldwide.

On 12 December 2019, the SCI dismissed 18 petitions against its verdict.

The GoI set up Shri Ram Janmabhoomi Teerth Kshetra (SRJTK) trust on 5 February 2020 for the construction and management of the Ram Mandir. On 19 February, the first meeting of SRJTK unanimously elected 'Ram Janmabhoomi Nyas' chief Mahant Nrityagopal Das Maharaj as chairman and VHP's Champat Rai as general secretary. Retired IAS officer and former Principal Secretary to the PM, Nripendra Mishra, was nominated as chairman of the construction committee.

On 23 March, the first phase of construction began to create a new place to keep *Ram Lalla*'s idol. The very next day, India's first lockdown was announced due to COVID-19. Construction had to be stopped.

Modi performed the *Bhoomi Pujan* (land worship or prayer) on 5 August 2020.

The Sompura family of Ahmedabad, who have contributed to the design of over 100 temples worldwide for at least 15 generations, designed the mandir based on *Vaastu* and *Shilpa Shashtras*. The entire structure is made with Rajasthan pink sandstone blocks, flooring is Makrana marble and walls also carved with Makrana. Fusing of stone blocks is done with about 10,000 copper plates. To ensure durability for 1,000 years, no iron was used, as iron has a life of 94 years. The 250ft x 380ft, 162ft high main structure was built on a 21ft-high raised granite platform to protect against ground moisture. There are three floors and 392 pillars with idols of deities carved on each. Apart from the octagonal *garbhagriha* (sanctum sanctorum), there are five *mandapas*. There are ramps and lifts for PwDs and elderly.

On every Ram Navami at noon, a system of mirrors and lenses will focus the sun's rays on *Ram Lalla's* idol, without using electricity. A 2500ft x 14ft rectangular compound wall with a *Parikrama* corridor surrounds Ram Mandir. The corners will have *mandirs* for Surya, Ganesha, Shiva, and Devi Bhagwati. There will be a *mandir* for Goddess Jagdamba on the north and Hanuman on the south.

Once complete, the 71ac temple complex (with 70 per cent green space, a 25,000-capacity pilgrim centre with medical facilities and lockers, educational facility, museum, and cafeteria) will be the world's 3rd largest Hindu temple. Over 70,000 people can be accommodated in the complex at any given time.

On 14 January 2021 (Makar Sankranti), SRJTK launched a 43-day donation drive aimed at reaching 55–60Cr people, the biggest crowdfunding drive in the world. About 2M VHP activists and volunteers collected donations. President Ram Nath Kovind became the first donor with ₹500,100. Several notable personalities and organisations followed.

The SRJTK ensured utmost transparency by issuing printed coupons and receipts of ₹10, ₹100, and ₹1,000. This lent credibility and encouraged individuals from all walks of life to contribute, including Muslims and Christians. Over ₹3,200Cr was collected and the inflow did not stop on 25 February 2021 when the drive ended. By April 2024, over ₹6,300Cr had come, leaving SRJTK with enough money for maintenance and other needs of the temple for several decades.

About ₹2,470Cr will be spent by SRJTK on the construction of the temple by the time it is fully complete by April 2025.

Contrary to the opposition's jibes, the GoI or the Government of Uttar Pradesh have not spent a single rupee on construction of the Ram Mandir.

The *pran pratishtha* (consecration) ceremony of a 51-inch-tall *Ram Lalla* idol was presided by Modi on 22 January 2024, and officiated by 121 priests, with 7,200 guests (including 4,000 sadhus from 151 orders) present, and more than 180M Indians watching on mobiles and TVs.

Guests included the entire Ambani family, Kumar Mangalam Birla, NRI tycoon Laxmi Mittal, Sachin Tendulkar, Saina Nehwal, Alia Bhat, Ranbir Kapoor, Katrina Kaif, Vicky Kaushal, southern superstars Rajinikanth, Chiranjeevi and Ram Charan, Sri Sri Ravishankar, and even the over 90-year-old former PM, HD Deve Gowda.

Amitabh and Abhishek Bachchan were there, Aishwarya Rai was not—but Rahul Gandhi said in a demeaning tone at over a dozen election rallies that he saw Aishwarya dancing at the ceremony.[1]

Many Hindus said that India has attained 'religious freedom' 76½ years after we got political Independence. Modi said in a voice choked with emotion as the crowd of 7,200 erupted[2]:

> *Sadiyon ki prateeksha ke baad, hamaare Ram aa gaye* (after waiting for ages, our Ram has come).
>
> Ram is the faith of India, Ram is the foundation of India; Ram is the idea of India, Ram is the son of India; Ram is the consciousness of India, Ram is the thought of India; Ram is the prestige of India, Ram is the glory of India; Ram is not a dispute, Ram is the solution; Ram is not only ours, Ram is for everyone; Ram is not just the present; Ram is eternal.

137

The 8th: Democracy Was in Danger

Rahul Gandhi and other opposition leaders keep saying that India's democracy is in danger under Modi. When was it in danger?

Article 356

As per Article 356 of the Constitution, President's Rule can be imposed in any state for failure of the constitutional machinery. The Congress used it 91 times in 54.4 years (average 1.673 times a year)—the most being 53 times by Indira Gandhi in 16 years (3.313/year), to dismiss state governments of opposition parties it did not get along with. Modi used it 7 times in 10.67 years (0.656/year).

Declaration of Emergency—25 June 1975

This was the darkest day for India's democracy. Indira Gandhi jailed hundreds of opposition leaders (including many who years later were part of UPA or the I.N.D.I.A. alliance), cut off newspapers electricity, and imposed press censorship. Her younger son Sanjay Gandhi virtually ran India with his friends. He recruited thousands of hooligans in the Congress. They used threats/force to intimidate those who opposed Sanjay. Without any official post, Sanjay exercised influence with cabinet ministers and senior government and police officers. When many ministers and officials resigned in protest, Sanjay appointed his supporters in their place.

About 6.2M–8.3M men (mostly Muslims) were forcibly sterilised, 16–21 times the number sterilised by Hitler's *Third Reich* during World War II. Accompanied by his crony, DDA Vice Chairman Jagmohan, Sanjay visited Old Delhi and got upset that he couldn't see the Jama Masjid due to a maze of tenements. The DDA bulldozed the tenements, displacing more than 70,000 persons. Police fired on demonstrators who were blocking the bulldozers, resulting in at least 150 deaths. When India's most popular singer Kishore Kumar refused to sing at an Indian Youth Congress function, his songs were banned on All India Radio (India's only radio network then) on Sanjay's insistence.

The SCI started 'obeying' Indira Gandhi, who promoted judges who gave judgments in her favour. She changed many laws—including the 42nd constitutional amendment. Indian history's most controversial constitutional amendment is called the 'Constitution of Indira'. It curtailed citizens' rights, stripped the SCI of many powers including the power to rule on the constitutional validity of laws, moved India towards parliamentary sovereignty, gave the PMO sweeping powers, transferred more power from states to the centre, eroding India's federal structure, and changed the description of India in the Preamble of the Constitution from 'sovereign democratic republic' to 'sovereign, socialist, secular democratic republic'.

Four Times from 1979 to 1998

Each of the 4 opposition PMs who took Congress's 'outside' support to form governments, were ousted in under a year.

Accidental Prime Minister

Sanjaya Baru was media advisor to Dr Singh from May 2004 to August 2008. In his book *The Accidental Prime Minister*, Baru suggests that the PM was a victim to multiple manoeuvres of Sonia Gandhi's political secretary Ahmed Patel ('AP').

After Patel died of COVID-19, *The Times of India* wrote in November 2020:[3]

> On paper, Manmohan Singh was PM, while Sonia was the power behind-the-throne. In reality, the reins were held by AP… he decided the make-up of the cabinet and of Sonia's team… terms of power sharing with coalition partners… influenced bureaucratic appointments including at the PMO. After Rajiv Gandhi, no one had so many Ministers, CMs, Governors… reporting to one person… his residence 23 Mother Teresa Marg… was the [source] of power.

The Economic Times wrote:

> Patel discreetly remained backstage while controlling the action. Theatrics played out at 24 Akbar Road [Congress headquarters] and decisions formalised at 10 Janpath [Sonia's home], but the realpolitik happened at 23 Mother Teresa Marg.[4]

The Congress 'core group' that comprised of Sonia Gandhi, Pranab Mukherjee, Arjun Singh, AK Antony, Ahmed Patel, and Dr Singh, met every week and took important decisions without consulting coalition partners. Traditionally, the CCPA takes high-level political decisions, but as Sonia was not a cabinet minister, she could not be in the CCPA, and this arm of the government hardly met in the UPA-era. The Congress core group was the *de facto* CCPA.

Sonia Gandhi's NAC

Right at the beginning of Dr Singh's tenure, in June 2004, a National Advisory Council (NAC) was set up with Sonia Gandhi as chairperson, to advise and sometimes even 'restrain' the PM from taking decisions. The NAC had 11–14 members from time to time. Most were foreign-funded Leftist activists, with zero administrative or governmental experience.

The extra-constitutional NAC took more crucial decisions than the PM or the cabinet. Sonia Gandhi and the NAC reserved the right to overrule the GoI when it was politically convenient for her. As many as 710 GoI files (majority from the PMO) were sent to get 'permission' from the NAC.

If the NAC was not murder of democracy, what was it? What was the role of the Parliament, the GoI, and the PM? Why were the existing procedures of parliamentary democracy or established systems of the passage of laws bypassed? The GoI had ministries that covered most topics that the NAC dealt with. Why did the NAC have the powers to obtain information from any ministry?

Under what provisions of the Constitution could the NAC submit policy or legislative recommendations to the PM? Though it did not have any executive powers and could only advise the PM and the GoI, given Sonia's power, ministers felt bound to follow the NAC's advice. An unelected NAC that was *de jure* (in law) an advisory body, was *de facto* (in fact) performing executive functions, thus violating the spirit of our Constitution.

The NAC's Communal and Targeted Violence Bill did not recognise communal violence by minorities against Hindus. It assumed only religious minorities and SCs/STs could be victims of communal violence. The NAC entrusted a 32-member panel to draft the Bill. Let's see the background of some of these 32 members:

- John Dayal bats for Rohingya Muslims, amongst many other activities that can be deemed as anti-national.
- Ram Puniyani opposed the hanging of convicted terrorist Afzal Guru.
- Roop Rekha Verma opposes the celebration of Indian culture such as Saraswati Puja in educational institutes.
- Shabnam Hashmi had a Church-funded NGO Anhad, whose FCRA registration was cancelled in 2016 due to 'undesirable activities'.
- Gautam Navlakha speaks and writes of so-called 'army and government atrocities in J&K'. He was arrested under UAPA for the 2018 Bhima Koregaon violence in Maharashtra. The SCI rejected his bail plea and asked him to surrender to the NIA. He met several times with Ghulam Nabi Fai, to 'unite intellectuals against government forces to defeat them physically and otherwise'. Due to bad health, the SCI allowed Navlakha to be under 'house arrest', with conditions like CCTV surveillance, 24x7 police guards at his expense, no computer/other communication device except a non-WiFi phone provided by police personnel once a day for maximum 10 minutes in police presence. His live-in partner Sabha Husain was allowed a non-WiFi phone with calls recorded by NIA. Kashmir-born US citizen Fai has been lobbying in the US for Kashmiri separatists and Pakistan for decades through an ISI front called Kashmiri American Council. He visits Pakistan regularly to meet the highest political, bureaucratic and military leaders. He was arrested by the FBI in

July 2011 for being an ISI agent and using at least $4M of Pakistani funds to influence the US position on Kashmir. As per prosecutors, he was in touch with ISI at least 400 times in 3 years. FBI says Pakistan paid Fai $500,000 to $700,000 per year. In December 2011, he pled guilty and gave specific details about the instructions and payments he got from ISI handlers that included three Pakistan Army officers.

- Teesta Setalvad is accused of witness tampering, getting illegal foreign funds, and misappropriating funds meant for survivors of the 2002 Gujarat riots. The SCI set up a Special Investigation Team (SIT) to reinvestigate the Godhra train burning and post-Godhra violence, with former CBI Director RK Raghavan as chairman. Zakia Jafri is the widow of a Congress MP burnt to death in the riots. Setalvad helped her file a petition before the Gujarat High Court to prosecute Modi (then Gujarat CM) and 62 others for allegedly conspiring to allow the massacre of Muslims. When Gujarat High Court dismissed it, Setalvad's legal team (led by UPA minister Kapil Sibal—he is also referred to in Chapters 136 and 139 in this book and is also Navlakha's lawyer) filed a petition before the SCI that told the SIT to look into the Jafri case. Without hearing Jafri, the SIT filed its closure report, clearing Modi and the 62 others of all charges, and rejecting claims that the Govt. of Gujarat did not do enough to prevent the riots. Setalvad's team filed a 'protest petition' before the SCI that ordered a magistrate to investigate the closure report and her protest petition. The magistrate dismissed her petition. Jafri protested again before the Gujarat High Court. The High Court refused to find fault in the SIT's report. Jafri filed a special leave petition before the SCI, challenged the magistrate's and Gujarat High Court's decisions and sought further investigation by the SCI. In June 2022, a 3-judge bench of the SCI upheld the clean chit given by the magistrate and the SIT to Modi and 62 others, accusing Setalvad of exploiting Jafri's emotions. She was arrested by the Gujarat ATS for allegedly conspiring to falsely implicate Modi and 62 others for the 2002 riots, but the SCI granted her bail. In RK Raghavan's autobiography *A Road Well Travelled*, he wrote that Setalvad and two police officers, one of whom has been sacked and jailed, targeted him during the probe. In its final report, the SIT had termed the three as 'liars'. Raghavan claimed there were efforts to 'dislodge' him from the SIT because he was 'politically inconvenient to those who were in great danger of being permanently eliminated from the Indian polity … I held my ground much to the annoyance of those who were opposed to the chief minister [Modi].'[5] *He was obviously referring to Sonia Gandhi and the Congress.* Licenses of both NGOs set up by Setalvad have been revoked. The UPA gave a Padma Shri to Setalvad in 2007.

- Dr Harsh Mander is a former IAS officer who supported mercy for the 26/11 terrorist Ajmal Kasab. In March 2018 he wrote, 'There has never been a harder time to be a Muslim in India, not since the stormy months that followed India's Partition.'[6] This was shared on social media by Pakistan's PM Imran Khan. Dr Mander is an apologist for Ishrat Jahan, an LeT operative killed in a police encounter in Gujarat. LeT has carried out minimum 14 attacks on India that have resulted in at least 657 deaths, with thousands injured. Mander runs an NGO that has received tens of crores from European

Catholics and US-based Islamist organisations. It's FCRA license was suspended twice in 2023 and finally revoked for good in January 2024. The CBI filed a chargesheet against him for various foreign exchange violations. He is also being investigated by the ED and the ITD on various charges.

- Others included Farah Naqvi, Dr Manzoor Alam and Maulana Niaz Farooqui.

Were these people expected to draft a fair and equitable Communal and Targeted Violence Bill? Is it surprising that the Bill was blatantly anti-Hindu, or that Sonia Gandhi chose such people to draft it?

In any case, their efforts went waste—after the Bill languished in Parliament for almost 9 years, the UPA had to withdraw it in February 2014.

'In the guise of protecting minorities, it attacks Hindu rights. This Bill will… legitimise criminal misdeeds of Muslims,' wrote Arindam Chaudhuri, Editor, *The Sunday Indian*.[7]

Former Chief Justice of Punjab and Haryana High Court, Dr M Rama Jois said,[8]

> It is astonishing that a Bill that is flagrantly violative of the right to equality and patently discriminatory could have been even thought of by the National Advisory Council under the chairmanship of Sonia Gandhi and introduced in Parliament by the Government headed by Dr Manmohan Singh.

138

The 7th: Dynasts Fall, Performers Rise

In 2016, he said in Firozabad (UP), 'You are demanding a potato factory, but you should understand that I am an Opposition leader. So, I cannot open a potato factory.'[9]

In 2018, he said, 'Coca-Cola company *ko shuru karne wala ek shikanji bechne wala vyakti tha*… America *mein shikanji bechta tha paani mein chini milata tha*.' (The man who started Coca Cola Company would mix water with sugar and sell lemonade.)[10]

He also said, 'Ford company *ka naam suna hai*? Mercedes *ka naam suna hai*? Honda *ka naam suna hai*? In *teen companyon ko kisne chaloo kiya*? *Kaun tha woh*? Mechanic *tha*, mechanic.' (Have you heard of Ford, Mercedes, and Honda? Who started these companies? Who was he? He was a mechanic!)

Former President of India Pranab Mukherjee said the man was 'yet to mature politically'. Mukherjee also questioned his ability to tell the difference between 'AM' and 'PM' (time).

Former US President Barack Obama wrote that he has 'a nervous, unformed quality about him, as if he were a student who'd done the coursework and was eager to impress the teacher but deep down lacked either the aptitude or the passion to master the subject'.[11]

Yet, his mother and his party workers and voters love him so much that they are willing to lose elections after elections for his sake.

Of course, you know who we are talking about.

Enough about Rahul Gandhi. Let's move on to his great-grandfather, the founder of India's most powerful political dynasty.

Jawaharlal Nehru said in his Independence Day address, 'We [Indians] do not work as hard as Europeans, Japanese, Chinese, Russians or Americans.'[12] He also said that these nationalities had intelligence, implying that Indians did not.

The average Indian works 5–6 days/week, while most Europeans work average 4.5 days/week. As far as intelligence is concerned, as many as 62 Fortune 500 have Indian CEOs and this includes Google, Microsoft, IBM, Adobe, Novartis, and Starbucks.

Pakistan captured 85,107km^2 of Indian territory in 1948, and China captured Ladakh's 37,244km^2 Aksai Chin region in 1962. Pakistan ceded the 6,993km^2 Shaksgam Tract to China in 1963. Pakistan continues to occupy 78,114km^2 of Indian territory and China 44,237km^2.

Put together, Nehru lost 122,351km^2, which is more than 3.72 per cent of India's current land area.

In 1950, the US floated the idea of India becoming a permanent member of the UNSC to India's permanent representative to the UN, Nehru's sister Vijaya Lakshmi Pandit. Nehru responded to his sister: 'India because of many factors is certainly entitled to a permanent seat. But we are not going in at the cost of China.'[13] In 1955, USSR's PM Nikolai Bulganin brought up the same issue during Nehru's visit to Moscow. Nehru responded that this would only create tensions between India and China, and it should not be done until China's admission into the UNSC. As a nation with about 14.8 per cent of world population, Nehru should have made all-out efforts to get India a permanent UNSC seat. We are still struggling for a permanent seat of the UNSC.

By 1950, jihadi rhetoric had started in J&K. During a visit of Pakistani PM Mohammad Ali Bogra to New Delhi in August 1953, a joint communiqué with Nehru reaffirmed India and Pakistan's commitment to a plebiscite (referendum of the public) to ascertain the will of the people of J&K, whether they want to (1) remain with India, (2) separate from India and merge with Pakistan or (3) become an independent nation. Thousands of Hindus and Sikhs have been killed. It took 69 years for Modi to solve the problem by repealing articles 370 and 35A.

Indira Gandhi said, 'When good work is approaching completion, we become complacent. When an obstacle comes, we lose hope. Sometimes, it seems the whole nation has accepted defeat.'[14]

Indian Armed Forces captured 15,010km^2 of Pakistani territory and 92,466 Pakistani prisoners in the 1971 war. In the July 1972 Shimla Agreement with Pakistan's PM, Indira gave back 14,127km^2 and all 92,466 prisoners, in exchange for nothing, despite Pakistan illegally occupying 78,114km^2 of Indian territory. *What did Indira Gandhi get from Pakistan and its (then) close ally, the US? Was it a big deposit in her Swiss Bank account?*

In 1974, Indira Gandhi gave away the 285ac Katchatheevu Island (22.3km from Rameshwaram in Tamil Nadu) to Sri Lanka, despite it being 36km away from their mainland, and therefore closer to India. With huge fishing income, the island's value is estimated at around ₹1,550Cr. Tamil Nadu fishermen frequently encounter conflicts with Sri Lankan Navy during their expeditions around Katchatheevu. Thousands have been arrested by Sri Lankan authorities in the last 50 years. *Once again, was there a big deposit in a Swiss Bank account?*

See the record of Sonia and Rahul Gandhi in the last six LS elections (including 2024):

Last 6 LS Elections	Congress and UPA / I.N.D.I.A.	BJP and NDA	BJP / NDA ⇧
Average Seats won by Party	110.0	210.2	▲ 91.1%
Average Seats won by Alliance	159.3	263.7	▲ 65.6%

In the only three (3) Lok Sabha elections in which Narendra Modi led the BJP and the NDA, their margins of victory over the Congress and the UPA were absolutely unreal.

LS Elections (2014, 2019, 2024)	Congress and UPA / I.N.D.I.A.	BJP and NDA	BJP / NDA ⇧
Average Seats won by Party	65	275	▲ 323.1%
Average Seats won by Alliance	118.67	327.33	▲ 175.8%

Prominent Congress leaders who left the party and joined the BJP include:

Senior LEADERS who LEFT CONGRESS and JOINED BJP	
Name of Leader	**POSTS in the Congress Party (current BJP post)**
SM Krishna	CM of Karnataka; Foreign Minister in UPA Govt
ND Tiwari	CM of Uttar Pradesh and CM of Uttarakhand
Jagadambika Pal	CM of Uttar Pradesh
Ashok Chavan	CM of Maharashtra

Senior LEADERS who LEFT CONGRESS and JOINED BJP	
Name of Leader	**POSTS in the Congress Party (current BJP post)**
Kiran Kumar Reddy	CM of (undivided) Andhra Pradesh
Capt Amarinder Singh	CM of Punjab
Vijay Bahuguna	CM of Uttarakhand
Digambar Kamat	CM of Goa
Ravi Naik	CM of Goa
Pema Khandu	CM of Arunachal Pradesh (Arunachal CM)
Himanta Biswa Sarma	Assam senior minister (Assam CM)
Jyotiraditya Scindia	UPA MoS, close aide of Rahul (Modi Govt cabinet minister)
Biren Singh	Manipur senior minister (Manipur CM)
Ranjit Singh Chautala	Haryana senior Minister (1987-90, 1999-2024), RS MP (1990-92)
Rao Inderjit Singh	LS MP (MoS IC n Modi Govt since 2014)
Suresh Pachouri	Rao Govt MoS, UPA MoS, Madhya Pradesh president
Jitin Prasada	UPA MoS (Yogi Govt cabinet minister in UP)
RPN Singh	UPA MoS
Ch. Birender Singh	LS MP, RS MP (RS MP)
Bhubaneswar Kalita	Assam president, LS MP, RS MP (RS MP)
Ashok Tanwar	Youth Congress president, LS MP, Haryana president
Sunil Jakhar	Punjab president, LS MP (Punjab BJP president)
Rita Bahuguna Joshi	UP president (LS MP, was Yogi Govt minister)
Arjun Modhwadia	Gujarat president, Gujarat MLA
Naveen Jindal	LS MP (2004-14), 33yrs in Congress, close to Rahul Gandhi

Another 6–8 MPs and more than 30 MLAs also left Congress and joined BJP.

Children of ex-Congress CMs/cabinet ministers who joined the BJP include Anil Antony, Kuldeep Bishnoi, Manish Khanduri, and Padmaja Venugopal. Some prominent Congress spokespersons such as CR Kesavan, Jaiveer Shergill,

Khushbu Sundar, Shehzad Poonawalla, and Tom Vadakkan have also moved to the BJP.

Others who left Congress and joined other parties or started their own, include UPA cabinet ministers Ghulam Nabi Azad (also J&K CM and RS leader of opposition), GK Vasan (his party in Tamil Nadu is now a BJP-ally), Kapil Sibal, and Mamata Banerjee; UPA ministers of state Jayanthi Natarajan and Milind Deora; Baba Siddique; Bubagra Pradyot Manikya (his party in Tripura is a BJP-ally); Ranjeet Deshmukh; Sushmita Dev; and Y.S. Jagan Mohan Reddy (current Andhra Pradesh CM).

Rise of the Performers

Modi went against convention and appointed several non-politicians as ministers. While most performed well, those who did not were shown the door. Let's look at some prominent names.

Name & Education	Background	Ministries
Dr S Jaishankar IFS (Indian Foreign Service)	Foreign Secretary of India. Speaks Tamil, Japanese, Mandarin, Russian, Hungarian. Ambassador to the US, China, Czechia; High Commissioner to Singapore; Dy Chief of Mission at Tokyo; served at Moscow, Colombo, Budapest.	Cabinet Minister—External Affairs since May 2019
Piyush Goyal CA, LLB	Worked as Investment Banker; Served on Boards of SBI and Bank of Baroda	Cabinet Minister—Finance, Railways, Commerce & Industry, Textiles, Coal, Consumer Affairs, Food and Public Distribution
Hardeep Singh Puri IFS (Indian Foreign Service)	India's PR to UN. Ambassador to Brazil; Deputy High Commissioner to Japan, UK, Sri Lanka. Also served in MOD and MEA. Coordinator of UNDP/UNCTAD project to help developing countries in multilateral trade negotiations. President, United Nations Security Council (UNSC) for 2 terms. Chairman, UNSC Counterterrorism Committee	Cabinet Minister—Housing and Urban Affairs, Petroleum & Natural Gas MoS (IC)—Civil Aviation MoS (IC)—Mines, New & RE MoS—Commerce & Industry
Ashwini Vaishnav IAS, MTech (IITK), MBA, Wharton, USA	MD (India), GE Transportation (Rail); VP (Locomotives) & Head (Urban Infrastructure Strategy), Siemens	Cabinet Minister—Railways, Communications, Electronics and Information Technology
Former Ministers till May 2024		
Raj Kr. Singh IAS, BA (Hons), English Lit., Dip. Management, Netherlands	Home Secretary of India	Cabinet Minister-—Power, New & Renewable Energy MoS- Skill Development and Entrepreneurship
General VK Singh PVSM, AVSM, YSM	Chief of Army Staff Attended US Army Ranger School (Special Forces) and US Army War College	MoS (IC)—DoNER, Statistics MoS—External Affairs MoS—MoRTH, Civil Aviation

The NITI Aayog serves as the apex public policy think tank of the GoI and the nodal agency to catalyse economic development and foster cooperative federalism through the involvement of state governments in economic policymaking using a bottom-up approach. It was set up by Modi on 1 January 2015 to replace the Congress-era Planning Commission that followed 'bargaining federalism' and a top-down approach.

The vice chairperson has cabinet rank and is assisted by a CEO (minister of state rank). Let's look at people who have held these positions:

Vice Chaiperson	Background
Suman Berry (Since May2022) PPE, Oxford University, UK Masters in Public Affairs, Princeton University, USA	Worked at World Bank for 28yrs, las as Lead Economist. Special Consultant, RBI. Director Gen, NCAER. Senior Visiting Fellow, Centre for Policy Research. Chief Economist, Royal Dutch Shell. Member, PMEAC. Member, Statistical Commission of India. Member, RBI's Technical Advisory Committee on Monetary Policy.
Dr Rajiv Kumar (Sep2017-Apr2022) PhD, Lucknow University DPhil, Oxford Univ., UK	Professor, IIFT; Economic Advisor, Dept of Economic Affairs, Min. of Finance; Principal Economist, ADB; Chief Economist, CII; Director & CEO, ICRIER; Secretary General, FICCI; Senior Fellow, Centre for Policy Research; Board Member, RBI and SBI.
Dr Arvind Panagriya (Jan2015-Aug2017) BA, MA, PhD in Economics, Princeton University, USA **Padma Bhushan (2012)**	Professor of Economics at University of Maryland; Jagdish Bhagwati Professor of Indian Political Economy at Columbia University; Chief Economist, Asian Development Bank; Worked at World Bank, IMF, WTO, UNCTAD; Non-Resident Senior Fellow, Brookings Institution; Member, Int'l Advisory Board, SEBI; Member, Board of Governors, ICRIER. Chancellor, Nalanda University, Bihar
CEO	**Background**
BVR Subrahmanyam (since Mar2023) IAS, BE (Mechanical) Management Degree, LBS	PS to PM Dr Manmohan Singh (2004-2008); Advisor, World Bank; Joint Secretary, PMO (Mar2012-Mar2015); Additional Chief Secretary (Home), Chhattisgarh (Jun2015-Jun2018); Chief Secretary, J&K (Jun2018-May2021); Commerce Secretary. to GOI (May2021-Sep2022).
Parameswaran Iyer IAS (Jul2022-Feb2023)	Water Resources Manager at World Bank. Head, Swachh Bharat Mission; Head, Jal Jeevan Mission. Was a Professor of Management Practices at IIMA.
Amitabh Kant IAS (Feb2016-Jun2022) MA in Int'l Relations, JNU	Tourism Secretary, Kerala (created the brand '**God's Own Country**'); Joint Secretary, Tourism, GOI (created '**Incredible India**' brand & campaign); Secretary, Department of Industrial Policy & Promotion (started '**Make in India**', '**Startup India**' and '**Ease of Doing Business**' initiatives).
Sindhushree Khullar IAS (Jan2015-Dec2015)	Worked at Intel as part of architectural team that designed the i486 processor. Founder, BPL Mobile. Founder, Jupiter Capital (AUM $1n); Founder, StarAsianet

Dr Panagriya is now Chairman of the 16th Finance Commission (2023–28), Parameswaran Iyer is India's nominee as executive director at the World Bank, and Amitabh Kant is the Indian emissary to G7 and G20.

It's not just the vice chairperson or CEO posts that have professionals of the highest pedigree, even lower posts have fantastic professionals.

For example, Urvashi Prasad who is director in the vice chairperson's office, was a consultant at the WHO, Cambridge University (UK), Imperial College (London), Michael & Susan Dell Foundation, worked at the World Economic Forum, and was a board member of Operation ASHA, an NGO that brings tuberculosis treatment at economically feasible rates to disadvantaged communities. She was a lateral hire in October 2016 and has worked there since then.

At the lowest level are 42 'young professionals'. We have dealt with young professionals and senior people at NITI and they match the best in the corporate world. They are also super helpful and fast.

Choice of CMs

As the BJP is not a dynastic party, apart from the centre, it is also very different from other parties in the selection of CMs, most of whom are young and dynamic. They are carefully chosen by a small team led by Modi himself and including Amit Shah and party president JP Nadda.

When a new BJP CM is announced, everyone is shocked, including BJP's state ministers and MLAs, opposition, and the media. Many a time, several ministers have to report to a person who is junior to them in age and experience, but that is the Modi style of developing future leaders.

Non-performing CMs are called to Delhi and politely told to make way for someone else that the party has selected.

Modi Is Changing the Bureaucracy

In an unprecedented act that shocked MPs and bureaucrats, Modi told the Parliament, 'What is this big power we have created? What will we achieve by handing reins of the nation to babus? Our babus are also citizens, and so are the youth of India.'[15]

All India Services or AIS include the IAS, IPS, and IRS.

CBI booked more than 1,200 AIS officers for corruption during FY15–FY24. It is not shocking that IAS officers were found with disproportionate assets of ₹25L to ₹650Cr per individual.

Since 2015, over 450 civil services officers have been forced to retire, deemed to have resigned or had cuts in remuneration/pensions.

- AIS rules were amended to provide specific timelines at different stages, to complete disciplinary proceedings against AIS officers.
- Modi government did away with interviews in recruitment for lower-level posts to curb corruption, bring more objectivity and transparency in the selection process and substantially ease problems of poor aspirants.
- Over 2,200 public authorities have aligned with the RTI online portal that shows pending RTI cases and reduces delays in responding to RTIs. The GoI is also persuading states to implement it.
- The Central Vigilance Commission (CVC) is developing an integrity index of 25 organisations.
- An e-service book is being implemented for all GoI employees.
- An online software now monitors departmental cases to complete inquiries in stipulated timeframes, and to fix

accountability. Initially adopted for IAS officers, it will subsequently extend to all civil services officers in the GoI as well as central group 'A' employees.

- To expedite PSE recruitments of senior executives at board-level or one level lower and reduce corruption, an online vigilance system provides the exact status in a timely, accurate and objective manner.
- Centralized Public Grievance Redress and Monitoring System (CPGRAMS) is very easy-to-use portal that helps you register any grievance against a GoI ministry, department or official and even private companies. If you are not satisfied with the closure, your appeal is escalated to seniors. CPGRAMS is monitored by a team of over 25 persons at the PMO. More than 7,620 public grievances are resolved daily.

Pay at higher levels of India's bureaucracy is relatively much lower than private sector jobs at similar levels, thereby reducing the government's ability to attract the right talent for the most important posts. Private sector salaries rise much faster than the government, based on the employee acquiring new skills and his/her performance. There is no incentive for government officers to acquire new skills or work hard as their promotions/increments are fixed in the civil services ecosystem based on British-era policies.

In the world's largest economy (the US), even 115 years ago, over 65 per cent of the federal (central government) workforce was appointed based on merit, measured by tests. Except posts in security/intelligence agencies like CIA, FBI, etc., the same is true today.

In June 2018, Modi government said it wanted to laterally hire 10 outstanding individuals with expertise in areas like finance, economic affairs, commerce, road transport and highways, shipping, civil aviation, agriculture, environment, and renewable energy, etc. A lateral hire is a candidate who is not from the AIS.

In August 2019, the Modi government laterally hired nine persons from the private sector as joint secretaries in various ministries. By March 2024, it had hired over 1,400 persons at the joint secretary, director, and deputy secretary levels.

More than 40 per cent of PMO's executive staff, over 60 per cent of the team at NITI Aayog, and over 90 per cent of the Invest India team are not from the AIS. Many are credited with the ideas Modi has implemented.

In comparison, Dr Singh's PMO had over 90 per cent people from the AIS. The Planning Commission of India that the NITI Aayog replaced had over 70 per cent from AIS. It also had politicians including the home, finance, agriculture, health, HRD (education), law, chemicals and fertilisers, and IT ministers, and the minister of state for planning as ex officio members.

While the planning ministry was under the PM in UPA, Modi brought the statistics and program implementation ministry also under himself, and a single minister of state handles both, as they have multiple synergies.

In 2012, the Planning Commission renovated two toilets at an expense of almost ₹35L.

The key differences between the Planning Commission and NITI Aayog are:

- The Commission could allocate funds to ministries and state governments, whereas NITI is a think tank and advisory body with no power to allocate funds.
- Role of state governments was limited to annual interactions during the Planning Commission's 5-Year

Plan meetings, whereas with NITI, the state governments play a more significant role.
- Policies were formed by the Planning Commission, after which states were consulted about fund allocation. The NITI Aayog consults states while the policy (to be sent as an advisory to the PM) is being formulated.
- Once the Planning Commission decided on a policy, it was imposed on states. The NITI Aayog has no power to impose any policies on states.

Was the purpose of the 'planning commission' to plan how Sonia Gandhi and her ministers would make commissions?

139

The 6th: Battling the Scumbags

Just have a look at what Modi is up against when it comes to the scumbags (the anti-national and corrupt) of India.

We are going to cover nine dynastic parties, and they have many things in common, the most important being:

- They hate Hindus and Hinduism.
- Founders' families are way more important than any party leaders.
- They don't follow the rule of the law or the Constitution.
- They paste their parties' branded stickers on free items that come from the GoI. They even release advertisements of Modi government welfare schemes that appear as if they are state government schemes.
- Their spokespersons speak lies on TV channels, are obnoxiously loud, and have no respect for fellow panellists.

DMK Party (Tamil Nadu)

Tamil Nadu's ruling DMK (*Dravida Munnetra Kazhagam*) was founded by the late M Karunanidhi (CM for 19 years). His son M.K. Stalin is CM since 7 May 2021. He is named after Josef Stalin, a ruthless dictator for 21 years of his 29-year-premiership of the Soviet Union. Over a million persons were imprisoned in forced labour camps (Gulag), and more than 700,000 were executed in 1934–39, under Stalin's 'Great Purge'.

MK's son Udhayanidhi Stalin is a minister since December 2022. In 2021, Udhayanidhi had alleged that Modi's cabinet ministers Sushma Swaraj and Arun Jaitley died as Modi caused them stress.

In September 2023, he said, 'Just like dengue, malaria, or coronavirus, we have to eradicate *Sanātana*.'[16] A few days later Udhayanidhi posted on 'X': 'Sanātan Dharma divides people in the name of caste and religion. Let me reiterate—like spread of Covid19, dengue, and malaria by mosquitoes, Sanātana is responsible for many social evils.'[17]

A letter by 262 notable citizens was sent to the CJI pressing the SCI to act. The Court reprimanded him and asked for a public apology.

Five days later, DMK's A. Raja (UPA minister who was jailed for 15.5 months for the 2G scam) said: '*Sanātan Dharma* should be compared to diseases such as HIV and leprosy.'[18] He said Stalin's comments were 'soft'.

In July 2022, Raja said that the GoI is not giving the state autonomy, and the PM and Home Minister Amit Shah should not force them to demand a '*thani nadu*' (separate nation).

In February 2024, Modi laid the foundation stone for ISRO's rocket launch complex in Thoothukudi district. DMK's fisheries minister released an advertisement with a picture of PM Modi, CM Stalin and two DMK ministers, and a rocket with China's flag on it.

Modi slammed DMK: 'They have not put India's flag but pasted a Chinese flag. They do not want to show India's achievements in the space sector. They have insulted our scientists and you.'[19]

In March 2024, Raja said:[20]

> Tamil Nadu will never accept chants of 'Jai Shri Ram' or 'Bharat Mata ki Jai'. India was never a nation. One nation means one language, one tradition, one culture. Here, Tamil is one nation and one country, Malayalam is one language, nation, and country, Oriya is a nation, language, and country. All these nations make up India. So, India is not a country, it is a subcontinent. There are so many traditions and cultures. In Manipur, they eat dog meat—that's a culture.

DMK minister Anitha Radhakrishnan called PM Modi a 'mo....f…er'.[21] DMK MP and CM's sister Kanimozhi sat on the stage and enjoyed his speech.

In March 2024, NCB arrested DMK office-bearer Jaffer Sadiq for a ₹2000Cr international drugs trafficking case (DMK sacked him when the scam became public). Sadiq said he had paid a huge sum to Udhayanidhi Stalin. Slogans like '*Drug Mafia Kazhagam*' (DMK) went viral on social media.

SCAMS OF DMK

Which Scam?	People Involved	Actions by Agencies	Amount
Illegal Sand Mining; Cash-for-Votes	Durai Murugan, TN minister and DMK general secretary; his son Kathir Anand; their associate Poonjolai Sreenivasan	ED attached assets & froze bank accounts; TN Govt appealed against ED's jurisdiction before MHC, saying sand mining is State subject & MHC gave Interim Stay; the SCI overruled MHC & allowed ED to continue	**₹4730cr; possibly up to ₹60,000cr**
BGR Energy Systems; Jobs Scam Money Laundering	V Senthil Balaji, TN minister	ED ARRESTED him in Jun2023, over ₹30cr land seized; Balaji resigned in Feb2024; Bail denied by MHC, Balaji in jail for 10+ months	**₹4900cr+**
Multiple Scams	S Jagathrakshakan, MP, UPA Govt MoS, and his family members	ED & ITD conducted multiple searches; ₹89.1cr assets seized;MHC rejected Jagath's petition against ED	**₹3500cr+**
Chennai One SEZ	DMK Govt, Former UPA home & finance minister P Chidambaram	Not Known	**₹2770cr+**
Reflector Stickers	Udhayanidhi Maran	Not Known	**₹2000cr+**
Tax Evasion	EV Velu, TN minister	ITD seized ₹29cr cash	**₹250cr+**
Disproportionate Assets; Forex Earning Non -Repatriation; Red Sand Quarrying	K Ponmudy, TN minister, his wife P Visalakshi, their son Gowthama Sigamani	MHC imposed 3yrs JAIL & ₹50L fine in one case; Disqualified as Minister & MLA; ED seized ₹8.60cr cash; One associate ARRESTED; Other Cases going on	**₹200cr+**

NOTE: Until Conviction by a Court, all scams/persons/amounts are alleged/estimated. Amounts are INFLATION-ADJUSTED to Apr2024.

Congressis say 'Pakistan Zindabad'

We wrote about former Congress MP D.K. Suresh saying that Karnataka should separate from India.

Government of Karnataka invited UK-based professor Natasha Kaul to deliver a lecture. She is a known India-hater and speaks of 'genocide in Kashmir' in many international fora and has even called J&K an 'India-occupied territory' and PoJK as a Pakistani territory.

Kannada and Culture Minister Shivaraj Tangadagi told Congress party workers to slap youth and students who chant 'Modi slogans'.

On 27 February 2024, the supporters of Congress MP Syed Naseer Hussain chanted 'Pakistan *Zindabad*' at the state secretariat 'Vidhana Soudha'. The MP smiled and even posed for photos with them.

On 1 March, there was a bomb blast at a café in Whitefield area of Bengaluru, one of India's largest tech hubs. Bengaluru police arrested three persons—there were photos of two near Hussain and forensic analysis confirmed they chanted 'Pakistan *Zindabad*'. On 14 April, both the person who planted the bomb and the mastermind were arrested from West Bengal.

'[CM] Siddaramaiah and [Deputy CM] D.K. Shivakumar's dangerous game of appeasement politics has enabled anti-national elements and the *tukde tukde* gang,' reacted BJP's R. Ashoka, leader of the opposition in Karnataka.[22]

What is the *tukde-tukde* gang?

Bharat tere tukde honge

On 9 February 2016, students from Kashmir, Kerala, and West Bengal gathered at JNU to pay tribute to Afzal Guru, a Kashmiri jihadi convicted for the 2001 Parliament attack (14 deaths) and hanged to death in 2013.

'*Bharat tere tukde honge, insha Allah, insha Allah*' (Allah willing, India, you will be broken into pieces); '*Kashmir ki azaadi tak, Bharat ki barbadi tak, jang rahegi jari*' (the war will continue till Kashmir gets freedom and India is destroyed); '*Allahu Akbar, Kashmir maange Azaadi, Kerala maange Azaadi*' (Allah is the greatest, Kashmir and Kerala are asking for freedom); '*Afzal tere khoon se inquilab aayega, Afzal hum sharminda hain, tere qatil jinda hain*' (Revolution will come due to your murder, Afzal, we are ashamed your murderers are still alive) were the slogans raised. They also asked people to raise voices against the Indian Army and CRPF.

On 12 February, Jawaharlal Nehru University Students' Union (JNUSU) President Kanhaiya Kumar (of Communist Party of India or CPI-affiliated All-India Students Federation) was arrested for sedition.

The Delhi Police tweeted: 'Abetment of any kind of anti-national activity is a punishable offence.' It referred to a 10 February tweet by an unverified Twitter handle @HafeezSaeedJUD (founder of LeT and Jama'at-ud-Da'wah): 'Requesting our Pakistani brothers to trend #SupportJNU for our pro-Pakistani JNUites brothers. #PakStandWithJNU.'[23]

On 14 February, teachers, students, alumni, and civil society activists, formed a human chain of about 2km to protest Kanhaiya's arrest.

Rahul Gandhi joined the protest and said: 'A youngster expressed himself and the government says he is anti-national. The most anti-national people are those who are suppressing the voice of this institution.'[24] Why was the 29-year-old 'youngster' still in college?

Hundreds of leftist students stay in subsidised hostels for years without graduating. JNU is a hotbed of anti-national activity, and most teachers are an integral part. We taxpayers pay for all this.

In April 2018, Kanhaiya Kumar was elected to CPI's National Council, fought the 2019 LS election from Bihar and lost by a huge margin. In July 2019, he was inducted in CPI's National Executive.

In September 2021, he joined Congress in Rahul Gandhi's presence. He actively participated in Rahul's 'Bharat Jodo Yatra' in September 2022–January 2023. In July 2023, he was appointed All India Congress Committee (AICC)'s in-charge of the National Students' Union of India, the Congress' students' wing. He was a spokesperson of Rahul's 'Bharat Jodo Nyay Yatra' in January–March 2024.

Not only did Rahul support the *tukde tukde* gang but he also made one of its initiators a key aide.

Three days after the 26/11 terrorist attack in Mumbai, when more than 450 hostages were still getting counselling and all of India was in shock, Rahul Gandhi was at a farmhouse, partying at his friend's wedding *sangeet*. Thousands had cancelled events and parties. But Rahul did not bother to mourn. He was 38.5 years old, an MP and a general secretary of the ruling party.

Rahul Gandhi is out of the country for 50–60 days a year. Allegedly, in every trip he meets enemies of India, be it the Chinese or Canadian/UK Sikhs, or Islamists, or even representatives of Pakistan's ISI. For example, in a visit to the US in September 2024, Rahul met US Congresswoman (MP) Ilhan Omar, who has been supporting Pakistan's agenda on J&K.[25] He addresses audiences at leftist universities/special-interest groups, where he mocks India. Among other things, he says:

- Make in India has failed (note: facts prove otherwise).
- India's economy is not growing as fast as Modi is 'advertising'—are IMF, World Bank, MSCI, JP Morgan,

Citigroup, Bank of America, JICA, and rulers of Saudi Arabia, Abu Dhabi and Dubai all fools?

- China captured thousands of square km of Indian land—perhaps he forgot it happened only twice in India's history (Nehru-era and UPA-era; see the chapter 'Handled the Dragon" in this book). In any case, should an MP say this abroad? Has Modi ever spoken of China capturing Indian land when Congress was in power?
- Democracy is dead in India—why is Rahul Gandhi still here? He can easily get Italian citizenship. Even China will happily make him their citizen and probably give him their highest civilian honour.
- At UK's Cambridge University, Rahul Gandhi said India is not a nation as per Article 1 of the Constitution, but a union of states. Siddhartha Verma, a 'Commonwealth scholar' in public policy countered Rahul: 'If you turn a page back and see the Preamble, it does mention India is a nation. Bharat finds its origin in the Vedas. Even when Chanakya made it clear to students in Taxila that they might belong to different *janapadas* but ultimately, they belong to the nation that is Bharat.' Gandhi replied: 'Rashtra is a kingdom.' Verma retorted: 'No, Rashtra is the Sanskrit word for nation.' Gandhi's last words were: 'The word nation is a Western concept.'
- The press, parliament, judiciary, and election commission are all under threat and are controlled by the Modi government.[26] Rahul's accusation of them controlling the judiciary is sedition, and 'contempt of court'.
- Europe and the US are not doing enough to restore democracy in India as they get trade and money from India. Yes, Rahul asked foreign powers to interfere in our internal affairs. This also amounts to sedition.

- Sikhs are not safe in India—Khalistani separatist Gurpatwant Singh Pannun (see chapter 'Don't Dare Bully India Now') lauded Rahul's statement.[27]
- BJP has spread kerosene all over the country, one spark can put us in big trouble.[28] Did a man who wants to become the PM (Rahul) want to burn the nation?

The Congress opposed Modi's development, revocation of Article 370 (they filed two appeals against revocation in the SCI, both were rejected), Make in India, Vande Bharat trains, new Parliament House, and the Ram Mandir at Ayodhya. Aren't these good for India?

Crimes of the Aam Aadmi Party

There are many controversies about Arvind Kejriwal's AAP.

- For several months, AAP did not give permission to Delhi Police to prosecute JNU's *tukde tukde* gang members.
- Soni Mishra killed herself after allegedly being sexually harassed by AAP activists. Kejriwal had told her to 'compromise'.
- When Gajendra Singh Kalyanwat hanged himself at an AAP rally, Kejriwal continued his speech even as the body was being brought down.
- There are allegations of AAP being funded by Khalistani groups. Terror group International Sikh Youth Federation (ISYF)'s chief operative Gurdial Singh campaigned for AAP in the 2017 Punjab election. Gurdial visited Pakistan many times. ISYF operatives were trained by the ISI to carry out terror attacks in India. Gurdial and 11 other ISYF operatives were arrested.

- AAP's former leader of opposition in Punjab SS Khaira and former MP Dr Dharamvir Gandhi supported a Khalistan Referendum.
- The party supported the (allegedly) Khalistani-funded farmer agitations both times.
- In March 2024, AAP MP Raghav Chadha met British MP Preet K Gill. She mobilises funds for the Khalistani separatist movement in the UK, funds violent protests outside India House in London and regularly posts anti-India/Modi/Hindu stuff on social media.
- Minister Kapil Mishra tried to expose Kejriwal's role in a ₹400Cr water tanker scam and AAP MLAs kicked his chest inside the assembly.
- MLA Somnath Bharti was arrested for beating and mentally torturing his wife for over 5 years. He also abused a lady journalist on live TV and told her she should be a prostitute.
- MLA Jarnail Singh beat an engineer of the Municipal Corporation of Delhi.
- Jitender Singh Tomar had four ministries. In June 2015, he was found guilty of faking his BSc and LLB degrees. He admitted the fakes, resigned, was arrested, and barred from contesting elections or practising law.
- AAP questioned the 2016 surgical strikes and asked the Army to provide proof of the strikes.
- Delhi's chief secretary was assaulted by AAP MLAs in Kejriwal's house.
- Kejriwal's close aide Bibhav Kumar assaulted the party's lady MP Swati Maliwal, also in the CM's residence.
- The Shunglu Committee indicted AAP on several appointments done in the Delhi government departments based on corruption and nepotism.

Delhi riots:[29] In December 2019–March 2020, there was a 101-day 24x7 anti-CAA sit-in protest at Delhi's Shaheen Bagh by Muslim women. They chanted '*Jinnah-waali azaadi*' and '*Pakistan Zindabad*'. Slogans and posters had provocative anti-Hindu content. Muslim mobs started riots on 15 December.

Chairman of Delhi Waqf Board and AAP MLA Amanatullah Khan was spotted near Jamia Milia Islamia University at Okhla. Chants of '*Hinduon se Azaadi*' (freedom from Hindus) were raised. Buses were set on fire.

Khan was declared a history-sheeter in March 2022. He was arrested several times but managed to get acquitted or get bail each time. There are 22 FIRs against this Kejriwal favourite. Apart from other misdeeds, as Waqf Board chairman, he is accused of illegal recruitment, illegally renting out Board properties and misappropriation of funds received from the Government of the NCT of Delhi. The SCI refused to stop the CBI or the ED from arresting Khan in Waqf Board scam cases and he was arrested by the ED in September 2024.

Massive riots broke out in Seelampur on 17 December. Stones were pelted at the police.

On 1 February, AAP's Kapil Gujjar fired three shots.

US President Trump was coming to Ahmedabad on 24 February. On the 22nd, 500–700 Muslim women blocked an important road near Jaffrabad Metro Station.

On the day Trump arrived, Muslim mobs went on a rampage and anarchy erupted across Delhi. A head constable died, and a DCP was injured. A petrol pump and many vehicles were torched. Amidst chants of '*Allahu Akbar*' and '*Nara-e-Takbeer*' (Pakistani version of *Allahu Akbar*), Hindus were killed mercilessly.

Islamists resorted to stone pelting, arson, vandalism, destroyed crores of property, and injured policemen and civilians. Around 250 Muslims came to AAP councillor Tahir Hussain's house at Moonga Nagar. From his terrace they chucked stones and petrol bombs. Sacks of bricks, stones, acid packs, and petrol bombs were found. Allegedly, Intelligence Bureau constable Ankit Sharma was dragged into Hussain's house, killed, and his body thrown in a drain behind the house.

In an adjacent building, Hindu women at a 'wedding house' would address their Muslim neighbours as '*Bhaijaan*' and greet them with '*Salaam*'. While a Hindu wedding was going on, Muslim women rained down acid and petrol bombs from Hussain's terrace.

A 19-year-old was attacked in his own shop and a drill bored into his head.

There are 2 schools in Shiv Vihar. Hindu-owned DRP was completely gutted. Muslim-owned Rajdhani sheltered the rioters, from where they pelted stones, hurled petrol bombs and fired guns.

Muslims took off clothes of adolescent Hindu girls and sent them naked to their homes. Some even took off their own clothes in front of the girls and gestured indecently, and some even masturbated.

A Muslim bike shop took hundreds of bikes to a safe place at 5am just before riots started. The rioters vandalised the shop to show themselves as victims, then took the counter out and set it on fire. Muslims collected their children from school beforehand.

More than 170 Hindu families put up 'House on Sale' signs as they were being terrorised by Muslims. They were warned against praying or even reciting Hanuman Chalisa—

by the same people who play '*azan*' from loudspeakers 5 times a day, 365 days a year.

Around 2,200 persons were arrested/detained.

Police registered a case against Tahir Hussain on 25 February 2020. He was on the run and was arrested on 5 March. He is still in jail for plotting the Delhi riots.

Muslims weaved stories of their innocence, tried to prove they were victims to claim compensation of ₹10L from the AAP government. Dozens vandalised their own shops to claim victimhood.

There was violence in 16 localities, most of which are Muslim-majority areas.

Fifty-three people died and more than 700 were injured in 101 days.

Had the riots not stopped due to COVID-19, how many more would have died?

It is clear Islamists were preparing for anti-Hindu riots for long under the pretext of anti-CAA protests. They stocked bricks, acid, and petrol bombs in advance.

Based on everything we heard from people in Delhi and read, we believe the riots were supported/funded by AAP.

The *tukde tukde* gang, notably Umar Khalid, was an integral part of the riots, and booked under UAPA for 'provocative speeches'. In September 2020, he was arrested as a conspirator. Police said Khalid met Tahir Hussain and activist Khalid Saifi on 8 January at Shaheen Bagh to plan the riots. Khalid has been in jail for over 4.5 years.

His lawyer is also Kapil Sibal, who has fought over 300 cases for terrorists, rioters, corrupt persons, and anyone against Hinduism for over 27 years.

AAP's senior leader Satyendar Jain was arrested in May 2022 by ED for laundering ₹16.39Cr through 4 'shell' companies; ₹3.16Cr cash and gold were seized. He had 8 ministries in the Delhi government at the time.

Liquorgate: The AAP government notified a Delhi Excise Policy in November 2020—849 liquor vends were sold for ₹8,911Cr. The Delhi government, which earlier ran 475 of the 864 liquor stores, was left with no control over sale of liquor.

Once licensees opened the shops, AAP reduced VAT on foreign liquor from 25 per cent to just 1 per cent, causing a huge loss to the exchequer. Shops could remain open for 18 hours against 14 hours earlier; dry days were reduced from 23 to just 3/year.

As many as 381 of the 849 shops closed within 5–7 months as they could not compete with giant wholesalers who had bought multiple licenses, and there was a revenue decline of ₹2,327.4Cr per year, against AAP's projection of an annual revenue increase of ₹9,500Cr.

In June 2022, the Congress (which later became AAP's ally in the I.N.D.I.A. alliance) wrote to Delhi Police seeking a probe into a 'multi-crore scam'.

In July 2022, Delhi's chief secretary alleged that Deputy CM and Excise Minister Manish Sisodia violated statutory provisions and caused a loss of over ₹580Cr to Delhi's exchequer.

Delhi's Lieutenant Governor (LG) recommended a CBI investigation.

Nine days later, the AAP government withdrew the Excise Policy, admitting the losses.

Businessmen lost hundreds of crores. One particular businessman lost almost ₹100Cr; and as it was borrowed, he even considered suicide.

In August 2022, CBI filed an FIR naming Sisodia and 14 others, claimed that crores were paid in kickbacks, and that the corruption goes to the 'highest levels' in the AAP government.

The ED filed a PMLA case, alleging that AAP hiked the profit margin for wholesalers to 12 per cent in lieu of a 6 per cent kickback, causing a loss of ₹2,873Cr to the Delhi government.

A liquor cartel known as 'South Group' (YSRCP MP Magunta Reddy, his son Raghav Reddy, K. Kavitha, Sarath Reddy, and others) was created to benefit from the Delhi Excise Policy. It allegedly gave advance kickbacks of ₹100Cr to AAP through AAP's media head Vijay Nair and was allotted over 28 per cent of the liquor shops.

Kavitha is the daughter of 'KCR', Telangana's then CM. She was LS MP in 2014–19 and is a Telangana MLC since October 2020.

In September 2022, the CBI arrested Nair, allegedly the main conduit for moving the bribe money.

In February 2023, the CBI arrested Manish Sisodia, and he joined his colleague Satyendar Jain in Tihar Jail.

After CBI recorded Arvind Kejriwal's statement on 16 April 2023, he said, 'The entire case is fabricated, and they do not have any proof. It is a result of dirty politics. AAP is a "*kattar imaandaar* party" (staunchly honest party). They want to finish AAP.'[30]

The ED claimed that the crime proceeds in the 'Liquor Gate' scam were over ₹600Cr.

Raghav Reddy, Sarath Reddy, and one other person became government approvers (one who admits his offence and agrees to testify against the others).

AAP's RS MP Sanjay Singh was arrested on 4 October 2023 and also lodged in Tihar. After six months, the SCI gave him conditional bail.

For a few months, the SCI denied bail to Sisodia saying a money 'transfer of ₹338Cr is tentatively established'.

In March 2024, the CAG said that Delhi government made a loss of ₹2,003Cr.

On 15 March 2024, the ED arrested K. Kavitha.

ED summoned Kejriwal 9 times, but he kept defying the law by not going for questioning. Three times a lower court and once the Delhi High Court asked him to go, but Kejriwal kept saying it was BJP's ploy to get him arrested before the 2024 elections, as they feared his popularity.

If he is a *kattar imaandaar*, why was he scared of being questioned?

ED arrested Arvind Kejriwal on 21 March 2024 when he failed the 9th summon. This was the 17th arrest in the Liquorgate scam.

Kejriwal is the only CM in history not to resign on being arrested. Despite saying multiple times that he does not want any post including swearing on his children's lives; such was his greed that he ran the Delhi government from Tihar Jail.

The SCI granted bail to Kejriwal, Sisodia, Kavitha, and several others accused in the case, in August and September 2024. However, Kejriwal was banned from going to the CM's office or sign any official documents. Four days after he got out of jail, Kejriwal finally resigned.

Funding from Ford Foundation: This American NGO that is allegedly a CIA-front and funds various individuals and organisations to secure US's world dominance, regularly gave money to Kejriwal and Sisodia's NGO 'Kabir'. Kavita Ramdas is a senior advisor to its president and has worked at the Ford Foundation for over 10 years. Her father (Late) Admiral L Ramdas was a former chief of Indian Navy. He was Arvind's godfather, and the internal 'Lokpal' of AAP.

SCAMS OF AAM AADMI PARTY			
Which Scam?	**People Involved**	**Actions by Agencies**	**Amount**
Unless mentioned otherwise, all persons are leaders of AAP			
Loss of Revenue to Delhi Govt due to AAP's FREE POWER scheme	**Arvind Kejriwal**, Manish Sisodia, Satyendra Jain	Did not find information	**₹60,000cr+**
Liquor Gate (Liquor Excise Case)	**Arvind Kejriwal**, Manish Sisodia, Sanjay Singh, Vijay Nair, Atishi Marlena, Saurabh Bhardwaj; BRS former MP & current MLC, K Kavitha; former BRS MLA Buchibabu Gorantla; YSRCP MP Magunta Sreenivasulu Reddy; Businessmen Amit Arora, Dinesh Arora, Binoy Babu, Abhishek Bonpalli, Rajesh Joshi, Sameer Mehendru, Magunta Raghav Reddy, Sharath Reddy; Gautam Malhotra (son of former Akali Dal MLA)	**CBI and/or ED arrested Arvind Kejriwal, Manish Sisodia, Sanjay Singh, Vijay Nair, and 12 other accused persons**	**₹3274cr**
Delhi Jal Board (DJB)	**Arvind Kejriwal**, Satyendra Jain and several DSB officials	CBI and ED have filed cases; ED is questioning Kejriwal	**₹600cr+**
Purchase of bad quality Panic Buttons for Buses and Taxis at highly inflated prices	**Arvind Kejriwal**, Kailash Gahlot	Did not find information	**₹1217cr**
Disappearance of Funds of Anna Hazare movement during Jantar Mantar protests in 2011	**Arvind Kejriwal**, Manish Sisodia	Although many associates alleged this scam, no one lodged formal complaints with the police or the Agencies	**₹256cr**
Various Scams at Mohalla Clinics and Delhi Govt Hospitals	**Arvind Kejriwal**, Manish Sisodia, Satyendra Jain	CBI is investigating	**₹60-100cr**
NOTE: *Until Conviction by a Court, all scams/persons/amounts are alleged/estimated. Amounts are INFLATION-ADJUSTED to Apr2024.*			

Anarchy and Melodrama: Kejriwal got himself slapped in public multiple times for public sympathy. Six days before Republic Day 2014 he did a *dharna* near Rajpath at night; he threatened to 'flood' Rajpath with lakhs of supporters and called himself an 'anarchist'. Have you seen his cry-baby tone in frequent TV addresses? Such a good actor and stunt man should have been in Bollywood.

Abuse of Power: AAP spent ₹1,586Cr of Delhi taxpayers' money on advertisements in 109 months at ₹47.6L per day! AAP's Punjab government spent ₹228.35Cr in a year at ₹62.6L per day!! Why does this small party need to spend over ₹110L/day to advertise nationally? AAP contested 39/40 seats in the 2022 Goa elections, got 6.77 per cent votes, and won 2 seats. In the 2023 Assembly elections in Madhya Pradesh, Karnataka, Rajasthan, and Chhattisgarh, AAP put up 412 candidates in 744 seats, of which 409 lost their deposits (99.3 per cent). How did the ad spend help? In any case, why should the taxpayers of Delhi and Punjab bear the costs of AAP's ads outside their states? Delhi's LG asked AAP to refund ₹164Cr out of this expenditure.

***Aam* CM**: Before Kejriwal became CM, he coughed incessantly, had a modest car, and said he would ban 'VIP culture' and not live like other CMs as he was 'an *Aam Aadmi*' (common man). He publicly stated time and again that he would not take a government car, a government bungalow or security if he gets any post.

After becoming CM, his cough went away, he spent over ₹11L for two lunch parties in February 2016, at ₹12,472 (Veg) and ₹16,025 (non-Veg) per plate[31] and has five cars for which the government paid ₹1.44cr.

The CM's residence was 'renovated' for ₹171Cr (including the cost of buying flats for officers whose houses had to be demolished to make way for the expansion of the AAM CM's 'Sheesh Mahal'). The sprawling bungalow even has an '*Aam Aadmi*' swimming pool, while many Delhi residents lack clean water, and the Yamuna has not been cleaned in 10 years since Kejriwal had promised to do it. And yes, he has security, in fact a lot of security.

Mamata Banerjee—the Vote Bank *Didi*

TMC and its leader Mamata Banerjee (aka *didi*) have systematically changed the demographics of West Bengal since 2011. From a 27 per cent Muslim population, it is estimated the state has 40–45 per cent Muslims now. Could Muslims really produce so many kids? The answer is no!

West Bengal's population was 91.276M in 2011. It grew only 13.84 per cent from 2011 against a national growth rate of 17.9 per cent. The 22.66 per cent lower growth rate (despite a 27 per cent Muslim population) was because there was no development, and therefore no jobs. As a result, lakhs migrated to cities that were creating new jobs.

Mamata Banerjee has allowed millions of illegal Bangladeshi migrants to settle down in West Bengal. An essential 'vote bank', they have voter IDs and ration cards. Many even have Aadhaar/Indian passports. Due to largesse of the Government of West Bengal, most are not poor. Fly in or out of Kolkata, and you will see 25 per cent or more Bangladeshi co-passengers.

Forget Hindus, even Bengali Muslims are unhappy. They say that Bangladeshis are preferred over Indian Muslims. No one in the state gets benefits of most GoI schemes because *didi* does not want Modi to become popular. A taxi driver or cart vendor cannot even register on the e-Shram portal as their pin codes are not accepted—God knows how she managed to do that on a central government portal.

We were shocked to hear the locals' estimates of the Bangladeshi population in just Kolkata and Howrah—between 2.5M to 5M.

POLL VIOLENCE IN WEST BENGAL

WHICH ELECTION	INCIDENTS	INJURIES	DEATHS
2018 Panchayat	451	1813	**98**
2019 Lok Sabha	1545	2489	**133**
2021 WB Assembly	686	2157	**128**
2023 Panchayat	429	1443	**76**
SOURCE: https://ga7a.short.gy/I3UpbO			

During elections, TMC goons seize colonies with higher BJP/CPM supporters and do not allow people to come out to vote. If central forces such as CRPF try to intervene, they are beaten up. Central Law Enforcement Agency (LEA) officers are obstructed from doing their duties in the state, and sometimes also beaten up by Kolkata Police/West Bengal state police.

TMC's scams are second only to the Congress.

SCAMS of Mamata Banerjee's TMC (current value ~₹5.88 lakh crores)			
Which Scam?	**People Involved**	**Actions by Agencies**	**Amount**
Unless mentioned otherwise, all persons are leaders of TMC (Trinamool Congress Party)			
Unfinished Projects but 100% money paid	**Mamata Banerjee, Abhishek Banerjee**	Not known	**$195,000cr+**
2.5mn Fake NREGA Job Cards	**Mamata Banerjee, Abhishek Banerjee**	In Jan2024, the CHC ordered a 4-member Committee to investigate; Centre is considering a CBI probe	**₹148,000cr+**
WBSSC (West Bengal School Service Commission) Recruitment Scam—over 21,000 persons Recruited illegally since 2014; Tampering of more than 9000 OMR sheets	**Abhishek Banerjee**; Manik Bhattacharya, Partha Chatterjee, Kuntal Ghosh, Jiban Krishna Saha; Sujay Krishna Bhadra who is working in **Abhishek Banerjee**'s office since 2009; actress Arpita Ghosh, a 'close associate' of Chatterjee; Bengali actress & President of TMC's student wing Saayoni Ghosh; WBSSE Chairman Kalyanmoy Gangopadhyay, former WBSSC Chairman Subiresh Bhattacharya, WBSSC Secretary Ashok Saha and Adviser Shanti Prasad Sinha; and 6-7 others	11 persons have been ARRESTED of whom 09 are in JAIL; ED recovered ₹64cr cash, gold & jewellery from Arpita. Soon after Chatterjee became minister, Arpita opened 04 'shell' companies for money laundering . By converting black money through these companies, Chatterjee bought properties worth 100s of crores in *benami* names. Assets of over ₹2500cr have been attached	**₹117,000cr+**
Rose Valley Chit Fund	**Mamata Banerjee**, Tapas Paul and Sudip Bandyopadhyay; Senior IPS Officer Rajeev Kumar; Promoter Gautam Kundu	GOI froze 2600 accounts of Rose Valley with ~₹800-1000cr.; Pal, Bandyopadhyay, and Kundu ARRESTED; Kumar chargesheeted by CBI but is defying even Supreme Court directions with support of Mamata	**₹71,720cr+**
Municipal Employee Recruitment Scam	**Mamata Banerjee, Abhishek Banerjee**, Shantanu Banerjee, Sujit Bose, Rathin Ghosh, Firad Hakim; Businessman Ayan Sil, a close associate of Shantanu	The CHC told CBI to investigate the scam and SCI endorsed it. ED is also doing a probe. The SCI endorsed ED's view that both recruitment scams are linked. ED ARRESTED Ayan Sil in Mar2023. ED seized ₹111cr.	**₹15,000cr+**
Ineligible Beneficiaries in PM Awaas Yojana	**Mamata Banerjee, Abhishek Banerjee**	The GOI has refused to release further funds to GoWB until action is taken.	**₹14,238cr**
Saradha Chit Fund	**Mamata Banerjee**, Kunal Ghosh, Madan Mitra, Shatabdi Roy, Srinjoy Bose; Senior IPS Officer Rajeev Kumar; Promoters Sudipta Sen and Debjani Mukherjee; Lawyer Nalini Chidambaram (w/o P Chidambaram)	An ED officer was beaten up by 8-9 TMC workers; Ghosh, Mitra, Bose, Sen, and Mukherjee ARRESTED; Ghosh repaid ₹2.67cr, Roy repaid ₹31-L; ₹690cr attached	**₹11,300cr+**
Siphoning of grains from the Public Distribution System	Jyotipriyo Mullick, Shahjahan Sheikh, hawala operator Sankar Addhya, rice miller Bakibur Rahaman, Biswajit Das, plus several others	ED attached 170+ properties worth over ₹450cr and seized around ₹20cr cash. All named persons ARRESTED	**₹10,830cr+**
Coal Smuggling Scam	**Abhishek Banerjee**, father Amit Banerjee, wife Rujira Narula Banerjee and sister-in-law Menaka Gambhir; Moloy Ghatak, Sushanta Mahato, Vinay Mishra, Chandranath Sinha; 08 Eastern Coalfield officials; 08 WBSP officers; businessman Anup Maji; and 20+ others	CBI had ARRESTED 12 persons till Feb2024. ED has attached cash and other assets of over ₹35cr.	**₹2665cr**
Cattle Smuggling Scam	Anubrata Mondal, **close aide of Mamata Banerjee**, and his daughter Sukanya; Md. Enamel Haque; former BSF commandant Satish Kumar; CA Manish Kothari	ED found properties of ₹77.65cr. Mondal's properties of ₹17cr attached. 54 accounts frozen. All the named persons are in JAIL.	**₹1330cr+**
SJDA Scam	Gautam Deb; IAS officer Godala Kiran Kumar who was CEO of SJDA Siliguri-Jalpaiguri Development Authority	ED is questioning the accused persons	**₹450cr+**
Narada Sting OP—52hrs' video footage of 13 senior TMC leaders and 01 SP accepting wads of currency	Suvendu Adhikari, Iqbal Ahmed, Sultan Ahmed, Prasun Bannerjee, Kakoli Ghosh Dastidar, Firhad Hakim, Madan Mitra, Aparupa Poddar, Mukul Roy, Saugata Roy, Sovan Chatterjee, and Subrata Mukherjee; PA of **Abhishek Banerjee** Sujay Bhadra; **Abhishek Banerjee**'s friend Karan Sharma; IPS Officer SMH Meerza	Chatterjee, Hakim, Mitra, and Mukherjee ARRESTED; CBI filed FIRs against 12 TMC leaders in April 2017, 04 of whom admitted taking ₹300,000 (current value ₹573,800) each	**₹1.55cr**
NOTE: *Until Conviction by a Court, all scams/persons/amounts are alleged/estimated. Amounts are INFLATION-ADJUSTED to Apr2024.*			

Saradha Scam: This Ponzi scheme cheated about 1.8M persons of about ₹4,000Cr during 2006–13. Saradha chairman Sudipta Sen bought paintings from *didi* (allegedly painted by her) for ₹1.86Cr. Sen wrote an

18-page confession letter to CBI, admitting he paid big money to politicians.

Rose Valley Chit Fund Scam: ED says that ₹17,520Cr was raised from investors in 1997–2013. All-India Small Depositors Association put the amount at ₹40,000Cr. The CBI arrested TMC MPs Tapas Pal and Sudip Bandyopadhyay. High drama unfolded after Bandyopadhyay's arrest. TMC members attacked the BJP office and severely injured around 15 BJP workers. They took to the streets in various parts of the state, did a rail blockade, and even staged a protest at the CBI's office at Kolkata.

Didi Does Drama: On 3 February 2019, a CBI team reached the house of Kolkata Police Commissioner Rajeev Kumar (Banerjee's ally) to question him about the Saradha and Rose Valley scams. Kumar had headed the state's SIT that had probed the scams before SCI handed over the cases to the CBI in 2014, along with other chit fund cases. CBI officers were detained by Kolkata Police. Banerjee rushed to Kumar's residence and then did a *dharna* for over 69 hours in the heart of Kolkata. Kumar sat right next to her in blatant disregard to the probity of his position. 'The Kolkata Police Commissioner is among the best in the world. His integrity, bravery and honesty are unquestioned,' tweeted *didi*.[32]

The CBI moved the SCI. On getting notices from the Court, West Bengal's chief secretary, DGP and Kumar replied that the Government of West Bengal and police never obstructed investigations, nor any official denied CBI cooperation. The trio claimed no police officer was at the CM's '*dharna manch*' despite TV footage of Kumar's presence. The SCI directed Kumar to 'appear before CBI at a neutral location and faithfully cooperate with the probe'. CBI interrogated Kumar in Shillong. He was also questioned with former MP Kunal Ghosh

(TMC had expelled him) on both scams. The CBI relied on a 91-page letter from Ghosh to the ED, detailing Kumar's role in handling the Saradha investigations.

Kumar was questioned for 39 hours over 5 days. The CBI requested the SCI for Kumar's 'custodial interrogation' as he was 'evasive and arrogant' in his answers. The Court withdrew protection from arrest and asked CBI to proceed as per law. Kumar suddenly disappeared. The CBI issued a 'lookout notice' instructing all immigration authorities to alert them if Kumar was fleeing India. Kumar moved the Calcutta High Court seeking quashing of CBI's notice and was granted 40 days' protection but was told to cooperate with CBI. Kumar was questioned again. By then, Banerjee had promoted him as additional director general in-charge of the CID department of the West Bengal state police. In August 2019, Kumar went on a month's leave and failed to attend 3 summons. On 1 Oct, the Calcutta High Court granted Kumar anticipatory bail. CBI moved the SCI. On 29 November, the SCI asked Kumar to reply on CBI's appeal challenging his bail. In December 2019, Kumar became principal secretary of West Bengal's IT department.

In December 2020, CBI told the SCI that West Bengal CM's Relief Fund paid ₹6.21Cr for salaries of Tara TV, which was part of Saradha group. Directly pointing the needle of suspicion at *didi*, CBI said there was a concerted effort to evade, avoid and escape the law, adding that the CM and Sudipta Sen had a very good relationship. Seeking custodial interrogation of Kumar, CBI said investigations had revealed that evidence connecting the TMC with Saradha were concealed by Bidhannagar Police when Kumar was the commissioner in that town. They said Kumar actively connived in shielding and protecting influential persons who promoted Saradha and benefited from illegally collected funds. The CBI said Saradha employee Safiqur Rehman had disclosed that Sudipta Sen was forced to sponsor all Pujas in Bhowanipore from where Mamata was contesting in 2011.

Narada Sting Operation: Senior journalist Mathew Samuel carried out a sting operation targeting high-ranking officials in West Bengal and politicians of TMC. After the 52-hour video footage surfaced, the Calcutta High Court ordered a probe by CBI. When West Bengal objected to CBI handling the probe, the Calcutta High Court and the SCI denied its appeal. The Government of West Bengal initiated a probe that booked Samuel for 'defamation', 'criminal conspiracy', 'forgery to harm reputation', etc. Kolkata Police was accused of heckling Samuel while interrogating him.

In August 2016, Calcutta High Court stayed West Bengal's probe for eternity, saying police cannot run a concurrent investigation alongside a court-monitored probe. When 4 TMC leaders were arrested, TMC supporters hurled stones at CBI's Kolkata office where they were kept. Central forces had to put up barricades and push back the agitators. *Didi* was also inside. The Calcutta High Court ordered house arrest of the 4 leaders. CBI told the SCI that TMC workers led by *didi* herself created a massive law and order situation to prevent it from producing the arrested before a trial court. The petition said the CM always created law and order situations with the help of antisocial elements to impede CBI officials from carrying out law-mandated duties. The Calcutta High Court granted interim bail to the 4 arrested TMC leaders. Investigations are ongoing.

PDS Scam and Sandeshkhali Rapist: Sheikh Shahjahan of Sandeshkhali village in North 24 Parganas Dist joined TMC in 2013, became '*up-pradhan*' of the gram panchayat in 2018 and his rise began. He was '*sabhapati*' of TMC's Sandeshkhali unit, and in 2023 won a zilla parishad seat. He owns 67ac fisheries, wholesale fish markets, a baby shrimp processing centre, and brick kilns. Sheikh is close to TMC leaders, particularly Jyotipriyo Mullick, then a minister in the Mamata government. The ED was investigating a ₹10,000Cr PDS scam—rice mills siphoned PDS grains in collusion with ration distributors, dealers and others; money was generated under the garb of paddy procurement under fake names and laundered via companies controlled by Mullick. An ED and CRPF team went to raid Sheikh's home on 5 January 2024 in connection with the PDS scam. A mob of 800–1,000 surrounded the ED–CRPF team, pelted stones and beat ED/CRPF personnel with *lathis*—three officers received head stitches.

On 8 February, local women carrying brooms and sticks blocked the main road and demanded immediate arrest of Sheikh and his aides Hazra and Sardar, whom they accused of sexual abuse and harassment. The next day, women attacked Hazra's properties and set fire to his poultry farm, which they said was on illegally grabbed land.

For over 5 years there were dozens of complaints against Sheikh and his cronies, for allegedly raping (including gang rape) hundreds of women several times inside the TMC office, but West Bengal state police did not act. There were also complaints about Sheikh grabbing lands to convert them into fish farms. After the fire, the women were threatened by TMC goons. The state police arrested Hazra and Sardar. The police initially denied rape allegations, but later filed cases against TMC leaders.

A 2-member NCW team visited Sandeshkhali. Its report talked of women's widespread fear and systematic abuse by police and TMC members. The report said: 'Women who dared to speak out against such atrocities faced immediate retaliation, including property confiscation, arrests of male family members, and further acts of brutality.'[33] NCW's findings revealed a distressing pattern of complicity by West Bengal state police.

If a woman complained about Sheikh or his goons, the state police would arrest her husband and/or other male family members and register a rape case against them. Sheikh's goons would break the husbands' bones and cripple them for life and set fire on their farm harvest.

NCW chairperson Rekha Sharma visited Sandeshkhali:

> Once Sheikh is arrested, more women will come out with complaints. Only one woman has registered her statement before a magistrate. We must instil confidence in them. West Bengal's officers are never allowed to meet teams of central officers as CM Mamata is trying to hide the truth … but the truth will come out.[34]

The West Bengal state police stopped a team of BJP MPs and two union ministers from visiting Sandeshkhali. A Congress-led team was also stopped. A 6-member independent fact-finding team led by former Patna High Court Chief Justice L.N. Reddy was detained. Reddy said,

> This is completely illegal. At least two of our women members should be allowed to visit females who bore the brunt of atrocities of musclemen enjoying political patronage and impunity from police action all these days till the media unravelled the shocking truth. [Government of West Bengal] cannot stop civil society members to interact with victims of human rights violations. What is the Government of West Bengal scared to hide?[35]

The West Bengal state police arrested Sheikh on 28 February, 54 days after the attack on the ED/CRPF team. 'The charges included "attempt to murder", "criminal force against public servant", and "grievous hurt", among others,' said an ADG of West Bengal state police. Apparently, there were 42 pending criminal cases against Sheikh that the West Bengal state police had not acted on for years. TMC immediately suspended Sheikh for 6 years. The TMC leadership, including Mamata initially came out in support of Sheikh but later distanced themselves. Denying that TMC was supporting Sheikh, Abhishek Banerjee (Mamata's nephew and successor) said TMC had always shunted ministers who were involved in scams. As soon as the news of the arrest reached Sandeshkhali, the villagers started distributing sweets and women hugged each other.

Sandeshkhali was tense for 3 weeks, with villagers protesting police inaction, and attacking TMC leaders' properties. There was widespread sexual assault and land grabbing attributed to Sheikh's followers. The CBI requested the Calcutta High Court to transfer the case and custody of Sheikh to itself, as it believed West Bengal state police's custody would defeat the investigation's purpose, as the state police was colluding with Sheikh, since it registered FIRs against ED officials on the same day they were assaulted, thereby not inspiring any confidence. The Government of West Bengal said the state CID was investigating 'all possible sections', including attempt to murder. The Calcutta High Court transferred the assault investigation to CBI. It directed West Bengal state police to forthwith transfer all papers to the CBI with the custody of Sheikh. The court said,

> 'The West Bengal state police are totally biased, and every attempt is being made to delay the investigation and protect him. The case merits a fair, honest and complete investigation

> for doing complete justice in general and people of the locality in particular. Attack occurred on members of Central agencies performing official duties, and had to be coordinated by the accused.

The Mamata government moved the SCI challenging the order, and refused to hand over Sheikh, saying the Calcutta High Court order violates West Bengal's legal right for a judicial review, and had cast 'unsubstantiated aspersions' on the state's investigating agency by transferring the probe to the CBI.

On 5 March 2024, NCW's Rekha Sharma met President Droupadi Murmu and recommended that 'President's Rule' be imposed in West Bengal.

On 6 March, the SCI denied any relief to the Government of West Bengal. The Calcutta High Court then ordered West Bengal state police to hand over Sheikh to the CBI the same day, and the state police was left with no choice.

Attack on the NIA: Personnel of the CBI, the ED, and the CRPF are not the only ones to bear the brunt of TMC's terrorism while performing their law-mandated duty. On 5 April 2024, after extensive searches at 5 locations, the NIA arrested 2 key conspirators for the bomb blast in Bhupatinagar, East Midnapore, in which 3 persons had died in 2022. As the NIA team started its search operation, a hostile mob launched an assault on the team, hurt 2 NIA officers, and broke their vehicle's windscreen. Mamata Banerjee alleged the NIA was working for the BJP:

> Why did they raid at midnight? Did they have police permission? Locals reacted how would have if any other stranger had visited at midnight. Why are they arresting people right before the elections? What right does NIA have? We call upon the entire world to fight against this BJP's dirty politics.[36]

The CM even accused NIA personnel of assaulting the villagers rather than the other way around.

Let us answer this: (1) Worldwide, LEA raids take place most often at night because it is easier for raid teams to get spotted during daylight, thus assisting in perpetrators escaping. The same is true for military warfare; (2) The NIA *does not* need police permission; (3) The locals knew they were not strangers as they came in clearly-marked police vehicles with blue beacon lights; (4) LEAs can conduct raids and make arrests when appropriate, not as per Mamata Banerjee's convenience; (5) The NIA has all the rights—does Mamata wish to challenge this before the SCI?; and (6) The 'entire world' does not know Mamata Banerjee.

With scams of almost ₹5.88LCr, and the atrocities on women (Shahjahan Sheikh is not the only one; there are several more allegations of TMC leaders across West Bengal sexually abusing women), Mamata and Abhishek Banerjee are also likely to get arrested—after all, more than 30 TMC leaders (including 11 ministers and MPs) have been arrested since 2021 alone. *Can Modi take on didi?*

Bihar's Jailman Lalu and Family

Despite being a Hindu, former Bihar CM and UPA Railways Minister Lalu Prasad Yadav of Rashtriya Janta Dal (RJD) allows senior party men to speak openly against Hinduism. Lalu has been involved in 11 scams. He has spent 89.2 months in jail and 31 months in hospital arrest (more than 10 years). The April 2024 value of scams he has been convicted is about ₹17,800Cr. Lalu was disqualified as an MP for 6 years and barred from contesting elections. On his 1st arrest in July 1997, he transferred the CM post to his uneducated wife, Rabri Devi. She has been convicted/accused in 5 scams, their son

Tejashwi Yadav in 5, their daughter Misa Bharti and son Tej Pratap Yadav in 2 each, and their daughters Ragini Yadav, Hema Yadav, and Chanda Singh in 1 scam each. In April 2024 value terms, properties of more than ₹14,800Cr have been seized from the family and total fines of over ₹18Cr paid by them. Some scams are still being investigated by CBI/ED, or being heard in courts, and Lalu may have to spend a few more years in jail.

UP's Muslim Friends, Samajwadi Party

Muslim appeasement by the dynastic Samajwadi Party is second only to India's 6 Islamic parties. Its founder Mulayam Singh Yadav (then CM of Uttar Pradesh) ordered police to fire on *kar sevaks* and 150 died. The party is also anti-women. Mulayam blocked the Women's Reservation Bill in Parliament in 2010. After a gang rape and murder of 2 teenage girls in 2014 which shocked India, he said, '*ladkon se galti ho jaati hai*' (boys make mistakes!). His son Akhilesh Yadav (CM of UP during March 2017–March 2022) told people not to take Covid vaccines, as they were BJP's vaccine.

Samajwadi Party is also known as a 'goonda party' as it not only shields mafia dons/other goons but also gives them tickets to contest elections. Some were even made ministers when the party was in power in UP. The party was a part of UPA for all 10 years and is a part of I.N.D.I.A. now.

YSRCP of Andhra Pradesh

This party was started by former CM of Andhra Pradesh, Y.S. Jagan Mohan Reddy. His father was a Congress CM of undivided Andhra Pradesh (it included Telangana till June 2014). As a Christian, Jagan openly supported churches and NGOs that convert Hindus to Christianity. He also ran many Christian-specific welfare programs. However, unlike most other opposition leaders, he never talks ill about Hinduism. Jagan changed names of Modi government schemes so that people think that he was doing the welfare. The PM-KISAN scheme was called Rythu Bharosa ('Rythu' is the 'R' in YSRCP). Since COVID-19, Modi government provides 5kg of free rice to poor people, and Jagan stuck his pictures on the GoI's rice bags. The state made massive losses of ₹145,614Cr during the 5 years he was CM. Here are some known scams:

SCAMS of Andhra Pradesh's YSRCP

Apart from the financial scams, YS Jagan Mohan Reddy and his colleagues are also involved in the illegal conversion of lakhs of Hindus (mainly in rural areas) to Christianity

Which Scam?	People Involved	What is the Sam about?	Amount
Unless mentioned otherwise, all persons are leaders of YSR Congress Party of YS Jagan Mohan Reddy			
Multiple TDR Scams	Many YSRCP Ministers, MLAs; and Municipal officers	Transferable Development Rights (TDR) purchased in several municipalities at inflated rates and most of the premium paid back to Party as kickbacks	**₹45,000cr**
JJM Scam	**YS Jagan Mohan Reddy**	No account for the funds spent in the State from GOI's Jal Jeevan Mission	**₹42,000cr**
NREGA Scam	**YS Jagan Mohan Reddy**	No account for NREGA funds spent	**₹32,000cr**
Liquor Scam	**YS Jagan Mohan Reddy**	Money Siphoned in liquor distribution by State	**₹30,000cr**
Sand Scam	Several people	Fake Way Bills for sand deals	**₹25,000cr**
GP Scam	**YS Jagan Mohan Reddy**	No account for Panchayat funds spent	**₹8600cr**
Vishakapatnam Land Scam	**YS Jagan Mohan Reddy** and several Party leaders	Party leaders purchased lands in Vizag for ₹10 lakhs per acre, which the AP Govt purchased from them for ₹50 lakhs per acre	**₹1000cr**
APDC Scam	**YS Jagan Mohan Reddy**	Andhra Pradesh Digital Corp. paid for Party ads	**₹500cr**
I-PAC Scam	**YS Jagan Mohan Reddy**	Govt money spent for Party's election strategy	**₹274cr**
***NOTE:** Until Conviction by a Court, all scams/persons/amounts are alleged/estimated. Amounts are INFLATION-ADJUSTED to Apr2024.*			

Rise and Fall of Shiv Sena's Uddhav Thackeray

Founded in 1966, the dynastic and formerly Hindu-centric Shiv Sena of Maharashtra was BJP's ally from 1989. It had two CMs in a Sena–BJP government from March 1995 to October 1999 and was a partner in BJP's Government of Maharashtra in October 2014–November 2019, and Modi government in May 2014–November 2019.

After the October 2019 Maharashtra elections, Uddhav Thackeray wanted to be CM despite winning only 56 seats against BJP's 105. When BJP did not concede, Uddhav formed an alliance with NCP (54 seats) and Congress (44 seats) despite knowing their anti-Hindu stand and became CM in November 2019. His greed did not last long. In June 2022, his colleague Eknath Shinde broke away with 40 of Sena's 56 MLAs, got the official Shiv Sena name and symbol from the Election Commission, and aligned with NDA. He became CM, with former CM Dev Fadnavis as his deputy—a huge sacrifice by BJP and personally by Fadnavis.

SCAMS of UDDHAV THACKERAY's SHIV SENA

Which Scam?	People Involved	Actions by Agencies	Amount
Unless mentioned otherwise, all persons are leaders of Shiv Sena (Uddhav Balasaheb Thackeray) faction			
Brihanmumbai Municipal Corp (BMC) Scam (76 works in 09 Depts)	**Uddhav Thackeray**, some Party colleagues and Brihanmumbai Municipal Corporation (BMC) officials	Special Investigation Team (SIT) led by the Mumbai Police Commissioner was formed in 20223 to probe this and many other scams	**₹15,400cr+**
BMC Covid Scam	Sujit Patkar, friend of Sanjay Raut (MP); BMC Commissioner Iqbal Chahal; 03 partners of Lifeline Hospital Managment Services; Dr Kishore Bisure of BMC; a PA of **Uddhav Thackeray**; and 05 others.	Sujit Patkar and Dr Bisure have been ARRESTED by ED, which has also seized assets of ₹12.24cr. Investigations are going on against several other persons	**₹14,700cr+**
Ajmera Builders—Municipal Corp. of Dahisar Scam	Uddhav Thackeray and MCD officials	The CAG and the State SIT are probing the case	**₹483cr**
Cash Withdrawal from Risod Urban Cooperative Credit Society	Bhavana Gawali, LS MP of SS (UBT)		**₹35.2cr**
Illegal conversion of Mahila Utkarsh Pratishthan Trust into a Company and siphoning funds	Bhavana Gawali, LS MP of SS (UBT) and her aide Saeed Khan	ED ARRESTED Khan in Sep2021, he was given Bail by MHC in Jul2022; ED attached Khan-owned office building of ₹3.75cr; Gawali under investigation	**₹23.83cr**
Remdesivir Purchase by BMC at inflated cost during Covid		The State SIT is investigating	**₹23.6cr**
Dapoli Illegal Resort Case	SS (UBT) Minister Anil Parab and his close associate Sadanand Kadam; and SDO Jayram Deshpande	Resort attached by ITD; ED attached Parab's assets of ₹10.2cr, ARRESTED Kadam (he got bail from SCI) and Deshpande (he got bail from BHC after 1yr JAIL)	**₹16cr+**
Khichadi Scam	Suraj Chavan, a close aide of SS (UBT) leader **Aaditya Thackeray**, son of **Uddhav**	ED has ARRESTED Chavan	**₹8.35cr**

NOTE: *Until Conviction by a Court, all scams/persons/amounts are alleged/estimated. Amounts are INFLATION-ADJUSTED to Apr2024.*

Pawar vs. Pawar

Nationalist Congress Party (NCP) was founded in 1999 by three Congress leaders—Maharashtra's Sharad Pawar (defence minister in Rao government and leader of opposition in LS), Meghalaya's P.A. Sangma (cabinet minister in Rao government, ex-LS Speaker), and Bihar's Tariq Anwar (LS MP), to protest against Congress nominating foreign-born Sonia Gandhi as PM candidate. Sangma died in 2016 and Anwar re-joined Congress in 2018 over differences with Pawar. The party was already Maharashtra-centric and after Tariq left, it became Pawar family-centric. NCP was allegedly in cahoots with India's 'most wanted' terrorist, Dawood Ibrahim (drug king of Mumbai from early 1980s till he organised the 1993 Bombay bomb blasts that killed 257 persons), and helped him escape to Pakistan. Allegedly, NCP is also involved in drug smuggling via the Maharashtra coastline. As CM for 3 stints in 1978–80, 1988–91, and 1993–95, Pawar was very corrupt.

Pawar made his daughter Supriya Sule party chief, ignoring the more apt claims of other senior leaders, including his nephew Ajit Pawar and his own right hand Praful Patel. This virtually finished his party. In July 2023, Ajit broke away with 40 of the 47 MLAs including Patel, got the NCP name and symbol from the Election Commission, and joined the Shinde Shiv Sena–BJP government as its 2nd deputy CM.

Modi—the Saviour of 'Bharat'

We hope you realise what Modi has fought against for the past 10 years, and why the Indian National Developmental Inclusive Alliance (I.N.D.I.A.) comprising all parties in this chapter (and many more) came together to fight the NDA in the 2024 LS elections. In Modi's own words, he has locked up their cash safes and thrown away the keys.

The I.N.D.I.A. bloc cannot survive if the BJP continues to be in power. That is why they are desperate and have tried a myriad of different tricks and schemes to malign Modi.

Of course, there are enough gullible people in India who believe their narratives, including well-educated urban middle-class and rich Indians, but most are ill informed.

Hopefully, even if 2 per cent of such people read this book, they will probably wake up and smell the coffee.

India, that is Bharat, is the reality of our nation. For centuries, the soul of India was burdened and scarred by the shackles of colonial impositions, but Bharat will be free from these. The name 'India' is merely a reflection of foreigners' understanding of Bharat—its wealth, its culture, and a little about its spirituality but they never understood Bharat fully. Therefore, they believed it could be evangelised. Unfortunately, they left behind dynasts such as the Gandhis, the Stalins, and the Yadavs.

For India to rise as 'Bharat' it needs a leader that understands Bharat and not someone lost in the mirage of 'India' because Bharat goes beyond the geographical boundaries of India. Bharat is the soul of our cultural ethos—the soul of our nation built on a foundation set by the principles of *Sanātan Dharma*. Modi lives and breathes Bharat. He is guiding India to rise as a 'Viksit Bharat' (developed India) by 2047, when we celebrate 100 years of freedom from the colonialists.

If our fortune was better, a leader like Netaji Subhas Chandra Bose or Sardar Patel would have been India's 1st PM instead of Jawaharlal Nehru. But such was our misfortune that we had Nehru and his family lording over us, just like the British, for 56.25 years out of 66.8 years since Independence, before Modi.

India reflects a lost soul, alive no doubt in the body but dead in the soul. The impact of centuries of foreign rule was that we lost our culture, we lost our history, our pride, our self-respect, our name, and more importantly, we lost our soul. India needs to shed its colonial past and rise to lead the world with a new world order built on the principles of One Earth, One Family, One Future, or simply put, *Vasudhaiva Kutumbakam*.

And Modi is spreading this message far and wide. He has set in motion a series of geopolitical strategies that will see Bharat taking pole position in global geopolitics.

Besides being a politician and a statesman, Modi is a warrior. In India, his role is that of governance, outside of India his role is one of a conqueror. He wants to conquer other nations not through war but through political diplomacy. His conscientious steps during the COVID-19 crisis in embarking on vaccine diplomacy was an act truly keeping with the spirit of humanity that *Sanātan Dharma* scriptures have extolled us to follow.

For almost 67 years since Independence, and even before our colonial strains, India was seen as a nation of economic and human resources to be exploited. Now under the leadership of Modi, Bharat is no doubt being seen as a nation of economic and human resources, but with caution, because now it cannot be exploited.

'India' was a '*Sone ki Chidiya*' (bird of gold), but 'Bharat' is not. This rekindling of Bharat's soul has found its stimulation because of Modi.

Modi at the G20 Leaders' Summit in New Delhi proudly displayed a 'Bharat' name plate to political leaders and people who watched on TV or mobiles around the world.

His intent was to condition global leaders into wilfully accepting that it is time for India to rise as 'Bharat' and take its true position on the world's geopolitical stage that had eluded it for decades because of the lack of deserving leadership.

140

The 5th: Rid of I.N.D.I.gestion

An opposition alliance of 28 political parties formed on 22 June 2023 was mischievously named by Rahul Gandhi as I.N.D.I.A. to confuse voters, as not only is it the name of our nation but also sounds like NDA.

Their only 'stated' purpose was to defeat the Modi-led BJP/NDA in the 2024 LS elections.

By the time the elections were underway, the alliance had 40 parties.

Some members say they came together to 'save democracy'. Could Modi have achieved so much without a functional democracy? Are global giants pumping billions of dollars into India because our democracy is in danger? We already wrote how democracy *was* in danger during Rahul Gandhi's grandmother's and mother's regimes.

If democracy means corruption, let democracy die.

If democracy means antinationalism, let's kill democracy.

If democracy means anti-Hinduism, we don't want democracy!

I.N.D.I.A. is just a new name for the Congress-led UPA that was voted out of power due to dozens of corruption scams and complete lack of governance, much of which we have covered, and some we will in the next chapter.

The 13 parties that were in the UPA in 2014 are all part of I.N.D.I.A. Knowing that the name UPA will bring back bad memories, they have assumed a new name.

The I.N.D.I.A. bloc has no single leader. Rahul Gandhi, Mamata Banerjee, Arvind Kejriwal, and Uddhav Thackeray—all these corrupt anti-nationalists wanted to be PM.

In 302 days since its founding and the beginning of the 2024 elections, I.N.D.I.A. leaders met only 5 times (average once in 60 days)—their 5th meeting was a 'virtual' one that was not even attended by key leaders Mamata Banerjee and Uddhav Thackeray.

The I.N.D.I.A. bloc was formed because Bihar CM Nitish Kumar wanted an anti-BJP pan-India alliance of opposition parties, with coordination and seat-sharing in all states. He too wanted to become the PM. Just 15 days after the 5th meeting (the virtual one), Kumar quit the bloc and re-joined the Modi-led NDA. He had been part of NDA earlier (1999–2014 and 2017–24).

Rashtriya Lok Dal also quit and joined the NDA.

In their first joint 'rally' in Patna on 3 March 2024, Lalu Prasad Yadav abused the PM: 'Who is Modi? He accuses us of doing dynastic politics. What can we do if Modi does not have a family? Why is he childless? He is not even a true Hindu ...'[37]

Rahul accused the GoI of working for only 'two-three super-rich people'. Kharge said removing Modi is 'a must to save the country'.

Despite supposedly being in alliance, Congress+CPM+CPI contested against each other in West Bengal, the CPM-led Left Democratic Alliance contested against the Congress-led United Democratic Front in Kerala, and AAP contested against Congress in Punjab. The TMC also contested against the Congress in 5 seats in other states, the Left parties contested against Congress in 76 seats, Samajwadi Party contested 9 seats against alliance partners (mainly Congress), Viduthalai Chiruthaigal Katchi contested 11 seats against I.N.D.I.A. bloc candidates, NCP (Sharadchandra Pawar) contested against Congress on 2 seats, and the AAP contested 2 seats in Assam on its own. As a result, there was no real seat-sharing in 180 seats (33.15 per cent of the total 543 LS seats).

Mamata Banerjee asked in public if Congress could win even 40 LS seats. She called Rahul Gandhi a 'migratory bird' and said that Congress wants to appease Muslims. Is only her party entitled to do Muslim appeasement?

Let us look at the history of how hotchpotch alliances without a clear leader have performed in India:

Alliance Governments without one party having 60% of the Alliance's Seats Do Not Survive

Prime Minister	Party or Alliance	Start Month	LS MPs	Outside Support	Days Lasted
Morarji Desai	Janata	Mar 1997	295	NA	**857**
Charan Singh	Janata	July 1999	64	154 Congress	**170**
VP Singh	National Front	Dec 1989	143	137 BJP + Left	**343**
Chandra Shekar	SJP (R)	Nov 1990	63	197 Congress	**223**
Atal Bihari Vajpayee	NDA	May 1996	210	NA	**13**
HD Deve Gowda	United Front	Jun 1996	178	140 Congress	**324**
IK Gujral	United Front	Apr 1997	178	140 Congress	**222**
Atal Bihari Vajpayee	NDA	Mar 1998	276	NA	**395**

Morarji's was the only government that crossed 13 months. Vajpayee came back stronger in 1999, with 299 MPs in his

13-party NDA, and provided a stable government for 4 years and 7.3 months.

Although the UPA did provide a stable 10-year government, it was primarily because Congress had 145 of the UPA's 218 MPs (66.5 per cent) in 2004 and 206/266 (77.4 per cent) in 2009.

Supposing that the I.N.D.I.A. bloc did manage to win 272 seats and form the government, could a weak Congress win 77.4 per cent (211 seats) or even 66.5 per cent (181 seats), especially considering that it contested just 327 seats (against 421 that it contested in 2019? Finally, it ended up with just 99.

Yet another 13/170/222/223/324/343/395-day government would have given severe I.N.D.I.gestion to 1.439B Indians.

THANK GOD not too many people fell for the opposition lies and voted the Modi-led NDA back to power, albeit with BJP not getting a majority on its own.

People in Maharashtra and Haryana realised their mistake and gave the BJP a majority of 48 seats out of 90 in the October 2024 Haryana Assembly elections (vs. 40 in 2019) and gave the NDA a thumping majority of 235 seats out of 288 in the November 2024 Maharashtra Assembly elections with the BJP alone getting 132 seats (vs. 105 in 2019).

In Jharkhand, which BJP lost, it managed to retain its vote share of over 33 per cent. In J&K, where BJP was not expected to win, it won 4 more seats than the previous elections.

After the embarrassing defeat in Maharashtra, non-Congress leaders of the I.N.D.I.A. bloc said they want a non-Congress person to lead the alliance. Some senior leaders even suggested disbanding I.N.D.I.A. altogether.

141

The 4th: ₹46LCr vs. Zero

Everyone knows that the UPA-era had massive corruption, but do you know the shocking numbers?

UPA's Scams of ₹46 lakh crores			
NAME	**WHAT UPA DID**	**PEOPLE INVOLVED**	**AMOUNT**
Recruitment of non-existent people as Teachers in Govt Schools		Arjun Singh, Kapil Sibal, MM Pallam Raju	**₹15.64 Lcr++**
CoalGate	Arbitrary Allotments of Coal Mines	Dr Singh, Shibu Soren, Sriprakash Jaiswal, BK Handique, Dinsha Patel	**₹632,500cr**
2G scam	Arbitrary allotments of 2G Spectrum	A Raja (DMK)	**₹567,246cr**
Delhi Airport Scam 240ac Land given to GMR at ₹160,550cr lower than market price–568ac Delhi Aerocity has used this 240ac.		Praful Patel (NCP)	**₹545,957cr**
80:20 Gold	Favouritism in Gold Import-Export	P Chidambaram	**₹206,007cr**
CWG Scam	Expenses in 2010 Commonwealth Games	Suresh Kalmadi, Sheila Dixit	**₹178,881cr**
Over 47,500 Cases of Public Sector Bank Loans Frauds		P Chidambaram, Dr Singh Pranab Mukherjee	**₹178,029cr**
Maharashtra Irrigation Scam		Ajit Pawar	**₹133,850cr**
Co-location	Market Manipulation at NSE by some Brokers who got stock prices before others	P Chidambaram	**₹106,719cr**
Fake NREGA Job Cards (~17.1% of total)		KCR (BRS), Dr. Singh, Oscar Fernandes, Mallikarjun Kharge	**₹103,836cr**
'Exotic' Forex Derivatives Scam		P Chidambaram	**₹102,230cr**
Ultra Mega Power Plant Award to Anil Ambani		Sushilkumar Shinde	**₹93,573cr**
Iron Ore Railway Freight Evasion Scam		Lalu Yadav, Mamata Banerjee, Dinesh Trivedi, Pawan Bansal, M Kharge	**₹68,248cr**
Fraud in Service Tax and Excise Duties		P Chidambaram, Dr Singh Pranab Mukherjee	**₹48,960cr**
Illegal Thorium Mining and Exports in Tamil Nadu		Dr Singh, Sis Ram Ola, BK Handique, Dinsha Patel	**₹43,440cr**
Illegal Land Deals in Haryana and Rajasthan		Bhupinder Singh Hooda, Ashok Gehlot	**₹24,450cr+**
GRAND TOTAL of 14 Mega Scams		▶▶▶	**₹45,97,926cr**
NOTE: Until Conviction by a Court, all scams/persons/amounts are alleged/estimated. Amounts are INFLATION-ADJUSTED to Apr2024.			

These totalled ₹15.69LCr at the time (2.4 per cent of 10 years' GDP).

There were dozens more, ranging from ₹6Cr to ₹27,000Cr per scam.

Total government expenditure was ₹204LCr, and a 25 per cent leakage would be ₹61LCr (7.8 per cent of 10 years' GDP).

Rajiv Gandhi (Rahul Gandhi's father) alluded to 85 per cent leakage in government expenditure when he was the PM, so our 25 per cent is conservative. The ₹61LCr equals more than ₹158LCr when adjusted for inflation.

Due to Coalgate, the Supreme Court cancelled 204 of the 218 coal blocks. The Modi government auctioned 107 coal mines in 9 rounds, that will generate revenue of over ₹4LCr for the Centre and states in 10 years. Many more will be auctioned. Coal production went up from 565.77MT in FY14 to 997.83MT in FY24 (up 76.4%). Earnings of states have grown manifold. Odisha had 860 per cent earnings growth in FY16–23, Chhattisgarh 620 per cent, Jharkhand 425 per cent, and Karnataka 316 per cent.

The Modi Government also auctioned 38 critical mineral blocs vital for renewable energy, defence and agriculture, that will contribute ₹30.40LCr to governments. It will auction another 100+ blocks of 24 critical minerals.

Rajiv Gandhi Trust and Gandhi family acquired hundreds of acres of land illegally or at 2–5 per cent of market prices from Congress-ruled state governments. Courts made them return several lands.

Within 3 years of coming to power, the Modi Government discovered this:

Duplicate / Non-existent / Ineligible Scam of UPA	Quantity
RATION Cards	442mn
BENAMI (fake name) Bank Accounts	52+mn
LPG connections	46+mn
NREGA Job Cards (FY11-FY14)	78.3+mn
Beneficiaries in Women & Child Development Ministry	9.88mn
Beneficiaries in Minority Affairs Ministry	2.79mn
PAN Cards	1.145mn
Beneficiaries in Rural Development Ministry	1.084mn
Beneficiaries of National Social Assistance Program	7,57,200
Scholarships	7,20,000
Shell Companies	3,41,000
Beneficiaries in Social Justice & Empowerment Ministry	1,98,000
Fake NGOs with FCRA Licences	26,700

All these 587.94M fake/duplicate names were deleted by the Modi government. This played a big role in the government saving ₹3.6LCr.

From April 2022, the GoI started pressurising states to pay NREGA wages via an Aadhaar-based payment system (ABPS). On 1 January 2023, GoI said ABPS would be mandatory by 1 February. This was extended till December 2023. Of 252.5M registered NREGA workers, 143.17M were categorised 'active' (those who worked at least a day in the last 3 financial years) as on 31 January 2024, and 88.915 per cent were ABPS-eligible. Facing pressure for 100 per cent ABPS-eligible job cards, in April 2022–December 2023, the states deleted about 76M ineligible cards.

The UPA was paying ₹350 per LED bulb; Modi government procured the same bulbs of the same brands for about ₹65/piece (down 81.4 per cent).

Corruption was the single biggest reason that the Congress and UPA had a massive rout in the 2014 elections.

Poor policy planning and execution resulted in large unspent welfare funds, crippling the impact of government schemes; 14 social and rural ministries had not spent ₹94,060Cr (6.4 per cent of the FY05–14 cumulative budget estimate). Less than 1 per cent of the cumulative budget estimate was unspent in the Modi-era.

Foreign travel expenditure:

Foreign Travel Expenditure	Countries Visited	Total Spend	Average per visit	Adjusted for Inflation till Apr2024
Dr Manmohan Singh	96	₹795.18cr	**₹8.283cr**	**₹25.03cr**
Narendra Modi	137	₹588.53cr	**₹4.296cr**	**₹6.03cr**
Dr Manmohan Singh spent 4.15 times more than Modi. On what? **Was money siphoned off?** Was it paid to Congress-friendly journalists who accompanied him on most foreign trips? **Or was it paid to Sonia Gandhi in return for her making him the PM?**				

Fake in India

Luk, Lifebody, Daily Milk, and Head & Shoulder are popular brands in rural India. Sound familiar?

They are fake and cheaper versions of popular brands Lux and Lifebuoy soaps, Dairy Milk chocolates, and Head & Shoulders shampoo, and look similar to the originals.

India is flooded with fakes that don't comply with price, quality or safety norms. Many don't even have prices, manufacturer names or expiry dates. They are often pasted separately on packs.

A 2015 FICCI (Federation of Indian Chambers of Commerce and Industry) study said that 31.6 per cent of FMCG goods and 21.7 per cent of packaged foods are sold in (figuratively speaking) several shades of grey. Fakes account for about 35 per cent of after-market auto component sales.

During 1999–2023, India's total retail market was ₹453LCr, and the GST collections were ₹76.54LCr.

Assuming 42.5 per cent of GST was for 'services', ₹44LCr GST came from 'goods', giving us an average GST rate of 9.7 per cent for goods (many goods are exempt or have lower GST rate such as 5 per cent).

If we conservatively assume 20 per cent of all goods were fake, it translates to ₹90.6LCr.

At average GST of 9.7 per cent, there was a loss of ₹8.79LCr to the exchequer. Without fakes, GST collections would be 11.5 per cent higher, and GDP almost 1.15 per cent higher.

To resolve pilferage, tracking and tracing of gas cylinders, almost 200,000 QR-tagged 14.2kg LPG cylinders were sent to distributors as a pilot study. Steps to prevent supply of underweight cylinders to consumers include random weight checks at bottling plants, tamper evident seals on cylinders, pre-delivery checks with portable weighing scales carried by delivery persons, and random checks by officials at warehouses, delivery points and en route.

The Modi government made it mandatory for all medicine strips and bottles to have QR codes, to curb counterfeit manufacturing and pilferage.

The Modi 3.0 government will soon launch central databases for citizens to track doctors' credentials.

Transparency

Everything was hidden behind *burkhas* in the UPA-era. Yes, RTI did come into force from October 2005, but for several years, citizens didn't even know who to contact for information based on RTI rights and even when contact details started getting added on ministry and Govt. Department websites, there were no responses to over 60 per cent of queries.

The Modi government has excelled in transparency. There are more than 135 portals and over 180 dashboards, about 90 per cent of which have daily or weekly data/information updates.

Via Swagatam (https://swagatam.gov.in/Public/Index.aspx) one can make an e-appointment to visit 16,467 officers in 547 departments and ministries. Almost 5.23M visitors had used it till 15 September 2024 and an average of 8,313 Daily Passes are issued. All visits are captured electronically, to ensure transparency. Soon it will be made mandatory for any visitor of a minister or government officer to use Swagatam.

The increased GoI expenditure of ₹548.37LCr (comprising around ₹504.837LCr on agriculture sector, social sector and citizens' welfare, and ₹43.532LCr on infrastructure), when compared with what UPA spent, was only possible due to a huge reduction in corruption.

We are not saying corruption is completely nil now, but it has reduced by 70–80 per cent compared with UPA and will reduce further in the 5 years of Modi 3.0.

In nine *India Today* polls from January 2020 to February 2024, average 10 per cent people voted that corruption-free government has been the biggest achievement of Modi.

We are sure most of the other 90 per cent are not even aware of what the Modi government has done for achieving 100 per cent transparency and corruption-free government.

142

The 3rd: Unemployment, Really?

The opposition has been screaming till the cows come home that Modi has failed to meet his promise of creating 2Cr jobs per year. What is the truth?

THE TRUTH ABOUT UNEMPLOYMENT			
SN	**PARAMETER**	**Added in 10 years**	**Total (March 2024)**
All numbers are in Millions (divide by 10 to get Crores)			
A	EPFO Contributing Members	**191.292 M**	**309.105 M**
B	NPS (National Pension Scheme) Subscribers	**66.735 M**	**73.241 M**
C	EPFO and NPS Members added in Modi-era	**258.027 M**	**Modi Govt's performance ▲217.3% better than UPA**
D	EPFO and NPS Members added in the UPA-era	**81.332 M**	
E	Employees of Micro Enterprises (<05 employees each) who are not in EPFO or NPS		**143.6 M**
F	Unorganised Sector Workers registered on e-Shram		**295.34 M**
G	Domestic Household Workers (DHWs) not registered anywhere (out of 86.15M)		**45.484 M**
H	Non-farmer and non-DHWs who are not registered on e-Shram (33.33% 176.7M)		**58.9M**
I	**TOTAL EMPLOYED PERSONS** (779.5M excluding Farmers) — A+B+E+F+G+H		**925.67 M**
J	**Number of Persons in India aged 15-62 (as of 31 March 2024)** *As India has no Census since 2011, we used 'PopulationPyramid' and 'Worldometers' data*		**957.42 M**
K	**Total Number of Unemployed Persons**		**31.75 M**
L	**INDIA'S UNEMPLOYMENT RATE** (K/J)		**3.316%**

These numbers completely bust the opposition narrative that Modi promised to create 2Cr (20M) jobs per year, but only achieved 10 per cent.

Is the average of 25.8027M/year less than 2Cr/year or more?

Is the opposition mixing up crores and millions?

Does the opposition not know that data researchers like Amit Bagaria and Savio Rodrigues will come out with the facts and expose their continuous lies?

The assumption in Row 'H' in the Table is substantiated by the fact that the professionals registered on e-Shram as of 31 March 2024 (taking a few samples) are only 2.985M car/taxi drivers against 52.613M registered cars and taxis (1663 per cent higher), 2.276M *kirana* shop assistants against more than 20M actual shops (779 per cent higher), 1.294M street vendors compared with 40M as per National Hawker Federation (2991 per cent higher), 1.167M auto drivers against 9.33M autos (700 per cent higher), 0.345M bus drivers and conductors compared with 1.64M buses (375 per cent higher), and 108,572 religious professionals of all religions against 1.28M places of worship (1079 per cent higher).

Some additional points to consider:

- Demand for NREGA jobs is continuously falling.
- The percentage of self-employed persons has gone up from 52.2 per cent in FY18 to 58.4 per cent in FY24.
- Of the 22.1M vacancies posted by the National Career Service, only 20.33M job seekers registered. Do the 1.77M persons who did not apply for these jobs want jobs or are they unemployable because of laziness or bad attitude (as per thousands of employers)?
- According to a survey of 3,000 employers in India by the leading global workforce solutions company

> ManpowerGroup of the US, as many as 80 per cent of businesses in India said that they are struggling to find the right talent in the country.

An International Labour Organization report said that 83 per cent of India's unemployed are youth. Opposition conveniently changed this to a narrative that 83 per cent of Indian youth is unemployed.

As per the IMF (https://bit.ly/IMF_UR), in 2024, Japan had a 2.5 per cent unemployment rate, Germany 3.4 per cent, the US 4.1 per cent, the UK 4.3 per cent, China 5.1 per cent, Canada 6.2 per cent, Italy 7.0 per cent, Brazil 7.2 per cent, and France 7.4 per cent.

India therefore has the second lowest unemployment rate among the world's top 10 economies.

143

The 2nd: Think Big, Do Bigger

'When the curse of incremental thinking infects you, you bind yourself into limits,'[38] Modi said, adding that this hampered India's progress for a long time. When he became PM in 2014, he found the bureaucracy was also suffering from this malaise and there was an urgent need to change their mindset.

He did exactly that and it led to unprecedented pace of infrastructure development and completion of ambitious projects in a time bound manner. 'People know this PM inaugurates the projects for which he lays the foundation stone,' Modi remarked.

Modi said:

> The trust of the whole world in India is constantly increasing. There is no place where India does not have clout today. Never was there so much positive sentiment for India. I said from the Red Fort, '*yahi samay hai, sahi samay hai*' (this is the time, the right time).[39]

From the world's tallest statue to the largest office complex, from the world's largest digital public infrastructure to the world's biggest statistical modelling and future trends forecasting software, from the world's 2nd largest convention and exhibition centre to the world's longest upgraded riverfront, from the world's highest airfield to the world's highest bridge and rail line, from the world's largest new capital infrastructure to the world's longest coastal road, Modi really thinks big.

We have witnessed a speed and scale of development made of dreams. The PM Gati Shakti National Master Plan (PMGS-NMP) is a unique, transformative approach for integrated planning across ministries and departments—more than 1,350 projects were completed in just 28 months. PMGS-NMP has 1,530 data layers. Until March 2024, 533 projects had been planned. Network Planning Group, an institutional mechanism of PMGS-NMP has evaluated 149 proposals with project cost of ₹13.3LCr.

While Vande Bharat trains and Amrit Bharat stations are a symbol of the success story of railways, driving on 12–16-lane highways makes us blink our eyes as we think we are in America or Europe. Bharat Mandapam makes us proud, but when three Indian astronauts go up to space in 2025, there will be tears of joy in our eyes.

Development Record of Modi vs. UPA (Sonia Gandhi)

PARAMETER	UPA	MODI	Change
Total Investment in Infrastructure	₹13.484 Lcr	₹57.016 Lcr	▲ 322.8%
Infra Investment as % of GDP	1.79%	3.3854%	▲ 89.1%
Airport Passenger Capacity (million/yr)	122mppa in FY14	580mppa in FY24	▲ 375.4%
Total Expenditure on Railways	₹1.072 Lcr	₹10.017 Lcr	▲ 834.4%
Track Length Added in 10yrs	6259 Rkm	27,058 Rkm	▲ 332.3%
Track Doubling / Tripling / Quadrupling	5077 Rkm	23,851 Rkm	▲ 369.8%
Track Electrification	8162 Rkm	44,199 Rkm	▲ 441.5%
LHB Coaches Produced	2584	32,662	▲ 1164%

Development Record of Modi vs. UPA (Sonia Gandhi)			
PARAMETER	UPA	MODI	Change
Cities with Metro Rail	5	23	▲ 360%
Metro / Rapid Rail Lines Added	189.3 km	758.5 km	▲ 300.7%
Investment on Roads & Highways	₹1.57 Lcr	₹13.02 Lcr	▲ 729.3%
National Highways Built	25,718 km	96,087 km	▲ 273.6%
Expressways Built	844 km	4605 km	▲ 445.6%
Universities Built	348	504	▲ 44.8%
Power Generation Capacity Added	117.889 GW	209.668 GW	▲ 77.9%
Inter-Regional Power Transfer Capacity	36 GW (FY14)	117 GW (FY24)	▲ 225%
Unpaid Dues of Generation Companied	₹1.40Lcr	₹44,000cr	▼ 68.6%
Solar Power Capacity	2.5 GW (FY14)	87.212 GW (FY24)	▲ 3388%
Wind Power Capacity	21 GW (FY14)	47.075 GW (FY24)	▲ 124.2%
PNG Connections (Domestic)	2.22 M	11.82 M	▲ 432.4%
Urban Homes built by GOI per month	6700	78,956	▲ 1078.4%
Household Latrines built per day	5749	33,169	▲ 477%

PMGS is seen at its best in these remarkable illustrations.

Not only is there a contrast in the sheer scale but intelligent people also realise that infrastructure built by the Modi government is much better planned, keeping expandability in mind, and is of far better quality, as work was done by capable contractors like L&T or Tata Projects, instead of cronies of the ruling dispensation during the UPA-era.

Money invested on infrastructure 'turns' minimum 2.5 times in the economy, so a rupee becomes ₹2.50. Job creation is also huge.

On 19 February 2024, Modi launched 14,000 projects of ₹10LCr in Uttar Pradesh and these are likely to generate 3.35M jobs. Yes, you read that right.

He has a roadmap to invest ₹135LCr on infrastructure by 2029, for which he consulted more than 15,000 people in the last 18 months of his 2nd term.

The UPA announced new projects and ambitious schemes but slept on the files after that. Modi did not just complete his projects but also those announced by UPA that never started or were not completed. How well or badly did Modi manage the economy?

Who Managed the Economy Better?

PARAMETER		Manmohan Singh (3 Economics degrees)	Narendra Modi (chai wala)	Change
Foreign Direct Investment		$305.277 B	$667.404 B	▲ 118.6%
Monthly Consumption Expense per person	URBAN	₹2630 (FY12)	₹ 6996 (Aug 2023-Jul 2024)	▲ 166.0%
	RURAL	₹1430 (FY12)	₹ 4122 (Aug 2023-Jul 2024)	▲ 188.3%
AatmaNirbhar Defence Production		₹258,868 Cr	₹713,619 Cr	▲ 175.7%
Petrol Price increase in 10 years		▲ 111.8%	▲ 32.6%	▼▼ 70.8%
Above figures are for the entire 10 years, whereas all the figures below are for FY14 (UPA) and FY24 (Modi)				
GDP in ₹ terms		₹113.55 LCr	₹295.36 LCr	▲ 160.1%
Per Capita Net Income (current prices)		₹79,118	₹184,205	▲ 132.8%
Forex Reserves		$304.223 B	$645.58 B	▲ 112.2%
Net Direct Tax Receipts		₹6.386 Lcr	₹19.58 Lcr	▲ 206.6%
Electronics & Telecom Products Export		$4.15 B	$28.534 B	▲ 587.6%
Number of Startups		350	157,300	▲ 44,843%
Net Worth of all PSEs		₹9.5 Lcr	₹71.4 Lcr	▲ 651.6%

Dr Singh was an expert in Economics and had worked at almost all the major economy-related posts in the GoI in his career, but a *chai wala* managed the economy much better than him. How?

Modi worked only in national interest, whereas Dr Singh worked only in Sonia Gandhi's interest and his own.

India's share of the world's total GDP (by PPP) has gone up from 6.18 per cent in 2014 to 7.51 per cent in 2023 and is projected to rise to 7.73 per cent in 2024 (up 25.1 per cent) and to 8.76 per cent by 2028, as per the IMF.

The IMF says that India's per capita income will reach ₹3.33L in 2028. Modi's target is ₹30L by 2047.

Modi improved or launched more than 450 schemes for citizens' welfare.

Sabka Saath, Sabka Vikas

PARAMETER	UPA	MODI	CHANGE
Job Created in Formal Sector	81.332 M	266.739 M	▲ 228.0%
Annual DBT Transfers	₹7,367.7cr	₹593,843cr	▲ 7960%
Loans Disbursed to Minorities	₹2,033.35cr	₹6,215.64cr	▲ 205.7%
Female Minority Students	1.044M (FY14)	1.711M (FY24)	▲ 63.9%
Agri & Social Sector Expenses	₹114.93 Lcr	₹504.84 Lcr	▲ 339.3%
National Pension Plan Subscribers	6.506 M	132.217 M	▲ 1932%
SC/ST/OBC in Higher Education	115.774 M	172.885 M	▲ 49.3%
Medical Colleges Built	153	351	▲ 129.4%
Jan Aushadi Kendra pharmacies	87	13,822 (Jun 2024)	▲ 15,787%
OFC in Villages	6,577km (FY14)	692,498km (Dec 24)	▲ 10,429%
Rural Homes without LPG	118.83 M	15.563 M	▼▼ 86.9%
Female Labour Force Participation	21.2%	44.3% (2023)	▲ 109.0%
Expenditure on Sports Infrastructure	₹419cr	₹2,704cr	▲ 545.3%
Expenditure on North East Region	₹23,300cr (FY14)	₹104,359cr (FY24)	▲ 347.9%
Tourist Arrivals in J&K	10.89 M (2013)	21.13 M (2023)	▲ 94.0%
Stranded Indians Evacuated from abroad	17,350	18,333,348	▲ 105,568%

In less than 6 years, *free* hospital treatments of ₹1.07LCr were given to 78M patients.

In 6 years, ₹3.46LCr was spent on PM-KISAN direct income support for an average of 96.121M farmers.

Let's look at some of Modi's achievements in various global indices for different parameters:

Improvement in India's Rankings and Scores in Global Indices			
Name of Index	**Organisation**	**Old Rank**	**New Rank**
Global Terrorism Index	Institute for Economics & Peace (Australia)	6 in 2014	14 in 2024
Ease of Doing Business Index	The World Bank	142 in 2014	63 in 2019
Logistics Performance Index	The World Bank	54 in 2014	38 in 2023
World Competitiveness Ranking	International Institute for Management Development (Switzerland)	44 in 2014	39 in 2024
Climate Change Performance Index	The World Bank	31 in 2014	7 in 2024
Energy Transition Index	World Economic Forum (Switzerland)	94 in 2014	63 in 2024
Renewable Energy Country Attractiveness Index	Ernst & Young	7 in 2014	3 in 2021
Global Innovation Index	World Intellectual Property Organization (USA)	66 in 2016	39 in 2024
E-Government Development Index	United Nations	118 in 2014	97 in 2024

Everything that Modi achieved was despite the economy being at a standstill for 19 months (15 months of continuous lockdowns with intermittent 'unlock' phases, and after-effect lasting another 5 months). This means Modi only had 99 months to do what he did. Therefore, his achievements should be multiplied by 1.21 to get a more realistic picture, especially when we compare with the UPA-era.

Modi's accomplishments become even more important when we realise that 70–80 per cent of the countries have still not recovered from the economic impact of COVID-19.

The IMF says India's GDP grew by 44.78 per cent from 2019 to 2024 compared with China's 29.43 per cent (India up 52.2 per cent) and the world's 25.65 per cent (India up 74.6 per cent).

It would be wrong to assume Modi has achieved so much without his excellent team of ministers and a core team of officers, especially in the PMO and NITI Aayog.

But unlike Board of Control for Cricket in India where a 5-member senior men's National Selection Committee (and not the captain) selects the team, in the case of most Indian PMs, it is the PM who selects the team. While there are several 'players of the match', Modi is the undisputed 'player of the series'.

Addressing a massive crowd of 60,000 PIOs and Arabs in Abu Dhabi (UAE) on 13 February 2024, Modi said, 'A Modi guarantee is a guarantee that the guarantee will be achieved.'[40]

In BJP's Sankalp Patra for the 2024 elections, Modi wrote:

> In the next five years, we will take our nation into the top three economies of the world, launch a final and decisive assault against poverty, open up newer avenues of growth in various sectors, further intensify our battle against corruption, unveil the next generation of reforms, and take a number of pro-people decisions and actions.

144

The 1st: Modi is Just Like a Wow

We like and respect Narendra Modi as he is a decent man, a good son of Bharat Mata. He is 'just like a wow!!'

Up to 26 January 2025, in the 4,154 days since he was appointed as the PM candidate of the BJP, Modi had not taken a single day of holiday. He had worked an average of 17 hours/day, or a total of 70,618 hours, which is equal to 37.56 years of the work done by a typical Indian corporate employee who works 8 hours/day for 235 days/year.

Modi works for all citizens across communities, not discriminating between Hindus, Muslims, Christians, Sikhs, Jains, or Buddhists, even though he is a Hindu and a politician from a party propagated as a Hindu-centric party.

The opposition and leftist media narrative that Muslims are living in fear in India is a bunch of hogwash.

In fact, with his secular approach, Modi has alienated quite a few core Hindutva proponents and organisations. They allege Modi is diluting his stance on issues important to Hindu leaders and groups. Some of them believe that in his effort to be recognised as a reputed global leader, he has taken a softer stand on critical issues that are seen as the bane of some religious communities in India.

Expecting Modi to focus only on Hindus' concerns and ignoring issues of other communities is unwise. He is not the PM of Hindus.

However, Modi has done more for Hindu Dharma as a PM than any other PM before him. Lord Ram has got a suitable home in Ayodhya after 496 years. He has restored/enhanced/modernised six other major temples and impact areas around them and will do many more in the next 4.25 years.

Modi's strengthening of ties with important Arab leaders is assisting India in dealing with Islamic terrorism.

Why is Modi India's best PM since independence?

Top 15 Achievements of Narendra Modi	
1	Worked Harder than any other Prime Minister
2	First PM to See the Potential for India to Become a Developed Nation and Work For It
3	Managed the Economy Well; Reduced Inflation & Bank NPAs; Boosted FDI & Forex Reserves
4	Got World Leaders, Business Tycoons, and Other Global Personalities to Finally Believe in India
5	Managed Pandemic Better than Most World Leaders; Executed World's Largest Vaccination Drive
6	Zero Personal Corruption; Zero Tolerance for Corruption
7	Tougher than any other PM on National Security, Terrorism, and Separatism
8	Increased Tax Compliance Collection Manifold and Got Money for Development & Welfare
9	Digitisation of Everything in Government for Ease of Living for Citizens and Transparency
10	Built Infrastructure at a Scale and Pace Bigger and Faster than Any Country in the World
11	First Indian PM to Boost Manufacturing Sector with 'Make-in-India' and 'AatmaNirbhar Bharat'
12	Hundreds of Welfare Schemes for Youth, Women, Farmers, Minorities, and Backward Classes
13	Worked for Every Segment of Society, from Senior Citizens to Divyangjan, from Muslims to Transgenders, from Pregnant Women to the Girl Child, from Tribals to Hill People
14	Developed the NE Region, J&K, Ladakh, and Islands, that had all been neglected for 66+ years
15	Grew PSBs and PSEs that were being used as piggy banks by earlier PMS

India will rise as 'Bharat' because of Narendra Modi's decency, his dedication, his passion, and his hard work.

Bharat Mata ki Jai!

Appendix: What the World Says about India

The world is talking about India, investing in India, creating jobs in India—why didn't this happen for 66.8 years before Modi became the prime minister?

'It is India's century. India is contributing 15 per cent to global growth. This is positioning India among the real leaders in the emerging economies. The contribution of the emerging economies.'

—**Borge Brende**, President, World Economic Forum

'It's not India's decade, it's India's century.'

—**Bob Sternfels**, global CEO, McKinsey & Co., world's most respected strategy consultants

'Perfect policy prescriptions, cast-in-stone execution schedules, and an unmatched ability to deliver development on a gigantic scale make India a unique investment destination. Citi is doing a huge amount of work in transformation and that is all happening in India.'

—**Jane Fraser**, CEO, Citibank

'India has become a place where more and more global investors are focused. It feels to me the momentum is building, not slowing.'

—**Jonathan Gray**, COO, Blackstone (world's No.1 PE firm)

'India is a high priority for us, the anchor for our Asia-Pacific investing. We're not pulling out of China, but India is probably the most important and the biggest opportunity.'

—**Henry Kravis**, Co-Executive Chairman, KKR (No. 2 PE firm)

'The development of infrastructure and stable business environment positions India well. When turnaround time at Indian ports went from 2½ months to seven days and eventually to 2-3 days; or India's average train speeds go from 20km an hour to 40 to 80, that makes a huge difference. People talk about India Stack and how the most basic needs of 800 million people are being met through digital tools. The changes in the last five years position India well for the next 10 to 20 years. India has made so much progress under Prime Minister Modi and we hope these continue. India will, in the foreseeable future, become the third largest economy. You won't have scarcity of capital with an environment for investors to feel confident, comfortable. Carlyle is one of the world's biggest private equity investors, and India is a very important component. It will become more and more important in the coming years.'

—**Ziang-Dong Yang**, Chairman of Carlyle Asia, (No. 5 PE firm)

'We are working to export $10B per year from India by 2027 and are committed to strengthening logistics, skills, and supply chains to make India a global export leader in toys, seafood, and other goods.'

— **Doug McMillan**, CEO, Walmart, world's largest retailer

'Discussed Amazon's commitment to invest $26B in India by 2030 with PM Modi; working together we will support startups, create jobs, enable exports, and empower individuals and small businesses to compete globally.'

—**Andy Jassy**, CEO, Amazon

'We share PM Modi's vision of the positive impact technology can make on India's future, from education and developers, to manufacturing and the environment, we are committed to growing and investing across the country.'

—**Tim Cook**, CEO, Apple

'The excitement here in terms of seeing the progress India has made, particularly around the prime minister's vision of Digital India and the economic opportunity. We are excited about India's fintech leadership thanks to UPI and Aadhaar and we are going to build on that foundation and take it global. With the advent of AI, the opportunity for India to make more progress is exciting and we're going to support the prime minister's vision there. His vision for Digital India was ahead of its time. I now see it as blueprint other countries are looking to do. It's exciting to see his commitment towards the economic growth of India.'

—**Sundar Pichai**, CEO, Google and its parent company, Alphabet

'The prime minister's passion for India's development, the welcome mat to business and investment and opportunity is obvious to pretty much everybody who has interacted with him. It's a big vision. He would like India to play a significant role in the region and at Boeing we support that a hundred percent. I think it's great when technologies and opportunities align with the vision that a leader has for a country. Boeing is proud to be playing a key role in the rapid expansion of India's aviation market, and in the mission readiness and modernisation of the nation's defence forces. We support the prime minister's Make in India initiative, with over 5,000 people in India's Boeing team pursuing high-quality careers doing innovative work.'

—**David Calhoun**, CEO, Boeing,
world No. 2 aircraft producer

'He [Modi] was more than willing to have a dialogue and I found it very productive, and we congratulate India on their tremendous programs and policies.'

—**Marillyn Hewson**, CEO, Lockheed Martin,
world's No.1 arms manufacturer

'He has an ability to inspire hope, to make us believe on what's possible. He builds confidence on what the future can be. Then he is amazingly good on execution and getting his team and other teams to work to a common goal, and then most importantly, he gets results. India will become the number one economy in the world.'

—**John Chambers**, former CEO, Cisco,
leader in networking/cloud computing/cybersecurity

'I inherited a structure with four regions in the world. We are taking India out of Asia-Pacific and making it a separate region—the world's only country that is a region on its own. I'm doing it as the ability of Indian market to go into hyper-growth is unique right now. Large economies are struggling. Everybody I talk to believes that this is the moment for India.'

—**Christoph Schell**, Executive Vice President and Chief Commercial Officer, Intel, world No. 2 chipmaker

'India ranks No. 1, 2 and 3 in Ikea's priority market list for investment, it has been incredibly interesting to see the speed of development in the last 5-10 years.'

—**Jesper Brodin**, CEO of Ingka Group (Sweden), the company that operates most of the Ikea stores worldwide. Ikea is the world's largest retailer of home furniture, furnishings, and other home products

'He [Modi] certainly believes that technology is the way to help move things forward. Our experience in investing in India has been outstanding. It's our secret weapon. We started in India well before it was fashionable to have a facility in India, and we said right from the beginning that we want to be able to file patents and do fundamental innovations. As an Indian American what could be more inspiring or a matter of pride than seeing what the prime minister is doing to really encourage startups, to really encourage investment in India. We will continue to invest heavily in India.'

—**Shantanu Narayen**, CEO, Adobe, creator of Adobe Photoshop, Document Cloud, and Acrobat Sign

'I appreciate the recent policy changes to accelerate defence and emerging tech manufacturing and augment capacity building in India.'

—**Vivek Lall**, CEO, General Atomics,
world's top manufacturer of military drones,
leader in fusion power for nuclear energy

'India is at an all-time high. Somebody has done a brilliant job. More and more people are realising it is not the same India it was 50 or even 30 years ago. India is becoming a better publicised and better-known country where positive changes are taking place. I will suggest people look at Indian equities if they want to be rich. Let the Americans buy the bonds, you buy the equities. If Modi does what he says he is going to do and he opens the currency and he opens the markets, China will have to watch out for the new India. Modi wants India to become a manufacturing hub. He thinks India has smart people. For a long time, smart Indians left India and went to other countries, but now it looks like they're staying. So, if Modi lets India open up more, and if smart Indians stay and help India do well, India could become one of the best economies in the world.'

—**Jim Rogers**, cofounder, Quantum Funds,
(till 1980, its portfolio gained 4200 per cent
when S&P was up only 47 per cent). He also created
the famous Rogers International Commodities Index

'If you want to see the future, come to India. If you want to feel the future, come to India. If you want to work on the future, come to India.'

—**Eric Garcetti**, US Ambassador to India

'I had an incredible opportunity to spend more than an hour and a half with Prime Minister Modi. He is the most popular world leader for a reason. He is unbelievable, visionary, and his level of commitment to the people of India is just indescribable and deep and passionate and real and authentic. And his desire to lift people out of poverty and move India forward as a global power is real, and it is happening. The best part of for me was this. Anyone who knows PM Modi, you know he is a tech guy, and he is deep into the details. So, I found myself at his home at 7:30pm on a Friday night, talking about details of radio access networks and artificial intelligence. It was just amazing. I told him: "In the years to come, there will be two ecosystems of technology. One consistent with our democratic values and another not, the US and India need to lead the world together in this technology ecosystem." Without missing a beat, after having travelled all week, he said: "Well, Secretary, AI doesn't stand for artificial intelligence, it is America-India technology." In India, I met with women, and I met with some of your unicorn entrepreneurs. I met with investors. I met with the biggest CEOs. India has arrived, India has more than arrived.'

— **Gina Raimondo**, former US Commerce Secretary

Notes

Introduction

1 https://time.com/6968332/modi-india-transformation-election/ (accessed 20 November 2024).
2 https://www.theguardian.com/commentisfree/2024/apr/17/the-guardian-view-on-indias-election-fixing-a-win-by-outlawing-dissent-damages-democracy (accessed 20 November 2024).
3 https://www.theguardian.com/world/2024/apr/19/messianic-spell-how-narendra-modi-created-a-cult-personality (accessed 20 November 2024).
4 https://www.theguardian.com/global-development/2024/apr/20/india-elections-democracy-corruption-modi-caste-inequality-poverty-development (accessed 20 November 2024).
5 https://www.theguardian.com/commentisfree/2023/apr/23/the-observer-view-on-narendra-modi-growing-threat-to-democracy (accessed 20 November 2024).
6 https://www.theguardian.com/commentisfree/2023/sep/08/biden-india-modi-g20-autocrat#:~:text=More%20broadly%2C%20since%20Modi%20took,by%20threatening%20their%20equal%20citizenship (accessed 20 November 2024).
7 https://www.reuters.com/breakingviews/india-can-grow-fast-with-or-without-narendra-modi-2024-04-10/ (accessed 20 November 2024).

8 https://www.bloomberg.com/opinion/features/2024-04-07/india-elections-progressive-south-is-rejecting-modi (accessed 20 November 2024).

9 https://www.deccanherald.com/opinion/indias-voting-machines-are-raising-too-many-questions-2975021 (accessed 20 November 2024).

10 https://www.bloomberg.com/opinion/articles/2023-12-21/modi-s-sledgehammer-politics-are-battering-indian-democracy (accessed 20 November 2024).

11 https://news.bloomberglaw.com/mergers-and-acquisitions/indias-press-barons-spend-millions-to-reshape-newsrooms (accessed 20 November 2024).

12 https://www.ft.com/content/c0daecb8-ae56-4721-877c-35550e095f39 (accessed 20 November 2024).

13 https://www.nytimes.com/2024/04/18/opinion/india-election-modi-religion.html (accessed 20 November 2024).

14 https://www.nytimes.com/2022/08/24/opinion/india-modi-democracy.html (accessed 20 November 2024).

15 https://www.nippon.com/en/in-depth/a09501/ (accessed 20 November 2024).

16 https://mondediplo.com/2024/04/03india (accessed 20 November 2024).

17 https://www.lemonde.fr/en/opinion/article/2024/04/20/india-s-elections-this-year-stand-out-for-their-undemocratic-nature_6668953_23.html# (accessed 20 November 2024).

18 https://www.lemonde.fr/en/opinion/article/2023/04/24/india-s-democratic-regression_6024042_23.html (accessed 20 November 2024).

19 https://www.economist.com/leaders/2024/01/18/narendra-modis-illiberalism-may-imperil-indias-economic-progress (accessed 20 November 2024).

20 https://www.youtube.com/watch?v=GGhwgD4VpWU (accessed 20 November 2024).

21 https://www.ndtv.com/india-news/pm-narendra-modi-speech-in-parliament-2019-mandate-came-after-a-trial-by-fire-2059102 (accessed 20 November 2024).

Part I: National Security Comes First

1 https://economictimes.indiatimes.com/news/politics-and-nation/congress-leaders-should-recall-antonys-statement-on-border-issue-during-upa-rule-kiren-rijiju/articleshow/86973159.cms?from=mdr
2 https://www.japantimes.co.jp/opinion/2013/05/11/commentary/world-commentary/chinas-land-grab-in-india/
3 Khurshid's visit took on such a rosy hue that it's difficult to believe India and China were on the verge of a border conflict just a week ago.
4 https://www.usnews.com/news/world-report/articles/2020-06-16/dozens-killed-as-india-china-face-off-in-first-deadly-clash-in-decades
5 https://www.thehindu.com/news/national/pm-modi-meets-qatars-ruler-discusses-well-being-of-indian-community/article67597750.ece
6 https://timesofindia.indiatimes.com/india/wouldnt-have-been-possible-freed-navy-veterans-praise-pm-modi-on-return-from-qatar/articleshow/107611272.cms
7 https://indianexpress.com/article/india/pm-modi-pulwama-crpf-convoy-attack-security-forces-full-freedom-respond-awantipora-5586635/
8 https://www.satp.org/datasheet-terrorist-attack/incidents-data/india
9 https://economictimes.indiatimes.com/news/elections/lok-sabha/india/terrorists-are-now-killed-in-their-turf-pm-modi/articleshow/109226449.cms?from=mdr
10 https://pib.gov.in/PressReleasePage.aspx?PRID=1985409

Part II: Managing the Economy

1 https://mospi.gov.in/sites/default/files/publication_reports/HCES%20FactSheet%202023-24.pdf
2 https://archive.doingbusiness.org/en/doingbusiness (accessed 30 November 2024).
3 bit.ly/FDI-RBI (accessed 30 November 2024).
4 bit.ly/I-chat (accessed 30 November 2024).
5 https://timesofindia.indiatimes.com/india/cant-outsource-natl-security-self-reliance-must-army-chief-manoj-pande/articleshow/107991346.cms (accessed 30 November 2024).
6 https://www.pressreader.com/india/the-indian-express/20240319/282213720808062 (accessed 30 November 2024).
7 https://www.indiatoday.in/india/story/raghuram-rajan-bad-loans-npa-crisis-1337357-2018-09-11 (accessed 30 November 2024).

Part IV: Unprecedented Infrastructure Development

1 https://www.pmindia.gov.in/en/government_tr_rec/namami-gange/ (accessed 30 November 2024).
2 https://timesofindia.indiatimes.com/india/pm-modi-building-a-palace-for-himself-while-farmers-protest-congress/articleshow/79672137.cms (accessed 30 November 2024).
3 https://www.thehindu.com/news/national/we-need-a-new-house-but-preserve-parliament-house-mps/article3640419.ece (accessed 30 November 2024).
4 https://www.theguardian.com/cities/2014/apr/17/india-smart-city-dholera-flood-farmers-investors#:~:text=Twice%20the%20size%20of%20Mumbai,utopian%20experiment%20end%20in%20chaos%3F (accessed 30 November 2024).
5 https://www.hindustantimes.com/assembly-elections/gujarat-elections-modi-s-dholera-dream-is-a-tale-of-delay-progress-

and-resistance/story-HKH2aY9U8BprFx4u2F1WbP.html (accessed 30 November 2024).

6 https://www.hindustantimes.com/assembly-elections/gujarat-elections-modi-s-dholera-dream-is-a-tale-of-delay-progress-and-resistance/story-HKH2aY9U8BprFx4u2F1WbP.html (accessed 30 November 2024).

Part VI: Women Empowerment

1 https://pib.gov.in/PressReleaseIframePage.aspx?PRID=2008770 (accessed 30 November 2024).

2 https://ga7a.short.gy/2PWBgA (accessed 30 November 2024).

3 https://ga7a.short.gy/d6DHjw (accessed 30 November 2024).

Part VII: Education, Skilling, Jobs

1 https://ga7a.short.gy/dKr3yT (accessed 30 November 2024).

Part VIII: Farmers, Backward Classes, and Special Groups

1 https://ga7a.short.gy/630Bf8 (accessed 30 November 2024).

2 https://ga7a.short.gy/TDKOtb (accessed 30 November 2024).

Part IX: *Duniya se Dosti*

1 https://ga7a.short.gy/MHOa6g (accessed 30 November 2024).

2 https://x.com/vonbrauckmann/status/1385622565272494081?lang=ar (accessed 30 November 2024).

3 https://www.dailypioneer.com/2021/columnists/incredible-india-deserves-respect.html (accessed 30 November 2024).

4 https://pib.gov.in/newsite/PrintRelease.aspx?relid=136733 (accessed 30 November 2024).

5 https://ga7a.short.gy/h3JUGn (accessed 30 November 2024).

6 https://ga7a.short.gy/dFgSnr (accessed 30 November 2024).

7 https://ga7a.short.gy/YSFXvM (accessed 30 November 2024).

Part XI: Modi Has Done So Much More

1 https://ga7a.short.gy/QkG8sM (accessed 30 November 2024).
2 https://ga7a.short.gy/JAZSfn (accessed 30 November 2024).
3 https://ga7a.short.gy/i1oYvQ (accessed 30 November 2024).
4 https://ga7a.short.gy/gtlGVm (accessed 30 November 2024).
5 https://ga7a.short.gy/7RddCw (accessed 30 November 2024).
6 https://ga7a.short.gy/7VVAXq (accessed 30 November 2024).
7 https://ga7a.short.gy/EEZYFP (accessed 30 November 2024).
8 https://ga7a.short.gy/9mvRJc (accessed 30 November 2024).
9 https://ga7a.short.gy/DdKtvX (accessed 30 November 2024).
10 https://ga7a.short.gy/ZVs99X (accessed 30 November 2024).
11 https://ga7a.short.gy/M1Ycvr (accessed 30 November 2024).
12 https://ga7a.short.gy/iL1VmN (accessed 30 November 2024).
13 https://ga7a.short.gy/m3Vkme (accessed 30 November 2024).
14 https://ga7a.short.gy/cRRkzK (accessed 30 November 2024).
15 https://ga7a.short.gy/RzN850 (accessed 30 November 2024).
16 https://ga7a.short.gy/kZoubD (accessed 30 November 2024).
17 https://ga7a.short.gy/ctuVeU (accessed 30 November 2024).
18 https://ga7a.short.gy/N6aAbs (accessed 30 November 2024).

Part XII: Myths vs Reality

1 https://ga7a.short.gy/JpUcfV (accessed 30 November 2024).
2 https://ga7a.short.gy/IvRpId (accessed 30 November 2024).
3 https://ga7a.short.gy/bnNjzi (accessed 30 November 2024).
4 https://ga7a.short.gy/Ue857g (accessed 30 November 2024).
5 https://ga7a.short.gy/QEyqWK (accessed 30 November 2024).

Part XIII: Top 10 Reasons Why We Wrote This Book

1 https://ga7a.short.gy/YGWpw0 (accessed 30 November 2024).
2 https://ga7a.short.gy/85GayN (accessed 30 November 2024).
3 https://ga7a.short.gy/nwQxUR (accessed 30 November 2024).

4 https://ga7a.short.gy/QEVQVF (accessed 30 November 2024).
5 https://ga7a.short.gy/cpnO4M (accessed 30 November 2024).
6 https://ga7a.short.gy/uEPsMM (accessed 30 November 2024).
7 https://ga7a.short.gy/z10cFe (accessed 30 November 2024).
8 https://ga7a.short.gy/z10cFe (accessed 30 November 2024).
9 https://ga7a.short.gy/6GYUlv (accessed 30 November 2024).
10 https://ga7a.short.gy/rnSmFu (accessed 30 November 2024).
11 https://ga7a.short.gy/WiHMpJ (accessed 30 November 2024).
12 https://ga7a.short.gy/JSF0nq (accessed 30 November 2024).
13 https://ga7a.short.gy/63tyf7 (accessed 30 November 2024).
14 https://ga7a.short.gy/2oPfax (accessed 30 November 2024).
15 https://thewire.in/government/reform-ias-but-dont-throw-the-baby-out-with-the-bathwater#google_vignette (accessed 30 November 2024).
16 https://ga7a.short.gy/1ssRud (accessed 30 November 2024).
17 https://ga7a.short.gy/JjiSJU (accessed 30 November 2024).
18 https://ga7a.short.gy/u6jbJL (accessed 30 November 2024).
19 https://ga7a.short.gy/liLIAI (accessed 30 November 2024).
20 https://ga7a.short.gy/b8gbSy (accessed 30 November 2024).
21 https://ga7a.short.gy/ZzFYd7 (accessed 30 November 2024).
22 https://ga7a.short.gy/JEivZj (accessed 30 November 2024).
23 https://ga7a.short.gy/gBkYOJ (accessed 30 November 2024).
24 https://ga7a.short.gy/nPCZhg (accessed 30 November 2024).
25 https://timesofindia.indiatimes.com/india/bjp-slams-rahul-gandhi-after-pannun-backs-his-remarks-on-sikhs/articleshow/113274019.cms (accessed 30 November 2024).
26 https://www.hindustantimes.com/india-news/in-london-rahul-gandhi-calls-rss-fascist-points-out-reasons-for-congress-decline-101678147505367.html (accessed 30 November 2024).
27 https://timesofindia.indiatimes.com/india/bjp-slams-rahul-gandhi-after-pannun-backs-his-remarks-on-sikhs/articleshow/113274019.cms (accessed 30 November 2024).

28 https://economictimes.indiatimes.com/news/politics-and-nation/bjp-has-spread-kerosene-all-over-the-country-one-spark-can-put-us-in-big-trouble-says-rahul-gandhi/videoshow/91705522.cms?from=mdr (accessed 30 November 2024).
29 https://ga7a.short.gy/UV0WOw (accessed 30 November 2024).
30 https://ga7a.short.gy/SmkMPf (accessed 30 November 2024).
31 https://ga7a.short.gy/J7Sz8S (accessed 30 November 2024).
32 https://ga7a.short.gy/UC35Ey (accessed 30 November 2024).
33 https://ga7a.short.gy/kfrvGW (accessed 30 November 2024).
34 https://ga7a.short.gy/IDxetT (accessed 30 November 2024).
35 https://ga7a.short.gy/JOzBSz (accessed 30 November 2024).
36 https://ga7a.short.gy/62L5TJ (accessed 30 November 2024).
37 https://ga7a.short.gy/IRlxmH (accessed 30 November 2024).
38 https://ga7a.short.gy/eV0IMM (accessed 30 November 2024).
39 https://ga7a.short.gy/ediQyB (accessed 30 November 2024).
40 https://ga7a.short.gy/kC7vzd (accessed 30 November 2024).

About the Authors

Amit Bagaria is a serial entrepreneur–turned author. He has authored 16 books, including eight no.1 bestsellers. He is also a columnist with more than 90 guest articles in various publications including *The Economic Times*, *The Indian Express,* and *DNA* as well as seven cover stories for retail magazines.

He was the news editor at his American university's weekly newspaper and was chosen 'Journalist of the Year' in his first year. He received the 'All American Journalist Award' from the American Scholastic Press Association, did a journalism course at Columbia University, and worked for *The New York Times*. He has also done two management courses at the famous Harvard Business School.

Amit was India's no. 1 hospital and mall development consultant and southern India's no. 1 residential realty consultant, apart from excelling in other sectors. During the 2008–09 financial crisis, he planned, designed, and marketed a mega 3,600-unit affordable apartment complex in Jaipur and followed it up with an even bigger 15,000-unit affordable complex in Bengaluru. He has invested in nine startups.

Amit and his businesses have featured in more than 290 articles and over 45 TV interviews in 19 countries, including more than 25 newspapers' front pages. He has been a guest lecturer at IIM, Bangalore; Symbiosis, Pune; and Tata Institute of Social Sciences, Mumbai. He has also been an anchor or panel moderator at 15 industry events in India, the UK, Dubai, and Spain; a member of CII and FICCI national committees; and a jury member for several award events worldwide. Amit has received 18 awards.

Savio Rodrigues is a Goa-based serial entrepreneur with business interests in media, IT, realty, and startups. He has over 28 years of work experience in journalism, media and communications. He is most respected for his role as the founder and editor-in-chief of *Goa Chronicle*, a globally recognised online news portal, for its hardcore factual reportage and investigative analyses.

Savio often appears on TV news debates and web talk-shows in India and abroad. His nationalistic views, progressive thinking, and dedication to the pursuit of truth on matters of social justice and corruption have been admired by many Indians globally.

Savio has authored a fiction book, *Karmic Ishq*, delving into the difficult subject of sexual abuse of children by family members and strangers, something that people in India are still shy of discussing openly in public. He has also co-authored a nonfiction with Amit Bagaria.